"An indispensable introduction to twentieth- and twenty-first-century Christian realism in international relations. Well-selected excerpts include familiar voices and new, showing development among thinkers over time. . . . The volume implicitly argues for Christian realism as a diverse, ecumenical, international, and contextual approach to politics. Essential reading in a world facing multiple threats and disruptions on the global stage."

—**Debra Erickson**, coeditor of *Jean Bethke Elshtain: Politics, Ethics, and Society*

"An invaluable and overdue resource, this anthology will be a vital point of reference for scholars of Christian realism. There is a deep wisdom at work in this masterfully compiled collection of essays."

—**Cian O'Driscoll**, Coral Bell School of Asia Pacific Affairs, ANU

"What has the faith of forgiveness and reconciliation to do with the cold realities of power that dominate geopolitics? Joustra and Patterson's volume traces a tradition of Christian political thought that studies the realities of power with clear eyes *and* a faithful commitment to order and neighborly love. What emerges is not denominational or partisan doctrine but a plurality of voices forming a compelling vision of international relations that is at once sober and hopeful."

—**Joshua Hastey**, Regent University

"*Power Politics and Moral Order* is the definitive reader on Christian realism. From Butterfield and Niebuhr to Elshtain and Weigle, the work includes a wide array of Christian realists addressing a host of topics. Edited by two contemporary and prominent Christian realists, Eric D. Patterson and Robert J. Joustra, the book is required reading for every student of international relations and those involved in making foreign policy."

—**Mark David Hall**, George Fox University

"For anyone interested in coming to a better understanding of Christian realism as manifested in foreign-policy circles—whether a scholar, student, policy maker, or the average reader—Patterson and Joustra's volume is essential reading. Providing historical context and conceptual elaboration about Christian realism, the volume includes key readings from each generation, including works by greats such as Reinhold Niebuhr, Kenneth Thompson, Paul Ramsey, George Weigel, Jean Elshtain, and others."

—**Gregory J. Moore**, Colorado Christian University

Power Politics and Moral Order

Power Politics and Moral Order

Three Generations of Christian Realism—A Reader

EDITED BY

Eric D. Patterson

AND

Robert J. Joustra

CASCADE *Books* • Eugene, Oregon

POWER POLITICS AND MORAL ORDER
Three Generations of Christian Realism—A Reader

Cascade Books
An Imprint of Wipf and Stock Publishers
199 W. 8th Ave., Suite 3
Eugene, OR 97401

www.wipfandstock.com

PAPERBACK ISBN: 978-1-7252-7884-4
HARDCOVER ISBN: 978-1-7252-7885-1
EBOOK ISBN: 978-1-7252-7886-8

Cataloguing-in-Publication data:

Names: Patterson, Eric, 1971– [editor]. | Joustra, Robert [editor].

Title: Power politics and moral order : three generations of Christian realism—a reader / edited by Eric D. Patterson and Robert J. Joustra.

Description: Eugene, OR: Cascade Books, 2022 | Includes bibliographical references.

Identifiers: ISBN 978-1-7252-7884-4 (paperback) | ISBN 978-1-7252-7885-1 (hardcover) | ISBN 978-1-7252-7886-8 (ebook)

Subjects: LCSH: Christianity and politics | Niebuhr, Reinhold, 1892–1971 | Christian ethics | Political ethics | Political theology | Church and state—Christianity

Classification: BR115.P7 P38 2022 (print) | BR115.P7 (ebook)

03/24/22

To our students, past and present,
wrestling with justice in God's world,

And especially to Abigail Lindner, Linda Waits,
Grace Lee Parr, Daniel Neven and Shua Kim,
for their careful eyes and hard labors

Contents

Part 2: Cold War Christian Realists

Part 3: Contemporary Christian Realists

Preface

REINHOLD NIEBUHR WROTE, "NOTHING worth doing is completed in our lifetime; therefore we must be saved by hope. Nothing true or beautiful makes complete sense in any immediate context of history; therefore we must be saved by faith." That sense of Christian hope and faith, and its application to the history being made around us in our own present, is what has drawn so many to Christian Realism.

Christian Realism is nothing new: it goes back to at least Augustine and has been transmitted down through the generations, via Aquinas and Calvin and Luther to our own time. This book demonstrates how an Augustinian (i.e., Christian Realism) approach to global politics captured the attention of those facing Nazi fascism and Soviet Communism in the twentieth century, and how this tradition continues to inform Christian thinking on war, peace, and security to this day.

We, the editors of the volume in your hands, have likewise been captivated by and contribute to this way of thinking. In my case (Eric), I was a young Master's candidate at the University of Wales at Aberystwyth. I kept coming across references in international relations theory texts that cited Christian political thinking that was pessimistic, cynical, or hopeless due to their emphasis on the fact of human sinfulness. The name associated with this "Christian Realism" was Reinhold Niebuhr.

When I read Niebuhr himself, rather than the attacks on him, I was inspired. Niebuhr recognized the spiritual elements that National Socialism and Communism represented and the political and moral threat they represented to the West, not just in terms of geopolitics, but in terms of human dignity and survival. I later discovered that Niebuhr and his friend John C. Bennett were not the only ones writing in this vein: the British historian Herbert Butterfield and his friend Martin Wight influenced similar approaches on the other side of the Atlantic. Moreover, over the next several decades, they influenced people who increasingly influenced me: Paul Ramsey, Jean Bethke Elshtain, and others. To this day, it is hard to find a more compelling voice than Niebuhr's when it comes to recognizing human fallenness *and* human potential, the blessing of democracy *and* its inherent weaknesses, the majesty of the U.S. *and* its sometimes conceit, the responsibility to use force *and* the moral complications it presents, and the call to love one's neighbor in a fallen world. Niebuhr was a dialectician, recognizing the tensions that are far more natural for the nuances of the human condition than the simplistic, and dangerous, idealisms that he fought.

Niebuhr and his contemporaries thus inspired elements of my career that include teaching and writing on the ethics of international affairs and a keen appreciation for the ethics of statecraft.

I (Robert) only first encountered Christian Realism when Justin Cooper, the President of Redeemer University, retired while I was in my Master's program at McMaster University. He invited me into his office, lined wall to wall with books after a long career in administration, and before that as a professor of international relations, and passed on the cultural lifeblood of a tradition. There I picked out books by authors I had only heard of—they were not really taught even at the graduate level at my university—Herbert Butterfield, Martin Wight, E. H. Carr, Hans Morgenthau, Reinhold Niebuhr, Kenneth Thompson, and others. In these, and the more to come, I found a serious, morally minded, scripturally rooted, tradition of foreign policy that offered a richness far better than the cul-de-sac in which I felt so trapped in international relations theory: the false dichotomies of foundationalism and anti-foundationalism, positivism and the epistemological turn, conviction and diversity. More than this, I found partner methods and concerns to my own religious tradition of neo-Calvinism, so much so that friends like Simon Polinder argue that—alongside an American School and an English School—we must also have an Amsterdam School of international relations, joined in the project of Christian Realism. I am the beneficiary and now enthusiastic ambassador of these traditions and the fruit they bear for justice in a world so famished for its taste.

This volume would not have been possible without the help of our research assistants and others. First, and foremost, Regent University student Abigail Lindner was a major organizing effort for this project. She worked with publishers to ascertain and secure copyrights, managed our database, and helped transfer old musty books from our shelves to clean electronic documents. Thank you, Abigail! Regent alumna Linda Waits provided excellent copy-editing services that professionalized the final draft. Other students from Regent University and Redeemer University assisted us, including Grace Lee Parr and Daniel Neven. We gratefully acknowledge financial support from our home institutions, Regent University and Redeemer University, which helped procure some of the copyrighted material. We are also grateful to the families of some of those whose work is featured herein who allowed us to utilize those works without charge.

Finally, we should point out that all spelling, capitalization, and punctuation have been reproduced as found in the original sources.

Eric Patterson, Regent University

Robert Joustra, Redeemer University

Introduction

IN THE WELL-TROD WORLD of power politics there is an ancient Greek maxim that young-sters too often learn intuitively on the playground: the strong will do what they can, and the weak will suffer what they must.[1] This was the motto of Athenian foreign policy that set so much context for Thucydides' famous *History of the Peloponnesian Wars*, but it also still summarizes much of the conventional wisdom about world affairs today.

Still in ancient Greece, for those yet reading Plato's *Republic*, we might remember the character Thrasymachus bursting into the scene of a debate on the nature of "justice," sweeping away what he thinks are naive and idealist arguments saying only that "justice is the advantage of the stronger." Nor must we be provincially Mediterranean about it. We could visit the Confucian sage Xunzi and the Legalists in Qin China or turn the Sanskrit pages of Kautilya's *Arthashastra* in ancient India. These are the origin stories of what has come to be called Realism—the morality of power politics—in international relations.

But Jean Bethke Elshtain says Realism only really gets down to "serious business" in the modern era.[2] The very adjective "Machiavellian" comes from the Italian states-man and advisor Niccolo Machiavelli (1469–1527), who passed down his wisdom in *The Prince*, in such fortune cookie quotables as "it is better to be feared than loved." Hot on his heels, Thomas Hobbes (1588–1679), writing in his implausibly titled *Leviathan*, argued that "the condition of man . . . is a condition of war of everyone against everyone." The nuclear age inaugurated a renaissance of Realist studies, as great power balance, national interest, and containment became matters not only of life and death but of the survival of the species. Names such as George F. Kennan, Hans Morgenthau, Kenneth Waltz, Henry Kissinger, and more recur for students of twentieth-century Realism.[3]

Realism is an enormous, complex, and influential school of thought in international relations. It is by far the most common way of looking at the world. If, as some salty philosophers have put it, all of philosophy is a footnote to Plato, then it is equally true

---

1. Rhodes and Hammond, *Peloponnesian War*.

2. Elshtain, *Just War Theory*, 261.

3 See classics such as Kennan and Mearsheimer, *American Diplomacy*; Morgenthau, *Politics Among the Nations*; Waltz, *Theory of International Politics* and *Man, the State, and War*, and finally the 2015 edition of Kissinger, *World Order*.

that all of international relations is a footnote to Thucydides, working out the dilemmas of power, anarchy, groups, and national interest.

One would not want to be mistaken for being dismissive of this grand tradition. There is wisdom in it, and what, after all, falls under the very broad and sweeping rubric of "Realism" is so diverse that it would be almost impossible to force the tradition into a box of easy criticisms.

But Christians can do better. The worldly Realism of Hobbes and Machiavelli, which we call *Pragmatic Realism,* has important insights, but also very fundamental flaws because it is limited to calculations and machinations that are materialistic and self-interested. The temptation is to accept that the rules of the game consist of anarchy, egoism, groupism, and power politics; rules we do not invent, but need to play by if we want to win.

The problem with this way of acting in the world, as Thucydides himself points out later in his *History of the Peloponnesian Wars,* for all the use of words like "realistic," it does not fit the world we live in. In that same *History* where Thucydides records the "Athens First" foreign policy, he finishes the story with a rather sober judgment in Pericles' majestic funeral oration. Athenian foreign policy is a wreck, its pride and its hubris have united the other Greek city states against it, imperial overstretch has taken its toll, internal turmoil has ripped apart what was once a democracy as its foreign policy crashed down around it, all in a cataclysm that can only be described in that age as a judgment by the gods. In sum, what we call the Pragmatic Realist quadrilateral—egoism, groupism, anarchy, and power politics[4]—tells us something important about the world, but it does not tell us *everything* important about the world. It builds an outlook on foreign affairs that can be dangerously *unrealistic,* one that gets a few important things right, but gets one fundamental thing wrong.

That thing is this: the driver of international politics is not *fear,* but *love.* For all of their prudential affinity, this is the fundamental difference between *Pragmatic Realism* and *Christian Realism,* e.g., Christian Realism reads to the end of Thucydides' *History* and hears in the funeral oration of Pericles a judgment of Athenian power and pride. Christian Realism holds not only the empirical problems of power and order together in one hand, but the book of Scripture and the ordering of God's creation in the other. Christian Realism labors, as John Calvin tells us, to hold the "Book of Creation" in one hand and the "Holy Scripture" in the other, *both* as revelations for our apocalyptic times to teach us about how and why to make justice in the international system.

Christian Realism, then, is nothing new. It is a political tradition[5] within Christianity with its roots in Scripture, applied and interpreted through church teachers like

---

4. Although versions of this quadrilateral exist in many places, the specific terms here are borrowed from Reus-Smit and Snidal, *The Oxford Handbook of International Relations.* Egoism is sometimes referred to as self-interest and groupism as statism. The basic argument is that under conditions of anarchy (where no sovereign authority exists) people will tend to group together out of common self-interest (fore among those interests is security).

5. *Christian Realism* is also a term used to describe a much broader moral or ethical perspective, which connects with our use of Christian Realism as a political perspective but is also a much more complete ethical framework. For a discussion of Christian Realism as a complete ethical framework see Stackhouse Jr., *Making the Best of It.* Our effort in this anthology is to elicit Christian Realism as a

Augustine, Aquinas, and Calvin, and revitalized in the twentieth century by resolute Christians who called for resolute action against Nazism, communism, and other diabolical programs of violence.

And so, this edited companion of classic, Cold War, and contemporary Christian Realists is more than a sourcebook of great writings. Its arrangement and curation also make three arguments, for three slightly different audiences.

First, we show that Christian Realism is *not* Pragmatic Realism, and that there is a difference in these approaches so fundamental that for all their prudential affinity it is a major mistake to pass off one for the other. The book is intended, perhaps foremost, for thinking Christians, whether American or not, whether academic or not; those for whom progressive liberal internationalism, on the one hand, or Pragmatic Realism, on the other, seem morally and politically wanting. For those considering foreign policy, Christian Realists may sometimes come to similar policy proposals to pragmatic, egocentric Realists—or progressive liberal internationalists—but that is not because they hold the same first principles (or that such principles do not therefore matter). Christian Realists are motivated by the sober obligations of *neighbor-love*, which calls for an ethic of political responsibility in a world that is typically irresponsible and self-centered. Responsible governments may go to war, or not go to war, but they should only do so, as Augustine said, from a perspective of love—to protect the weak, to punish wrongdoers, or to right past wrongs. Christian Realism calls for policies of order and justice; Pragmatic Realism calls for power-maximization and ruthless competition.

Second, for students new to the world of international relations, we want to offer a tradition with moral language and moral arguments from *within* Realism. So often, introductions to Realism offer amoral caricatures, a world not far removed from a simple reading of the Melian Dialog, where the pragmatic Realist quadrilateral exhausts foreign policy. Rather than showing a diverse and theologically profound tradition, students can immediately be turned off by crass power politics, so far removed from their hopes for justice, development, human rights, and missions in the international system. Although this is not quite the point the church father Tertullian was trying to make, in this context we could ask his same question with different emphasis: What *has* (Thucydides') Athens to do with Jerusalem?[6] Today's students are tomorrow's practitioners, so a volume that deals with Christian Realist responses to nuclear weapons, terrorism, genocide, and the other challenges of international life offer critical tools for not only statecraft, but for followers of Jesus.

Finally, we also offer an original *generational* organization of Christian Realists, which is both trans-Atlantic (including not only the American School, but also the English School and the emerging Amsterdam School) as well as contemporary. Christian Realism, in other words, is not a one-time American tradition, settled and archived in foreign

---

framework for *international politics*, rather than to make larger arguments about the entirety of ethics for the Christian believer.

6. When the church father Tertullian asked his original question, "What has Jerusalem to do with Athens?" he was referencing the divide between the church and the academy, the Christian and the heretic, or the thoughts of "man's philosophy" and "God's words." Athens was a stand in for Greek philosophy and Jerusalem for religion.

policy history. It is dynamic, evolving, and has a story. We want to tell that story through this anthology, in part to show that Christian Realism is *not* a school of thought that begins and ends "primarily with the ethicist and public intellectual Reinhold Niebuhr."[7] The tether that grounds Christian Realists, we argue, is not American, but Roman-Christian, in the person of Augustine. And, in fact, some exceptional work in Christian Realism is British, coming out of what is called the early English School in international relations, or even Dutch—as in the emerging Amsterdam School.

And while not only American, it is also not only mid-twentieth century. Our anthology shows three distinct periods. First, a generation of Christian Realists facing fascism and communism, primarily—though not only—in the writings of great Americans such as Reinhold Niebuhr. Second, a generation of Cold War Christian Realists, whose concerns shift to new technologies of warlike weapons of mass destruction, multilateral institutions, proxy conflicts and insurgencies, and, of course, the Vietnam War. Finally, a third generation of Christian Realists—contemporary scholars—takes shape in the multilateral world of the new millennium, theologically orthodox, but politically and increasingly internationally diverse.

Christian Realism answers the questions of every power and every age in a slightly different way. But it is our conviction that Christian Realism is especially well suited for *our* power, and *our* age, for a new, albeit very different Augustine, to speak to the pessimists and the declinists, but also the optimists and the utopians, and center the search for a just international order in the kingship of Christ.[8]

Be Not Afraid: The Key to Christian Realism

In 2015, Alissa Wilkinson and I (Robert Joustra) opened a book on the "apocalypse" with the arresting claim that "the world was going to hell."[9] We certainly have that *feeling* as casual observers of international relations: weapons of mass destruction proliferate, dangerous and nefarious international networks—of terrorists, smugglers, crime syndicates, and human traffickers—abound, trade talks collapse, our climate swings back and forth, none of which is to even scratch the surface on the anxiety of pandemics and lockdowns. Moderation is rare.

Fear permeates our age.

What is more, we also suffer the feeling that most of these things are *our fault*. Here we are, say the modern Nehemiahs and Isaiahs, carrying on with our injustices and idolatries, and around us the world burns. Here we are carrying on with our smutty secularism,[10] our hypersexualized pleasures and pursuits, oblivious to the collateral violence and destruction. Our pessimism and fear—of each other as much as of our problems—are the harvest of generations of callous indifference, of rapacious politics and economics.

---

7. Patterson, "Enduring Value of Christian Realism," 28.

8. For an expansion, see Joustra, "Public Justice after the Resurrection."

9. Joustra and Wilkinson, *How to Survive the Apocalypse*.

10. Douthat, *The Decadent Society*.

"Fear," said the historian and Christian Realist Herbert Butterfield, "is a thing which is extraordinarily vivid while we are in its grip; but once it is over, it leaves little trace on our consciousness."[11] The historian has to work especially hard, argued Butterfield, because it is almost impossible to capture *feeling* in history: how to understand and interpret the terror Napoleon inspired, or the German dread of Russia, the atmosphere of Robespierre and his reign of terror? "Through such pinholes there leaks evidence of a terror which clearly underlies a wider area of the narrative than the single episode that drew our attention to it." How will history capture the *feeling* of our age, and what pinholes will historians' peek through to feel the larger narrative? 9/11? Sure. The financial collapse of 2007/2008, probably: the Rohingya, Syria, Yemen, the Islamic State, nuclear proliferation, coral reefs, COVID-19, . . . the list goes on.

"We do not always realize—and sometimes we do not like to recognize"—Butterfield noted—"how often a mistaken policy, an obliquity in conduct, a braggart manner, or even an act of cruelty, may be traceable to fear."[12]

Writing as though he were observing today's polarized politics, Butterfield argued in *Christianity, Diplomacy, and War*:

> . . . the greatest menace to our civilization today is the conflict between giant organized systems of self-righteousness—each system only too delighted to find that the other is wicked—each only too glad that the sins give it the pretext for still deeper hatred and animosity.[13]

What is true of individuals, he goes on to argue, is even more the case for nations.

> There is aggression; there is tyranny; there is revolutionary ferment; but if we wish to civilize international affairs we must do more than arrogantly hold our own against the barbarians, merely meeting them with their own weapons. Everything is going to depend in fact upon what we do over and above the work of self-defense. There can be no international system until somebody finds a way of relieving the pressure and begins the task of creating confidence.[14]

And yet, none of this would seem especially new to either the godfather of American Christian Realism, public theologian and counselor to presidents Reinhold Niebuhr, or to the fourth-century church father Augustine, from whom Niebuhr took so many of his most profound insights. How uniquely do our problems and anxieties, after all, stack up against the ailing collapse of the Roman world, or the cataclysm of National Socialism, the communistic Soviets, and the holocausts of the Second World War? Our guides, Niebuhr and Augustine, were no strangers to our current affairs, which too often exaggerate—as those caught in them do—the unique danger and terror of the present moment.

But surely *love is* too weak a thing to hang our geopolitical hats on in the Atomic Age, we hear the present-day complaint. Love, we may remember John the Evangelist

---

11. Butterfield, *International Conflict in the Twentieth Century*, 81–82.

12. Butterfield, *Christianity, Diplomacy, and War*, 90.

13. Butterfield, *Christianity, Diplomacy, and War*, 90.

14. Butterfield, *Christianity, Diplomacy, and War*, 90.

saying, casts out fear,[15] but this is surely a fine teaching for church mice, not soldiers and platoons. Amid the ruins of Rome, Augustine did not think so. Augustine said a commonwealth was *defined* by our common love. Reinhold Niebuhr agreed:

> Man, according to the biblical view, may use his freedom to make himself falsely the center of existence; but this does not change the fact that love rather than self-love is the law of existence, in the sense that man can only be health, and his communities at peace, if man is drawn out of himself and saved from the self-defeating consequences of self-love.[16]

None of this dismisses our problems out of hand, as though to say that placing *love* at the center of our politics magically resolves sin and its institutional depredations. It is simply to name that our anxiety is often out of pace with the reality of the world. Maybe we watch too much cable news. Maybe we spend too much time on social media. Maybe the scale of world affairs dwarfs what we imagine we, little individuals, can do. Yet through our civil, social, and religious institutions, even as individuals within our society, we can potentially do a great deal. And there is a profound story to tell. It is not all bad news. Love does not blind us to the scourge of sin and evil, but it motions us beyond them, to see the beautiful and restored, not just ugly and the broken: of Hope International building savings banks in Burundi, of the President's Emergency Preparedness Plan for HIV/AIDS (PEPFAR) beating back the scourge of AIDS in Sub-Saharan Africa, of Giant Pandas taken off the Endangered Species List in 2018. This is still our Father's world. And though the wrong seems oft so strong, God is the ruler yet.

The first word of the arrival of the King was given by the angels of Bethlehem. As we consider life, *pro Rege*, "for the King" today, we could do worse than start with the first words of his heralding angels: "Do not be afraid." These are the first words about the arriving King; and the last of the King's triumphant finish in Revelation are just like it, "Behold, I am making all things new," (Rev 21:5 ESV).

"We seem unable to subdue the demon of frightfulness in a head-on fight," according to Butterfield, who continues: "Let us take the devil by the ear, and surprise him with a dose of those gentler virtues that will be poison to him. At least when the world is in extremities, the doctrine of love becomes the ultimate measure of our conduct."[17]

What Is Christian Realism?

These *feelings* of an age are one of the reasons that Reinhold Niebuhr described Realism as a *disposition*, not doctrine; more a feeling about the world than a set of ideological abstractions. Eric Patterson calls Christian Realism a "community of discourse" rather than a formal ideology or school of thought.[18] John D. Carlson calls Christian Realism a "middle path" between "two untenable alternatives: on one hand, amoral and a-religious

---

15. See 1 John 4:18.

16. Niebuhr, "Augustine's Political Realism," In *Christian Realism and Political Problems*, 130.

17. Butterfield, *Christianity, Diplomacy, and War*, 98.

18. Patterson, "Enduring Value of Christian Realism," 28.

forms of political Realism and, on the other, sentimental or perfectionist forms of idealism."[19] Roger Shinn describes Christian Realism as:

> ... Christian in its appropriation of biblical motifs and classical doctrines, such as sin; it was realistic in its criticism of naïve idealism or utopianism, and it was in confrontation with the brute facts and power struggles of the contemporary world. It was alert to both the word of God and the latest news from the European and Asiatic battlefronts.[20]

So, what are the basic dispositions that hold this thing called Christian Realism together as a "community of discourse"? In a way, this whole book of sources is an answer to that question, but to shape our approach we want to first offer several broad ideas.[21]

First, Christian Realism stands within a broader set of assumptions about Realism more generally, including what we have called the Pragmatic Realist quadrilateral: egoism, groupism, anarchy, and power politics. Christian Realism does not *deny* that these conditions exist, but it offers profoundly different accounts of them, and sees them as among the features, not the natural identity, of the international system. As Niebuhr himself said:

> ... realism becomes morally cynical or nihilistic when it assumes that the universal characteristic in human behavior must also be regarded as normative. The biblical account of human behavior, on which Augustine bases his thought, can escape both illusion and cynicism because it recognizes that corruption in human freedom may make a behavior pattern universal without making it normative.[22]

Second, Christian Realism is *theologically Augustinian*, most especially, as Niebuhr above argues, in the way it thinks about human nature. Following the biblical account, Christian Realism gives a picture not only of how sin and misery permeate human affairs, but also how God's graces (Calvinists want to add special *and* common graces among them) provide the possibility for how such egotistical human persons can manage to make justice and beauty. It gives us a picture of the world, in other words, that explains how human beings can murder at Auschwitz *but also* how human beings can paint the Mona Lisa; it does not rob us of Isaiah's picture of beating our swords into plowshares, even on this side of the eschaton. A *seriously theological* account of human nature, therefore, does not leave Christian Realism stranded, like Pragmatic Realism, without a path to cooperation and justice apart from egoistic, material self-interest. Such an account also presumes real attention to all three "images" of International Relations Theory (individual domestic politics, international politics), as Kenneth Waltz calls them in *Man, the State, and War*.

Third, Christian Realism therefore offers an *Augustinian politics*. In both classical Realism and Liberalism, part of the argument for political order has always been to

19. Carlson, "What Is Christian about Christian Realism?" 37.

20. Shinn quoted in Patterson, "Enduring Value of Christian Realism," 29.

21. The following adaptation provided here from Patterson, "Enduring Value of Christian Realism," 29–32.

22. Niebuhr, "Augustine's Political Realism," In *Christian Realism and Political Problems*, 130.

7

"restrain the licentiousness of man," an argument following from Rom 13:4, where Paul reminds the Roman church that the government does not "bear the sword for nothing" (NIV). Interestingly, broadly pragmatic and secular approaches agree with Paul's reasoning, if not his presumption that God has ordained the business of government: the government's monopoly on coercive power enables it to restrain the worst of human behavior. But Augustinian politics gives one further account of political authority that is not just about controlling our worst behaviors. If we think of this "restraining authority" as a *negative* authority, then Augustine might say political authority also has a *positive* dimension: the pursuit of public justice. At the heart of a great political community, what Augustine calls a *commonwealth*, are not common fears but *common loves*. Commonwealths are *for* things, and it is only in the process of what they are for, that we know what they are also *against*. The United States is *for* life, liberty, and the pursuit of happiness. Canada is *for* peace, order, and good government. This implies things we are against, but the cornerstone of political order is not *fear*, says Augustine, but *love*. *Both* political duties imply the use of force, at the domestic level, but also—contra pacifists—a morally engaged armed force at the foreign level, to protect and to cultivate the virtues of the commonwealth. Broadly, such an Augustinian politics overlaps somewhat with what is called the Just War tradition.

Fourth, despite international anarchy, institutions and systems are very important to Christian Realists. Of course, most world affairs take place within the context of institutions and systems, whether states or otherwise. But what the Christian Realist is especially interested in is how those systems and institutions are shaped by *power* and by *religion*, or—to put it in Augustinian terms—by how our systems and institutions are structured and oriented toward loves and fears. Abraham Kuyper called this an "architectonic critique," by which he meant "understanding and explaining systems and institutions by examining their incurably religious roots and functions."[23] What we love and what we fear has a way of being powerfully structured into our common life, and by studying those same systems and institutions we can sometimes be surprised to discover that what we *say we love* is not always the same as what *we really do love*. Christian Realism penetrates beyond high-minded rhetoric to ask this *cui bono*: who or what really benefits? Who or what is this system or process really aimed toward? Students of today's deconstructionist politics may be surprised to find that early Christian Realists such as Niebuhr and Bennett were dissecting power relations well before it became fashionable.

Fifth, Christian Realists are therefore skeptical of but also recognize the importance of power in groups. Eric Patterson says, Christian Realism "criticizes the potency of collective chauvinism," especially nationalism (a form of groupism). If, as John Calvin says, the heart is a factory of idols, then the Christian Realist sees world affairs as an idol industrial complex. Individuals may well often make self-interested choices, but groups are even *more* likely to make self-interested decisions, where restraint is lower because consequences and benefits are collectivized. Environmentalists often point to the old sheep parable from Scotland to help us understand the "tragedy of the commons." In that

23. Joustra, "Globalization and the Kingdom of God," 9. See online at https://www.cpjustice.org/public/public_justice_review/article/56.

parable, common pastures shared between farmers are over-exploited because small, self-interested acts around a common resource eventually grow into a collapse of the pasture. This may seem like a benign enough problem in the bucolic highlands, but when the logic of such collective chauvinism is applied to nuclear proliferation or ocean acidification, we can see that things get very dangerous, very quickly.

Sixth, Christian Realism rejects many "isms,'" both abstract ideological accounts of the world—that try to take the world "as the ideology believes it to be" rather than "as it is"—and also states, systems, institutions, and ideologies that have at their heart a kind of corruption (*Christian* Realists would say, idolatrous tendencies, or egoism). Augustine said that a commonwealth is bound together by its common loves. Niebuhr agreed, saying "commonwealths are bound together by a common love, or collective interest."[24] The *higher* or *lower* the political order, the more moral and just the love toward which the commonwealth bends. No commonwealth bends perfectly, to be sure, and no system or institution is inoculated from idolatrous intrusion. What Russian novelist Alexander Solzhenitsyn said about the human heart could be a Christian Realist confession about states and global institutions: the line between good and evil cuts right through its center.

Finally, Christian Realism emphasizes limits and restraint. It is not revolutionary, and it has a tendency to prudence and skepticism. Niebuhr's most famous book, *The Irony of American History* (1952), emphasizes how egotistical pride clouds human judgment and leads to tragedy. This is a special challenge for rich, powerful, technocratic societies in the North Atlantic world. Such powers can sometimes fool our citizens and policy makers into believing that they have the power to stop and redress many evils in the world that, in fact, they do not. The *tragedy* of great power politics, as John Mearsheimer put it, cannot be patched by the wizards of Silicon Valley. It is a perennial part of human and political nature, this side of the eschaton. Just so, moderation, restraint, and prudence are among Christian Realism's canonical virtues.

Here is then an introductory picture of Christian Realism, as follows:

1. Pragmatic Realism (and its quadrilateral: egoism, groupism, anarchy, and power politics) as features, not as fundamental.

2. Augustinian picture of human nature, and a broad picture of international relations (humanity, the state, and war).

3. Augustinian politics, not only to restrain evil but *also* to build positive public justice, tools for which include the use of force (Just War).

4. Architectonic critique, understanding and explaining systems and institutions by their (sometimes undisclosed) religious visions of human life and politics.

5. Skepticism of groups and group decision making, especially states.

6. Alertness to abstract ideologies, and *lower* loves that groups sometimes bend toward, i.e., ethno-nationalism.

7. Restraint and prudence in foreign affairs, emphasizing order and justice rather than power-maximization or utopian governmental structures.

24. Niebuhr, "Augustine's Political Realism," 123.

A great deal of this picture strikes us as Christian, but interestingly Christian Realism's critics, and certainly Niebuhr's strongest critics, were often fellow Christians. Here, they found a "religio-ethical framework too comfortably accommodated to power structures, [which] justified American power and policies, and reinforced liberal and democratic values at the expense of authentic Christian belief, commitment, and community." In short, for such critics, Christian Realism is not nearly "Christian enough: it is more Realism than Christian."[25]

In his essay entitled "Why War is a Moral Necessity for America," Stanley Hauerwas lays out a Christian pacifist's criticism of Niebuhr and Christian Realism.[26] These tend to center on the tradition of Just War, a religious school of thinking which lays out conditions under which warfare can take place (*jus ad bellum*, right criteria for going to war, and *jus in bello*, right conduct within war). Hauerwas argues that Just War itself is too *idealist*, a false set of ideological abstractions which naively presumes any moral theory can restrain war. "War," he argues, "has become the altar of sacrifice to a false idol—the nation."[27] Niebuhrian Realism, he goes on, "provides more a legitimating ideology for America's political arrangements than it does a faithful explication of a Political Theology rooted in Scripture."[28]

William T. Cavanaugh even argues that the modern nation-state is an "apostasy of Christendom," and that its Westphalian origin (1648) is a story not about restraining evil and public justice, but rather about enabling princes to make total war.[29] The tragic, genocidal history of the twentieth century, says Cavanaugh, is not an accident of the state and its powers, but rather the logical consequence of an idolatrous nationalism captive to the very idols of power, self-interest, and war that Christian Realism pretends to moderate. Finally, its abstractions of Scripture overlook direct commands of Jesus, turning his command to "turn the other cheek" into carpet bombing the Vietnamese with startling ease.

Interestingly, Christian Realists tend to take this kind of criticism very seriously. Niebuhr, for example, "shared Hauerwas's apprehensions, not only about just war but about American idolatry as well."[30] John D. Carlson argues that "Niebuhr was not a just war thinker per se" and that "the distinctive contributions of Christian Realism fall from view when conceived through a narrow just war lens."[31] The Christian Realist skepticism of human nature and groups and its alertness to abstract ideologies and prudential moderation *all* suggest a healthy skepticism toward any "checklist" application of a just war doctrine. Christian Realism, especially outside of the United States, in its Greco-Roman origin, its English and Dutch expressions, also finds a ready partner to Hauerwas's important criticisms of American nationalism and hubris. And while Christian Realists would differ meaningfully from Hauerwas on any thoroughgoing pacifism, and typically are

25. Carlson, "What Is Christian about Christian Realism?" 38.

26. Carlson and Ebel, *From Jeremiad to Jihad*.

27. See also Cavanaugh, *Migrations of the Holy*, especially his essay "Killing for the Telephone Company," 52–64.

28. Hauerwas and Broadway, *Wilderness Wanderings*.

29. Cavanaugh, *The Myth of Religious Violence*.

30. Carlson, "What Is Christian about Christian Realism?" 45.

31. Carlson, "What Is Christian about Christian Realism?" 46.

supportive of a restrained just war framework, there is plenty of room within Christian Realism for skeptics of government intentions, idolatrous nationalism, and unrestrained power. This critique, in fact, is one of Christian Realism's defining features.

It is finally important to say that Christian Realism is *a* Christian view on world affairs. It is not *the* Christian view, though obviously we find it the most convincing and constructive. In this book, we will survey those views from not only classic Christian Realists, like Niebuhr, Butterfield, Ramsey, and others, but also a later generation of Christian Realists, who apply and extend the tradition to contemporary issues. Here we will find Eric Patterson's "community of discourse," and—we hope—a meaningful and serious attempt to offer this Christian Realism as a pattern and a paradigm of "hope in troubled times."

Christian Realists: A Generational Anthology

Our final argument is born out in the structure of the book itself, which we split into three parts, what we call the three generations of Christian Realists. A great deal of Christian Realism has been footnotes to Niebuhr, the man who virtually defines the tradition. And there is good cause to argue, as we said above, that much of Christian Realism comes down to the agenda set by Reinhold Niebuhr. But, ultimately, while Niebuhr was undoubtedly a giant of his time, he was still *of his time*, and the tradition to which he gave voice was far older, and far more perennial, than both his critics and his advocates sometimes admit.

Our generational structure is therefore anchored to events and periods, not just persons. We begin, undoubtedly, with Niebuhr. But it is not Niebuhr himself who defines this "first generation" but rather the nature of the challenges he faced: the interwar period, the Second World War itself, fascism, communism, and the emergence of weapons of mass destruction. This first generation, roughly 1932–65, is characterized not only by these challenges abroad but also by the collateral challenges at home, idealistic policies rooted in utopian views of human progress, whether it be in terms of science, education, the Social Gospel, or the transforming power of human intellectual and reason to upend the logic of the international system. Niebuhr undoubtedly had every one of these challenges front of mind when he published *Moral Man, Immoral Society* in 1932, an opening salvo against the idealists just as fascism and Soviet communism were on their march to domination and to war.

Niebuhr is joined in trans-Atlantic fashion by great preachers, pundits, and practitioners like Herbert Butterfield, John C. Bennett, Martin Wight, and theologians like Dietrich Bonhoeffer, Paul Tillich, and apologists like C. S. Lewis. Contrary to the appeasers and the idealists, this generation gave a clear-eyed account of sin, both individual and institutional, the consequence of which was vigilance on the part of not just citizens but Christians to act responsibly in the face of real danger and evil. Niebuhr himself employed "irony" as a crucial category for the Christians in the United States of America, whose power and privilege were so extraordinary that their origin was either forgotten or denied. Such innocence was not a happy one, tragically, and its naiveté was a cause Christian Realists laid at the feet of the cataclysm of the Second World War.

Postwar reconstruction and international order beget the line into what we call our second generation of Christian Realists (1965–90), dominated by the proliferation of nuclear weapons, the Cold War proxy escalations in conflicts, especially Vietnam, and the machinery of bipolarity that so quickly became an existential threat to civilization. The lieutenants of the Second World War had become the world's leaders, not only in the United States (Kennedy, Johnson, Nixon, Reagan) but also abroad (Mitterand, Helmut Schmidt, Jaruzekski).

Much seemed new to this generation of Christian Realists, but much—most—also was the same. The ethics of power politics were hardly original to the Princeton ethicist Paul Ramsey (1913–88), or foreign policy experts like Ernest W. Lefever (1919–2009), or political scientists like Kenneth W. Thompson (1921–2013). The recovery and update of doctrines like just war were a key piece of work in a world that many thought had suspended traditional rules of conflict, with weapons of mass destruction. Ramsey and others labored to show that while tactics had shifted, the moral fulcrum had not. The questions were undoubtedly different for this generation, the challenges of positivism and secularism were different from the idealism of the generation before, but the answers were rooted in the same constancy of Augustinian thought. Jean Bethke Elshtain (1941–2013) cited both Augustine and Niebuhr with regularity, whom she called the greatest public theologian of our time.

Finally, the third generation of Christian Realists (1990–present) is perhaps most characterized by its commitment to theological orthodoxy as a ready resource to answer often forgotten questions. A *theological* recovery, argue those like Keith Pavlischek, is long overdue, not only from the easy positivism of the Cold War, but from the liberal theology of the first generation, Niebuhr fore among them. *La Revanche de Dieu* is not original to the Christian Realists, but a return to the sources of the tradition has proven fecund for this generation struggling to make sense of a world transforming from bipolarity, to multipolarity, and (perhaps?) back again. The questions of this generation tend to be more theological in part because of the resurgence of tribalism and ethnonationalism after the Cold War, a resurgence that finds its catalysts not only abroad, but also at home. The question of polarization persists, not only the old rivalries of the international system, but the newly exposed rivalries within liberal-democratic states themselves. Now, as then, the work of Augustinian realism, what we call Christian Realism, seems powerful and fresh. Now, as then, trans-Atlantic collaboration brings voices from over the ocean, and increasingly around the world, to answer questions of *justice*, of *order*, and of *right* and *wrong*, in newly urgent ways.

Conclusion: Against the Water Monsters

The Leviathan is an unlikely metaphor. It is mentioned only a handful of times in the Bible, and then often in passing or itself a metaphor for strength, power, or mystery. As best we can tell, it refers to a sea monster or serpent. Job 41 gives us the most complete picture, where

God himself asks if Job can "pull in Leviathan with a fishhook" or "put a cord through its nose or pierce its jaw with a hook"—"Will it keep begging you for mercy? Will it speak to you with gentle words?"—"Flames stream from its mouth; sparks of fire shoot out. Smoke pours from its nostrils, as from a boiling pot over burning reeds" (NIV)—and so on. In Psalm 104 God is praised for creating all things, including the Leviathan. Chapter 60 of the book of Enoch in the Pseudepigrapha calls it a female monster dwelling in the watery abyss (while the Behemoth is a male monster living in the desert east of Eden).

What an usual choice, then, for Thomas Hobbes to have made on what has becoming the driving metaphor of international politics since his publication of *The Leviathan* (1651). This, after all, is the image that Hobbes and the Realists (and Liberals) give us for how to imagine the state: a Leviathan, a powerful beast unmatched by any but God, a terror to all who encounter it. Our picture of international relations becomes clear if we accept this starting point. A great big ocean, dominated by Leviathans of varying size and scale, destined to hunt, hurt, and overpower each other. It is the setting of a *Godzilla* movie, or a big budget *Pacific Rim*—the clash of the Leviathans.

We do not think Abraham Kuyper had Godzilla in mind, we doubt he was even thinking of Thomas Hobbes, when he argued in his *Lectures on Calvinism* that "the state is not an octopus."[32] But his point fits the metaphor: the state is neither all powerful, nor all encompassing. Even politics, precious and profound as it may be, is hardly the full picture of human life. In the beginning was the Word, not the nation-state.

We must contend with states, but maybe we can find a better metaphor that matches the perspective of Christian Realism, with its skepticism of groups, power, and its prudential approach. Mariano Barbato has argued that this metaphor should be "the pilgrim":

> Hobbes offered with the Leviathan, a metaphor taken from the religious semantics of the Bible, to illustrate the new concept of the "modern state." My pilgrim is like the Leviathan a metaphor taken from religious semantics and the task is the same: offering a new root metaphor for global politics.[33]

A pilgrim posture toward our politics sounds suspiciously like the fifth verse of Canada's national anthem, which at some (Canadian) universities they still sing with gusto:

> Ruler Supreme, who hearest humble prayer,
> Hold our Dominion in thy loving care.
> Help us to find, O God in Thee, our lasting rich reward,
> As waiting for a better day, we ever stand on guard.

Can we do better than the terror-inspired water monsters that Pragmatic Realism offers? We think we can. And we think these generations of Christian Realists such as Reinhold Niebuhr, Herbert Butterfield, Paul Ramsey, John C. Bennett, Jean Bethke Elshtain, and Rebecca Heinrichs are just the guides to get us there.

---

32. Kuyper, *Lectures on Calvinism*.
33. Barbato, *Pilgrimage, Politics, and International Relations*, xi-xii.

Part 1: **Classical Christian Realists**

Classical Christian Realists: An Introduction

THE FIRST GENERATION OF Christian Realism began as a reaction to political idealism in the lead-up to the Second World War and ended at the time of U.S. escalation in Vietnam, roughly the period 1932–65.[1,2] The interwar period (1918–39) was characterized by idealistic policies rooted in utopian views of human progress, whether in terms of science, education, the Social Gospel, or, in international affairs, by a conviction that democracy, international law, and international institutions could transform power politics by mandating peace. Reinhold Niebuhr (1892–1971) published what some consider to be the opening salvo of Christian Realism, *Moral Man and Immoral Society,* in 1932, just as the Nazis were on the rise, the Soviets were ending their first Five-Year Plan, and as the Japanese were preparing to rape Nanking.

The events that the first generation of Christian Realists observed, interpreted, and reacted to were of global consequence: the diabolical ideologies of National Socialism and communism, the responsibility of government for order and justice at home and abroad, the responsibility of citizens and governments to reject irresponsible pacifism and undertake just wars, the complex issues of weapons of mass destruction. In a moment, more will be said about a few of these themes because they perennially show up in the Christian Realist literature, to this very day.

Christian Realism provided thinkers like Niebuhr, Bennett, and Butterfield a lens, or an approach, for understanding not just the phenomena itself, but how to properly think about it. As elaborated in the introduction to this volume, there are certain consistent presuppositions that guide these individuals, rooted in orthodox Augustinian thinking, even if the individuals do not necessarily agree on the best specific policy course of action at a given moment.

Henry Pitney Van Dusen gave us the term "middle axioms" to describe the informed, policy relevant approach of Christian Realism. Van Dusen, longtime president of Union Theological Seminary while Niebuhr and Bennett were teaching there, was a notable ecumenical leader during the middle part of the twentieth century. He turned against the

1. This distinction between realism and idealism is associated with E. H. Carr's important book, *The Twenty Years Crisis, 1919–1939,* which argued that the Nazis and their allies were allowed to strengthen due to the naive, idealistic policies of the West.

2. Tillich and Lewis both made radio addresses during the war. See Stone and Weaver, eds. *Against the Third Reich: Paul Tillich's Wartime Radio Broadcasts into Nazi Germany;* C. S. Lewis published some of those addresses, including "The Conditions for a Just War" and "Why I Am Not a Pacifist." Dietrich Bonhoeffer ended up in prison after joining an assassination attempt against Hitler. See his letters, particularly "After Ten Years."

liberal idealism of the 1920s–30s, recognizing the need for robust structures against the evil possible in political life. Thus, he was a proponent of the United Nations as a bulwark against future wars. In his introduction to the "Six Pillars of Peace," composed primarily by future U.S. Secretary of State John Foster Dulles, Van Dusen notes an important policy point. Christian Realism typically provides what he calls, "middle axioms":

> The attempt of Christians to discover the limits within which they may speak with authority in the political and economic realm has been greatly furthered in recent years by the recognition of "middle axioms." The attempt of middle axioms are propositions midway between broad general goals which are likely to claim ready acceptance but may easily be neglected in practice, and concrete plans which are the province of technical experts.

This is a recurring theme throughout Christian Realism, from Niebuhr to Ramsey to today's Christian Realists: we can provide a thoughtful, prophetic set of principles ("middle axioms") but we also respect the expertise of technical experts to inform policy practicalities.

These first-generation Christian Realists emphasized individual sin and the sinful chauvinism of collectives and societies, which means that Christians, and all citizens, must act responsibly to challenge and thwart evil. Herbert Butterfield (1900–1979) consistently lectured about the role of sinful human nature in history, particularly as regards self-interestedness and war-making, summarized in his "International Conflict in the 20th Century: A Christian View." Niebuhr called on the "Children of Light" to counter the antagonistic evil of "The Children of Darkness." This is why Bennett, Niebuhr, and others called on Americans to join the fight during the Second World War. One will find similar themes during that time in the speeches and essays of theologians such as Dietrich Bonhoeffer, Paul Tillich, and the popular apologist C. S. Lewis.[3] John C. Bennett (1902–95) reflected on the need for a sober, but responsible, appraisal of the Second World War in his essay "American Christians and the War." His book, *Christian Realism*, argued that Christians cannot bow out of society, but must take up their vocations, including service as statesmen, soldiers, and law-enforcement officials, in order to live out the "law of love" in a fallen world.

Tragedy and Irony in Postwar Liberations

There is a vocabulary the recurs in the writings of the Christian Realists that includes terms such as sin, order, hope, justice, ambiguity, responsibility, and the like. One set of descriptors that arises across the generations of Christian Realism, but is associated with Reinhold Niebuhr in particular, is "irony" and "tragedy." From Niebuhr through Elshtain, U.S. foreign policy choices are defined in these terms and it is helpful to the student of Christian Realism to see how different this terminology is from what one reads in other forms of political commentary (e.g., secular, Catholic social teaching).

---

3. In Part 2 of this book, we will see Christian Realist Ernest Lefever's distinction between sturdy "morality" (ethics) and immature, or irresponsible, "moralism" (platitudes).

In *The Irony of American History.* Niebuhr defines three different ways for observing contemporary situations. The first is *pathos*. Niebuhr says that the "pathetic" situation "elicits pity, but neither deserves admiration nor warrants contrition." An example is suffering caused by "purely natural evil," such as an outbreak of bubonic plague in the Congo.

The second and third are more significant for the moral policy maker who has the responsibility for making decisions and taking action in the real world. *Tragedy* is when a "conscious choice for evil" is made for the sake of some good, or some higher good. The threat of annihilation in nuclear deterrence is tragic: it defends civilization by promising massive destruction. Niebuhr writes, "tragedy elicits admirations as well as pity." The ethical statesman willing to make such terrible choices is worthy of Niebuhr's respect.

Irony, for Niebuhr, is when "apparently fortuitous incongruities in life," which appear to be random or unplanned, "are, upon closer examination, realized to be *not* merely fortuitous." Often in literature such hidden relationships are the making of comedy, such as in Shakespeare's plays where the misunderstanding of identities and relationships is the foundation of the humor. Hidden relationships, such as how strength can be a vulnerability, go beyond the comedic to the ironic. The hubris of heroes can likewise be ironic. Where selfishness overlaps with goodwill, where self-sacrifice intersects with self-interest, is usually a gray area, one that Christian Realists tend to call "ambiguous." Niebuhr argues that when one becomes aware of such ironies in political life, one must grapple with that pretense or vanity with contrition, because the temptation will be to defend oneself and one's prerogatives, accentuating it to the "point of pure evil."

The Irony of American History goes on to a thoughtful evaluation of American motives and morality. Niebuhr argues that America has long congratulated itself for its morality: eventually overcoming slavery, avoiding an overseas empire like the European powers, and eschewing international entanglements. But there is a conceit here that is prideful and dishonest, because a careful scrutiny of U.S. history shows much good but also plenty of moral failure. Even good deeds are often motivated by a mixture of self-interestedness and idealistic intentions.

In *The Irony of American History* Niebuhr made an important statement about responsibility, statecraft, and early atomic diplomacy. The U.S. did not come to World War II with a large military or overseas empire, but it ended the war as a superpower. Few Americans could have imagined in 1941 the global responsibilities the US would have to shoulder just four years later as the bulwark of freedom, peace, and security. Such responsibility exemplifies the principle of stewardship in political life: to protect political order and advance justice. Niebuhr also points to the dilemma of nuclear weapons. He, and most Christian Realists, believed that WMDs were a tragic necessity for deterring rapacious, Soviet-led communism, but they did not shy away from the "moral ambiguities" presented by an apocalyptic nuclear showdown.

In contrast to the ironies of American history, such as the chasm between the "ideal and reality of freedom" in the American South, the Soviet Union's ethic was truly evil. Niebuhr argued that Moscow embraced an idealistic morality of equality and liberation that justified a rapacious, totalitarian politics. The ends justified the means. In later chapters, we will see a similar use of the language of tragedy, irony, and ambiguity by

Christian Realists, one that recognizes both the positive aspects and the shortcomings of U.S. foreign policy as well as the moral nature of the Cold War struggle

Theologians of a New World Order

The Christian Realists had a clear-eyed relationship with justifications for representative government, democracy, and human rights, the latter a term that surged into international relations after WWII, in the wake of the Nuremburg and Tokyo trials. The war crimes tribunals called Germany to account for crimes against the peace (waging war) in a way similar to the Treaty of Versailles in 1918. The Nazis, and similarly the Japanese leadership, were also held accountable for crimes against individual persons as well groups (e.g., "crimes against humanity") and, ultimately, the 1949 Genocide Convention was adopted. Alongside the revitalized Geneva Conventions of 1949 (e.g., protections for prisoners of war, the shipwrecked, and wounded soldiers), a regime of trials and new laws sought to re-establish a moral center in international politics that was decimated by the depredations of the Axis Powers.

Especially for Americans, the notion of robust civil liberties and civil rights was an expectation of political life. For Christians, the value of the human person, rooted in the doctrine of the *imago dei* and Christ's Great Commandment, were already important. But the industrial-scale atrocities of the Second World War, from Manchuria to Auschwitz, galvanized many—including the Christian Realists—to vociferously speak out on the topic of human rights.

It is important to recognize that the Christian Realists did not make the case for democracy, civil liberties, and human rights in vague, moralistic terms. One key argument was that robust individual liberties are the first check on the power of the state, in other words, civil liberties and civil rights are a balancing of powers, a check on centralized power. Moreover, some Christian Realists argued, when human rights have been recognized in law and practice, it has often been the result of an exhausting battle of some sort. Niebuhr made such arguments in favor of labor movements and the rights of black Americans as early as the 1920s. He later explicated the value of international law and institutions, including a strong United Nations, as a similar republican check on any country having too much power in international relations. These types of argument were important to those drafting the UN Charter and its successor, the legally-binding International Covenant on Civil and Political Rights (1966), which protects religious freedom and other human rights.

Beyond Moralism and Imperialism

John C. Bennett's mid-1943 "American Christians and the War" was addressed to students—students who were moralistically opposed to war and deeply skeptical of U.S. involvement on behalf of the British and French Empires. Bennett counters that two wrong-headed Christian responses to the war are aiding the Axis evil. The first is a form of political pacifism that enervates the West's war effort. The second is a somewhat reasonable concern that in the past Washington and other governments painted the Great War (the First World War) as a "crusade," and that the "holy war" motif covered up sin and destruction.

Bennett is patient with the pacifism of his student audience, desiring to galvanize them to understand that the United States must thwart fascist tyranny. Bennett argues, as Niebuhr does, that Americans are a bit naive and enjoy playing the naif in order to avoid responsibility, but if Americans really knew just how bad it was in Europe and Asia at the time, they would feel called to action. Ignorance, feigned or real, is no excuse for forsaking moral responsibility. Bennett notes that there is a wide, shared middle ground for pacifists and those who think the war is just. His four areas of agreement are ones that are echoed throughout the Christian Realist literature. First, both just war advocates and pacifists refuse to label the world war a "holy war." Second, both sides "support opportunities for conscientious objectors," which is consonant with the American founding. Moreover, both sides want to "keep government policy under Christian criteria" and both sides know that one must begin preparing now—in the midst of hot war (1943)—to establish an enduring and just peace. Bennett's is a reasoned argument and, over time, arguments like his—when combined with the atrocities of the Nazis and Imperial Japan—galvanized young Americans to serve and to fight.

During the 1930s, attorney John Foster Dulles was heavily involved in efforts to explicate Christian responses to global insecurity, such as at the ecumenical Oxford Conference of 1937. A devout Presbyterian, lay leader within the Federal Council of Churches (predecessor to the National Council of Churches), and future U.S. Secretary of State (his brother, Avery, became CIA director), Dulles led the drafting of "Six Pillars of Peace" that he famously outlined in a speech in March, 1943 in New York City. With an eye toward a just and durable post-war peace, Dulles begins, "We are about to address ourselves to the citizens of this country and say to them that . . . considerations of *morality* and *enlightened self-interest* combine to require this nation now to commit itself to a future of organized international collaboration."[4] Dulles goes on to articulate a set of principles for what today we call the "liberal international order," the important role for U.S. leadership, and the establishment of the United Nations. He does not do so idealistically, but as matters of grave necessity: we must cooperate, we must work together, and these institutional arrangements will check the power of any evil actor such as Germany or Japan. Dulles would, as President Eisenhower's Secretary of State, be a staunch anti-Communist focused on buttressing the Western alliance against Soviet and Chinese domination in Asia and Europe.

Apostasy at Home, Not Just Abroad

Martin Wight's "The Church, Russia, and the West" (1948) foreshadowed Samuel Huntington's *The Clash of Civilizations* (1992) by outlining a historic struggle between the Orthodox East and the Latin West that has been handed down to their respective

---

4. Dulles, "Six Pillars of Peace" original speech at http://www.ibiblio.org/pha/policy/1943/1943–03–18a.html.

descendants: Russia's secular Marxism and the West's secular bourgeoisie liberalism. These were the "organized systems of self-righteousness" that Wight's friend Butterfield warned were destined to violently—and perhaps apocalyptically—clash for global order. Yet the real problem, argued Wight, is not the power-balancing of East and West, rather, it is "the emancipation of power from moral restraints." In other words, the breakdown of Christian morality, whether in the East or West, has emancipated the raw power of these civilizations from the restraining influence of religion.

Wight echoes several key Christian Realist themes in his essay. Most importantly, should the Christian give up when it seems that power politics is taking the world in the direction of secular, anti-Christian totalitarianism and/or war? The answer is a resounding, "NO." The reason that Christians have hope is because they understand history to be sacred: "Between history as power only and history as purpose . . . [between] secular history as the surface of time-process, dead and gone, and sacred history as the sacred true power, transparent against the light of eternity!"[5] Wight wrote that Augustine's two cities are our lived reality and as such represent a tension that believers must engage and live through. He castigates the normal response of liberal Christians, to either hope for the best and muddle through without a concern for expertise or responsible action (which he called Pelagianism) or a secular-liberal faith in progress as a reified force in and of itself. He further observed, "neither of these beliefs are Christian" and indicated they do not take into account the realities of human fallenness nor of human responsibility for neighbor-love. In short, a careful reading of Wight reintroduces, from a British perspective, many of the themes popularized by Niebuhr and the American Christian Realists: hubris, secularism, Augustine's two cities, and calls for resolution and hope.

Conclusion

In conclusion, as the reader turns to the select readings by Niebuhr and others, one may ask: why is so much of this focused on the United States in terms of U.S. power and U.S. responsibility? In part this is due to the fact that Niebuhr himself was a colossus of Christian Realist thinking, who dominated the discourse to such an extent that he advised the U.S. State Department, the White House, and was prominently displayed as the cover portrait for *Time* magazine's twenty-fifth anniversary issue! Second, whereas post-war European capitals were struggling to rebuild in the aftermath of 1945, the United States was undeniably the only superpower in the West. Moreover, because the United States had never had a colonial empire and because Americans had told themselves that they had a uniquely moral foreign policy, including past isolationism, Christian Realists and others called, coaxed, and castigated Washington to step up to the global responsibility that was in harmony with its unique level of power. Finally, on the Continent and elsewhere (e.g., Canada), many Christian thinkers were not thinking about power politics, but rather influenced by the Christian Democratic movement to focus on consensual politics at home and (Western) European integration. These governments were either absorbed with their own reconstruction or with a middle

5. Wight, "The Church, Russia, and the West," 33.

power path of diplomacy, tied to the institutions and order of the superpower's making after the war. Partly for that reason, the dilemma of power—the tragedy and irony as Niebuhr himself would put it—was a burden that fell most heavily on the architects of international order after WWII, primarily the United States of America. Why and to what extent America's allies quietly quit the field of great power politics, after vigorous and substantial investments into its struggles in the twentieth century, is a fascinating if somewhat off-topic question. But for whatever reason, Realism generally, and Christian Realism certainly, found a home most readily in the post-imperial United Kingdom and in the newly ascendant United States of America.

1 – 1

"Human Nature and the Dominion of Fear"[1]

Herbert Butterfield

FEAR IS A THING which is extraordinarily vivid while we are in its grip; but once it is over, it leaves little trace of itself in our consciousness. It is one of the experiences that we can never properly remember—one, also, which since we may be ashamed of it we may have reason for not wishing to remember. We are in the position of those unsympathetic parents who, though they can recall the concrete things that happened in their lives, have forgotten what it really felt like to be in love. It is curious that moods and sensations which mastered us in the past, and which may almost consume a man, are so difficult to recover or to reimagine afterward.

Because it is so hard for us to recapture the feeling in our imagination, we can be thoroughly nonparticipating when there is question of a fear that is not our own. If another person is the victim of it, we may fail—or it may never occur to us to try—to apprehend either the thing in itself or the range of its possible consequences. It would seem that we are not always easily convinced of the existence of fear in other people, especially when the other people are political rivals or potential enemies. At any rate historians are not easily convinced when they deal at a later time with former enemies of their country. Above all, if the thing which the other party dreaded is a danger that never materialized, it becomes easy to be skeptical about the genuineness of the fear itself. When the historian cannot escape recording the terror that Napoleon inspired, or the German dread of Russia at one time and another, or the apprehension of a people in the face of imminent attack, he may produce a factual statement that gives little impression of the force and the effect of the emotion actually experienced. Sometimes he is jolted into a realization of his deficiency as he finds himself confronted by an event and sees that the rest of his picture provides only an inadequate context for it. It turns out that there was some standing factor in the story—a terrible feeling of thunder in the atmosphere—which he had imperfectly apprehended or merely failed to keep in mind. We read of Londoners who, during the Gordon Riots, pandered to the forces of anarchy; they felt it safer to don the blue cockade of the rioters than to rely on government protection. We learn that when Robespierre spoke before the revolutionary Convention on the day preceding his fall,

---

1. "Human Nature and the Dominion of Fear" appeared as chapter 4 in Herbert Butterfield's *International Conflict in the Twentieth Century*.

his vague charges and threats against unspecified traitors left every man in apprehension—wondering whether his own life was safe; and for this reason he lost his majority. When we meet such things as these we are sometimes forced to the sudden realization of the fact that the story has been going on for some time in an atmosphere of fear which we have been failing to take sufficiently into account. Through such pinholes there leaks evidence of a terror which clearly underlies a wider area of the narrative than the single episode that drew our attention to it.

The student of history needs to consider this question, therefore. Some aspects of the past—and these perhaps the ones most related to men's minds and moods—are particularly difficult to recapture. The atrocities of our own day, for example, are naturally more vivid to us than those of a century/ago. The world tends to judge a present-day revolution merely by its atrocities and an ancient one much more by its ideals and purposes. This is partly because the sufferings and terrors of a former generation are more easily overlooked. We need to possess something of the art of the dramatist in order to enter into the sensations of other people—to recover, for example, the "feel" of some terror that once possessed a nation or a ministry. And it must not be said that we ought to leave our imagination out of our history, for the minds of men, and even the mood of society, may have their part in accounting for human conduct.

Even when the student of the past is really bent on analysis, he must recapture the fear, and the attendant high pressure, which so greatly affect the actions of men and the policy of governments. Yet the historical imagination is never so defective as when it has to deal with the apprehension and insecurity of frightened people. It is a point to remember, therefore, that the historian, surveying the past (like the statesman surveying rival powers in his own contemporary world), is apt to do less than justice to the part played by fear in politics, at any rate so far as concerns governments other than his own.

We do not always realize—and sometimes we do not like to recognize—how often a mistaken policy, an obliquity in conduct, a braggart manner, or even an act of cruelty, may be traceable to fear. What is true of individual people is likely to be still more true of great agglomerations of humanity, where further irrational factors always come into play. With nations, even more than with individuals, in fact, the symptoms of fear may be unlike fear—they may even be the result of an attempt to convince us of the reverse. Apart from all this, fear may exist as a more constant and less sensational factor in life, perpetually constricting very reasonable people in their conduct in the world. It may curb their natural desire to react against injustice, or (if only by the production of wishful thinking) prevent them from recognizing the crimes of their own government. It can lead to small compliances and complicities, the production of "yes men," the hardening of inherited orthodoxies and accepted ideas. It may cause a man to halt in the course of his own speculations, and shrink from the dreadful audacity of pushing his thought to its logical conclusion. Even in the field of scholarship, writers may be too frightened of one another; historians may be too anxious to play safe. There can also be a generalized fear that is no longer conscious of being fear, and hangs about in the form of oppressive dullness or heavy cloud, as though the snail had retreated into its shell and forgotten the reason, but had not the spirit to put out its feelers anymore.

Sir Edward Grey said that it was unwise for a diplomat to be oversuspicious. It is possible that he himself was most unfortunate in the region where he failed to follow his own teaching.

During the French Wars of Religion, the fear, the whisperings and the rumors of atrocities—the deadlock of suspicion and counter-suspicion—produced the atmosphere of melodrama; and this psychological fever seems to have had the effect of multiplying the atrocities. There was a time when ministers in France were formidable potentates, who knew that on their fall they would be pursued for their enormities or persecuted for their mistakes. So long as this situation endured, the ministers, therefore, would try to entrench themselves in dynastic systems; they would resort to desperate measures in order to keep their power. The result was that when Mazarin engaged in intrigue, Louis XIV rather charitably excused him on the ground that this was natural for a man in his position. Later, when Louis had drawn the claws of ministers and put them on something more like their modern footing, he said that they actually preferred the new conditions of things, because they could work in greater confidence and security. Political strife must have been mitigated even in England when ministers could retire from office without having to fear that they would be impeached by those who supplanted them. Here, too, the transition from the politics of melodrama, the politics of the *coup d'état*, was achieved in proportion as fear was reduced. The extreme case, however, is the situation that Hobbes seems to have had in mind—a situation in which men are not absolutely brutish, and do not want to be brutish, but are made brutish by their fear and suspicion of one another. Each may be wanting peace above all things, but no single one of them can be certain about the intentions of the rest, They are like two men in a room, both anxious to throw their pistols away, but in a state of deadlock because each must be sure that he does not disarm himself before the other.

In other words, fear and suspicion are not merely factors in the story, standing on a level with a lot of other factors. They give a certain quality to human life in general, condition the nature of politics, and imprint their character on diplomacy and foreign policy. Over and over again during the course of the French Revolution fear and suspicion—fear of the foreign invader, but also suspicion of aristocratic plots—underlie the development of the story and decide the turn of events.

It is the realm of international affairs, however, which comes closest to the last situation that has been mentioned, the situation of Hobbesian fear. Since the war of 1914, our predicament in this respect has become worse, not better, because, till that time, a considerable region of Europe had long enjoyed the benefit of stability and traditional acceptance. Here frontiers had been comparatively settled and a country like Norway had not needed to be greatly preoccupied with its security. Much of that region has now been thrown into the melting pot. It is doomed to suffer further dislocations if ever there is a change in the distribution of power. The demand for security, and the high consciousness that we now have of this problem of security, have increased the difficulty, and increased the operation of fear in the world. Hitler demanded security for Germany, and I am not sure that he did not show more discernment about this matter than many other people. It was impossible, however, for Germany to acquire the degree of security she thought she ought to have, without herself becoming a menace to her neighbors. This universe always was unsafe, and those who demand a watertight security are a terrible danger in any period of history. I wonder if it could not be formulated as a law that no state can ever achieve the security it desires without so tipping the balance that it becomes a menace to its neighbors. The great aggressors of modern times, France, and then Germany and then Russia, began by resisting aggressors, then demanding guarantees and more guarantees, until they had come almost imperceptibly to the converse position. Then the world (always rather late in the day) would wake up and find that these powers were now aggressors themselves. The French Revolution, like the Russian one, established client-republics around its frontiers, but then these had to be guaranteed, and constantly it transpired that the aggressor needed to go further in order to keep what he had already got. Napoleon, when he brought all this to a climax by going to Moscow, made arrogant assertions in his public pronouncements. In more private statements, however, one meets the hint that he knew himself to be making a gamble. Even Napoleon could be moved by fear—for he felt that everything would collapse if he failed to go forward and meet the Russian challenge.

There was a time when it was impossible to convince people that any power except Germany would be so wicked as to keep up armaments and force everybody else to be armed. It was considered meanness to suggest that another power—particularly Soviet Russia—could possibly behave in the same way; and because of that fallacy we have to face the emergence of Russian power in the twentieth century in conditions unusually disadvantageous for us. Yet, if Russia were to promise to abolish all armaments, even bows and arrows, I doubt whether we would make an agreement with her on those terms, much as we might imagine ourselves to be ready for it. We should say that the Russians, by virtue of their excess in population and by virtue of geographical contiguity, would be able to march into Europe, though they only had sticks and stones with which to fight. Indeed, there is no security for Western Europe unless America has the power to make Russia insecure. And this gives us one of the patterns of those terrible dilemmas which seem always to be confronting us in international affairs.

Further than this, the United States at the present day must be vividly aware of the fact that when a country enjoys power and predominance, even its own virtues do not exempt it from suspicion and undeserved mistrust. If this can happen when America is so necessary for the defense of the rest of the world against the Communist menace, what would happen if Communism collapsed, and if the United States were left as a single giant, lording it alone in the world? Stalin might have been the most virtuous of rulers in 1945, but the fear and suspicion would still have existed, because, for one thing, how easy it would have been for us to say that we could never be sure about the character of his successors. When a country achieves a position of predominance—a position which enables it to assert its will in many regions with impunity—not only does it imagine that its will is more righteous than it really is, but internal forces are likely to throw to the top the kind of man who will exploit the opportunity for aggression. We do not need to deny that one state, one government or one ruler may be more wicked than another; but this is simply an additional factor in the case, and it is better to regard it as superimposed upon an initial fundamental dilemma. We cannot penetrate to the roots of fear if we merely condemn the other party moralistically. It is necessary to attack rather the structure of that fundamental dilemma which is the prime cause of international deadlock.

One of the most terrible consequences of fear and war fever is a melodramatic kind of myth-making which has been the curse of international relations since 1914. This is the source of the blight which makes compassion wither out of the world; and its results are before our eyes. Because we thought that there could never be an aggressor so wicked as Germany under the Kaiser, we determined to fight the First World War to the point of total surrender. We thereby conjured into existence two menaces still more formidable for ourselves—the Communist on the one hand, the Nazi on the other. Some men realized, even in 1914, that all we needed to do was to hold off Germany till the Russian Bear became a more formidable threat to all of us. To judge by the writings of some leading members of the British Foreign Office at the time, the intervening period would not have had to be long. In general, however, we can say that, until 1914, the world was perhaps proceeding very tolerably, save that it was beginning to get a little fevered, because, already, it had come somewhat under the dominion of fear. Those who made dark and dismal prophecies about Germany could claim in the days of Hitler that their predictions had come true. But these people had their part in the producing of that nightmare situation in which their prophecies were almost bound to come true.

Fear, then, plays a greater part in life and in the course of history than we often realize, and sometimes we know that it is fear which is in operation when individuals and nations are bullying or bragging, or taking a crooked course. It may even be fear that is at work when a nation is desperately engaged in trying to convince us that it is not afraid. In spite of this (or perhaps rather because of it) one may feel a little anxious about the way in which the great powers of the earth appear to be relying on fear today. On the one hand, statesmen ought never to be too sure about the efficacy of fear in the last resort. On the other hand it is always dangerous to assume that fear can be used to cast out fear. The mere dread of having to suffer the consequences of the hydrogen bomb is not going to deter governments and peoples from starting warlike action, or intensifying this once it has begun. In the critical instance—the case of the ruthless man who knows that he is beaten—the mere fear of retaliation will not in itself prevent desperate policies, including the actual use of the bomb.

The world can hardly ever have been so apprehensive as since the days when statesmen proclaimed that by victory in war they could bring about "freedom from fear." Those who can boast of their stocks of hydrogen bombs are not exempt from this fear, which numbs people and makes them think that they must take their fate passively, that their opinions and resolves can make no difference. We must not imagine that all is well if our armaments make the enemy afraid; for it is possible that, at least in the twentieth century, it is fear more than anything else which is the cause of war. Until very recently we ourselves had not lost the realization of the fact that mounting armaments, because they intensified fear and poisoned human relations, operated rather to provoke war than to prevent it. Under the high pressure which fear induces, any minor and peripheral issue can seem momentous enough to justify a great war.

Those who refuse to recognize squarely the dominion of fear and the play of necessity in the world (especially during times of war, revolution and unsettlement) are often the very ones who refuse to do justice to man's freedom when they are called upon for an act of will. It is for this reason that a world as intellectually advanced as ours stands mute and paralyzed before a great issue; and we grind our way, content to be locked in historical processes, content just to go digging our thought deeper into whatever happens to be the accustomed rut. There comes a moment when it is a healthy thing to pull every cord tight and make an affirmation of the higher human will. When we seem caught in a relentless historical process, our machines enslaving us, and our weapons turning against us, we must certainly not expect to escape save by an unusual assertion of the human spirit. The intensified competition in armaments embodies movements which have been mounting through the centuries, and providing mankind with its chief headache for a number of decades. Those who once thought it cynical to imagine that any power save Germany could be responsible for keeping the world still in arms, and now think that only Communists could be so wicked, do not realize that if Russia and China were wiped out, the world would soon be rearming again, and, as likely as not, the United States would be getting the blame for it. In other words, the problem of armaments is a bigger one than is generally realized, and we cannot begin to put the initial check upon the evil—we cannot begin to insert the first wedge—unless we make a signal call upon every human feeling we possess. We wait, perhaps, for some Abraham Lincoln who will make the mightiest kind of liberating decision.

Here is a spacious and comprehensive human issue, at what may well be one of the epic stages in the world's history. It is a matter not to be settled in routine consultations between governments and their military experts who are always bent on going further and further in whatever direction they have already been moving. At such a crisis in the world's history, even those of us who never had any superstitious belief in human rectitude will have some faith in humanity to assert—some heart-throb to communicate—so that, across all the Iron Curtains of the world deep may call unto deep. There is aggression; there is tyranny; there is revolutionary ferment; but if we wish to civilize international affairs we must do more than arrogantly hold our own against the barbarians, merely meeting them with their own weapons. Everything is going to depend in fact upon what we do over and above the work of self-defense. There can be no international system until somebody finds a way of relieving the pressure and begins the task of creating confidence.

If it is possible to put a personal opinion without claiming any authority for it, or asserting that it ought to have any weight, but regarding it as one of the varied views that are thrown up in a democracy, one might suggest that what is most terrifying of all in the present situation is not to have to keep discovering the crimes of the Communists; it is something much more inconvenient to us: namely, having to recognize the services which Communism has rendered in various parts of the globe. Those services have been accompanied by tyranny and oppression; but, again, it is terrifying to have to remember that this was once the chief objection to revolutionary democracy. It is not even clear that Communism, though it can be so oppressive today, does not possess colossal potentialities for future liberty—a liberty that we must not expect to be achieved before an international *détente* has made it more possible to have a relaxation at home. I think that, in this modern world, which in some ways is worse than people think but in some ways is better, all systems are going to move in the direction of liberty, if only somebody will open a window so that the world can breathe a more relaxed air and we can end the dominion of fear. If, however, we are unable to achieve this, the very measures which we are taking to preserve liberty in the world are bound to lead to the loss of liberty even in the regions that most prize it. They are bound—if we go on intensifying them—to make us become in fact more and more like the thing we are opposing. Even those who customarily try to guard themselves against a facile and unrealistic idealism in politics might well wonder whether—now that the hydrogen bomb has been super added—their anti-doctrinairism is not becoming too doctrinaire. When there is a question of a weapon so destructive, the risk which accompanies one kind of action has to be balanced against the risks involved in the opposite policy, or attendant upon inaction itself. When the hazard is very great in either case, it may be useful to take account also of the end for the sake of which one chooses to accept the hazard.

The hydrogen bomb will presumably always have at least a potential existence in our civilization, since the knowledge of how to make the weapon can hardly be un-learned, except in a disaster that would follow its drastic use. If we were to resort to the most destructive kind of bomb, we could hardly claim privilege for our generation or rely on any possibility of restricting the use of the weapon to a single war. We cannot argue still again that no generation past or future could possibly have to face an enemy as wicked as our present enemy. We should have to conclude that ours is a civilization that took a wrong turn long ago, and now, by the hydrogen bomb, had to be rolled back to its primitive stages, so that, in a second Fall of Man, the world could unload itself of knowledge too dangerous for human possession. It is not necessary to take a very high perspective on these matters; it is just too crazy and unseemly when a civiliza-tion as lofty as ours (pouring the best of its inventive genius into the task) carries the pursuit of destructive ness to the point at which we are now carrying it. Let us be clear about one important fact: the destructiveness which some people are now prepared to contemplate is not to be justified for the sake of any conceivable mundane object, any purported religious claim or supramundane purpose, or any virtue that one system of organization can possess as against another. It is very questionable whether, when it comes to the point, any responsible leader of a nation will ever use the hydrogen bomb in actual warfare, however much he may have determined in advance to do so. The weapon is dangerous to the world because it is a weapon only for men like the falling Hitler—desperate men making their last retreat. The real danger will come from the war leader who will stick at nothing because he knows that he is defeated and doomed in any case. He may be reckless even of his own nation, determined to postpone his own destruction for a week, or to carry the rest of the world down with him. As in the case of Germany when Hitler was falling, war may be protracted by the will of a handful of wicked and desperate men. On these terms we are going to be more afraid of defeating our enemy than of suffering ordinary military defeat ourselves.

It is not clear that there is much point in having the equality (or even the superiority) in terroristic weapons if, as is sometimes asserted, the enemy has the ruthlessness and the organization to carry on a war with less regard for the sufferings of his people than is possible in the democracies. If Communism is a monstrous sadistic system, the gentle and the urbane will not easily outdo it in the use of terroristic device. By a reversal of all previous ideas on the subject of armaments, however, some people have imagined that the hydrogen bomb is the climax of blessing, the magical "deterrent" which will paralyze the guns and neutralize the numbers of the potential enemy. Such reasoning is precarious; and we ought to be very careful before we accept the view that ten years ago it was only the atomic bomb which deterred the Russians from a major war. A country in the position that Russia held after 1945 tends to seek to make use of its interim advantage up to any point short of a renewal of general war. It seeks to step in wherever there is a power vacuum and it probes for a power vacuum even where none exists—probes until it meets an uncomfortable degree of resistance. There seems to be no reason for believing that Russia would have meditated a full-scale war, even if she had had to meet only pre-atomic weapons, the weapons of Hitler's war. Short of such a conflict, I wonder what power ever went further in the type of aggrandizement in question than Russia at a time when the West held the atomic bomb while the East was still without it. It is even possible that we hoaxed ourselves with the atomic bomb, which was too monstrous a weapon for peripheral regions and problems, too terrible to use in a cause that was in any way dubious, too cumbrous for dealing with a power that was ready to skirmish with any danger short of actual war. In such a case one can even conceive the possibility of the Russians realizing the situation in advance, and calling our bluff while we ourselves were not yet aware that we were merely bluffing. Whether this has already happened or not, it is just this situation—with the West deceived and the Russians undeceived—that we ought to be careful to avoid at the present day. We cannot contemplate—we cannot even plausibly threaten—a nuclear war over some of the mixed and mongrel issues which are arising (and are going to arise) in sundry sections of the globe. If it is argued that we can, and that the dread of this will be effective with the Russians, then, beyond question, the Russians are in a more general sense under the dominion of fear; for in such a case they have a right also to fear a willful and capricious use of nuclear weapons.

Some men say that the world must perish rather than that Justice should ail—as though we were not leaving sufficient injustices unremedied on our own side of the Iron Curtain. The justice of man has less mercy than the justice of God, who did not say that because of the sin of some men the whole human race should lose even the chance of bettering itself in future. Even in peacetime the hydrogen bomb has made such a deep impression as to suggest enormous evils (greater than the evils of Communism itself) if the weapon is ever used by either party in a war. The demoralizing effect on the user as well as the victim might well include a hysteria beyond all measure, the dissolution of loyalty to the state, and anarchy or revolution of an unprecedented kind. Even the sense of the possible proximate use of the hydrogen bomb—short of an actual explosion—will have the effect of creating a deep separation between peoples and their governments. We may know that war is near by two signs: firstly, when people begin to say that the hydrogen bomb is not so terrible after all; and secondly, when we are told that it is better to destroy civilization than to tolerate some piece of barbarism on the part of that nation which happens to be the potential enemy at the moment. In fact, we have reached that point at which our own weapons have turned against us, because their destructiveness is so out of relation with any end that war can achieve for mankind.

There is so great a risk in having the hydrogen bomb that there can hardly be greater risk if we unplug the whole system, and if our governments refuse to have anything to do with the weapon. Even if there were, the radical difference in the quality of these risks would cancel it; for with modern weapons we could easily put civilization back a thousand years, while the course of a single century can produce a colossal transition from despotic regimes to a system of liberty. I am giving a personal view; but I am not sure that the greatest gift that the West could bring to the world would not be the resolution neither to use the hydrogen bomb nor to manufacture it any further. Certainly, the East would hardly believe us (at least for some time) if we said that we were not going to resort to this weapon for any conceivable end. We should have to take the line, therefore, that our determination was not dependent on anything that other people believed. Even if the East refused to join us in the assertion, we can declare that the hydrogen bomb is an unspeakable atrocity, not to be used in any war, and not even to be the basis of any form of threat. It is a thing not to be used even if the enemy has used it first, since the situation is a new one—the right of retaliation could mean no more than the right to multiply an initial catastrophe that could not be undone. While it is still open to us in time of peace, we might ask ourselves whether there is no conceivable weapon that we will brand as an atrocity, whether there is no horror that we should regard as impermissible for winning a war, because so incommensurate with the limited objects that can ever be secured by war. When we talk about using the hydrogen bomb to defeat aggression, we are using dangerous language. Someday, no doubt, a wiser world than ours will use the term "aggressor" against any people who enjoy rights, powers and possessions in a country that is not its own, and exploits these against the will of the population concerned. Sometimes we seem to be using the term in respect of peoples who are merely seeking to be freed from such oppression; in this sense I have seen the Algerian rebels described as aggressors, using violence for the purpose of securing a change in the *status quo*. The Anglo-French action at Suez should open our eyes to the fact that a so-called "invasion" (though it be by armies in full array) can arise from something much more complicated than a mere cruel lust for conquest. The United Nations condemned the Anglo-French enterprise; but, even so, a hydrogen bomb on London or Paris would have been an unspeakable form of punishment.

It is sometimes argued that those who refuse to resort to the hydrogen bomb may be declining to risk themselves for the liberty of others. But nobody can calculate—and perhaps only accidental circumstances would decide in a given case—whether the use of the bomb or its repudiation would carry the greater immediate risk. In any case, we cannot say that we will not receive the bomb—we can only say that we will not be responsible for the sin and the crime of delivering it. Supposing we do have to receive it, the one thing we can do is to choose the end for which we will consent to be sacrificed. We can choose the cause on behalf of which we will die if we are going to have to die. We can do this instead of being the blind victims of historical processes, which will end by making us more and more like the thing that we are opposing. However hard we have tried in the twentieth century to make allowances in advance for the unpredictable consequences of war, we have always discovered that the most terrible of these had been omitted from our calculations or only imperfectly foreseen. One of the examples of the fact is the loss of liberty in various countries in Eastern Europe and the Balkans—the very regions whose freedom was the primary issue for which we were supposed to have undertaken two world wars.

If it is wrong to tip the balance slightly in favor of humanity and faith at such a point as this, the fact is so monstrous as to imply the doom of civilization, whatever decision we take on the present issue. If we picture a long line of future generations we can hardly help feeling that, even if wars of some sort continue (human nature remaining very much as it is now), we would want our successors not to hate one another so much as to think it justifiable to use the hydrogen bomb. The fact that we can contemplate such an atrocity is a symptom of a terrible degeneracy in human relations—a degeneracy which the predicament itself has no doubt greatly helped to produce. But if all this is not correct, and if we do not signally repudiate the hydrogen bomb, it is still true that in the last resort some strong human affirmation of a parallel kind may be the only way of stopping the tension and deflecting the course of development to which we are now enslaved. Some other kind of affirmation might serve a similar purpose; and amongst the possibilities at our disposal there is one which to many earnest people would come no doubt as a serious test. We have talked a great deal about the crimes of Communism, and those who are chiefly concerned with militaristic propaganda would like us to think of nothing else. We do not always realize what a tremendous area of our thinking is affected by the fact that we refuse to recognize also the services which Communism has rendered in various parts of the globe. At the very beginning of all our arguments and decisions, it matters very much if we consent to say that Communism is a benevolent thing gone wrong—it is not mere unredeemed and diabolical evil. For anything I know, its chief error may even be the same as that of both Catholics and Protestants in the age of the religious wars and persecutions—an error which has been responsible for terrible massacres and atrocities in history—namely, a righteousness that is too stiff-necked and a readiness to believe that one can go to any degree in the use of force on behalf of a cause that one feels to be exclusively right. In such a case it is possible that we ourselves are making even the identical error, especially in any contemplation of the use of the hydrogen bomb. When there is a terrible *impasse,* it is sometimes useless to go on battering against the obstruction—one must play a trick on fatality by introducing a new factor into the case. We seem unable to subdue the demon of frightfulness in a head-on fight. Let us take the devil by the rear, and surprise him with a dose of those gentler virtues that will be poison to him. At least when the world is in extremities, the doctrine of love becomes the ultimate measure of our conduct.

All this represents in any case the kind of way in which to assert the human will, against the machinery of relentless process, in history. It represents also the way in which one would like to see the Christian religion working softly and in silence upon the affairs of the world at large. It illustrates the way in which religious activity may get a purchase on the wheels of a human destiny which otherwise now appears to be directionless.

1-2

"American Christians and the War"

John C. Bennett[1]

THE AMERICAN CHURCHES HAVE approached this war and the issues that lie behind it with a divided mind. They have a bad conscience because of their "all out" support of the last war. For years, the characteristic Christian teaching in America was influenced by disillusionment concerning the results of the last war and by various forms of pacifism. Distance from the armies and the secret police of the Axis powers created a situation in which it was easy for these two factors—disillusionment about the last war and pacifism—to control the minds of Christians.

Influence of Pacifism

The attack upon Pearl Harbor and the actual belligerency of this country made a difference, but not as great a difference among the leaders of the Churches as might have been expected. The pacifists ceased to be obstructionists in most cases but they retained their essential outlook. They steeled themselves against the temptation to change their minds because of public pressure. As time went on and the pacifists found themselves pastors of men who were in the armed services and their families, many of them came to take a very different attitude. They allowed some of their doctrinaire positions to fall into the background and they overcame any tendencies that they may have had toward self-righteousness and identified themselves with those who are in the war without in most cases changing their judgments concerning the issues of the war. There have been surprisingly few cases of pacifist ministers who have lost their churches because of their stand in this war. The most influential Protestant journal, *The Christian Century*, after a long record of opposition to the interventionist tendencies in the Church and to the foreign policy of the government, a record that was characterized by a combination of isolationism and Christian scruples about war which gave the impression of pacifism, suddenly changed and became a supporter of the war effort. It developed a whole theology about war which combined some important religious insights with unconscious journalistic ingenuity that enabled it to retain its blind spots, to support the war without taking back anything that it had said before Pearl Harbor. Judging from the letters that it has published it made few converts among its pacifist admirers.

---

1. Bennett, "American Christians and the War," 81–89.

The Roman Catholic Church and the War

It should be said that the Roman Catholic Church switched overnight and clothed itself with the garb of conventional patriotism. It became quite unreserved in its support of the war both in its public prayers and in its pronouncements. This attitude is all the more remarkable because of the very strong anti-Russian and anti-British sentiments in that Church. Probably its shift is the result of its traditional teaching about the support of the state, its freedom from the influence of Christian pacifism, and its desire to compensate for its minority status by avoiding offence to the majority. I confess that while I agree with its leaders about the importance of military victory I think that it has taken this position in such a way as to sacrifice important Christian insights of which it as the Church with greatest claim to universality might have remained the guardian.

It is very natural for the observer of the American Churches to exaggerate the influence of pacifism among them. There are very few pacifists among the laymen. A majority of the clergy are convinced supporters of the government and have never been pacifists. In some denominations, such as the Episcopal Church, pacifism has never been very strong. I think that it would be a safe generalisation to say that among the ministers under fifty who are "progressive" in their theological and social views pacifism is the majority opinion. Also, it is probably true that if one were to select the twenty-five preachers of greatest national influence, a majority would be pacifists. Recently I had occasion to write to a group of preachers and professors of Homiletics. I chose somewhat at random thirteen men for my purpose which had nothing to do with the question of pacifism but with their competence as preachers. I discovered after making the selection that of those thirteen eight were on record as pacifists. It has often been said that there is a marked difference between preachers and theologians in regard to pacifism. A great many of our most influential theologians were strong interventionists before America entered the war. A writer who consulted many theologians and preachers with the idea of interpreting this fact came to this conclusion before America's entrance into the war: "By and large, however, the weight of personal testimony would seem to indicate that there is probably an even division among both theologians and ministers, with the non-interventionists leaving a slight edge." But he adds: "Probably the most vocal theologians are interventionists and the most vocal ministers are the non-interventionists."[2] That last statement agrees with my impression, but I should want the word "vocal" used in a neutral rather than in a derogatory sense and to associate it on both sides with extent of influence.

The Ecumenical Mind

There is one very interesting fact about the distribution of opinions about the war that should be emphasised. Those who have had most experience of the ecumenical Church, who have most responsibility within the ecumenical movements, are not pacifists and were interventionists before Pearl Harbor. I can think of very few exceptions to this generalisation. My interpretation may be biased because I agree with those who are

2. George, "Opinions on the War," 33–42.

in this group but it is difficult for me to resist the conclusion that it is their sense of solidarity with the sufferings of people in the conquered countries of the world and their vivid realisation of what an Axis victory would mean to everything for which the world Church stands, that have led them to this point of view. One has found the same tendency among those who have been missionaries in China. For them, as for those who are in close contact with Europe, the kind of aggression that leads to the extension of totalitarian tyranny is not an abstraction but a concrete horror which seems even greater than the concrete horror of war.

Divided Mind of Protestant Churches

The pronouncements of the Protestant Churches have in most cases shown the divided mind to which I referred at the beginning of this article. Though the pacifists are numerically in a minority they have had great influence on the resolutions of Church bodies. They have had this influence in part because they are in strategic positions in the denominations. Also, the non-pacifists in many denominations have sought to avoid any action that completely overrides the convictions of the minority. The point of view of the Oxford Conference report that recognises that there are at least three points of view about war which have a place in the Christian Church is generally accepted. On the other hand, the lack of clear statements by the Churches in relation to the issues of the war has misled the country into thinking that pacifism is stronger in the Church as a whole (ministers and laymen) than it actually is and it has prevented the Church from giving adequate guidance at the point of most urgent need. It was largely to correct this situation that the Federal Council of Churches at its biennial session in December 1942, made a statement which was clearer in its assertion of what is at stake in this war than any previous statement by as representative a body. Because of this statement, the Federal Council was strongly attacked by *The Christian Century* on the ground that it had put the Church into the war. The statement actually is written with great discrimination. The fact that the Federal Council has taken this lead confirms what I have said about the attitudes of those who are identified with the ecumenical Church because the leadership of the Council is closely associated with the ecumenical movements.

"Christianity in Crisis"

To counteract the well organised pacifist influence in the Churches, those who have long-believed that Christians as Christians should support the struggle against the Axis and who before Pearl Harbor were strongly "interventionist" in their political views, established the journal, *Christianity and Crisis,* a bi-weekly publication that is edited by a committee of which Reinhold Niebuhr is the chairman. The platform of this journal is as far removed from conventional nationalism or militarism as it is from pacifism. It sees the war as a world-wide struggle for freedom. It is as much concerned as are the pacifists to prepare now for the peace though it stresses the preparation that will come through strengthening the ties between the United Nations as the nucleus of a new world order rather than paper plans for a distant future. It keeps the government under criticism and seeks at all times to preserve a Christian perspective on the war. It is significant that its editor, Reinhold Niebuhr, is also chairman of an organisation that is called "The Friends of German Freedom". *Christianity and Crisis* always opposes the one-sided anti-German attitude of a Vansittart. British readers may be able to place the point of view of *Christianity and Crisis* if I say that it is very close to that of Archbishop Temple. On the whole it resembles that of *The Christian News-Letter* though it does differ from the latter in tone largely because *The Christian News-Letter* was established within a nation that was already a belligerent, and hence sought to counteract some of the aspects of belligerency from a Christian point of view, whereas *Christianity and Crisis* had the job from the beginning of counteracting the opposite tendency to evade the issues of the war in the interests of neutrality.

The differences within the American Churches and the confusion in many individual minds should not hide the fact that there are important common attitudes which both pacifists and non-pacifists share. In fact I believe that inconvenient and wrong-headed as much pacifism is, the twenty years of pacifist influence have left very good deposits in the thought of American Christians. Twenty years from now it may be easier to recognise this than it is today. My impression is that the restraint that is characteristic of Christians today is in part the result of years of pacifist teaching.

Certain Attitudes Shared by Christians

We can see the common attitudes which most Christians share in four areas: (1) The refusal on all sides to turn this war into a "Holy War"; (2) the general support of the opportunities that are given to conscientious objectors; (3) the willingness to keep the policy of the government under Christian criticism; (4) the emphasis upon the importance of preparing now for the peace. I shall discuss briefly each of these points.

This Is Not a Holy War

(1) The unwillingness to identify the Church as a Church with the war without reservation and the realisation that in some respects the war is a judgment upon our nation and its allies represent a gain upon the attitude of the Churches of America in the last war. There is a difference of emphasis here, of course, between pacifists and non-pacifists. Many pacifists dwell upon the past sins of the United Nations and seem to be almost unaware of the monstrous evils that are now perpetrated by the Axis powers. But few Christian leaders see this war as a struggle between righteous and unrighteous nations. The non-pacifists believe that there is a righteous cause at stake and that this cause depends upon a military victory for the United Nations but they realise that this cause would be betrayed by nations that fight with self-righteous fury. There is a religious dimension in the life and thought of most American Christians which enables them to think of all nations as under the judgment of God. For the most part, Christian leadership sees the moral conflict that war brings to any sensitive conscience and there is no tendency to idealise war.

Attitude to Conscientious Objectors

(2) Before the beginning of this war most American Churches had developed a policy which provides for the defence of the conscientious objectors. They have been in large part responsible for the very liberal policy of the government in regard to conscientious objectors in this war. The national Church bodies have passed innumerable resolutions recognising the rights of the Christian conscience, and both pacifists and non-pacifists among the clergy have adhered to this position. It is true that the so-called "Peace Churches" (the Friends, the Mennonites and the Church of the Brethren) have borne more than their share of the expense of supporting the conscientious objectors in the Public Service Camps. That cost has to be carried by private agencies. The larger denominations have been unwilling to use undesignated funds for this purpose because of the possible repercussions from laymen who do not yet share the official attitudes of the Churches on this matter.

Christian Criticism of the Government

(3) The Churches in this country have not allowed themselves to become an echo of the government. One illustration of the agreement of pacifists and non-pacifists is their attitude toward the evacuation of the Japanese Americans (most of whom are American citizens) from their west coast homes. I have been unable to discern any important difference between pacifists and non-pacifists on this issue. Individuals disagree as to whether or not the original evacuation was a necessity but there is no serious disagreement among Christian leaders about the policy of detention. To keep American citizens in internment camps is abhorrent to all, and not least to the Christian leaders on the coast who know the Japanese best. I asked the executive of one large denomination if there were any ministers in his denomination on the coast who took an unsympathetic attitude toward these Japanese Americans and he answered that not more than one per cent, took such an attitude. That is remarkable when you consider the large amount of public prejudice that exists. One of the most violent attacks on the government, not only for the detention of the Japanese Americans but even for the evacuation policy, was an editorial in *Christianity and Crisis*. On this matter there is no difference between *Christianity and Crisis* and *The Christian Century*.

Problems of the Post-War World

(4) The American Churches are united in their realisation that at best military victory can do no more than stop something. They also realise that war in itself is a bad training for the tasks of construction that will come with the peace. The pacifists and the non-pacifists are united in their conviction that they should prepare now to lay the foundations for the post-war world. They are at one in rejecting policies of vengeance, American isolationism and American imperialism. The Federal Council of Churches appointed a commission two years ago, headed by Mr. John Foster Dulles, to guide the Churches in this task of preparing for peace. This commission sponsored the Conference at Delaware, Ohio, in

March, 1942, the report of which is the most important utterance of American Christians about the problems of the post-war world. This report had behind it the work of both pacifists and non-pacifists and seems to be acceptable to both.

The Federal Council commission is handicapped in some respects by the disagreement between these two groups. It must completely ignore the fact that the just and durable peace that it seeks is impossible without a military victory for the United Nations. Also, it is inclined to ignore the urgent problems that will face the victorious nations at the conclusion of hostilities. Such matters as the treatment of Germany and Japan and the policing of parts of Europe are too controversial to be frankly faced. Another difficulty has been that as a commission it has only recently been able to emphasise the importance of solidarity with the other nations among the United Nations though many of its members, including Mr. Dulles, have seen this very clearly. There is a fear on the part of many non-pacifists that when the war is over the pacifists will still be too perfectionist to support the measures that are necessary to provide for order and security. On this point American pacifists would be divided and I am quite sure that the majority would not oppose such measures in principle if they had the sanction of most of the world community. But many will still be negative about these things, either because of perfectionist principles or because of their distrust of our European Allies, a distrust that has been built up through the years as a defence of their pacifism. In order to set forth a clear position about the peace which is not confused by pacifism, isolationism or imperialism, a movement has been formed which is called: "Christian Conference on War and Peace". It is entirely unofficial and it has the backing of the people who support *Christianity and Crisis.* This movement was not founded to oppose the Federal Council Commission but to supplement the latter which is handicapped by its official status and the differences of opinion among its members.

Reconciliation between Christians

Readers of this article who know at firsthand what Axis aggression means to persons around the world may be shocked at the evidence that it presents of a strange detachment on the part of many Christians in America. The minds of many of the most sensitive and most deeply committed Christians were formed before it became as apparent as it is today that the violence that accompanies resistance to totalitarian tyranny is less evil than the tyranny itself. It is difficult for such minds to change until they know as much as our friends in Europe and Asia know about this tyranny. It is often assumed that they are chiefly controlled by a too simple theological liberalism and that it is this that accounts for their pacifism. Personally, I believe that this influence is exaggerated. There are many liberals who are not pacifists. Liberalism did not develop many pacifists in the last war. Moreover, one of the most convincing statements of the idea that in the modern world war is the greatest of all possible evils is in Brunner's *The Divine Imperative,* an idea that Brunner himself has abandoned not for theological reasons but because of what events have taught him. When this war is over there will be a problem of reconciliation not only between enemies but between those who have suffered most and those who have seemed to live in a detached and unreal world when the great issues of the struggle were being decided. I hope that Americans who are not pacifists but who understand the influences that have produced so many pacifists (perhaps they have in the past contributed to those influences!), and who retain a good deal of sympathy with the young American Christian who has been subjected to these influences in the Church and the Student Christian Movement, may help in this reconciliation. On all sides there will be needed a realisation of the contradictions in any Christian decision in regard to war and there will be needed the grace of humility.

"The Ironic Element in the American Situation"[1]

Reinhold Niebuhr

I

EVERYBODY UNDERSTANDS THE OBVIOUS meaning of the world struggle in which we are engaged. We are defending freedom against tyranny and are trying to preserve justice against a system which has, demonically, distilled injustice and cruelty out of its original promise of a higher justice. The obvious meaning is analyzed for us in every daily journal; and the various facets of this meaning are illumined for us in every banquet and commencement-day speech. The obvious meaning is not less true for having become trite. Nevertheless it is not the whole meaning.

We also have some awareness of an element of tragedy in this struggle, which does not fit into the obvious pattern. Could there be a clearer tragic dilemma than that which faces our civilization? Though confident of its virtue, it must yet hold atomic bombs ready for use so as to prevent a possible world conflagration. It may actually make the conflict the more inevitable by this threat; and yet it cannot abandon the threat. Furthermore, if the conflict should break out, the non-communist world would be in danger of destroying itself as a moral culture in the process of defending itself physically. For no one can be sure that a war won by the use of the modern means of mass destruction would leave enough physical and social substance to rebuild a civilization among either victors or vanquished. The victors would also face the "imperial" problem of using power in global terms but from one particular center of authority, so preponderant and unchallenged that its world rule would almost certainly violate basic standards of justice.

Such a tragic dilemma is an impressive aspect of our contemporary situation. But tragic elements in present history are not as significant as the ironic ones. Pure tragedy elicits tears of admiration and pity for the hero who is willing to brave death or incur guilt for the sake of some great good. Irony however prompts some laughter and a nod of comprehension beyond the laughter; for irony involves comic absurdities which cease to be altogether absurd when fully understood. Our age is involved in irony because so many dreams of our nation have been so cruelly refuted by history. Our dreams of a pure virtue are dissolved in a situation in which it is possible to exercise the virtue of

1. Niebuhr, *The Irony of American History*, 1–16.

responsibility toward a community of nations only by courting the prospective guilt of the atomic bomb. And the irony is increased by the frantic efforts of some of our idealists to escape this hard reality by dreaming up schemes of an ideal world order which have no relevance to either our present dangers or our urgent duties.

Our dreams of bringing the whole of human history under the control of the human will are ironically refuted by the fact that no group of idealists can easily move the pattern of history toward the desired goal of peace and justice. The recalcitrant forces in the historical drama have a power and persistence beyond our reckoning. Our own nation, always a vivid symbol of the most characteristic attitudes of a bourgeois culture, is less potent to do what it wants in the hour of its greatest strength than it was in the days of its infancy. The infant is more secure in his world than the mature man is in his wider world. The pattern of the historical drama grows more quickly than the strength of even the most powerful man or nation.

Our situation of historic frustration becomes doubly ironic through the fact that the power of recalcitrance against our fondest hopes is furnished by a demonic religio-political creed which had even simpler notions than we of finding an escape from the ambiguity of man's strength and weakness. For communism believes that it is possible for man, at a particular moment in history, to take "the leap from the realm of necessity to the realm of freedom." The cruelty of communism is partly derived from the absurd pretension that the communist movement stands on the other side of this leap and has the whole of history in its grasp. Its cruelty is partly due to the frustration of the communist overlords of history when they discover that the "logic" of history does not conform to their delineation of it. One has an uneasy feeling that some of our dreams of managing history might have resulted in similar cruelties if they had flowered into action. But there was fortunately no program to endow our elite of prospective philosopher-scientist-kings with actual political power.

Modern man's confidence in his power over historical destiny prompted the rejection of every older conception of an overruling providence in history. Modern man's confidence in his virtue caused an equally unequivocal rejection of the Christian idea of the ambiguity of human virtue. In the liberal world the evils in human nature and history were ascribed to social institutions or to ignorance or to some other manageable defect in human nature or environment. Again the communist doctrine is more explicit and therefore more dangerous. It ascribes the origin of evil to the institution of property. The abolition of this institution by communism therefore prompts the ridiculous claim of innocency for one of the vastest concentrations of power in human history. This distillation of evil from the claims of innocency is ironic enough. But the irony is increased by the fact that the so-called free world must cover itself with guilt in order to ward off the peril of communism. The final height of irony is reached by the fact that the most powerful nation in the alliance of free peoples is the United States. For every illusion of a liberal culture has achieved a special emphasis in the United States, even while its power grew to phenomenal proportions.

We were not only innocent a half century ago with the innocency of irresponsibility; but we had a religious version of our national destiny which interpreted the meaning of our nationhood as God's effort to make a new beginning in the history of mankind. Now we are immersed in world-wide responsibilities; and our weakness has grown into strength. Our culture knows little of the use and the abuse of power; but we have to use power in global terms. Our idealists are divided between those who would renounce the responsibilities of power for the sake of preserving the purity of our soul and those who are ready to cover every ambiguity of good and evil in our actions by the frantic insistence that any measure taken in a good cause must be unequivocally virtuous. We take, and must continue to take, morally hazardous actions to preserve our civilization. We must exercise our power. But we ought neither to believe that a nation is capable of perfect disinterestedness in its exercise, nor become complacent about particular degrees of interest and passion which corrupt the justice by which the exercise of power is legitimatized. Communism is a vivid object lesson in the monstrous consequences of moral complacency about the relation of dubious means to supposedly good ends.

The ironic nature of our conflict with communism sometimes centers in the relation of power to justice and virtue. The communists use power without scruple because they are under the illusion that their conception of an unambiguously ideal end justifies such use. Our own culture is schizophrenic upon the subject of power. Sometimes it pretends that a liberal society is a purely rational harmony of interests. Sometimes it achieves a tolerable form of justice by a careful equilibration of the powers and vitalities of society, though it is without a conscious philosophy to justify these policies of statesmanship. Sometimes it verges on that curious combination of cynicism and idealism which characterizes communism, and is prepared to use any means without scruple to achieve its desired end.

The question of "materialism" leads to equally ironic consequences in our debate and contest with communism. The communists are consistent philosophical materialists who believe that mind is the fruit of matter; and that culture is the product of economic forces. Perhaps the communists are not as consistently materialistic in the philosophical sense as they pretend to be. For they are too Hegelian to be mechanistic materialists. They have the idea of a "dialectic" or "logic" running through both nature and history which means that a rational structure of meaning runs through the whole of reality. Despite the constant emphasis upon the "dignity of man" in our own liberal culture, its predominant naturalistic bias frequently results in views of human nature in which the dignity of man is not very clear.

It is frequently assumed that human nature can be manipulated by methods analogous to those used in physical nature. Furthermore it is generally taken for granted that the highest ends of life can be fulfilled in man's historic existence. This confidence makes for utopian visions of historical possibilities on the one hand and for rather materialistic conceptions of human ends on the other. All concepts of immortality are dismissed as the fruit of wishful thinking. This dismissal usually involves indifference toward the tension in human existence, created by the fact that "our reach is beyond our grasp," and that every sensitive individual has a relation to a structure of meaning which is never fulfilled in the vicissitudes of actual history.

The crowning irony in this debate about materialism lies in the tremendous pre-occupation of our own technical culture with the problem of gaining physical security against the hazards of nature. Since our nation has carried this preoccupation to a higher degree of consistency than any other we are naturally more deeply involved in the irony. Our orators profess abhorrence of the communist creed of "materialism" but we are rather more successful practitioners of materialism as a working creed than the communists, who have failed so dismally in raising the general standards of well-being.

Meanwhile we are drawn into an historic situation in which the paradise of our domestic security is suspended in a hell of global insecurity; and the conviction of the perfect compatibility of virtue and prosperity which we have inherited from both our Calvinist and our Jeffersonian ancestors is challenged by the cruel facts of history. For our sense of responsibility to a world community beyond our own borders is a virtue, even though it is partly derived from the prudent understanding of our own interests. But this virtue does not guarantee our ease, comfort, or prosperity. We are the poorer for the global responsibilities which we bear. And the fulfillments of our desires are mixed with frustrations and vexations.

Sometimes the irony in our historic situation is derived from the extravagant emphasis in our culture upon the value and dignity of the individual and upon individual liberty as the final value of life. Our cherished values of individualism are real enough; and we are right in preferring death to their annulment. But our exaltation of the individual involves us in some very ironic contradictions. On the one hand, our culture does not really value the individual as much as it pretends; on the other hand, if justice is to be maintained and our survival assured, we cannot make individual liberty as unqualifiedly the end of life as our ideology asserts.

A culture which is so strongly influenced by both scientific concepts and technocratic illusions is constantly tempted to annul or to obscure the unique individual. Schemes for the management of human nature usually involve denials of the "dignity of man" by their neglect of the chief source of man's dignity, namely, his essential freedom and capacity for self-determination. This denial is the more inevitable because scientific analyses of human actions and events are bound to be preoccupied with the relations of previous causes to subsequent events. Every human action ostensibly can be explained by some efficient cause or complex of causes. The realm of freedom which allows the individual to make his decision within, above and beyond the pressure of causal sequences is beyond the realm of scientific analysis. Furthermore the acknowledgment of its reality introduces an unpredictable and incalculable element into the causal sequence. It is therefore embarrassing to any scientific scheme. Hence scientific cultures are bound to incline to determinism. The various sociological determinisms are reinforced by the general report which the psychologists make of the human psyche. For they bear witness to the fact that their scientific instruments are unable to discover that integral, self-transcendent center of personality, which is in and yet above the stream of nature and time and which religion and poetry take for granted.[2]

2. In his comprehensive empirical study of human personality Gardner Murphy nicely suggests the limits of empiricism in dealing with the self. He declares: "We do not wish to deny the possibility suggested by James Ward that all awareness is colored by selfhood. . . . Least of all do we wish to attempt to

Furthermore it is difficult for a discipline, whether philosophical or scientific, oper-ating, as it must, with general concepts, to do justice to the tang and flavor of individual uniqueness. The unique and irreplaceable individual, with his . . .

> Thoughts hardly to be packed
> Into a narrow act,
> Fancies that broke through language and escaped.[3]
> (Browning)

[Rabbi Ben Ezra] with his private history and his own peculiar mixture of hopes and fears, may be delineated by the poet. The artist-novelist may show that his personality is not only unique but subject to infinite variation in his various encounters with other individuals; but all this has no place in a strictly scientific account of human affairs. In such accounts the individual is an embarrassment.

If the academic thought of a scientific culture tends to obscure the mystery of the individual's freedom and uniqueness, the social forms of a technical society frequently endanger the realities of his life. The mechanically contrived togetherness of our great urban centers is inimical to genuine community. For community is grounded in per-sonal relations. In these the individual becomes most completely himself as his life enters organically into the lives of others. Thus our theory and our practice tend to stand in contradiction to our creed.

But if our academic thought frequently negates our individualistic creed, our so-cial practice is frequently better than the creed. The justice which we have established in our society has been achieved, not by pure individualism, but by collective action. We have balanced collective social power with collective social power. In order to pre-vail against our communist foe we must continue to engage in vast collective ventures, subject ourselves to far-reaching national and international disciplines and we must moderate the extravagance of our theory by the soberness of our practice. Many young men, who have been assured that only the individual counts among us, have died upon foreign battlefields. We have been subjected to this ironic refutation of our cherished creed because the creed is too individualistic to measure the social dimension of human existence and too optimistic to gauge the hazards to justice which exist in every com-munity, particularly in the international one.

It is necessary to be wiser than our creed if we would survive in the struggle against communism. But fortunately we have already been somewhat better in our practice than in our quasi-official dogma. If we had not been, we would not have as much genuine community and tolerable justice as we have actually attained. If the prevailing ethos of a bourgeois culture also gave itself to dangerous illusions about the possibilities of managing

---

set aside the still unsolved philosophical question whether the process of experiencing necessitates the existence of a non-empirical experiencer. . . . Nothing could be gained by a Gordian-knot solution of such a tangled problem. We are concerned solely with the immediate question: Should the student of personality at the present stage of research postulate a non-empirical entity distinct from the organism and its perceptual responses? . . . To this limited question a negative answer seems advisable." Murphy, *Personality,* 491. There can of course be no "non-empirical entity." But there may be an entity which cannot be isolated by scientific techniques.

3. Excerpted from Robert Browning's poem "Rabbi Ben Ezra."

the whole of man's historical destiny, we were fortunately and ironically saved from the evil consequences of this illusion by various factors in our culture. The illusion was partly negated by the contradictory one that human history would bear us onward and upward forever by forces inherent in it. Therefore no human resolution or contrivance would be necessary to achieve the desired goal. We were partly saved by the very force of democracy. For the freedom of democracy makes for a fortunate confusion in defining the goal toward which history should move; and the distribution of power in a democracy prevents any group of world savers from grasping after a monopoly of power.

These ironic contrasts and contradictions must be analyzed with more care presently. Our immediate prefatory concern must be the double character of our ironic experience. Contemporary history not merely offers ironic refutation of some of our early hopes and present illusions about ourselves; but the experience which furnishes the refutation is occasioned by conflict with a foe who has transmuted ideals and hopes, which we most deeply cherish, into cruel realities which we most fervently abhor.

II

One of the great works of art in the western tradition, which helped to laugh the culture of chivalry and the ideals of medieval knight errantry out of court, was Cervantes' Don Quixote. Quixote's espousal of the ideals of knighthood was an absurd imitation of those ideals; and *it* convicted the ideals themselves of absurdity. The medieval knights had mixed Teutonic class pride and the love of adventure of a military caste with Christian conceptions of suffering love. In Quixote's imitation the love becomes genuine suffering love. Therefore, while we laugh at the illusions of this bogus knight, we finally find ourselves laughing with a profounder insight at the bogus character of knighthood itself.

Our modern civilization has similarities with the culture of medieval knighthood. But its sentimentalities and illusions are brought to judgment, not by a Christ-like but by a demonic fool; and not by an individual but a collective one. In each case a mixture of genuine idealism with worldliness is disclosed. The medieval knights mixed pride in their military prowess with pretenses of coming to the aid of the helpless. However, the helpless were not those who really needed help but some fair ladies in distress. Our modern commercial civilization mixes Christian ideals of personality, history and community with characteristic bourgeois concepts. Everything in the Christian faith which points to ultimate and transcendent possibilities is changed into simple historical achievements. The religious vision of a final realm of perfect love in which life is related to life without the coercion of power is changed into the pretension that a community, governed by prudence, using covert rather than overt forms of power, and attaining a certain harmony of balanced competitive forces, has achieved an ideal social harmony. A society in which the power factors are obscured is assumed to be a "rational" rather than coercive one. The knight of old knew about power. He sat on a horse, the symbol of military power. But the power of the modern commercial community is contained in the "counters" of stocks and bonds which are stored in the vaults of the bank. Such a community creates a culture in which nothing is officially known about power, however desperate may be the power struggles within it.

The Christian ideal of the equality of all men before God and of equality as a regulative principle of justice is made into a simple historical possibility. It is used by bourgeois man as a weapon against feudal inequality; but it is not taken seriously when the classes below him lay claim to it. Communism rediscovers the idea and gives it one further twist of consistency until it becomes a threat to society by challenging even necessary functional inequalities in the community. The Christian idea of the significance of each individual in God's sight becomes, in bourgeois civilization, the concept of a discrete individual who makes himself the final end of his own existence. The Christian idea of providence is rejected for the heady notion that man is the master of his fate and the captain of his soul.

Communism protests against the sentimentalities and illusions of the bourgeois world-view by trying a little more desperately to take them seriously and to carry them out; or by opposing them with equally absurd contradictory notions. The bourgeois world is accused of not taking the mastery of historical destiny seriously enough and of being content with the mastery of nature. To master history, declares Engels, requires a "revolutionary act." "When this act is accomplished," he insists, "—when man not only proposes but also disposes, only then will the last extraneous forces reflected in religion vanish away." That is to say, man will no longer have any sense of the mystery and meaning of the drama of history beyond the limits of his will and understanding; but he will be filled with illusions about his own power and wisdom.

For the bourgeois idea of a society in which the morally embarrassing factor of power has been pushed under the rug, communism substitutes the idea of one final, resolute and unscrupulous thrust of power in the revolution. This will establish a society in which no coercive power will be necessary and the state will "wither away." The notion of a society which achieves social harmony by prudence and a nice balance of competitive interests, is challenged by communism with the strategy of raising "class antagonisms" to a final climax of civil war. In this war the proletariat will "seize the state power" and thereby "put an end to itself as a proletariat" (Engels). This is to say, it will create a society in which all class distinctions and rivalries are eliminated.

For the liberal idea of the natural goodness of all men it substitutes the idea of the exclusive virtue of the proletariat, who, according to Lenin, are alone capable of courage and disinterestedness. Thus it changes a partially harmful illusion about human nature into a totally noxious one. As if to make sure that the illusion will bear every possible evil fruit, it proposes to invest this allegedly virtuous class with precisely that total monopoly of power which is bound to be destructive of every virtue. Communism challenges the bourgeois notion of a discrete and self-sufficing individual with the concept of a society so perfect and frictionless that each individual will flower in it, and have no desires, ambitions and hopes beyond its realities. It thinks of this consummation as the real beginning of history and speaks of all previous time as "pre-history." Actually such a consummation would be the end of history; for history would lose its creative force if individuals were completely engulfed in the community. Needless to say the change of this dream into the nightmare of a coercive community, in which every form of individual initiative and con-science is suppressed, was an inevitable, rather than fortuitous, development. It proved that it is even more dangerous to understand the individual only in his social relations than to deny his social substance.

In every instance communism changes only partly dangerous sentimentalities and inconsistencies in the bourgeois ethos into consistent and totally harmful ones. Com-munism is thus a fierce and unscrupulous Don Quixote on a fiery horse, determined to destroy every knight and lady of civilization; and confident that this slaughter will purge the world of evil. Like Quixote, it imagines itself free of illusions; but it is actually driven by twofold ones. Here the similarity ends. In the Quixote of Cervantes the second illusion purges the first of its error and evil. In the case of the demonic Quixote the second illu-sion gives the first a satanic dimension.

Our own nation is both the participant and the victim of this double irony in a special way. Of all the "knights" of bourgeois culture, our castle is the most imposing and our horse the sleekest and most impressive. Our armor is the shiniest (if it is legitimate to compare atom bombs with a knight's armor); and the lady of our dreams is most opulent and desir-able. The lady has been turned into "prosperity." We have furthermore been persuaded by our success to formulate the creed of our civilization so passionately that we have sup-pressed its inconsistencies with greater consistency than any of our allies. We stand before the enemy in the first line of battle but our ideological weapons are frequently as irrelevant as were the spears of the knights, when gunpowder challenged their reign.

Our unenviable position is made the more difficult because the heat of the battle gives us neither the leisure nor the inclination to detect the irony in our own history or to profit from the discovery of the double irony between ourselves and our foe. If only we could fully understand that the evils against which we contend are frequently the fruit of illusions which are similar to our own, we might be better prepared to save a vast uncom-mitted world, particularly in Asia, which lies between ourselves and communism, from being engulfed by this noxious creed.

"The Church, Russia and the West"[1]

Martin Wight

THE AMSTERDAM ASSEMBLY WILL meet in the shadow of the conflict between Russia and the West, and part of its task will be to define the Christian position towards it. We think of this first of all as being a work of contributing to the reconciliation of the opposing blocs, and of showing that the Church abolishes the Iron Curtain. There is truth in this, but since it resembles the kind of thing the Church has been saying for years without appreciable effect, we may wonder whether it goes deep enough, or what is the right way to interpret it.

The question is whether we are speaking politically or theologically. It is imperative that the Amsterdam Assembly should not become a function of the international struggle. Nevertheless it is a political fact that Amsterdam is a Western and not a Soviet city. On the other hand, the Church is no more identified with the West than it is with Russia; nor is the Church *between* Russia and the West. The Church is within and without and above Russia and the West: this is a theological fact overriding the political circumstances of which churches may or may not come to Amsterdam.

Any statement about the Church's position in the present international crisis, therefore, will be true in proportion to its theological depth. We have the double task of analysing the crisis in historical terms and of assessing it in theological terms. The latter is much the more important: it includes the former in a way in which the former does not include *it,* for it means reconsidering the nature of the Church's action in history and politics.

But let us begin by examining the immediate context of the Church's action, the rival historical phenomena that we call Russia and the West.

The Apostasy of Christendom

When we consider these two blocs or groupings or civilisations whose antagonism determines world politics today, two things become apparent at the outset. It is an antagonism

1. This chapter was presented as an address by Martin Wight at a conference of Christian politicians at the Ecumenical Institute, Bossey, on June 4, 1948 and then published as Wight, *The Ecumenical Review,* 25–45.

between two parts of what was once Christendom; and the conflict has reached its present dimensions because Christendom, of which these were parts, is dead.

It is not a conflict in which one party is China or India or even Islam, that is to say a culture or civilisation which has no historical connection with Christianity. For more than a thousand years the conflict which occupied Christian men was of this kind, the conflict with Islam. But that conflict was triumphantly or shamefully won by Christendom, and Islam is now moribund. Our conflict is fratricidal. It is a continuation, in another form, of the ancient conflict between Byzantine and Latin Christianity, with Russia as the inheritor and organiser of the Byzantine East, America as the inheritor and organiser of the Catholic and Protestant West.

This conflict between the twin Christendoms is a very ancient thing, more ancient than their formal schism over the doctrine of the Procession of the Holy Ghost in 1054, more ancient indeed than their common conflict against Islam.[2] It repeatedly broke into open warfare, and this warfare culminated in the Fourth Crusade (1201–1204), when the Western Crusaders turned their weapons aside from Islam against their Orthodox Christian brethren, conquering and sacking Constantinople and destroying the Byzantine Empire—predecessors and exemplars of the Turks. 250 years later, when the Byzantine Empire, restored and enfeebled, was fighting its last desperate battle against the Turks, the West failed to come to its assistance. The ecclesiastical and imperial claims of Constantinople passed to Moscow, the Third Rome; but this only opened a new chapter in the struggle. Russia had already had her own experience of conflict with the West, in the attempt of the Teutonic Knights to conquer Novgorod which was defeated by St. Alexander Nevski in 1242. Four times since Russia succeeded Byzantium as the head of Orthodox Christendom the West has hurled itself upon Russia in an attempt at conquest. The Poles at the beginning of the seventeenth century, the Swedes at the beginning of the eighteenth, the French at the beginning of the nineteenth, the Germans in the present decade of the twentieth, have successively followed the road to Moscow. There is another side to this, of course: Ivan the Terrible and Catherine the Great were not good neighbours. But it is not on the part of Eastern Christendom that the historical record shows a balance of aggression; throughout the common history of the two Christendoms, except perhaps at the very beginning, the Eastern has been the weaker, and the victim.[3]

---

2. The first important political expression of the conflict was the controversy between John IV the Faster, Patriarch of Constantinople (582–595) and Pope Gregory the Great (590–603) over John's assumption in 588 of the title "The Ecumenical Patriarch"—a piece of insolent pride which to Gregory showed the approach of Antichrist.

3. Cf. Stalin's speech to the First All-Union Conference of Managers of Socialist Industry, February 4, 1931: "One feature of the history of old Russia was the continual beatings she suffered for failing behind, for her backwardness. She was beaten by the Mongol khans. She was beaten by the Turkish beys. She was beaten by the Swedish feudal lords. She was beaten by the Polish and Lithuanian gentry. She was beaten by the British and French capitalists. She was beaten by the Japanese barons. All beat her for her backwardness: for military backwardness, for cultural backwardness, for political backwardness, for industrial backwardness, for agricultural backwardness," Stalin, *Problems of Leninism,* 356. The Byzantine princess Anna Comnena in the twelfth century describes the Latins' military advantage in possessing the crossbow in terms that suggest a Soviet reference to the atomic bomb, though the language of political invective was then neither stereotyped nor degrad: *Alexiad,* bk. x, ch. 8.

But Russia and the West are not [sic] longer Christendoms; they are post-Christian civilisations; for Christendom, Eastern and Western alike, is dead. Let us try to define our terms: what do we mean by Christendom? Something like this: a society in which—1. the majority are practising Christians; 2. the Church is therefore the most venerated and influential of all institutions; 3. the Church itself is vigorous and uncorrupted—and are we to add, united? 4. social and political organisation is therefore saturated with Christian presuppositions. These conditions are no longer found anywhere in the world. Christians are everywhere a dwindling minority with decreasing influence in a society whose presuppositions are non-Christian and increasingly anti-Christian. Marxism has become the secular substitute for Orthodox Christianity as bourgeois liberalism was already the secular substitute for Western Christianity.[4] Since about the French Revolution in the West, since the Russian Revolution in the East, the Church has been adapting itself, slowly and uncertainly and with many mistakes, to the unknown circumstances of post-Christendom and neo-paganism. Does this mean a simple reversion to conditions before Constantine? Is there something to learn from the precedent of Israel in the Exilic and post-Exilic periods? Or does the Church, taking what courage it can from the extraordinary transformation of human history in the Christian Era, and above all by the unification of the world, go forward to new syntheses? None of these questions has a simple answer, but they lead to the heart of our problem.

The last thing to be noticed about Russia and the West is the most astonishing of all, and that which most clearly puts the Church in an unprecedented position. These two descendants of Christendom have expanded to partition the world between them. "Their line is gone out through all the earth, and their words to the end of the world."[5] The only parts of the earth that have not in the past hundred years come under their direct political control are China on the one hand and fragments of Islam—Persia, Saudi Arabia, and modern Turkey—on the other; and these exceptions have all in some degree been partitioned or made spheres of influence. The present state of China, divided between the Communists and the American-backed Kuomintang, is the most obvious example. Thus the evangelical command, that repentance and the remission of sins should be preached in Christ's name among all nations,[6] has received an inverted and terrifying fulfilment: there is no nation and no part of the earth that lies beyond the range either of the American businessman or of the Communist Party organiser.[7]

4. This is not to overlook the Western origin of the Marxist creed, a circumstance that sharply underlines the interdependence of the two civilisations. See Heimann. "U.S.A. and U.S.S.R.," *Christianity and Crisis.*

5. Ps 19:4; Rom 10:18.

6. Luke 24:47.

7. Tocqueville with astonishing insight predicted this partition of the world in the concluding words of the second volume of *De la Démocratie en Amérique.*

"Il y a aujourd'hui sur la terre deux grands peuples qui, partis de points différents, semblent s'avancer vers le même but : ce sont les Russes et les Anglo-Américains.

"Tous deux ont grandi dans l'obscurité, et, tandis que les regards des hommes étaient occupés ailleurs, ils se sont places tout à coup au premier rang des nations, et le monde a appris presque en même temps leur naissance et leur grandeur.

"Our Iniquities, and the Iniquities of Our Fathers Together"

We are accustomed to look back to the French Revolution and the Industrial Revolution in analysing the historical background of the Church's task today. But is it relevant, it may be asked, to extend our view to such forgotten events as the Fourth Crusade or the Polish occupation of Moscow in 1610–1612? I think we must. We know that no event however remote in place is beyond the Church's responsibility, and there is an application of the same principle to events remote in time. There is a real sense in which the United States is as old as Magna Carta, and the Soviet Union as old as that ecclesiastical revolution under the Isaurian Emperors of Byzantium which we call the Iconoclastic Movement. There is a real sense—Soviet propaganda found it in the recent War—in which the conflict between Russia and the West is as old as the victory of Alexander Nevski. Civilisations are coherent moral entities, in whose history retribution is not without its part. "I will not keep silence," it was said of apostate Israel, "but will recompense, even unto their bosom, Your iniquities, and the iniquities of your fathers together."[8] We are bound up today in the conflict between Russia and the West, because we are burdened by the heritage of sin which in Hindu philosophy is known as *Karma*—our corporate destiny decided by the sum of our corporate actions in the past.[9] We have inherited the sins of schism and war, of reunion unaccomplished, of the necessity for the Reformation and the Reformation's failure, of the apostasy of Christendom. Recognition, understanding, above all repentance, these alone can free us. Ellis Gibbs Arnall, the ex-Governor of Georgia, has put some profound words in the mouth of an old preacher in the North Georgia hill country: "Everything you do today, or I do, affects not only what is going to happen but what already has happened, years and centuries ago. Maybe you cannot change what has passed, but you can change all the meaning of what has passed. You

---

"Tous les autres peuples paraissent avoir atteint a peu près les limites qu'l tracées la nature, et n'avoir plus qu'à conserver ; mais eux sont en croissance: tous les autres sont arrêtes ou n'avancent qu'avec mille efforts ; eux seuls marchent d'un pas aise et rapide dans une carrière dont l'œil ne saurait encore apercevoir la borne.

"L'Américain lutte contre les obstacles que lui oppose la nature; le Russe est aux prises avec les hommes. L'un combat le désert et la barbarie; l'autre la civilisation revêtue de toutes ses armes: aussi les conqu8tes de l'Américain se font-elles avec le soc du laboureur, celles du Russe avec l'épée du soldat.

"Pour atteindre son but, le premier s'en repose sur l'intert personnel, et laisse agir sans les diriger la force et la raison.

"Le second concentre en quelque sorte dans un homme toute la puissance de la société. L'un a pour principal moyen d'action la liberté ; l'autre, la servitude.

"Leur point de départ est différent, leurs voies sont diverses ; néanmoins, chacun d'eux semble appelé par un dessein secret de la Providence a tenir un jour dans ses mains les destinées de la moitié du monde."

These words were first published in January 1835.

8. Isa 65:6–7; cf. Lam 5:7, 16.

9. On the approximation of the law of Karma to the Christian doctrine of divine justice see Radhakrishnan, *The Hindu View of Life*, 71–77; on its falling short of the Christian doctrine, cf Gore, *The Philosophy of the Good Life*, chapter 3. The development of the theory of historical retribution and corporate guilt in the Bible is subtle and complex, but the degree of it that we are here concerned with is contained in the Second Commandment.

can even take all the meaning away."[10] And you can even contribute meaning to that part of the past that seems meaningless. This is something of the truth enshrined in the doctrine of the Communion of Saints.

But there remains the heritage of sin to expiate, the inevitability of retribution. It is in the international sphere that the demonic concentrations of power of the modern neo-pagan world have their clearest expression. Russia and America are the last two Great Powers within the Westernised system of sovereign states. And the characteristic of that system, after centuries in which the Church has had no influence upon its development, is the emancipation of power from moral restraints. Leviathan is a simple beast: his law is self-preservation, his appetite is for power.[11] The process of international politics that has followed from this is equally simple: the effective Powers in the world have decreased in number and increased in size, and the method has been war. In the present century this has gone on at an accelerated pace. In 1914 there were eight Great Powers in the world. In 1919, after the disappearance of Austria-Hungary, there were seven. By 1941, with the conquest of France and the vassalisation of Italy, there were five. By 1948, with the conquest of Germany and Japan and the decline of Britain, there were two left, each of them thinking of the day when there will be only one, each of them claiming to be the world state *in posse*.

Hence the ambiguity of international politics: they have ultimately turned out to be power-politics. Our attempts at international cooperation have succeeded only where they conformed to the pattern of power. The League of Nations, the Kellogg Pact, the Disarmament Conference, the Atlantic Charter, the United Nations, the Baruch Plan for the control of atomic energy—they have been a procession of wraiths. (It is true that the United Nations continues to exist, but it is not what it was at San Francisco.) On the other hand, the contemporary examples of successful international cooperation are the American organisation of Western Europe through the Marshall Plan and the prospective American guarantee to the Western Union, and the Soviet organisation of Eastern Europe through the Cominform and the Molotov Plan. And these two achievements are dialectically connected: they derive their principle of growth from their mutual hostility.

So that if we are to make a realistic analysis of the existing crisis, if we are to assess the present weight of historical retribution, we must face these two conclusions.

1. No thorough-going cooperation between Russia and the West is possible within the foreseeable future, that is, so long as Russia and the West remain what they distinctively are. It may be possible however to establish a balance of power which might last a generation. This very broadly has been the objective of American policy since the War. But here at once the ambiguity of international politics appears: what

10. Arnall, *The Shore Dimly Seen*, 128.

11. Cf. one of the earliest and greatest textbooks of Western post-Christendom: ". . . the nature of Power, is in this point, like to Fame, increasing as it proceeds; or like the motion of heavy bodies, which the further they go, make still the more hast. . . . So that in the first place, I put for a general inclination of all mankind, a perpetual and restless desire of Power after power, that ceaseth only in Death. And the cause of this, is not always that a man hopes for a more intensive delight, than he has already attained to; or that he cannot be content with a moderate power: but because he cannot assure the power and means to live wen, which he hath present, without the acquisition of more." Hobbes, *Leviathan,* chapters x, xi.

in one view would be a balance of power, in another view would be the stabilisation of America's present military preponderance through the monopoly of the atomic bomb; and the second view is inevitably Russia's.

2. The Third World War is therefore humanly speaking inevitable. A balance of power is no substitute for international order: it is inherently unstable. Within a generation Russia will have the atomic bomb, and the growth of her population will give her an overwhelming preponderance in manpower.[12] From that point onwards any balance of power that may have been constructed will dissolve. And if the inevitability of the next war is admitted, as far as a human assessment can go, some subsidiary probabilities are easily discerned. Such a war would be fought with the fullest employment of atomic weapons and what other post-atomic weapons may be thought militarily decisive, and with the smallest moral restraint. In the short run the odds are probably in favour of America, but decreasingly so as the war is delayed, by reason of the certain growth of the Soviet population, the probable development of Soviet industry, and on the American side those weaknesses and irregularities in a society with parliamentary democracy and an uncontrolled economy which will always give opportunities for Communist exploitation and penetration. (This is speculative; we are unable to see whether there are corresponding weaknesses and irregularities of Soviet society; but there is no reason to suppose that they would be important so long as the Soviet state can be held together by the doctrine of the hostile capitalist world.) Whichever won, Russia or America, would establish upon the ruins a world state.

The Christian Dialectic of History

To say that war between Russia and the West is humanly speaking inevitable is so far from fashionable among Christians today that it seems improper. "Our people should reject fatalism about war. War is not inevitable. If it should come, it would be because of conditions that men could have changed."[13] The position is put with more precision

12. The United States President's Air Policy Commission reported on January 13, 1948, that "it would be an unreasonable risk for our present planning purposes to assume that other nations will not have atomic weapons in quantity by the end of 1952" (*New York Times*, January 14, 1948). This is a guess, though presumably an informed one. Population changes are susceptible of more accurate and detailed forecast. See Notestein et al., *The Future Population of Europe and the Soviet Union*. "By 1970 the U.S.S.R., in its 1937 boundaries, has as large a source of primary military manpower as Germany, the United Kingdom, Italy, France, Poland, Spain, and Roumania combined, these being the seven European countries with the greatest forces of manpower outside of the Soviet Union," Notestein et al., *The Future Population of Europe and the Soviet Union*, 134. An economist who reviewed this book in the London *Observer* of September 10, 1944, made a still more startling comparison: "By 1970, with about 32 million men in the industrially and militarily vital group aged 20 to 34, the Soviet Union will have only slightly fewer of these men than the United Kingdom, the Dominions, France, Germany, and the United States put together."

13. *A Positive Program for Peace*, statement approved by the Executive Committee of the Federal Council of Churches of Christ in America in special session, April 26, 1948, para. 3. There is a touch of Christian Science in the American Churches, denying that evil really exists and that disaster can

by Visser 't Hooft: "It goes without saying that we must resolutely refuse to participate in criminally irresponsible or cynically defeatist talk about the inevitability of war."[14] Does this mean that there is no way of declaring the inevitability of war which is *not* criminally irresponsible or cynically defeatist? Surely not. There is a way of foretelling the inevitability of disaster which is theologically responsible and informed with—not optimism, but with hope. It is the way in which the Prophets repeatedly predicted the doom of Israel and of the nations of the Gentiles, and a greater than the Prophets predicted the doom of Jerusalem. Prediction rises to prophecy when it becomes the vehicle of judgment, and it becomes the vehicle of judgment when it carries the rider "Except ye repent."[15] Prediction is not illegitimate; there is a sense in which it is too easy; the catastrophes of secular history are so obvious as they approach that they cannot be ignored.[16] It is the duty of Christians to analyse the secular situation with ruthless realism, and without the timidity, distaste and self-deception that Communists attribute to bourgeois culture in decline. The Church was enjoined to cultivate the wisdom of the serpent as well as the simplicity of the dove, and the Pharisees were condemned for not being able to discern the signs of the times.[17] Ruthlessly realistic analysis is not incompatible with hope, for hope is a theological not a political virtue. "Humanly speaking inevitable," we say, but this omits the humanly incalculable factor of God's grace. And even if it is not God's purpose to intervene, it does not invalidate hope, because the object of hope is not particular things God may allow in history, but God himself.

On our side, we have no technique for making catastrophes avoidable and diverting the onrush of history. We only know that we are called to repentance. All prophecy carries the exhortation to flee from the wrath to come,[18] but it is a spiritual flight, and does not afford an escape from the necessities of secular history. These are to be endured as sufferings from the hand of God. They are what Luther called the *left hand* of God, suggesting how there are depths in destiny and God's purpose is ultimately served even by the forces of history that defy him.[19]

---

really be imminent. Cf. *Soviet-American Relations*, statement submitted by the Commission on a Just and Durable Peace and adopted by the Executive Committee of the Federal Council of Churches of Christ in America, October 11, 1946: "War with Russia can be avoided and it must be avoided without compromise of basic convictions." The corresponding tendency in the British Churches is that of the ostrich, admitting that evil exists and that disaster may be imminent, but refusing to look at them. "It may be that the larger problem of human relations will prove insoluble. It may be our fate to fight and die for our faith or to perish in someone else's quarrel. It may be that we shall not see peace in our time. We have to accept these possibilities as real, and not give them a further thought," *The Christian News-Letter*, December 11, 1946: 16. It is difficult to find a Biblical foundation for either of these attitudes.

14. Niebuhr, "The Christian in World Affairs," 121.

15. Luke 13:5. Cf. Ezek 18:30.

16. "A great and advanced society has . . . a powerful momentum; without destroying the society itself you cannot suddenly check or divert its course. Thus it happens that years beforehand detached observers are able to predict a coming clash of societies which are following convergent paths in their development." Mackinder, *Democratic Ideals and Reality*, 12.

17. Matt 10:16; 16:3.

18. Matt 3:7; Luke 3:7; 1 Thess 1:10. Cf. Niebuhr, *Discerning the Signs of the Times*, 66–67.

19. Cf. De Pury, *Journal from My Cell*, 30–33.

The distinction between secular and sacred history is the stuff of our argument— between history as process only and history as purpose, between history aetiological and history teleological. If we use one metaphor we may say that secular and sacred history interpenetrate; if we use another, and perhaps a truer one, we will see secular history as the surface of the time-process, dead and glassy, and sacred history as the same time-process transparent against the light of eternity, the sum of all the depths of destiny. It is the distinction between St. Augustine's two cities, the earthly city which is built by the love of self to the contempt of God, and the heavenly city which is built by the love of God to the contempt of self.[20] The two cities are always mixed up in this world, but there is a rhythm in their interaction, and sometimes it is their coincidence and sometimes their divergence that is more apparent.

And the Church itself, the bearer of sacred history, of whom the heavenly city is the nuclear core, is also involved in secular history, is an organisation with institutional needs and institutional vices. It is perhaps the distinction we make in our minds when we are not quite sure whether to refer to the Church as 'she' or 'it.' On the one side, the indefectible Church, the body and members of whom Christ is the head, uniting all generations dead and living in the communion of saints, the Church whose mode of operation is perpetual prayer, the Church that abolishes the Iron Curtain. On the other side, the historical churches, with their divisions, their hierarchies, their orders, their councils, their statesmanlike calculations and their negligences and blunders. It was to the first, the mystical Church, that the promise was given that the gates of hell should not prevail against it;[21] the second, the historical church, can betray its vocation like the historical Israel before it, and is as much in need of repentance. The churches of the Reformation tradition emphasise this distinction (though they have not always done so in their history); and their most important disagreement with Roman Catholicism is their belief that Roman Catholicism identifies the empirical with the mystical Church, which is the theocratic heresy. In history these two aspects of the Church can never coincide, and in the course of history the emphasis between them swings and shifts. Institutionally the Church must always seek to preserve itself as a fortress in the world; but when as an institution it is faltering and crumbling, it is then that the volume of prayer and the manifestation of sanctity of the mystical Church can become most vivifying.

If we look at the trajectory of the Church's history, the two thousand years in which it has made its first attempt at a Christian civilisation and failed, we can see that the Christian dialectic has worked out thus: 1. In the pagan world, the greatest alienation of the Church from secular history, the predominance of the Church's mystical aspect, the ascendancy of the saints and martyrs. Consequently: 2. The Church's greatest penetrative power over secular history, which led to: 3. The approximation of the Church to the secular world, the zenith of Christendom, the predominance of the Church's institutional aspect. Consequently: 4. A weakening hold on secular society, the dissolution of Christendom. Interwoven with this dialectic has been the ambivalence of the Church's attitude towards the state, whose classic expression we find in the contrast between Romans xiii and Revelation xiii.

20. Augustine, *De Civitate Dei,* bk. 14, ch. 28.
21. Matt 16:18.

To the Church in general St. Peter wrote, "Submit yourselves to every ordinance of man for the Lord's sake; whether it be to the King as supreme; or unto governors, as unto them that are sent by him for the punishment of evildoers, and for the praise of them that do well." But to the Sanhedrin, when at a particular crisis they had forbidden him to preach, he said, "We ought to obey God rather than men."[22] This tension and latent contradiction has always existed in the Christian doctrine of the state, though here again at different times now one and now the other has tended to predominate. What we seem to hear, then, if we listen to the history of the Church, is a treble counterpoint: the melody of the Church's defiance and submission towards the state, and the melody of the mystical and the institutional Church, above the plainsong of sacred and secular history.

The Meaninglessness of Secular History

Two beliefs have hitherto underlain the ordinary non-Christian attitude towards the present crisis, the attitude of the ordinary secular liberal in our post-Christian Western world. One is a broad pelagianism—the belief that we are on the whole well-meaning people doing our best, who will somehow muddle through. The other is secular optimism—the belief that because we are well-meaning and doing our best, things will therefore tend to come right; or (for optimism sidesteps subtly in fatalism) that what does happen will be for the best anyway. Hence, perhaps, the way in which it has been usual in modem times to see public affairs as a succession of "questions" or "problems" (from the venerable Eastern Question down to the Palestine Question, one of its contemporary progeny, the problem of sovereignty, the problem of Veto, the exports problem, and so on) with the implication that they have answers and solutions, being incidents in the broad if irregular trend of progress.

Neither of these beliefs are Christian. We are not well-meaning people doing our best; we are miserable sinners, living under judgment, with a heritage of sin to expiate. We are doing our best like Caiaphas, for our idolatrous loyalties; we are well-meaning like Pilate, everyday crucifying Christ afresh. We will not somehow muddle through; if we repent and cast ourselves upon God's mercy we have the promise that we shall be saved—a totally different thing, which carries no assurance of muddling through in this world. Nor do we find in the Bible anything resembling the secular theory of progress. What we find there is a scheme of purification through catastrophe and redemption through suffering, the rediscovery in our individual lives and our corporate histories of resurrection after passion and death.

But these two beliefs are dying out among non-Christians, and being gradually replaced by philosophies of despair. Existentialism is only the most fashionable of them. The ordinary man's area of confidence and meaningfulness is rapidly contracting, and the basis of agnosticism contracts with it. The past forty years have shown, in a way in which

22. 1 Pet 2:13–14; Acts 5:29. St. Peter before the Sanhedrin was echoing what had been said four hundred years earlier by Socrates at his trial: "Men of Athens, I honour and love you; but I shall obey God rather than you, and while I have life and strength I shall never cease from the practice and teaching of philosophy," Plato, *Apology*, 29d. Cf. Amos 7:10–17; Jer 26:12–15.

the modern world thought no longer possible, the meaninglessness of secular history. "For how we can, how can anyone anywhere, who has his eyes open, suppress the insistent question: what does my life, what does my work mean, if we are constantly confronted and threatened by political or economic chaos and by total war?"[23] The alternative to an agnostic despair is submission to Leviathan; for the demonic mass-state in both its Fascist and its Communist forms, gives freedom from meaninglessness. A Communist writer has described the Moscow front in 1941 as being sustained by the conviction that "Hitler had not, nor could have, history's right to victory";[24] and Goebbels in 1943 declared that Germany was bound to win the war, because without a German victory history would lose its meaning, and history was not meaningless.[25]

Christianity has points of contact with these three attitudes, dying liberalism, despair, and the idolatry of Leviathan; and it is sometimes infected by them. It is a paradox that the post-Christian beliefs of liberalism have attached themselves to Christianity, of which they were in origin a perversion, and are likely to survive among Christians after they have become obviously untenable by anybody else. And Christianity will often touch its cap respectfully to Leviathan: the Russian Revolution, we are told, and the new regimes in Eastern Europe, though in many aspects they are deplorable, have abolished feudalism and racialism and so proved themselves the agents of a historical process. It is difficult to see what recommendation in a Christian sense this is. The abolition of feudalism and racialism, however necessary in itself, can only be accounted a good in relation to what has succeeded them. The replacement of the old-fashioned and inefficient tyrannies in Eastern Europe by modem stream-lined efficient tyrannies does not confer meaning upon the historical process. It suggests rather the ancient meaninglessness of a cyclical process, the historical philosophy of the ancient world, by which the author of Ecclesiastes was oppressed, and from which Christianity liberated men. The only concern of the Church with historical processes of this sort is to bring them under judgment, which may mean also that for those involved in them the processes are themselves the bearers of a judgment—the left hand of God. It is with despair, the state of mind lying between the liberalism that no longer sustains and the demonic mass-movements that beckon and terrify the individual, and which lies again on the other side of those demonic mass-movements when they have collapsed—it is with agnosticism verging on despair that Christianity can work best. The greatest living English novelist, the most sensitive and courageous of liberal humanists, wrote just before the War: "There is nothing disgraceful in despair. In 1938–1939 the more despair a man can take on board without sinking, the more completely is he alive."[26] This is an attitude congenial to Christianity. It has loyalty to principles in the face of meaninglessness; it has the beginnings of humility; it is capable of the Gospel.

---

23. Visser 'T Hooft, "The Christian in World Affairs," 108–9.

24. "To imagine for a moment the possibility of Hitler's victory meant to forego all reason; if it were to happen then there could be no truth, logic, nor light in the development of human society, only chaos, darkness and lunacy; and it would be better not to live," Krieger, *From Moscow to the Prussian Frontier*, 8.

25. Speech in the Berliner Sportpalast, October 3, 1943; *Yiilkischer Beobachter*, October 4, 1943.

26. Forster, *The New Statesman and Nation*, 972.

The Christian Meaning of History

What then is the Christian meaning of history? If it carries no promise of progress, what promise does it carry? And how does it show the meaning of the crisis in which we live?

The theory of history to which the Church has always been committed, and from which only in the last century perhaps some churches allowed their attention to be distracted, is the Biblical theodicy. History is not an autonomous process which secretes its own meaning as it goes along, like a cosmic endocrine gland. (This view of history as an autonomous process, by the way, is hard to separate from determinism and the denial of man's moral freedom). History is a process with an author, who lies outside it, that is to say outside time. It had a beginning and will have an end, both of them determined by its author; and it is only in relation to what lies outside itself that it has a meaning. But it is a process whose moving force is the moral freedom of the human individuals involved in it; and consequently its meaning is identical with *judgment* by the author, a verdict on the exercise of that freedom both general and particular, a sifting of the good elements from the bad. After an agelong preparation and expectation, at a certain point in the historical process (a point defined in the Creed by the reference to Pontius Pilate) meaning and judgment appeared inside history, with the incarnation of history's author. The meaning thus made apparent was God in human terms.[27] But the judgment was *implicit* judgment, in that the forces of unmeaning history immediately rushed upon the incarnate meaning to destroy it, thereby inadvertently passing judgment on themselves. This point was the fulfilment of history since the meaning of history was there shown; but there still remained an epilogue in which that meaning might be fully proclaimed—the epilogue in which we live. And with the end of the epilogue history will end too: our air-bubble in eternity will collapse. We imagine the end of history as the last event of the temporal series; we know it doctrinally as the Second Coming of Christ; but in the sense in which we are considering it, it is the final verdict by the author of history, the act of *explicit* judgment, which will separate the evil from the good and afford the ultimate meaning.

Three characteristics in particular are to be remarked about this epilogue we live in, which we call the Christian Era. They are closely interwoven, but for clarity we must consider them separately.

The first is the imminence of the Second Coming. The Second Coming is always imminent. Christ said three things about it: that it would be sudden, catching mankind unawares;[28] that it was unpredictable, and must not be made a factor in human speculations;[29] and that it was to be expected by the Church with the watchful humility of good servants expecting the return of an absent master.[30] This provides one of the most concentrated intellectual paradoxes in the New Testament, but it is morally simple. The end of human history is by definition outside the range of human knowledge; speculation about it is therefore foolish; we should not allow ourselves to be diverted either by attempts at certainty or by the absence of certainty from our moral

27. John 14:9; Heb 1:1–3.

28. Matt 24:42—25:13; Luke 21:34–36. Cf. Rev 3:3; 16:15.

29. Matt 24:36; Mark 13:32; Acts 1:6–7.

30. Mark 13:33–37; Luke 12 35–40. Cf. 1 Thess 5:1–4.

responsibilities *within* history. "Take ye heed, watch and pray: for ye know not when the time is."[31] The New Testament is saturated with this awareness, at once alert and submissive, of the imminence of the end.

For the time between the Resurrection and the Second Coming is indeed an epilogue. Upon us "the ends of the world are come."[32]

"When once the Christ had come," says Newman, in one of the most exquisite passages in his sermons,

> . . . as the Son over His own house, and with His perfect Gospel, nothing remained but to gather in His saints. No higher Priest could come—no truer doctrine. The Light and Life of men had appeared, and had suffered, and had risen again; and nothing more was left to do. Earth had had its most solemn event, and had seen its most august sight; and therefore it was the last time. And hence, though time intervene between Christ's first and second coming, it is not *recognized* (as I may say) in the Gospel scheme, but is, as it were, an accident. For so it was, that up to Christ's coming in the flesh, the course of things ran straight towards that end, nearing it by every step; but now, under the Gospel, that course has (if I may so speak) altered its direction, as regards His second coming, and runs, not towards the end, but along it, and on the brink of it; and is at all times equally near that great event, which, did it run towards, it would at once run into. Christ, then, is ever at our doors; as near eighteen hundred years ago as now, and not nearer now than then; and not nearer when He comes than now. When He says that He will come soon, "soon" is not a word of time, but of natural order. This present state of things, "the present distress" as St. Paul calls it, is ever *close upon* the next world, and resolves itself into it. As when a man is given over, he may die any moment, yet lingers; as an implement of war may any moment explode, and must at some time; as we listen for a clock to strike, and at length it surprises us; as a crumbling arch hangs, we know not how, and is not safe to pass under; so creeps on this feeble weary world, and one day, before we know where we are, it will end.[33]

In eschatological expectation as in other things, the history of the Church has shown a rhythm between alternate points of view. The early Christians, in their eagerness, looked forward across history as it were through a telescope, exaggerating the closeness of the end. In modern times we have done the opposite. Applying the wrong end of the telescope to our eyes, we have decided that the Second Coming is so far away that we cannot detect it and need not worry about it; it is probably connected with the cooling down of the earth and the second law of thermodynamics, and can be left to astronomers; and so we may settle comfortably to the real business of life, doing good to one another and to ourselves, correcting social maladjustments, and keeping civilisation greased and refuelled. "Their inward thought is that their houses shall continue forever, and their dwellings places to all generations; they call their lands after their own names."[34] We have not really believed in the epilogue-theory at all. It has seemed obvious to us that Christ was not the fulfilment

31. Mark 13:33.

32. 1 Cor. 10:11. Cf. Heb 9:26, 1 Pet 1:20.

33. Newman, "Waiting for Christ," *Parochial and Plain Sermons,* 240–41.

34. Ps 69:11.

of history but the beginning of any history that mattered, that the Reformation marked a new crest, the American Revolution another, the League of Nations a third, and that history increases in importance as it approaches ourselves—a philosophy which it is the business of every daily newspaper to inculcate. The denouement of the atomic bomb is so crudely theatrical as to seem specially devised for the children we have shown ourselves to be. It is indeed a singular mark of divine mercy; for the imminence of judgment would still be there without the atomic bomb, but it is difficult to imagine anything less than the atomic bomb that might have made us realise it.

The second characteristic to be noted in the development of history is that the tares grow up with the wheat.[35] Evil and good grow alongside, towards the final judgment: the Church spreads, but the forces that hate the Church spread too, their hostility evoked by and growing *pari passu* with her own growth. The notion that the Christian Era should be a period of the gradual perfection of men and society is the opposite of what we find in the New Testament. Jewish apocalyptic had generally supposed an age of bliss within history, a restored Kingdom of David, to come after the final catastrophes. Jesus revolutionised this, pointing instead to ultimate bliss in the transcendent order beyond space and time.[36] He described the remainder of history in terms which suggested that it would be even more full of tumult and confusion, of wars and famines than what had gone before; and a marked feature of it was to be the appearance of antichrists and of apostasies among the faithful.[37] So history moves, not only towards the divine act of judgment that will bring it to an end, but also towards a final concentration of Satanic evil within history,[38] immediately preceding the Second Coming, when the prince of this world will for the last time have his hour, as he had it during the Passion, and for the last time will be judged.[39]

And the third characteristic of the epilogue, circumscribed always as it is by the imminence of the end, and impelled by the mounting struggle of the opposing forces within it, is the continuous recurrence, even before the end, of crisis and redemption, of judgment and the giving of life to those who will respond to judgment. The archetypal pattern of the Incarnation, the Crucifixion and the Resurrection is repeated continually in all human lives and all human situations. If there is a "progress" about this repetition, it seems to be only in the sense that the crises increase in magnitude, as the Church expands in the world, and increase in depth, as the consciousness of human sin is deepened and therefore the corresponding salvific power of God. So to believe that the end of the world is potentially imminent is no mark of a childish and defective analysis of the course of history, as might be supposed by those who would point out that the world has in fact *not* come to an end.[40] Indeed it is plain in the Church's history that expectation

---

35. Matt 13:24–30, 37–43; cf. 47–50. See Dodd, *The Parables of the Kingdom*, 183–86.

36. Dodd, *The Parables of the Kingdom*, 71–74.

37. Mark 13; Matt 24; Luke 21.

38. 2 Thess 2:3–4; Rev 13. Cf. 1. Maritain, *St. Thomas Aquinas*, 87–88; Berdyaev, *The Meaning of History*, 204; Niebuhr, *The Nature and Destiny of Man*, 327–30

39. Luke 22:53; John 12:31; 14:30; 16:11.

40. It is familiar that the history of Christian apocalyptic has been reflected in a debased form in the history of Marxist apocalyptic. The Russian Revolution was the parallel to the Incarnation, the realisation of meaning within history, with an implicit judgment on the world at large. There followed an exaggerated

of the end has always been one of the marks of a high spiritual culture; though this does not mean that we can regain a high spiritual culture by cultivating apocalyptic fantasies. To expect the end is to recognise the deeper truth that judgment is always imminent, is latent in every crisis—personal as well as public, and that at any moment our lives may be sliced off and we may be judged.[41] Every immediate crisis, therefore, is a transparency of the last crisis; as when Our Lord predicted the destruction of Jerusalem, but only as a prefiguring of the end. "To the Christian the world is always ending, and every historical crisis is, as it were, a rehearsal for the real thing."[42]

Repentance and Prophecy

The revival of the eschatological elements in Christianity has been one of the main achievements of the theologians of this century. It has been the real response of the Church to the contemporary upheaval. Our age has had many boasts for itself, and holds many records, but its essential uniqueness lies perhaps in the sphere where it has not been accustomed to make claims. The crisis we have been living through since 1939 or 1933 or 1914, whichever date we may choose, is possibly more exactly a transparency, more nearly a rehearsal for the real thing, than any of which we have historical record. It has become the consensus of all our historians and secular prophets that we are living at the end of an age, and even the newspaper reader is being forced to realise that the forces of growth are now entirely overbalanced by the forces of destruction. The Communist interprets this with satisfaction as the last epilepsy of capitalist society, but the Christian sees the working of a deeper dialectic, and the clash of contradictions in a dimension the Communist does not know of. The "questions" and "problems" of dissolving Christendom can now be seen for what they are, as judgments. They are judgments taking the form of demonic perversions: judgment on war, which is no longer a purposive and preservative activity governed by the doctrine of the just war, but has become an indiscriminate social convulsion;[43] judgment on the state, in the form of an impending world

expectation of the world revolution, which would be the final and explicit judgment. When the world revolution did not happen, the Communist movement turned its attention to the tactics of an indefinitely prolonged epilogue. The historical parallel is a subject of great importance that needs to be worked out in detail. The fundamental difference between the two apocalyptics is that Marxism denies the extra-historical category and therefore forces the fulfilment of history within the historical process itself.

41. ". . . the Last Judgment will supervene unexpectedly and unpredictably upon a world showing no indication of its approach, unless it be that 'the sky grows darker yet and the sea rises higher.' That seems to imply that there is no moment in the world's history which by historical necessity leads up to the Judgment. Doomsday simply takes a cut across the timestream at any point and reveals the triumph of the divine purpose in it." Dodd, *History and the Gospel*, 170.

42. Dawson, *Beyond Politics*, 136.

43. "L'Europe est pleine de guerres, mais le plus nigaud commence a se rendre compte que ces guerres sont le prétexte et l'alibi d'une guerre, qui sera la Guerre, la Guerre absolue, ni politique, ni sociale, ni religieuse au sens strict du mot, la Guerre qui n'ose pas dire son nom peut-être parce qu'elle n'en a aucun, qu'elle est simplement l'état naturel d'une société humaine dont l'extraordinaire complexité est absolument sans proportion avec les sentiments élémentaires qui l'animent, et qui expriment les plus basses formes de la vie collective: vanité, cupidité, envie." (Bernanos, *Les Grands Cimetières sous la Lune*, 172–73). Leon Bloy used similar words 25 years earlier: "Pour qui voit dans l'Absolu, la guerre n'a de sens

state which may well be a more frightful concentration of tyrannical power than any we have yet experienced; judgment on nationalism, which has long been again a form of idolatry that was denounced by the prophets of the Old Testament; judgment on revolution, which has been swollen into the decisive fact of contemporary secular history, and has produced a giant debased substitute for the Church.

In these circumstances it is inevitable that the emphasis of the Church's teaching should once more be upon the eschatological elements of her creed; but the problem, which is perhaps the special problem for Amsterdam, is that little of them has yet filtered through to Christian political thinking. The revival of Christian eschatology has been the real response to the contemporary crisis, but except among the churches of the European Continent it has been, so to speak, only half-conscious, instinctive rather than reasoned. And how is Christian eschatology relevant to Christian political thinking; how would it be expressed if its influence became conscious?

First, by throwing the Church back upon the task which is at once the centre and the circumference of its attempts to build a Christian civilisation: the proclaiming of the gospel of the crucified and risen Christ. Then, by applying the call to repentance with which the gospel was first heard among men *to itself,* the Church to the Church. For within the Church too there are the tensions of history, the struggle between nature and grace; and the historical Church has its share of guilt for the collapse of Christendom. Here its task now may be to see how its own position carries some degree of determination, some inescapable accumulation of retribution due.

· This inner reorientation, this *metanoia,* precedes the proclamation of the gospel by the Church to the world. And there the task today is perhaps especially prophetic judgment in its negative sense. To the Gentiles Christ crucified is always folly: he brings not peace but tribulation, not progress but crisis. The Church must know its own position against the abysses of an un-Christed world. It is under the commission to Ezekiel, that it will be judged, not by whether the wicked die in their iniquity, for this it cannot control, but according to whether it spoke to warn the wicked from their wicked way.[44] And this means that the Church must know not only its own position but also the depth of the crisis of the world. It must know that the area of effective contact between the Church and the secular world is contracting, and that the front along which the Church has to open up its artillery of prophetic condemnation is extending. Nor does the language of prophecy say, "This time the perils are seen; possible defences are at hand and the vigorous and dynamic spirit which produces the peril can also produce an era of unprecedented progress. Thus, men have great opportunity at the price of measurable risk."[45] The language of prophecy says, "Woe unto you that desire the day of the Lord! to what end is it for you?; the day of the Lord is darkness, and not light. As if a man did flee from a lion, and a bear met him; or went into the house, and leaned his hand on the wall, and a serpent bit him. Shall not the day of the Lord be darkness, and not light?;

que si elle est *exterminatrice,* et l'avenir très prochain nous le montrera," (Bloy, *L'Ame de Napoléon,* 114).

44. Ezek 3:17–21.

45. *Soviet-American Relations,* a statement submitted by the Commission on a Just and Durable Peace and adopted by the Executive Committee of the Federal Council of the Churches of Christ in America, October 11, 1946, conclusion.

even very dark, and no brightness in it?"[46] The first kind of language has its proper place, but it must always be subordinated to the second kind of language; for the second kind includes the first kind, and repentance may in God's mercy bring the things that the first looks to, but the first kind by itself cannot do this.

As the present crisis deepens and the historical prospect grows darker, their meaninglessness and terror will increase for everybody except the Christian. The Church alone knows all about this;—has been here before; this is where she comes in. "And when these things begin to come to pass, then look up, and lift up your heads; for your redemption draweth nigh."[47] The future observer, looking back, may see the Church now as standing at the farthest possible point from secular history, of which only a minimum comes at this moment within the reach of her sacramentalising power. He may see her shifting her emphasis and insight from Romans xiii to the Apocalypse xiii. He may see her once more confronting Antichrist, as she so often has before. He may see her once more with eagerness awaiting the coming of her Lord, watching and praying, lest that day should overtake her as a thief.[48] He may see the mystical Church once more radiating forth her spiritual beams, outshining the feeble and divided institutional Church, like the corona round the sun in eclipse: spiritual beams which may or may not reach down the future to fertilise a new Christendom ten centuries hence—it does not matter. But first of all we today must clear our minds about the point at which we have arrived; and perhaps this is what Amsterdam can do.

46. Amos 5:8–20.
47. Luke 21:28.
48. 1 Thess 5:4.

1–5

"Augustine's Political Realism"[1]

REINHOLD NIEBUHR

I

THE TERMS "IDEALISM" AND "realism" are not analogous in political and in metaphysical theory; and they are certainly not as precise in political, as in metaphysical, theory. In political and moral theory "realism" denotes the disposition to take all factors in a social and political situation, which offer resistance to established norms, into account, particularly the factors of self-interest and power. In the words of a notorious "realist," Machiavelli, the purpose of the realist is "to follow the truth of the matter rather than the imagination of it; for many have pictures of republics and principalities which have never been seen." This definition of realism implies that idealists are subject to illusions about social realities, which indeed they are. "Idealism" is, in the esteem of its proponents, characterized by loyalty to moral norms and ideals, rather than to self-interest, whether individual or collective. It is, in the opinion of its critics, characterized by a disposition to ignore or be indifferent to the forces in human life which offer resistance to universally valid ideals and norms. This disposition, to which Machiavelli refers, is general whenever men are inclined to take the moral pretensions of themselves or their fellowmen at face value; for the disposition to hide self-interest behind the facade of pretended devotion to values, transcending self-interest, is well-nigh universal. It is, moreover, an interesting human characteristic, proving that the concept of "total depravity," as it is advanced by some Christian realists, is erroneous. Man is a curious creature with so strong a sense of obligation to his fellows that he cannot pursue his own interests without pretending to serve his fellowmen. The definitions of "realists" and "idealists" emphasize disposition, rather than doctrines; and they are therefore bound to be inexact. It must remain a matter of opinion whether or not a man takes adequate account of all the various factors and forces in a social situation. Was Plato a realist, for instance, because he tried to guard against the self-interest of the "guardians" of his ideal state by divesting them of property and reducing their family responsibilities to a minimum? Does this bit of "realism" cancel out the essential unrealism, inherent in ascribing to the "lusts of the body" the force of recalcitrance against the moral norm; or in attributing pure virtue to pure mind?

1. Niebuhr, "Augustine's Political Realism," In *Christian Realism and Political Problems*, 119–46.

Augustine was, by general consent, the first great "realist" in western history. He deserves this distinction because his picture of social reality in his *civitas dei* gives an adequate account of the social factions, tensions, and competitions which we know to be well-nigh universal on every level of community; while the classical age conceived the order and justice of its *polis* to be a comparatively simple achievement, which would be accomplished when reason had brought all sub-rational forces under its dominion.

This difference in the viewpoint of Augustine and the classical philosophers lies in Augustine's biblical, rather than rationalistic, conception of human selfhood with the ancillary conception of the seat of evil being in the self. Augustine broke with classical rationalism in his conception of the human self, according to which the self is composed of mind and body, the mind being the seat of virtue because it has the capacity to bring all impulses into order; and the body, from which come the "lusts and ambitions," being the cause of evil. According to Augustine the self is an integral unity of mind and body. It is something more than mind and is able to use mind for its purposes. The self has, in fact, a mysterious identity and integrity transcending its functions of mind, memory, and will. "These three things, memory, understanding, and love are mine and not their own," he declares, "for they do what they do not for themselves but for me; or rather I do it by them. For it is I who remember by memory and understand by understanding and love by love."[2] It must be observed that the transcendent freedom of this self, including its capacity to defy any rational or natural system into which someone may seek to coordinate it (its capacity for evil) makes it difficult for any philosophy, whether ancient or modern, to comprehend its true dimension. That is why the classical wise men obscured it by fitting its mind into a system of universal mind and the body into the system of nature; and that is also why the modem wise men, for all their rhetoric about the "dignity" of the individual, try to cut down the dimension of human selfhood so that it will seem to fit into a system of nature. This conception of selfhood is drawn from the Bible, rather than from philosophy, because the transcendent self, which is present in, though it transcends, all of the functions and effects, is comprehensible only in the dramatic-historical mode of apprehension which characterizes biblical faith. Augustine draws on the insights of neo-Platonism to illustrate the self's power of self-transcendence; but he rejects Plotinus' mystic doctrine, in which the particular self, both human and divine, is lost in a vast realm of undifferentiated being.

Augustine's conception of the evil which threatens the human community on every level is a corollary of his doctrine of selfhood. "Self-love" is the source of evil rather than some residual natural impulse which mind has not yet completely mastered. This excessive love of self, sometimes also defined as pride or *superbia,* is explained as the consequence of the self's abandonment of God as its true end and of making itself "a kind of end." It is this powerful self-love or, in a modem term, "egocentricity," this tendency of the self to make itself its own end or even to make itself the false center of whatever community it inhabits, which sows confusion into every human community. The power of self-love is more spiritual than the "lusts of the body," of which Plato speaks; and it corrupts the processes of the mind more than Plato or Aristotle knew. That is why

2. Augustine, *De Trinitate,* 15.22.

Augustine could refute the classical theory with the affirmation that "it is not the bad body which causes the good soul to sin but the bad soul which causes the good body to sin." At other times Augustine defines the evil in man as the "evil will"; but with the understanding that it is the self which is evil in the manifestation of its will. "For he who extols the whole nature of the soul as the chief good and condemns the nature of the flesh as if it were evil, assuredly is fleshly both in the love of the soul and in the hatred of the flesh."[3] This concise statement of the Christian position surely refutes the absurd charge of moderns that the Christian faith is "dualistic" and generates contempt for the body. It also established the only real basis for a realistic estimate of the forces of recalcitrance which we must face on all levels of the human community, particularly for a realistic estimate of the spiritual dimension of these forces and of the comparative impotence of "pure reason" against them. Compared with a Christian realism, which is based on Augustine's interpretation of biblical faith, a great many modem social and psychological theories, which fancy themselves anti-Platonic or even anti-Aristotelian and which make much of their pretended "realism," are in fact no more realistic than the classical philosophers. Thus modem social and psychological scientists are forever seeking to isolate some natural impulse such as "aggressiveness and to manage it: with equal vanity they are trying to find a surrogate for Plato's and Aristotle's disinterested "reason" in a so-called "scientific method." Their inability to discover the corruption of self-interest in reason or in man's rational pursuits; and to measure the spiritual dimension of man's inhumanity and cruelty, gives an air of sentimentality to the learning of our whole liberal culture. Thus we have no guidance amid the intricacies of modem power politics except as the older disciplines, less enamored of the "methods of natural science," and the common sense of the man in the street supplies the necessary insights.

II

Augustine's description of the social effects of human egocentricity or self-love is contained in his definition of the life of the "city of this world," the *civitas terrena,* which he sees as commingled with the *civitas dei.* The "city of this world" is dominated by self-love to the point of contempt of God; and is distinguished from the *civitas dei* which is actuated by the "love of God" to the point of contempt of self. This "city" is not some little city-state, as it is conceived in classical thought. It is the whole human community on its three levels of the family, the commonwealth, and the world. A potential world community is therefore envisaged in Augustine's thought. But, unlike the stoic and modem "idealists," he does not believe that a common humanity or a common reason gives promise of an easy actualization of community on the global level. The world community, declares Augustine, "is fuller of dangers as the greater sea is more dangerous."[4] Augustine is a consistent realist in calling attention to the fact that the potential world community may have a common human reason but it speaks in different languages and "Two men, each ignorant of each other's language" will find that "dumb animals, though of a different

3. Augustine, *De Civ. Dei,* 15.5.
4. Augustine, *De Civ. Dei,* 19.7.

species, could more easily hold intercourse than they, human beings though they be."[5] This realistic reminder that common linguistic and ethnic cultural forces, which bind the community together on one level, are divisive on the ultimate level, is a lesson which our modem proponents of world government have not yet learned.

Augustine's description of the *civitas terrena* includes an emphasis on the tensions, frictions, competitions of interest, and overt conflicts to which every human community is exposed. Even in the family one cannot rely on friendship "seeing that secret treachery has often broken it up."[6] This bit of realism will seem excessive until we remember that our own generation has as much difficulty in preserving the peace and integrity in the smallest and most primordial community, the family, as in integrating community on the highest global level.

The *civitas terrena* is described as constantly subject to an uneasy armistice between contending forces, with the danger that factional disputes may result in "bloody insurrection" at any time. Augustine's realism prompts him to challenge Cicero's conception of a commonwealth as rooted in a "compact of justice." Not so, declares Augustine. Commonwealths are bound together by a common love, or collective interest, rather than by a sense of justice; and they could not maintain themselves without the imposition of power. "Without injustice the republic would neither increase nor subsist. The imperial city to which the republic belongs could not rule over provinces without recourse to injustice. For it is unjust for some men to rule over others."[7]

This realism has the merit of describing the power realities which underlie all large scale social integrations whether in Egypt or Babylon or Rome, where a dominant city-state furnished the organizing power for the Empire. It also describes the power realities of national states, even democratic ones, in which a group, holding the dominant form of social power, achieves oligarchic rule, no matter how much modern democracy may bring such power under social control. This realism in regard to the facts which underlie the organizing or governing power refutes the charge of modem liberals that a realistic analysis of social forces makes for state absolutism; so that a mild illusion in regard to human virtue is necessary to validate democracy. Realistic pessimism did indeed prompt both Hobbes and Luther to an unqualified endorsement of state power; but that is only because they were not realistic enough. They saw the dangers of anarchy in the egotism of the citizens but failed to perceive the dangers of tyranny in the selfishness of the ruler. Therefore they obscured the consequent necessity of placing checks upon the ruler's self-will. Augustine's realism was indeed excessive. On the basis of his principles he could not distinguish between government and slavery, both of which were supposedly the rule over man by man and were both a consequence of, and remedy for, sin; nor could he distinguish between a commonwealth and a robber band, for both were bound together by collective interest; "For even thieves must hold together or they cannot effect what they intend." The realism fails to do justice to the sense of justice in the constitution of the Roman Empire; or for that matter to the sense of justice in a robber band.

5. Augustine, *De Civ. Dei,* 19.7.

6. Augustine, *De Civ. Dei,* 19.5.

7. Augustine, *De Civ. Dei,* 19.21.

For even thieves will fall out if they cannot trust each other to divide the loot, which is their common aim, equitably. But the excessive emphasis upon the factors of power and interest, a wholesome corrective to Cicero's and modern Ciceronian moralistic illusions, is not fatal to the establishment of justice so long as the dangers of tyranny are weighed as realistically as the dangers of anarchy.

Augustine's realistic attitude toward government rests partly upon the shrewd observation that social peace and order are established by a dominant group within some level of community; and that this group is not exempt from the corruption of self-interest merely because the peace of society has been entrusted to it. (One thinks incidentally how accurately the Augustinian analysis fits both the creative and the ambiguous character of the American hegemony in the social cohesion of the free world.) The realism is partly determined by his conception of a "natural order" which he inherited from the early Christian fathers, who in turn took it from that part of the Stoic theory which emphasized the primordial or primitive as the natural. This Stoic and Christian primitivism has the merit of escaping the errors of those natural law theories which claim to find a normative moral order amid the wide variety of historic forms or even among the most universal of these forms. The freedom of man makes these Stoic conceptions of the "natural" impossible. But it has the weakness which characterizes all primitivism, whether Stoic, Christian, or Romantic, for it makes primitive social forms normative. A primitive norm, whether of communal property relations or unorganized social cohesion, may serve provisionally as an occasion for the criticism of the institutions of an advancing civilization, more particularly the institutions of property and government; but it has the disadvantage of prompting indiscriminate criticism. This lack of discrimination is obvious in primitivistic Stoicism, in early Christianity, in seventeenth-century Cromwellian sectarianism, in Romanticism, and in Marxism and anarchism.

Augustine expressed this idea of a primitive social norm as follows: "This is the prescribed order of nature. It is thus that God created man. For 'let them,' He says, 'have dominion over the fish of the sea and the fowl of the air and over every creeping thing, which creepeth on the earth.' He did not intend that His rational creature, made in His image, should have dominion over anything but irrational creation—not man over man but man over beasts. And hence the righteous men of primitive times were made shepherds of cattle rather than kings of men."[8] This primitivism avoids the later error of the absolute sanctification of government. But its indiscriminate character is apparent by his failure to recognize the difference between legitimate and illegitimate, between ordinate and inordinate subordination of man to man. Without some form of such subordination the institutions of civilization could not exist.

III

If Augustine's realism is contained in his analysis of the *civitas terrena,* his refutation of the idea that realism must lead to cynicism or relativism is contained in his definition of the *civitas dei,* which he declares to be "commingled" with the "city of this word" and

---

8. Augustine, *De Civ. Dei,* 19.15.

which has the "love of God" rather than the "love of self" as its guiding principle. The tension between the two cities is occasioned by the fact that, while egotism is "natural" in the sense that it is universal, it is not natural in the sense that it does not conform to man's nature who transcends himself indeterminately and can only have God rather than self for his end. A realism becomes morally cynical or nihilistic when it assumes that the universal characteristic in human behavior must also be regarded as normative. The biblical account of human behavior, upon which Augustine bases his thought, can escape both illusion and cynicism because it recognizes that the corruption of human freedom may make a behavior pattern universal without making it normative. Good and evil are not determined by some fixed structure of human existence. Man, according to the biblical view, may use his freedom to make himself falsely the center of existence; but this does not change the fact that love rather than self-love is the law of his existence in the sense that man can only be healthy and his communities at peace if man is drawn out of himself and saved from the self-defeating consequences of self-love. There are several grave errors in Augustine's account of love and of the relation of love to self-love; but before considering them we might well first pay tribute to his approach to political problems. The virtue of making love, rather than justice, into the norm for the community may seem, at first blush, to be dubious. The idea of justice seems much more relevant than the idea of love, particularly for the collective relationships of men. The medieval tradition which makes the justice of a rational "natural law" normative even for Christians when they consider the necessities of a sinful world, seems much more realistic than modem forms of sentimental Protestantism which regards love as a simple alternative to self-love, which could be achieved if only we could preach the idea persuasively enough to beguile men from the one to the other. Augustine's doctrine of love as the final norm must be distinguished from modem sentimental versions of Christianity which regard love as a simple possibility and which think it significant to assert the obvious proposition that all conflicts in the community would be avoided if only people and nations would love one another. Augustine's approach differs from modem forms of sentimental perfectionism in the fact that he takes account of the power and persistence of egotism, both individual and collective, and seeks to establish the most tolerable form of peace and justice under conditions set by human sin. He inherited the tradition of monastic perfection; and he allows it as a vent for the Christian impulse toward individual perfection, without however changing the emphasis upon the duty of the Christian to perfect the peace of the city of this world. Furthermore, he raises questions about monastic perfection which, when driven home by the Reformation, were to undermine the whole system. "I venture to say," he writes:

> . . . that it is good for those who observe continence and are proud of it, to fall that they may be humbled. For what benefit is it to anyone in whom is the virtue of continence, if pride holds sway? He is but despising that by which man is born in striving after that which led to satan's fall . . . holy virginity is better than conjugal chastity, . . . but if we add two other things, pride and humility, . . . which is better, pride or humility? . . . I have no doubt that a humble married woman is to be preferred to a proud virgin . . . a mother holds a lesser place in the Kingdom of God because she has been married, than the daughter, seeing that she is a virgin.

. . . But if thy mother has been proud and thou humble, she will have some sort of place and thou none.[9]

While Augustine's doctrine of love is thus not to be confused with modem sentimentalities which do not take the power of self-love seriously, one may well wonder whether an approach to politics which does not avail itself of the calculations of justice, may be deemed realistic. We have already noted that Augustine avails himself of the theory of the "natural law," only in the primordial version of the theory. If primordial conditions of a "natural order" are not to be defined as normative, the only alternative is to assume a "rational order" to which the whole of historical life conforms. Aquinas, in fact, constructed his theory of the natural law upon classical, and primarily Aristotelian, foundations. It was the weakness of both classical and medieval theories that they assumed an order in history, conforming to the uniformities of nature. Aristotle was aware of deviations in history, greater than those in nature; but he believed that there was nevertheless one form "which was marked by nature as the best." There is, in other words, no place in this theory of natural law for the endlessly unique social configurations which human beings, in their freedom over natural necessity, construct. The proponents of "natural law" therefore invariably introduce some historically contingent norm or social structure into what they regard as God's inflexible norm. That was the weakness of both classical and medieval social theory; and for that matter of the natural law theories of the bourgeois Parties of the eighteenth century, who had found that they regarded as a more empirically perceived "natural law"; but the modem empirical intelligence was no more capable than the deductive rational processes of classical and medieval times to construct a social norm, not colored by the interests of the constructor, thus introducing the taint of ideology into the supposed sanctities of law. We must conclude therefore that Augustine was wise in avoiding the alleged solution of a natural law theory, which was the basis of so much lack of realism in both the classical and the medieval period, and which can persist today long after the Aristotelian idea of fixed form for historical events has been overcome, as the dogma of a religious system which makes its supposed sanctities into an article of faith. His conception of the radical freedom of man, derived from the biblical view, made it impossible to accept the idea of fixed forms of human behavior and of social organization, analogous to those of nature, even as he opposed the classical theory of historical cycles. Furthermore, his conception of human selfhood and of the transcendence of the self over its mind, made it impossible to assume the identity of the individual reason with a universal reason, which lies at the foundation of the classical and medieval natural law theories. It is in fact something of a mystery how the Christian insights into human nature and history, expressed by Augustine, could have been subordinated to classical thought with so little sense of the conflict between them in the formulations of Thomas Aquinas; and how they should have become so authoritative in Roman Catholicism without more debate between Augustinian and Thomistic emphases.

Augustine's formula for leavening the city of this world with the love of the city of God is more adequate than classical and medieval thought, both in doing justice to the

9. Augustine, Sermon CCCIIV, ix, 9.

endless varieties of historical occasions and configurations and in drawing upon the resources of love rather than law in modifying human behavior.

Every "earthly peace," declares Augustine, is good as far as it goes. "But they will not have it long for they used it not well while they had it." That is, unless some larger love or loyalty qualifies the self-interest of the various groups, this collective self-interest will expose the community to either an overt conflict of competing groups or to the injustice of a dominant group which "when it is victorious it will become vice's slave." Let us use some examples from current national and international problems to illustrate the Augustinian thesis. There is, or was, a marked social tension between the middle classes of industrial owners and the industrial workers in all modern industrial nations. In some of them, for instance in Germany and France, this tension led to overt forms of the class conflict. In others such as Britain, the smaller European nations and America, this tension was progressively resolved by various accommodations of interest. Wherein lay the difference? It did not lie in the possession of more adequate formulae of justice in some nations than in others. The difference lay in the fact that in some nations the various interest groups had, in addition to their collective interest, a "sense of justice," a disposition to "give each man his due" and a loyalty to the national community which qualified the interest struggle. Now, that spirit of justice is identical with the spirit of love, except at the highest level of the spirit of love, where it becomes purely sacrificial and engages in no calculation of what the due of each man may be. Two forms of love, the love of the other and the love of the community, were potent in short in modifying the acerbities and injustices of the class struggle. The two forms of love availed themselves of various calculations of justice in arriving at and defining their *ad hoc* agreements. But the factors in each nation and in each particular issue were too variable to allow for the application of any general rules or formulae of justice. Agreements were easier in fact if too much was not claimed for these formulae. Certain "principles" of justice, as distinguished from formulas or prescriptions, were indeed operative, such as liberty, equality, and loyalty to covenants; but these principles will be recognized as no more than the law of love in its various facets.

In the same manner the international community is exposed to exactly the tensions and competitions of interest which Augustine describes. There are no formulas of justice or laws which will prevent these tensions from reaching overt conflict if the collective interest of each nation is not modified by its loyalty to a higher value such as the common civilization of the free nations. Where this common loyalty is lacking, as in our relations with Russia, no formula can save us from the uneasy peace in which we live. The character of this peace is just as tentative as Augustine described it. Whenever common loves or loyalties, or even common fears, lay the foundation for community, it must of course be our business to perfect it by calculations of justice which define our mutual responsibilities as exactly as possible.

It must be noted that the Augustinian formula for the leavening influence of a higher upon a lower loyalty or love, is effective in preventing the lower loyalty from involving itself in self-defeat. It corrects the "realism" of those who are myopically realistic by seeing only their own interests and failing thereby to do justice to their interests where they are involved with the interests of others. There are modern realists, for instance, who, in their reaction to abstract and vague forms of international idealism, counsel the nation to consult only its own interests. In a sense collective self-interest is so consistent that it is superfluous to advise it. But a consistent self-interest on the part of a nation will work against its interests because it will fail to do justice to the broader and longer interests, which are involved with the interests of other nations. A narrow national loyalty on our part, for instance, will obscure our long range interests where they are involved with those of a whole alliance of free nations. Thus the loyalty of a leavening portion of a nation's citizens to a value transcending national interest will save a "realistic" nation from defining its interests in such narrow and short range terms as to defeat the real interests of the nation.

IV

We have acknowledged some weaknesses in the Augustinian approach to the political order which we must now define and examine more carefully. Non-Catholics commonly criticize Augustine's alleged identification of the *civitas dei* with the visible Church But we must absolve him of this charge or insist on a qualification of the criticism. He does indeed accept the Catholic doctrine, which had grown up before his day; and he defines the visible Church as the only perfect society. There are passages in which he seems to assume that it is possible to claim for the members of the Church that they are solely actuated by the *amor dei*. But he introduces so many reservations to this assertion that he may well be defined in this, as in other instances, as the father of both Catholicism and the Reformation. Of the Church, Augustine declared, "by faith she is a virgin. In the flesh she has few holy virgins"[10] or again: "God will judge the wicked and the good. The evil cannot now be separated from the good but must be suffered for a season. The wicked may be with us on the threshing floor . . . in the barn they cannot be."[11] The reservations which he made upon the identification of the Church and the kingdom laid the foundations for the later Reformation position. But these reservations about the sinners who might be present in the visible Church cannot obscure a graver error in his thought. This error is probably related to his conception of grace, which does not allow for the phenomenon, emphasized by the Reformation, that men may be redeemed in the sense that they consciously turn from self to Christ as their end, and yet they are not redeemed from the corruption of egotism which expresses itself, even in the lives of the saints. This insight is most succinctly expressed in Luther's phrase "*fustus et peccator simul*" (righteous and sinners at once). When Augustine distinguished between the "two loves" which characterize the "two cities," the love of God and the love of self, and when he pictured the world as a commingling of the two cities, he does not recognize that the co-mingling is due, not to the fact that two types of people dwell together but because the conflict between love and self-love is in every soul, It is particularly important to recognize this fact in political analyses; for nothing is more obvious than that personal dedication is no guarantee against the involvement of the dedicated individual in some form of collective egotism.

10. Niebuhr is citing Augustine's Sermon CCXIII, vii, 7.
11. Niebuhr is citing Augustine's *Comm. on Ps.*, CXIX, 9.

We have frequency referred to Augustine's definition of the "two loves" which inform the "two cities" of which "the one is selfish and the other social," the one loving self to the point of the contempt of God and the other loving God to the point of contempt of self. The question is whether Bishop Nygren[12] is right in defining the Augustinian conception of *amor dei* as rooted in a classical rather than a biblical concept.

In defense of Augustine it must be said that he is not insensible to the two facets of the love commandment and therefore does not define the *amor dei* in purely mystical terms as a flight from this world. He insists on the contrary that the *amor dei* is "social" and he offers the concord among brethren as a proof of the love of God. But nevertheless Nygren is right in suggesting that the thought of Plotinus has colored Augustine's conceptions sufficiently so that the *agape* of the New Testament is misinterpreted by Augustine's conception of *caritas* and *amor dei*. The *agape* form of love in the New Testament fails to be appreciated particularly in two of its facets: A) the equality of the "two loves," the love of the neighbor and the love of God (enforced in the Scripture by the words "the Second is like unto it") is violated by Augustine under the influence of Plotinus even as a later medieval Catholic mystic, St. John of the Cross, violates it when he regarded the love of the creature as a ladder which might lead us to the love of God, but must be subordinated to the latter. Augustine wants us to love the neighbor for the sake of God, which may be a correct formulation; but he wants us to prove the genuineness of our love of God in the love of the neighbor, or by leading him to God. Thus the meeting of the neighbor's need without regard to any ultimate religious intention is emptied of meaning. The love of the neighbor is for him not part of a double love commandment but merely the instrument of a single love commandment which bids us flee all mortality including the neighbor in favor of the immutable good. B) The second facet of the *agape* concept of the New Testament which tends to be obscured is the notion of sacrificial love, the absurd principle of the Cross, the insistence that the self must sacrifice itself for the other. It is not fair to Augustine to say that he neglects this facet of meaning for he seems to emphasize it so constantly. He comes closest to its meaning when he deals with the relation of humility to love. Yet it seems fair to say that he was sufficiently imbued by classical mystical thought forms so that the emphasis lies always upon the worthiness or unworthiness of the object of our love; the insistence is that only God and not some mutable "good" or person is worthy of our love. This is a safeguard against all forms of idolatry. But it does not answer another important question: when I love a person or a community do I love myself in them or do I truly love them? Is my love a form of alter-egoism? The Augustinian *amor dei* assumes that the self in its smallness cannot contain itself within itself and therefore it is challenged to go out from itself to the most ultimate end. But it hardly reveals the full paradox of self-realization through self-giving which a scandal in the field of rational ethics as the Cross is a scandal in the field of rational religion. Yet it is the source of ultimate wisdom. For the kind of self-giving which has self-realization as its result must not have self-realization as its conscious end; otherwise the self by calculating its enlargement will not escape from itself completely enough to be enlarged. The weakness of Augustine in obscuring these facets of the *agape* principle may be illustrated, without unfairness I hope,

12. Anders Nygren, in *Agape and Eros*.

by referring to his treatment of family love. He questions the love of mate or children as the final form of love, but not for New Testament reasons. He does not say: "When you love your wife and children are you maybe really loving yourself in them and using them as the instruments of your self-aggrandisements?" He declares instead, in effect, you must not love your family too unreservedly because your wife and children are mortal. They also belong to the "rivers of Babylon," and, if you give them absolute devotion, the hour of bereavement will leave you desolate. Of course Augustine is too much the Christian to engage in a consistent mystic depreciation of the responsibilities and joys of this earthly life. After all, his whole strategy for the "commingling" of the two cities revolves around the acceptance of the ordinary responsibilities of home and state but in performing these tasks for the ultimate, rather than the immediate end. "What then?" he asks. "Shall all perish who marry and are given in marriage, who till the fields and build houses? No, but those who put their trust in these things, who prefer them to God, who for the sake of these things are quick to offend God, these will perish. But those who either do not use these things or who use them as though they used them not, trusting more in Him who gave them than in the things given, understanding in them His consolation and mercy, and who are not absorbed in these gifts lest they fall away from the giver. These are they whom the day will not overtake as a thief unprepared."[13] We must not, in criticizing Augustine for neo-Platonic elements in his thought, obscure the Christian elements which will be equally an offense to modem men who regard the world as self-sufficing and self-explanatory, who reject as absurd the Christian faith that there is not only a mystery behind and above the world of observed phenomena and intelligible meanings, but that it is a mystery whose meaning has been disclosed as a love which elicits our answering love. This modem generation with its confidence in a world without mystery, and without meaning beyond simple intelligibility, will not be beguiled from its unbelief by a reminder that its emancipation from God has betrayed it into precisely those idolatries, the worship of false gods, the dedication to finite values as if they were ultimate, of which Augustine spoke. But it must be recorded nevertheless as a significant fact of modern history. While it is an offence to regard communism as the inevitable end-product of secularism, as some Christians would have us believe, it is only fair to point out that the vast evils of modem communism come ironically to a generation which thought it would be easy to invest all the spiritual capital of men, who mysteriously transcend the historical process, in some value or end within that process; and communism is merely the most pathetic and cruel of the idolatrous illusions of this generation.

We must be clear about the fact that all the illusions about man's character and history which made it so difficult for either the classical or the modern age to come to terms with the vexing problems of our togetherness, seem to stem from efforts to understand man in both his grandeur and his misery by "integrating" him into some natural or rational system of coherence. Thereby they denied the mystery of his transcendence over every process which points to another mystery beyond himself without which man is not only a mystery to himself but a misunderstood being.

13. Augustine, *Comm. on Ps.* CXX, 3.

We cannot deny that from a Christian standpoint the world is like a "river of Babylon" to use Augustine's symbol; and that Augustine is right in suggesting that ultimately we cannot find peace if we are merely tossed down the river of time. We must find security in that which is not carried down the river. "Observe however," declares Augustine in a simile which will seem strange to generations which have made the "rivers of Babylon," the stream of temporal events, into forces of redemption; but which will not seem so strange as the modem experience proves history as such to be less redemptive than we had believed.

> The rivers of Babylon are all things which are here loved, and pass away. For example, one man loves to practice husbandry, to grow rich by it, to employ his mind on it, to get his pleasure from it. Let him observe the issue and see that what he has loved is not a foundation of Jerusalem, but a river of Babylon. Another says, it is a grand thing to be a soldier; all farmers fear those who are soldiers, are subservient to them, tremble at them. If I am a farmer, I shall fear soldiers; if a soldier, farmers will fear me. Madman! thou hast cast thyself headlong into another river of Babylon, and that still more turbulent and sweeping. Thou wishest to be feared by thy inferior; fear Him Who is greater than thou. He who fears thee may on a sudden become greater than thou, but He Whom thou oughtest to fear will never become less. To be an advocate, says another, is a grand thing; eloquence is most powerful; always to have clients hanging on the lips of their eloquent advocate, and from his words looking for loss or gain, death or life, ruin or security. Thou knowest not whither thou hast cast thyself. This too is another river of Babylon, and its roaring sound is the din of the waters dashing against the rocks. Mark that it flows, that it glides on; beware, for it carries things away with it. To sail the seas, says another, and to trade is a grand thing—to know many lands, to make gains from every quarter, never to be answerable to any powerful man in thy country, to be always travelling, and to feed thy mind with the diversity of the nations and the business met with, and to return enriched by the increase of thy gains. This too is a river of Babylon. When will the gains stop? When wilt thou have confidence and be secure in the gains thou makest? The richer thou art, the more fearful wilt thou be. Once shipwrecked, thou wilt come forth stripped of all, and rightly wilt bewail thy fate *in* the rivers of Babylon, because thou wouldest not sit down and weep *upon* the rivers of Babylon.
>
> But there are other citizens of the holy Jerusalem, understanding their captivity, who mark how human wishes and the diverse lusts of men, hurry and drag them hither and thither, and drive them into the sea. They see this, and do not throw themselves into the rivers of Babylon, but sit down upon the rivers of Babylon and upon the rivers of Babylon weep, either for those who are being carried away by them, or for themselves whose deserts have placed them in Babylon.[14]

Whatever the defects of the Augustine approach may be, we must acknowledge his immense superiority both over those who preceded him and who came after him. A part of that superiority was due to his reliance upon biblical rather than idealistic or naturalistic conceptions of selfhood. But that could not have been the only cause, else Christian systems before and after him would not have been so inferior. Or were they inferior either

14. Augustine, *Comm. on Ps* CXXXVI, 3, 4.

because they subordinated the biblical-dramatic conception of human selfhood too much to the rationalistic scheme, as was the case with medieval Christianity culminating in the thought of Thomas Aquinas? or because they did not understand that the corruption of human freedom could not destroy the original dignity of man, as was the case with the Reformation with its doctrines of sin, bordering on total depravity and resulting in Luther's too pessimistic approach to political problems? As for secular thought, it has difficulty in approaching Augustine's realism without falling into cynicism or in avoiding nihilism without falling into sentimentality. Hobbes' realism was based on an insight which he shared with Augustine, namely, that in all historical encounters the mind is the servant and not the master of the self. But he failed to recognize that the self which thus made the mind its instrument was a corrupted and not a "normal" self. Modern "realists" know the power of collective self-interest as Augustine did; but they do not understand its blindness. Modem pragmatists understood the irrelevance of fixed and detailed norms; but they do not understand that love must take the place as the final norm for these inadequate norms. Modem liberal Christians know that love is the final norm for man; but they fall into sentimentality because they fail to measure the power and persistence of self-love. Thus Augustine, whatever may be the defects of his approach to political reality, and whatever may be the dangers of a too slavish devotion to his insights, nevertheless proves himself a more reliable guide than any known thinker. A generation which finds its communities imperiled and in decay from the smallest and most primordial community, the family, to the largest and most recent, the potential world community, might well take counsel of Augustine in solving its perplexities.

1–6

"The Children of Light and the Children of Darkness"

Reinhold Niebuhr[1]

I

DEMOCRACY, AS EVERY OTHER historic ideal and institution, contains both ephemeral and more permanently valid elements. Democracy is on the one hand the characteristic fruit of a bourgeois civilization; on the other hand it is a perennially valuable form of social organization in which freedom and order are made to support, and not to contradict, each other.

Democracy is a "bourgeois ideology" in so far as it expresses the typical viewpoints of the middle classes who have risen to power in European civilization in the past three or four centuries. Most of the democratic ideals, as we know them, were weapons of the commercial classes who engaged in stubborn, and ultimately victorious, conflict with the ecclesiastical and aristocratic rulers of the feudal-medieval world. The ideal of equality, unknown in the democratic life of the Greek city states and derived partly from Christian and partly from Stoic sources, gave the bourgeois classes a sense of self-respect in overcoming the aristocratic pretension and condescension of the feudal overlords of medieval society. The middle classes defeated the combination "of economic and political power of mercantilism by stressing economic liberty; and, through the principles of political liberty, they added the political power of suffrage to their growing economic power. The implicit assumptions, as well as the explicit ideals, of democratic civilization were also largely the fruit of middle-class existence. The social and historical optimism of democratic life, for instance, represents the typical illusion of an advancing class which mistook its own progress for the progress of the world.

Since bourgeois civilization, which came to birth in the sixteenth to eighteenth centuries and reached its zenith in the nineteenth century, is now obviously in grave peril, if not actually in *rigor mortis* in the twentieth century, it must be obvious that democracy, in so far as it is a middle-class ideology, also faces its doom.

This fate of democracy might be viewed with equanimity, but for the fact that it has a deeper dimension and broader validity than its middle-class character. Ideally democracy is a permanently valid form of social and political organization which does justice

---

1. Niebuhr, *The Children of Light and the Children of Darkness*, chapter 1.

to two dimensions of human existence: to man's spiritual stature and his social character; to the uniqueness and variety of life, as well as to the common necessities of all men. Bourgeois democracy frequently exalted the individual at the expense of the community; but its emphasis upon liberty contained a valid element, which transcended its excessive individualism. The community requires liberty as much as does the individual; and the individual requires community more than bourgeois thought comprehended. Democracy can therefore not be equated with freedom. An ideal democratic order seeks unity within the conditions of freedom; and maintains freedom within the framework of order. Man requires freedom in his social organization because he is "essentially" free, which is to say, that he has the capacity for indeterminate transcendence over the processes and limitations of nature. This freedom enables him to make history and to elaborate communal organizations in boundless variety and in endless breadth and extent. But he also requires community because he is by nature social. He cannot fulfill his life within himself but only in responsible and mutual relations with his fellows.

Bourgeois democrats are inclined to believe that freedom is primarily a necessity for the individual, and that community and social order are necessary only because there are many individuals in a small world, so that minimal restrictions are required to prevent confusion. Actually the community requires freedom as much as the individual; *and* the individual requires order as much as does the community.

Both the individual and the community require freedom so that neither communal nor historical restraints may prematurely arrest the potencies which inhere in man's essential freedom and which express themselves collectively as well as individually. It is true that individuals are usually the initiators of new insights and the proponents of novel methods. Yet there are collective forces at work in society which are not the conscious contrivance of individuals. In any event society is as much the beneficiary of freedom as the individual. In a free society new forces may enter into competition with the old and gradually establish themselves. In a traditional or tyrannical form of social organization new forces are either suppressed, or they establish themselves at the price of social convulsion and upheaval.

The order of a community is, on the other hand, a boon to the individual as well as to the community. The individual cannot be a true self in isolation. Nor can he live within the confines of the community which "nature" establishes in the minimal cohesion of family and herd. His freedom transcends these limits of nature, and therefore makes larger and larger social units both possible and necessary. It is precisely because of the essential freedom of man that he requires a contrived order in his community.

The democratic ideal is thus more valid than the libertarian and individualistic version of it which bourgeois civilization elaborated. Since the bourgeois version has been discredited by the events of contemporary history and since, in any event, bourgeois civilization is in process of disintegration, it becomes important to distinguish and save what is permanently valid from what is ephemeral in the democratic order.

If democracy is to survive it must find a more adequate cultural basis than the philosophy which has informed the building of the bourgeois world. The inadequacy of the presuppositions upon which the democratic experiment rests does not consist merely in the excessive individualism and libertarianism of the bourgeois world view; though it must be noted that this excessive individualism prompted a civil war in the whole western world in which the rising proletarian classes pitted an excessive collectivism against the false individualism of middle-class life. This civil conflict contributed to the weakness of democratic civilization when faced with the threat of barbarism. Neither the individualism nor the collectivism did justice to all the requirements of man's social life, and the conflict between half-truth and half-truth divided the civilized world in such a way that the barbarians were able to claim first one side and then the other in this civil conflict as their provisional allies.[2]

But there is a more fundamental error in the social philosophy of democratic civilization than the individualism of bourgeois democracy and the collectivism of Marxism. It is the confidence of both bourgeois and proletarian idealists in the possibility of achieving an easy resolution of the tension and conflict between self-interest and the general interest. Modem bourgeois civilization is not, as Catholic philosophers and medievalists generally assert, a rebellion against universal law, or a defiance of universal standards of justice, or a war against the historic institutions which sought to achieve and preserve some general social and international harmony. Modern secularism is not, as religious idealists usually aver, merely a rationalization of self-interest, either individual or collective. Bourgeois individualism may be excessive and it may destroy the individual's organic relation to the community; but it was not intended to destroy either the national or the international order. On the contrary the social idealism which informs our democratic civilization had a touching faith in the possibility of achieving a simple harmony between self-interest and the general welfare on every level.

It is not true that Nazism is the final fruit of a moral cynicism which had its rise in the Renaissance and Reformation, as Catholic apologists aver. Nazi barbarism is the final fruit of a moral cynicism which was only a subordinate note in the cultural life of the modern period, and which remained subordinate until very recently. Modern civilization did indeed seek to give the individual a greater freedom in the national community than the traditional feudal order had given him; and it did seek to free the nations of restraints placed upon their freedom by the international church. But it never cynically defied the general interest in the name of self-interest, either individual or collective. It came closer to doing this nationally than individually. Machiavelli's amoral "Prince," who knows no law beyond his own will and power, is made to bear the whole burden of the Catholic polemic against the modern world. It must be admitted that Machiavelli is the first of a long line of moral cynics in the field of international relations. But this moral cynicism only qualifies, and does not efface, the general universalistic overtone of modern liberal idealism. In the field of domestic politics the war of uncontrolled interests may have been the consequence, but it was certainly not the intention, of middle-class individualists. Nor was the conflict between nations in our modern world their intention. They did demand a greater degree of freedom for the nations; but they believed that it was possible to achieve an uncontrolled

2. The success of Nazi diplomacy and propaganda in claiming the poor in democratic civilization as their allies against the "plutocrats" in one moment, and in the next seeking to ally the privileged classes in their battle against "communism," is a nice indication of the part which the civil war in democratic civilization played in allowing barbarism to come so near to a triumph over civilization.

harmony between them, once the allegedly irrelevant restrictions of the old religio-political order were removed. In this they proved to be mistaken. They did not make the mistake, however, of giving simple moral sanction to self-interest. They depended rather upon controls and restraints which proved to be inadequate.

II

In illumining this important distinction more fully, we may well designate the moral cynics, who know no law beyond their will and interest, with a scriptural designation of "children of this world" or "children of darkness." Those who believe that self-interest should be brought under the discipline of a higher law could then be termed "the children of light." This is no mere arbitrary device; for evil is always the assertion of some self-interest without regard to the whole, whether the whole be conceived as the immediate community, or the total community of mankind, or the total order of the world. The good is, on the other hand, always the harmony of the whole on various levels. Devotion to a subordinate and premature "whole" such as the nation, may of course become evil, viewed from the perspective of a larger whole, such as the community of mankind. The "children of light" may thus be defined as those who seek to bring self-interest under the discipline of a more universal law and in harmony with a more universal good.

According to the scripture "the children of this world are in their generation wiser than the children of light." This observation fits the modern situation. Our democratic civilization has been built, not by children of darkness but by foolish children of light. It has been under attack by the children of darkness, by the moral cynics, who declare that a strong nation need acknowledge no law beyond its strength. It has come close to complete disaster under this attack, not because it accepted the same creed as the cynics; but because it underestimated the power of self-interest, both individual and collective, in modern society. The children of light have not been as wise as the children of darkness.

The children of darkness are evil because they know no law beyond the self. They are wise, though evil, because they understand the power of self-interest. The children of light are virtuous because they have some conception of a higher law than their own will. They are usually foolish because they do not know the power of self-will. They underestimate the peril of anarchy in both the national and the international community. Modern democratic civilization is, in short, sentimental rather than cynical. It has an easy solution for the problem of anarchy and chaos on both the national and international level of community, because of its fatuous and superficial view of man. It does not know that the same man who is ostensibly devoted to the "common good" may have desires and ambitions, hopes and fears, which set him at variance with his neighbor.

It must be understood that the children of light are foolish not merely because they underestimate the power of self-interest among the children of darkness. They underestimate this power among themselves. The democratic world came so close to disaster not merely because it never believed that Nazism possessed the demonic fury which it avowed. Civilization refused to recognize the power of class interest in its own communities. It also spoke glibly of an international conscience; but the children of darkness meanwhile skillfully set nation against nation. They were thereby enabled to despoil one nation after another, without every nation coming to the defence of each. Moral cynicism had a provisional advantage over moral sentimentality. Its advantage lay not merely in its own lack of moral scruple but also in its shrewd assessment of the power of self-interest, individual and national, among the children of light, despite their moral protestations.

While our modern children of light, the secularized idealists, were particularly foolish and blind, the more "Christian" children of light have been almost equally guilty of this error. Modern liberal Protestantism was probably even more sentimental in its appraisal of the moral realities in our political life than secular idealism, and Catholicism could see nothing but cynical rebellion in the modern secular revolt against Catholic universalism and a Catholic "Christian" civilization. In Catholic thought medieval political universalism is always accepted at face value. Rebellion against medieval culture is therefore invariably regarded as the fruit of moral cynicism. Actually the middle-class revolt against the feudal order was partially prompted by a generous idealism, not unmixed of course with peculiar middle-class interests. The feudal order was not so simply a Christian civilization as Catholic defenders of it aver. It compounded its devotion to a universal order with the special interests of the priestly and aristocratic bearers of effective social power. The rationalization of their unique position in the feudal order may not have been more marked than the subsequent rationalization of bourgeois interests in the liberal world. But it is idle to deny this "ideological taint" in the feudal order and to pretend that rebels against the order were merely rebels against order as such. They were rebels against a particular order which gave an undue advantage to the aristocratic opponents of the middle classes.[3] The blindness of Catholicism to its own ideological taint is typical of the blindness of the children of light.

Our modern civilization, as a middle-class revolt against an aristocratic and clerical order, was irreligious partly because a Catholic civilization had so compounded the eternal sanctities with the contingent and relative justice and injustice of an agrarian-feudal order, that the new and dynamic bourgeois social force was compelled to challenge not only the political-economic arrangements of the order but also the eternal sanctities which hallowed it.

If modern civilization represents a bourgeois revolt against feudalism, modern culture represents the revolt of new thought, informed by modern science, against a culture in which religious authority had fixed premature and too narrow limits for the expansion of science and had sought to restrain the curiosity of the human mind from inquiring into

---

3. John of Salisbury expresses a quite perfect rationalization of clerical political authority in his *Policraticus* in the twelfth century. He writes: "Those who preside over the practice of religion should be looked up to and venerated as the soul of the body. . . . Furthermore since the soul is, as it were, the prince of the body and has a rule over the whole thereof, so those whom our author calls the prefects of religion preside over the entire body." Book V, ch. ii.

A modern Catholic historian accepts this justification of clerical rule at its face value as he speaks of Machiavelli's politics as a "total assault upon the principles of men like John of Salisbury, preferring to the goodness of Christ, the stamina of Caesar." (Emmet John Hughes, *The Church and the Liberal Society*, 33.) John of Salisbury's political principles were undoubtedly more moral than Machiavelli's. But the simple identification of his justification of clericalism with the "goodness of Christ" is a nice illustration of the blindness of the children of light, whether Christian or secular.

"secondary causes." The culture which venerated science in place of religion, worshipped natural causation in place of God, and which regarded the cool prudence of bourgeois man as morally more normative than Christian love, has proved itself to be less profound than it appeared to be in the seventeenth and eighteenth centuries. But these inadequacies, which must be further examined as typical of the foolishness of modem children of light, do not validate the judgment that these modern rebels were really children of darkness, intent upon defying the truth or destroying universal order.

The modern revolt against the feudal order and the medieval culture was occasioned by the assertion of new vitalities in the social order and the discovery of new dimensions in the cultural enterprise of mankind. It was truly democratic in so far as it challenged the premature and tentative unity of a society and the stabilization of a culture, and in so far as it developed new social and cultural possibilities. The conflict between the middle classes and the aristocrats, between the scientists and the priests, was not a conflict between children of darkness and children of light. It was a conflict between pious and less pious children of light, both of whom were unconscious of the corruption of self-interest in all ideal achievements and pretensions of human culture.

III

In this conflict the devotees of medieval religion were largely unconscious of the corruption of self-interest in their own position; but it must be admitted that they were not as foolish as their secular successors in their estimate of the force of self-interest in human society. Catholicism did strive for an inner and religious discipline upon inordinate desire; and it had a statesmanlike conception of the necessity of legal and political restraint upon the power of egotism, both individual and collective, in the national and the more universal human community.

Our modern civilization, on the other hand, was ushered in on a wave of boundless social optimism. Modern secularism is divided into many schools. But all the various schools agreed in rejecting the Christian doctrine of original sin. It is not possible to explain the subtleties or to measure the profundity of this doctrine in this connection. But it is necessary to point out that the doctrine makes an important contribution to any adequate social and political theory the lack of which has robbed bourgeois theory of real wisdom; for it emphasizes a fact which every page of human history attests. Through it one may understand that no matter how wide the perspectives which the human mind may reach, how broad the loyalties which the human imagination may conceive, how universal the community which human statecraft may organize, or how pure the aspirations of the saintliest idealists may be, there is no level of human moral or social achievement in which there is not some corruption of inordinate self-love.

This sober and true view of the human situation was neatly rejected by modern culture. That is why it conceived so many fatuous and futile plans for resolving the conflict between the self and the community; and between the national and the world community. Whenever modern idealists are confronted with the divisive and corrosive effects of man's self-love, they look for some immediate cause of this perennial tendency, usually in some specific form of social organization. One school holds that men would be good if only political institutions would not corrupt them; another believes that they would be good if the prior evil of a faulty economic organization could be eliminated. Or another school thinks of this evil as no more than ignorance, and therefore waits for a more perfect educational process to redeem man from his partial and particular loyalties. But no school asks how it is that an essentially good man could have produced corrupting and tyrannical political organizations or exploiting economic organizations, or fanatical and superstitious religious organizations.

The result of this persistent blindness to the obvious and tragic facts of man's social history is that democracy has had to maintain itself precariously against the guile and the malice of the children of darkness, while its statesmen and guides conjured up all sorts of abstract and abortive plans for the creation of perfect national and international communities.

The confidence of modern secular idealism in the possibility of an easy resolution of the tension between individual and community, or between classes, races and nations is derived from a too optimistic view of human nature. This too generous estimate of human virtue is intimately related to an erroneous estimate of the dimensions of the human stature. The conception of human nature which underlies the social and political attitudes of a liberal democratic culture is that of an essentially harmless individual. The survival impulse, which man shares with the animals, is regarded as the normative form of his egoistic drive. If this were a true picture of the human situation man might be, or might become, as harmless as seventeenth- and eighteenth-century thought assumed. Unfortunately for the validity of this picture of man, the most significant distinction between the human and the animal world is that the impulses of the former are "spiritualized" in the human world. Human capacities for evil as well as for good are derived from this spiritualization. There is of course always a natural survival impulse at the core of all human ambition. But this survival impulse cannot be neatly disentangled from two forms of its spiritualization. The one form is the desire to fulfill the potentialities of life and not merely to maintain its existence. Man is the kind of animal who cannot merely live. If he lives at all he is bound to seek the realization of his true nature; and to his true nature belongs his fulfillment in the lives of others. The will to live is thus transmuted into the will to self-realization; and self-realization involves self-giving in relations to others. When this desire for self-realization is fully explored it becomes apparent that it is subject to the paradox that the highest form of self-realization is the consequence of self-giving, but that it cannot be the intended consequence without being prematurely limited. Thus the will to live is finally transmuted into its opposite in the sense that only in self-giving can the self be fulfilled, for: "He that findeth his life shall lose it; and he that loseth his life for my sake shall find it."[4]

On the other hand the will-to-live is also spiritually transmuted into the will-to-power or into the desire for "power and glory." Man, being more than a natural creature, is not interested merely in physical survival but in prestige and social approval. Having the intelligence to anticipate the perils in which he stands in nature and history, he invariably

4. Matt 10:39 (KJV).

seeks to gain security against these perils by enhancing his power, individually and collectively. Possessing a darkly unconscious sense of his insignificance in the total scheme of things, he seeks to compensate for his insignificance by pretensions of pride. The conflicts between men are thus never simple conflicts between competing survival impulses. They are conflicts in which each man or group seeks to guard its power and prestige against the peril of competing expressions of power and pride. Since the very possession of power and prestige always involves some encroachment upon the prestige and power of others, this conflict is by its very nature a more stubborn and difficult one than the mere competition between various survival impulses in nature. It remains to be added that this conflict expresses itself even more cruelly in collective than in individual terms. Human behaviour being less individualistic than secular liberalism assumed, the struggle between classes, races and other groups in human society is not as easily resolved by the expedient of dissolving the groups as liberal democratic idealists assumed.

Since the survival impulse in nature is transmuted into two different and contradictory spiritualized forms, which we may briefly designate as the will-to-live-truly and the will-to-power, man is at variance with himself. The power of the second impulse places him more fundamentally in conflict with his fellowman than democratic liberalism realizes. The fact he cannot realize himself, except in organic relation with his fellows, makes the community more important than bourgeois individualism understands. The fact that the two impulses, though standing in contradiction to each other, are also mixed and compounded with each other on every level of human life, makes the simple distinctions between good and evil, between selfishness and altruism, with which liberal idealism has tried to estimate moral and political facts, invalid. The fact that the will-to-power inevitably justifies itself in terms of the morally more acceptable will to realize man's true nature means that the egoistic corruption of universal ideals is a much more persistent fact in human conduct than any moralistic creed is inclined to admit.

If we survey any period of history, and not merely the present tragic era of world catastrophe, it becomes quite apparent that human ambitions, lusts and desires, are more inevitably inordinate, that both human creativity and human evil reach greater heights, and that conflicts in the community between varying conceptions of the good and between competing expressions of vitality are of more tragic proportions than was anticipated in the basic philosophy which underlies democratic civilization.

There is a specially ironic element in the effort of the seventeenth century to confine man to the limits of a harmless "nature" or to bring all his actions under the discipline of a cool prudence. For while democratic social philosophy was elaborating the picture of a harmless individual, moved by no more than a survival impulse, living in a social peace guaranteed by a pre-established harmony of nature, the advancing natural sciences were enabling man to harness the powers of nature, and to give his desires and ambitions a more limitless scope than they previously had. The static inequalities of an agrarian society were transmuted into the dynamic inequalities of an industrial age. The temptation to inordinate expressions of the possessive impulse, created by the new wealth of a technical civilization, stood in curious and ironic contradiction to the picture of essentially moderate and ordinate desires which underlay the social philosophy of the physiocrats and of Adam

Smith. Furthermore a technical society developed new and more intensive forms of social cohesion and a greater centralization of economic process in defiance of the individualistic conception of social relations which informed the liberal philosophy.[5]

The demonic fury of fascist politics in which a collective will expresses boundless ambitions and imperial desires and in which the instruments of a technical civilization are used to arm this will with a destructive power, previously unknown in history, represents a melancholy historical refutation of the eighteenth- and nineteenth-century conceptions of a harmless and essentially individual human life. Human desires are expressed more collectively, are less under the discipline of prudent calculation, and are more the masters of, and less limited by, natural forces than the democratic creed had understood.

While the fury of fascist politics represents a particularly vivid refutation of the democratic view of human nature, the developments within the confines of democratic civilization itself offer almost as telling a refutation. The liberal creed is never an explicit instrument of the children of darkness. But it is surprising to what degree the forces of darkness are able to make covert use of the creed. One must therefore, in analyzing the liberal hope of a simple social and political harmony, be equally aware of the universalistic presuppositions which underlie the hope and of the egoistic corruptions (both individual and collective) which inevitably express themselves in our culture in terms of, and in despite of, the creed. One must understand that it is a creed of children of light; but also that it betrays their blindness to the forces of darkness.

In the social philosophy of Adam Smith there was both a religious guarantee of the preservation of community and a moral demand that the individual consider its claims. The religious guarantee was contained in Smith's secularized version of providence. Smith believed that when a man is guided by self-interest he is also "led by an invisible hand to promote an end which is not his intention."[6] This "invisible hand" is of course the power of a pre-established social harmony, conceived as a harmony of nature, which transmutes conflicts of self-interest into a vast scheme of mutual service.

Despite this determinism Smith does not hesitate to make moral demands upon men to sacrifice their interests to the wider interest. The universalistic presupposition which underlies Smith's thought is clearly indicated for instance in such an observation as this: "The wise and virtuous man is at all times willing that his own private interests should be sacrificed to the public interest of his own particular order of society—that the interests of this order of society be sacrificed to the greater interest of the state. He should therefore be equally willing that all those inferior interests should be sacrificed to the greater interests of the universe, to the interests of that great society of all sensible and intelligent beings, of which God himself is the immediate administrator and director."[7]

5. Thus vast collective forms of "free enterprise," embodied in monopolistic and large-scale financial and industrial institutions, still rationalize their desire for freedom from political control in terms of a social philosophy which Adam Smith elaborated for individuals. Smith was highly critical of the budding large-scale enterprise of his day and thought it ought to be restricted to insurance companies and banks.

6. Smith, *Wealth of Nations*, Book IV, ch. 7.

7. Smith, *Wealth of Nations.*, Book V, ch. i, part 3.

It must be noted that in Smith's conception the "wider interest" does not stop at the boundary of the national state. His was a real universalism in intent. *Laissez faire* was intended to establish a world community as well as a natural harmony of interests within each nation. Smith clearly belongs to the children of light. But the children of darkness were able to make good use of his creed. A dogma which was intended to guarantee the economic freedom of the individual became the "ideology" of vast corporate structures of a later period of capitalism, used by them, and still used, to prevent a proper political control of their power. His vision of international harmony was transmuted into the sorry realities of an international capitalism which recognized neither moral scruples nor political restraints in expanding its power over the world. His vision of a democratic harmony of society, founded upon the free play of economic forces, was refuted by the tragic realities of the class conflicts in western society. Individual and collective egotism usually employed the political philosophy of this creed, but always defied the moral idealism which informed it.

The political theory of liberalism, as distinct from the economic theory, based its confidence in the identity of particular and universal interests, not so much upon the natural limits of egotism as upon either the capacity of reason to transmute egotism into a concern for the general welfare, or upon the ability of government to overcome the potential conflict of wills in society. But even when this confidence lies in reason or in government, the actual character of the egotism which must be restrained is frequently measured in the dimension of the natural impulse of survival only. Thus John Locke, who thinks government necessary in order to overcome the "inconvenience of the state of nature," sees self-interest in conflict with the general interest only on the low level where "self-preservation" stands in contrast to the interests of others. He therefore can express the sense of obligation to others in terms which assume no final conflict between egotism and the wider interest: "Everyone," he writes, "as he is bound to preserve himself and not to quit his station willfully, so by the like reason, when his own preservation comes not into competition, ought as much as he can preserve the rest of mankind."[8] This is obviously no creed of a moral cynic; but neither is it a profound expression of the sense of universal obligation. For most of the gigantic conflicts of will in human history, whether between individuals or groups, take place on a level, where "self-preservation" is not immediately but only indirectly involved. They are conflicts of rival lusts and ambitions.

The general confidence of an identity between self-interest and the commonweal, which underlies liberal democratic political theory, is succinctly expressed in Thomas Paine's simple creed: "Public good is not a term opposed to the good of the individual; on the contrary it is the good of every individual collected. It is the good of all, because it is the good of everyone; for as the public body is every individual collected, so the public good is the collected good of those individuals."[9]

While there is a sense in which this identity between a particular and the general interest is ultimately true, it is never absolutely true in an immediate situation; and such identity as could be validly claimed in an immediate situation is not usually recognized by

8. Locke, *Two Treatises on Government*, Book II, ch. 2, para. 6.

9. Paine, *Dissertations on Government, The Affairs of the Bank, and Paper-Money* (1786).

the proponents of particular interest.[10] Human intelligence is never as pure an instrument of the universal perspective as the liberal democratic theory assumes, though neither is it as purely the instrument of the ego, as is assumed by the anti-democratic theory, derived from the pessimism of such men as Thomas Hobbes and Martin Luther.

The most naive form of the democratic faith in an identity between the individual and the general interest is developed by the utilitarians of the eighteenth and nineteenth centuries. Their theory manages to extract a covertly expressed sense of obligation toward the "greatest good of the greatest number" from a hedonistic analysis of morals which really lacks all logical presuppositions for any idea of obligation, and which cannot logically rise above an egoistic view of life. This utilitarianism therefore expresses the stupidity of the children of light in its most vivid form. Traditional moralists may point to any hedonistic doctrine as the creed of the children of darkness because it has no real escape from egotism. But since it thinks it has, it illustrates the stupidity of the children of light, rather than the malice of the children of darkness. It must be observed of course that the children of darkness are well able to make use of such a creed. Utilitarianism's conception of the wise egotist, who in his prudence manages to serve interests wider than his own, supported exactly the same kind of political philosophy as Adam Smith's conception of the harmless egotist, who did not even have to be wise, since the providential laws of nature held his egotism in check. So Jeremy Bentham's influence was added to that of Adam Smith in support of a *laissez-faire* political philosophy; and this philosophy encouraged an unrestrained expression of human greed at the precise moment in history when an advancing industrialism required more, rather than less, moral and political restraint upon economic forces.

It must be added that, whenever the democratic idealists were challenged to explain the contrast between the actual behaviour of men and their conception of it, they had recourse to the evolutionary hope; and declared with William Godwin, that human history is moving toward a form of rationality which will finally achieve a perfect identity of self-interest and the public good.[11]

Perhaps the most remarkable proof of the power of this optimistic creed, which underlies democratic thought, is that Marxism, which is ostensibly a revolt against it, manages to express the same optimism in another form. While liberal democrats dreamed of a simple social harmony, to be achieved by a cool prudence and a calculating egotism, the actual facts of social history revealed that the static class struggle of agrarian societies had been fanned into the flames of a dynamic struggle. Marxism was the social creed

10. The peril of inflation, which faces nations in war-time is a case in point. Each group seeks to secure a larger income, and if all groups succeeded, the gap between increased income and limited consumer goods available to satisfy consumer demand would be widened to the point at which all groups would suffer from higher prices. But this does not deter shortsighted groups from seeking special advantages which threaten the commonweal. Nor would such special advantage threaten the welfare of the whole, if it could be confined to a single group which desires the advantage. The problem is further complicated by the fact that an inflationary peril never develops in a "just" social situation. Some groups therefore have a moral right to demand that their share of the common social fund be increased before the total situation is "frozen." But who is to determine just how much "injustice" can be redressed by a better distribution of the common fund in war-time, before the procedure threatens the whole community?

11. Godwin, *Political Justice,* Book VIII, ch. ix.

and the social cry of those classes who knew by their miseries that the creed of the liberal optimists was a snare and a delusion. Marxism insisted that the increasingly overt social conflict in democratic society would have to become even more overt, and would finally be fought to a bitter conclusion. But Marxism was also convinced that after the triumph of the lower classes of society, a new society would emerge in which exactly that kind of harmony between all social forces would be established, which Adam Smith had regarded as a possibility for any kind of society. The similarities between classical *laissez-faire* theory and the vision of an anarchistic millennium in Marxism are significant, whatever may be the superficial differences. Thus the provisionally cynical Lenin, who can trace all the complexities of social conflict in contemporary society with penetrating shrewdness, can also express the utopian hope that the revolution will usher in a period of history which will culminate in the Marxist millennium of anarchism. "All need for force will vanish," declared Lenin, "since people will grow accustomed to observing the elementary conditions of social existence without force and without subjection."[12]

The Roman Catholic polemic against Marxism is no more valid than its strictures against democratic liberalism. The charge that this is a creed of moral cynicism cannot be justified. However strong the dose of provisional cynicism, which the creed may contain, it is a sentimental and not a cynical creed. The Marxists, too, are children of light. Their provisional cynicism does not even save them from the usual stupidity, nor from the fate, of other stupid children of light. That fate is to have their creed become the vehicle and instrument of the children of darkness. A new oligarchy is arising in Russia, the spiritual characteristics of which can hardly be distinguished from those of the American "go-getters" of the latter nineteenth and early twentieth centuries. And in the light of history Stalin will probably have the same relation to the early dreamers of the Marxist dreams which Napoleon has to the liberal dreamers of the eighteenth century.

IV

Democratic theory, whether in its liberal or in its more radical form, is just as stupid in analyzing the relation between the national and the international community as in seeking a too simple harmony between the individual and the national community. Here, too, modern liberal culture exhibits few traces of moral cynicism. The morally autonomous modern national state does indeed arise; and it acknowledges no law beyond its interests. The actual behaviour of the nations is cynical. But the creed of liberal civilization is sentimental. This is true not only of the theorists whose creed was used by the architects of economic imperialism and of the more covert forms of national egotism in the international community, but also of those whose theories were appropriated by the proponents of an explicit national egotism. A straight line runs from Mazzini to Mussolini in the history of Italian nationalism. Yet there was not a touch of moral cynicism in the thought of Mazzini. He was, on the contrary, a pure universalist.[13]

12. Lenin, *Toward the Seizure of Power,* Vol. II, 214.
13. "Your first duty," wrote Mazzini, "first as regards importance, is toward humanity. You are men before you are citizens and fathers. If you do not embrace the whole human family in your affections, if

Even the philosophy of German romanticism, which has been accused with some justification of making specific contributions to the creed of German Nazism, reveals the stupidity of the children of light much more than the malice of the children of darkness. There is of course a strong note of moral nihilism in the final fruit of this romantic movement as we have it in Nietzsche; though even Nietzsche was no nationalist. But the earlier romantics usually express the same combination of individualism and universalism which characterizes the theory of the more naturalistic and rationalistic democrats of the western countries. Fichte resolved the conflict between the individual and the community through the instrumentality of the "just law" almost as easily as the utilitarians resolved it by the calculations of the prudent egotist and as easily as Rousseau resolved it by his conception of a "general will," which would fulfill the best purposes of each individual will. This was no creed of a community, making itself the idolatrous end of human existence. The theory was actually truer than the more individualistic and naturalistic forms of the democratic creed; for romanticism understood that the individual requires the community for his fulfillment. Thus even Hegel, who is sometimes regarded as the father of state absolutism in modern culture, thought of the national state as providing "for the reasonable will, insofar as it is in the individual only implicitly the universal will coming to a consciousness and an understanding of itself and being found."[14]

This was not the creed of a collective egotism which negated the right of the individual. Rather it was a theory which, unlike the more purely democratic creed, understood the necessity of social fulfillment for the individual, and which, in common with the more liberal theories, regarded this as a much too simple process.

If the theory was not directed toward the annihilation of the individual, as is the creed of modern religious nationalism, to what degree was it directed against the universal community? Was it an expression of the national community's defiance of any interest or law above and beyond itself? This also is not the case. Herder believed that "fatherlands" might "lie peaceably side by side and aid each other as families. It is the grossest barbarity of human speech to speak of fatherlands in bloody battle with each other." Unfortunately, this is something more than a barbarity of speech. Herder was a universalist, who thought a nice harmony between various communities could be achieved if only the right would be granted to each to express itself according to its unique and peculiar genius. He thought the false universalism of imperialism, according to which one community makes itself the standard and the governor of others, was merely the consequence of a false philosophy, whereas it is in fact one of the perennial corruptions of man's collective life.

Fichte, too, was a universalist who was fully conscious of moral obligations which transcend the national community. His difficulty, like that of all the children of light, was that he had a too easy resolution of the conflict between the nation and the community

---

you do not bear witness to the unity of that family, if—you are not ready, if able, to aid the unhappy,— you violate your law of life and you comprehend not that religion which will be the guide and blessing of the future." Mazzini held kings responsible for national egotism: "The first priests of the fatal worship [of self-interest] were the kings, princes, and evil governments. They invented the horrible formula: everyone for himself. They knew that they would thus create egoism and that between the egoist and the slave there is but one step." *The Duties of Man*, ch. xii.

14. Hegel, *Philosophy of Mind*, Sect. II, para. 539.

of nations. He thought that philosophy, particularly German philosophy, could achieve a synthesis between national and universal interest. "The patriot," he declared, "wishes the purpose of mankind to be reached first of all in that nation of which he is a member. . . .This purpose is the only possible patriotic goal. . . .Cosmopolitanism is the will that the purpose of life and of man be attained in all mankind, Patriotism is the will that this purpose be attained first of all in that nation of which we are members."[15] It is absurd to regard such doctrine as the dogma of national egotism, though Fichte could not express it without insinuating a certain degree of national pride into it. The pride took the form of the complacent assumption that German philosophy enabled the German nation to achieve a more perfect relation to the community of mankind than any other nation. He was, in other words, one of the many stupid children of light, who failed to understand the difficulty of the problem which he was considering; and his blindness included failure to see the significance of the implicit denial of an ideal in the thought and action of the very idealist who propounds it.

Hegel, too, belongs to the children of light. To be sure he saw little possibility of constructing a legal structure of universal proportions which might guard the interests of the universal community and place a check upon the will of nations. He declared "states find themselves in a natural, more than a legal, relation to each other. Therefore there is a continuous struggle between them. . . . They maintain and procure their rights through their own power and must as a matter of necessity plunge into war."[16] It may be observed in passing that this is a more accurate description of the actual realities of international relations than that of any of the theorists thus far considered. But the question is whether Hegel regarded this actual situation as morally normative. Hegel's thought upon this matter was ambiguous. On the one hand he tended to regard the demands of the state as final because he saw no way of achieving a legal or political implementation of the inchoate community which lies beyond the state. But on the other hand he believed that a more ultimate law stood over the nation, that it "had its real content in *Weltgeschichte,* the realm of the world mind which holds the supreme absolute truth."[17] This mind, he believed, "constitutes itself the absolute judge over states."[18] The nation is thus politically, but not morally, autonomous. This is no doctrine of moral cynicism. Rather it is a sentimental doctrine. Hegel imagined that the nation, free of political but not of moral inhibitions, could nevertheless, by thinking "in Weltgeschichte" (that is, by becoming fully conscious of its relation to mankind), thereby "lay hold of its concrete universality."[19] The error is very similar to that of Fichte and of all the universalists, whether naturalistic or idealistic, positivist or romantic. It is the error of a too great reliance upon the human capacity for transcendence over self-interest. There is indeed such a capacity. If there were not, any form of social harmony among men would be impossible; and certainly a democratic version of such harmony would be quite unthinkable. But the same man who

15. Fichte, "Patriotische Dialoge," in *Nachgelassene Werker,* Vol. III, 226.

16. Hegel, *Saemmtliche Werker,* Vol. III, 74.

17. Hegel, *Philosophy of Right,* para. 33.

18. Hegel, *Philosophy of Right,* para. 33.

19. Hegel, *Philosophy of Mind,* Sect. II, para. 552.

displays this capacity also reveals varying degrees of the power of self-interest and of the subservience of the mind to these interests. Sometimes this egotism stands in frank contradiction to the professed ideal or sense of obligation to higher and wider values; and sometimes it uses the ideal as its instrument.

It is this fact which a few pessimists in our modern culture have realized, only to draw undemocratic and sometimes completely cynical conclusions from it. The democratic idealists of practically all schools of thought have managed to remain remarkably oblivious to the obvious facts. Democratic theory therefore has not squared with the facts of history. This grave defect in democratic theory was comparatively innocuous in the heyday of the bourgeois period when the youth and the power of democratic civilization surmounted all errors of judgment and confusions of mind. But in this latter day, when it has become important to save what is valuable in democratic life from the destruction of what is false in bourgeois civilization, it has also become necessary to distinguish what is false in democratic theory from what is true in democratic life.

The preservation of a democratic civilization requires the wisdom of the serpent and the harmlessness of the dove. The children of light must be armed with the wisdom of the children of darkness but remain free from their malice. They must know the power of self-interest in human society without giving it moral justification. They must have this wisdom in order that they may beguile, deflect, harness and restrain self-interest, individual and collective, for the sake of the community.

"Why the Christian Church Is Not Pacifist"

Reinhold Niebuhr[1]

WHENEVER THE ACTUAL HISTORICAL situation sharpens the issue, the debate whether the Christian Church is, or ought to be, pacifist is carried on with fresh vigor both inside and outside the Christian community. Those who are not pacifists seek to prove that pacifism is a heresy; while the pacifists contend, or at least imply, that the Church's failure to espouse pacifism unanimously can only be interpreted as apostasy, and must be attributed to its lack of courage or to its want of faith.

There may be an advantage in stating the thesis, with which we enter this debate, immediately. The thesis is, that the failure of the Church to espouse pacifism is not apostasy, but is derived from an understanding of the Christian gospel which refuses simply to equate the gospel with the "law of love." Christianity is not simply a new law, namely, the law of love. The finality of Christianity cannot be proved by analyses which seek to reveal that the law of love is stated more unambiguously and perfectly in the life and teachings of Christ than anywhere else. Christianity is a religion which measures the total dimension of human existence not only in terms of the final norm of human conduct, which is expressed in the law of love, but also in terms of the fact of sin. It recognizes that the same man who can become his true self only by striving infinitely for self-realization beyond himself is also inevitably involved in the sin of infinitely making his partial and narrow self the true end of existence. It believes, in other words, that though Christ is the true norm (the "second Adam") for every man, every man is also in some sense a crucifier of Christ.

The good news of the gospel is not the law that we ought to love one another. The good news of the gospel is that there is a resource of divine mercy which is able to overcome a contradiction within our own souls, which we cannot ourselves overcome. This contradiction is that, though we know we ought to love our neighbors as ourselves, there is a "law in our members which wars against the law that is in our mind," so that, in fact, we love ourselves more than our neighbor.

The grace of God which is revealed in Christ is regarded by Christian faith as, on the one hand, an actual "power of righteousness" which heals the contradiction within our hearts. In that sense Christ defines the actual possibilities of human existence. On the

1. Niebuhr, "Why the Christian Church Is Not Pacifist," 1–47.

other hand, this grace is conceived as "justification," as pardon rather than power, as the forgiveness of God, which is vouchsafed to man despite the fact that he never achieves the full measure of Christ. In that sense Christ is the "impossible possibility." Loyalty to him means realization in intention, but does not actually mean the full realization of the measure of Christ. In this doctrine of forgiveness and justification, Christianity measures the full seriousness of sin as a permanent factor in human history. Naturally, the doctrine has no meaning for modern secular civilization, nor for the secularized and moralistic versions of Christianity. They cannot understand the doctrine precisely because they believe there is some fairly simple way out of the sinfulness of human history.

It is rather remarkable that so many modern Christians should believe that Christianity is primarily a "challenge" to man to obey the law of Christ; whereas it is, as a matter of fact, a religion which deals realistically with the problem presented by the violation of this law. Far from believing that the ills of the world could be set right "if only" men obeyed the law of Christ, it has always regarded the problem of achieving justice in a sinful world as a very difficult task. In the profounder versions of the Christian faith the very utopian illusions, which are currently equated with Christianity, have been rigorously disavowed.

Nevertheless, it is not possible to regard pacifism simply as a heresy. In one of its aspects modern Christian pacifism is simply a version of Christian perfectionism. It expresses a genuine impulse in the heart of Christianity, the impulse to take the law of Christ seriously and not to allow the political strategies, which the sinful character of man makes necessary, to become final norms. In its profounder forms this Christian perfectionism did not proceed from a simple faith that the "law of love" could be regarded as an alternative to the political strategies by which the world achieves a precarious justice. These strategies invariably involve the balancing of power with power; and they never completely escape the peril of tyranny on the one hand, and the peril of anarchy and warfare on the other.

In medieval ascetic perfectionism and in Protestant sectarian perfectionism (of the type of Menno Simons, for instance) the effort to achieve a standard of perfect love in individual life was not presented as a political alternative. On the contrary, the political problem and task were specifically disavowed. This perfectionism did not give itself to the illusion that it had discovered a method for eliminating the element of conflict from political strategies.

On the contrary, it regarded the mystery of evil as beyond its power of solution. It was content to set up the most perfect and unselfish individual life as a symbol of the Kingdom of God. It knew that this could only be done by disavowing the political task and by freeing the individual of all responsibility for social justice.

It is this kind of pacifism which is not a heresy. It is rather a valuable asset for the Christian faith. It is a reminder to the Christian community that the relative norms of social justice, which justify both coercion and resistance to coercion, are not final norms, and that Christians are in constant peril of forgetting their relative and tentative character and of making them too completely normative.

There is thus a Christian pacifism which is not a heresy. Yet most modern forms of Christian pacifism are heretical. Presumably inspired by the Christian gospel, they have really absorbed the Renaissance faith in the goodness of man, have rejected the Christian doctrine of original sin as an outmoded bit of pessimism, have reinterpreted the Cross so that it is made to stand for the absurd idea that perfect love is guaranteed a simple victory over the world, and have rejected all other profound elements of the Christian gospel as "Pauline" accretions which must be stripped from the "simple gospel of Jesus." This form of pacifism is not only heretical when judged by the standards of the total gospel. It is equally heretical when judged by the facts of human existence. There are no historical realities which remotely conform to it. It is important to recognize this lack of conformity to the facts of experience as a criterion of heresy.

All forms of religious faith are principles of interpretation which we use to organize our experience. Some religions may be adequate principles of interpretation at certain levels of experience, but they break down at deeper levels. No religious faith can maintain itself in defiance of the experience which it supposedly interprets. A religious faith which substitutes faith in man for faith in God cannot finally validate itself in experience. If we believe that the only reason men do not love each other perfectly is because the law of love has not been preached persuasively enough, we believe something to which experience does not conform. If we believe that if Britain had only been fortunate enough to have produced 30 per cent instead of 2 per cent of conscientious objectors to military service, Hitler's heart would have been softened and he would not have dared to attack Poland, we hold a faith which no historic reality justifies.

Such a belief has no more justification in the facts of experience than the communist belief that the sole cause of man's sin is the class organization of society and the corollary faith that a "classless" society will be essentially free of human sinfulness. All of these beliefs are pathetic alternatives to the Christian faith. They all come finally to the same thing. They do not believe that man remains a tragic creature who needs the divine mercy as "much at the end as at the beginning of his moral endeavors. They believe rather that there is some fairly easy way out of the human situation of "self-alienation." In this connection it is significant that Christian pacifists, rationalists like Bertrand Russell, and mystics like Aldous Huxley, believe essentially the same thing. The Christians make Christ into the symbol of their faith in man. But their faith is really identical with that of Russell or Huxley.

The common element in these various expressions of faith in man is the belief that man is essentially good at some level of his being. They believe that if you can abstract the rational-universal man from what is finite and contingent in human nature, or if you can only cultivate some mystic-universal element in the deeper levels of man's consciousness, you will be able to eliminate human selfishness and the consequent conflict of life with life. These rational or mystical views of man conform neither to the New Testament's view of human nature nor yet to the complex facts of human experience.

In order to elaborate the thesis more fully, that the refusal of the Christian Church to espouse pacifism is not apostasy and that most modern forms of pacifism are heretical, it is necessary first of all to consider the character of the absolute and unqualified demands which Christ makes and to understand the relation of these demands to the gospel.

II

It is very foolish to deny that the ethic of Jesus is an absolute and uncompromising ethic. It is, in the phrase of Ernst Troeltsch, an ethic of "love universalism and love perfectionism." The injunctions "resist not evil," "love your enemies," "if ye love them that love you what thanks have you?" "be not anxious for your life," and "be ye therefore perfect even as your father in heaven is perfect," are all of one piece, and they are all uncompromising and absolute. Nothing is more futile and pathetic than the effort of some Christian theologians who find it necessary to become involved in the relativities of politics, in resistance to tyranny or in social conflict, to justify themselves by seeking to prove that Christ was also involved in some of these relativities, that he used whips to drive the money-changers out of the Temple, or that he came "not to bring peace but a sword," or that he asked the disciples to sell cloak and buy a sword. What could be more futile than to build a whole ethical structure upon the exegetical issue whether Jesus accepted the sword with the words: "It is enough," or whether he really meant: "Enough of this"?[2]

Those of us who regard the ethic of Jesus as finally and ultimately normative, but as not immediately applicable to the task of securing justice in a sinful world, are very foolish if we try to reduce the ethic so that it will cover and justify our prudential and relative standards and strategies. To do this is to reduce the ethic to a new legalism. The significance of the law of love is precisely that it is not just another law, but a law which transcends all law. Every law and every standard which falls short of the law of love embodies contingent factors and makes concessions to the fact that sinful man must achieve tentative harmonies of life with life which are less than the best. It is dangerous and confusing to give these tentative and relative standards final and absolute religious sanction.

Curiously enough the pacifists are just as guilty as their less absolutist brethren of diluting the ethic of Jesus for the purpose of justifying their position. They are forced to recognize that an ethic of pure non-resistance can have no immediate relevance to any political situation; for in every political situation it is necessary to achieve justice by resisting pride and power. They therefore declare that the ethic of Jesus is not an ethic of non-resistance, but one of nonviolent resistance that it allows one to resist evil provided the resistance does not involve the destruction of life or property.

There is not the slightest support in Scripture for this doctrine of non-violence. Nothing could be plainer than that the ethic uncompromisingly enjoins non-resistance and not non-violent resistance. Furthermore, it is obvious that the distinction between violent and non-violent resistance is not an absolute distinction. If it is made absolute, we arrive at the morally absurd position of giving moral preference to the non-violent power which Doctor Goebbels wields over the type of power wielded by a general. This absurdity is really derived from the modern (and yet probably very ancient and very Platonic) heresy of regarding the "physical" as evil and the "spiritual" as good. The *reductio*

---

2. Luke 22:36.

ad absurdum of this position is achieved in a book which has become something of a textbook for modern pacifists, Richard Gregg's *The Power of Non-Violence*. In this book nonviolent resistance is commended as the best method of defeating your foe, particularly as the best method of breaking his morale. It is suggested that Christ ended his life on the Cross because he had not completely mastered the technique of non-violence, and must for this reason be regarded as a guide who is inferior to Gandhi, but whose significance lies in initiating a movement which culminates in Gandhi.

One may well concede that a wise and decent statesmanship will seek not only to avoid conflict, but to avoid violence in conflict. Parliamentary political controversy is one method of sublimating political struggles in such a way as to avoid violent collisions of interest. But this pragmatic distinction has nothing to do with the more basic distinction between the ethic of the "Kingdom of God," in which no concession is made to human sin, and all relative political strategies which, assuming human sinfulness, seek to secure the highest measure of peace and justice among selfish and sinful men.

III

If pacifists were less anxious to dilute the ethic of Christ to make it conform to their particular type of non-violent politics, and if they were less obsessed with the obvious contradiction between the ethic of Christ and the fact of war, they might have noticed that the injunction "resist not evil" is only part and parcel of a total ethic which we violate not only in wartime, but every day of our life, and that overt conflict is but a final and vivid revelation of the character of human existence. This total ethic can be summarized most succinctly in the two injunctions "Be not anxious for your life" and "love thy neighbor as thyself."

In the first of these, attention is called to the fact that the root and source of all undue self-assertion lies in the anxiety which all men have in regard to their existence. The ideal possibility is that perfect trust in God's providence ("for your heavenly father knoweth what things ye have need of") and perfect unconcern for the physical life ("fear not them which are able to kill the body") would create a state of serenity in which one life would not seek to take advantage of another life. But the fact is that anxiety is an inevitable concomitant of human freedom, and is the root of the inevitable sin which expresses itself in every human activity and creativity. Not even the most idealistic preacher who admonishes his congregation to obey the law of Christ is free of the sin which arises from anxiety. He may or may not be anxious for his job, but he is certainly anxious about his prestige. Perhaps he is anxious for his reputation as a righteous man. He may be tempted to preach a perfect ethic the more vehemently in order to hide an unconscious apprehension of the fact that his own life does not conform to it. There is no life which does not violate the injunction "Be not anxious." That is the tragedy of human sin. It is the tragedy of man who is dependent upon God, but seeks to make himself independent and self-sufficing.

In the same way there is no life which is not involved in a violation of the injunction, "Thou shalt love thy neighbor as thyself." No one is so blind as the idealist who tells us that war would be unnecessary "if only" nations obeyed the law of Christ, but who remains unconscious of the fact that even the most saintly life is involved in some measure of contradiction to this law. Have we not all known loving fathers and mothers who, despite a very genuine love for their children, had to be resisted if justice and freedom were to be gained for the children? Do we not know that the sinful will-to-power may be compounded with the most ideal motives and may use the latter as its instruments and vehicles? The collective life of man undoubtedly stands on a lower moral plane than the life of individuals; yet nothing revealed in the life of races and nations is unknown in individual life. The sins of pride and of lust for power and the consequent tyranny and injustice are all present, at least in an inchoate form, in individual life. Even as I write my little five-year-old boy comes to me with the tale of an attack made upon him by his year-old sister. This tale is concocted to escape paternal judgment for being too rough in playing with his sister. One is reminded of Germany's claim that Poland was the aggressor and the similar Russian charge against Finland.

The pacifists do not know human nature well enough to be concerned about the contradictions between the law of love and the sin of man, until sin has conceived and brought forth death. They do not see that sin introduces an element of conflict into the world and that even the most loving relations are not free of it. They are, consequently, unable to appreciate the complexity of the problem of justice. They merely assert that if only men loved one another, all the complex, and sometimes horrible, realities of the political order could be dispensed with. They do not see that their "if" begs the most basic problem of human history. It is because men are sinners that justice can be achieved only by a certain degree of coercion on the one hand, and by resistance to coercion and tyranny on the other hand. The political life of man must constantly steer between the Scylla of anarchy and the Charybdis of tyranny.

Human egotism makes large-scale co-operation upon a purely voluntary basis impossible. Governments must coerce. Yet there is an element of evil in this coercion. It is always in danger of serving the purposes of the coercing power rather than the general weal. We cannot fully trust the motives of any ruling class or power. That is why it is important to maintain democratic checks upon the centers of power. It may also be necessary to resist a ruling class, nation or race, if it violates the standards of relative justice which have been set up for it. Such resistance means war. It need not mean overt conflict or violence. But if those who resist tyranny publish their scruples against violence too publicly the tyrannical power need only threaten the use of violence against non-violent pressure to persuade the resisters to quiescence. (The relation of pacifism to the abortive effort to apply non-violent sanctions against Italy in the Ethiopian dispute is instructive at this point.)

The refusal to recognize that sin introduces an element of conflict into the world invariably means that a morally perverse preference is given to tyranny over anarchy (war). If we are told that tyranny would destroy itself, if only we would not challenge it, the obvious answer is that tyranny continues to grow if it is not resisted. If it is to be resisted, the risk of overt conflict must be taken. The thesis that German tyranny must not be challenged by other nations because Germany will throw off this yoke in due time, merely means that an unjustified moral preference is given to civil war over international war, for internal resistance runs the risk of conflict as much as external resistance. Furthermore, no consideration is given to the fact that a tyrannical State may grow too powerful to be successfully resisted by purely internal pressure, and that the injustices which it does to other than its own nationals may rightfully lay the problem of the tyranny upon other nations.

It is not unfair to assert that most pacifists who seek to present their religious absolutism as a political alternative to the claims and counter-claims, the pressures and counter-pressures of the political order, invariably betray themselves into this preference for tyranny. Tyranny is not war. It is peace, but it is a peace which has nothing to do with the peace of the Kingdom of God. It is a peace which results from one will establishing a complete dominion over other wills and reducing them to acquiescence.

One of the most terrible consequences of a confused religious absolutism is that it is forced to condone such tyranny as that of Germany in the nations which it has conquered and now cruelly oppresses. It usually does this by insisting that the tyranny is no worse than that which is practised in the so-called democratic nations. Whatever may be the moral ambiguities of the so-called democratic nations, and however serious may be their failure to conform perfectly to their democratic ideals, it is sheer moral perversity to equate the inconsistencies of a democratic civilization with the brutalities which modern tyrannical States practise. If we cannot make a distinction here, there are no historical distinctions which have any value. All the distinctions upon which the fate of civilization has turned in the history of mankind have been just such relative distinctions.

One is persuaded to thank God in such times as these that the common people maintain a degree of "common sense," that they preserve an uncorrupted ability to react against injustice and the cruelty of racial bigotry. This ability has been lost among some Christian idealists who preach the law of love but forget that they, as well as all other men, are involved in the violation of that law; and who must (in order to obscure this glaring defect in their theory) eliminate all relative distinctions in history and praise the peace of tyranny as if it were nearer to the peace of the Kingdom of God than war. The overt conflicts of human history are periods of judgment when what has been hidden becomes revealed. It is the business of Christian prophecy to anticipate these judgments to some degree at least, to call attention to the fact that when men say, "peace and quiet" "destruction will come upon them unaware," and reveal to what degree this overt destruction is a vivid portrayal of the constant factor of sin in human life. A theology which fails to come to grips with this tragic factor of sin is heretical, both from the standpoint of the gospel and in terms of its blindness to obvious facts of human, experience in every realm and on every level of moral goodness.

IV

The gospel is something more than the law of love. The gospel deals with the fact that men violate the law of love. The gospel presents Christ as the pledge and revelation of God's mercy which finds man in his rebellion and overcomes his sin.

The question is whether the grace of Christ is primarily a power of righteousness which so heals the sinful heart that henceforth it is able to fulfil the law of love; or whether it is primarily the assurance of divine mercy for a persistent sinfulness which man never overcomes completely. When St. Paul declared: "I am crucified with Christ; nevertheless I live, yet it is no more I that live but Christ that dwelleth in me," did he mean that the new life in Christ was not his own by reason of the fact that grace, rather than his own power, enabled him to live on the new level of righteousness? Or did he mean that the new life was his only in intention and by reason of God's willingness to accept intention for achievement? Was the emphasis upon sanctification or justification?

This is the issue upon which the Protestant Reformation separated itself from classical Catholicism, believing that Thomistic interpretations of grace lent themselves to new forms of self-righteousness in place of the Judaistic-legalistic self-righteousness which St. Paul condemned. If one studies the whole thought of St. Paul, one is almost forced to the conclusion that he was not himself quite certain whether the peace which he had found in Christ was a moral peace, the peace of having become what man truly is; or whether it was primarily a religious peace, the peace of being "completely known and all forgiven," of being accepted by God despite the continued sinfulness of the heart. Perhaps St. Paul could not be quite sure about where the emphasis was to be placed, for the simple reason that no one can be quite certain about the character of this ultimate peace. There must be, and there is, moral content in it, a fact which Reformation theology tends to deny and which Catholic and sectarian theology emphasizes. But there is never such perfect moral content in it that any man could find perfect peace through his moral achievements, not even the achievements which he attributes to grace rather than the power of his own will. This is the truth which the Reformation emphasized and which modern Protestant Christianity has almost completely forgotten.

We are, therefore, living in a state of sorry moral and religious confusion. In the very moment of world history in which every contemporary historical event justifies the Reformation emphasis upon the persistence of sin on every level of moral achievement, we not only identify Protestant faith with a moralistic sentimentality which neglects and obscures truths in the Christian gospel (which it was the mission of the Reformation to rescue from obscurity), but we even neglect those reservations and qualifications upon the theory of sanctification upon which classical Catholicism wisely insisted.

We have, in other words, reinterpreted the Christian gospel in terms of the Renaissance faith in man. Modern pacifism is merely a final fruit of this Renaissance spirit, which has pervaded the whole of modern Protestantism. We have interpreted world history as a gradual ascent to the Kingdom of God which waits for final triumph only upon the willingness of Christians to "take Christ seriously." There is nothing in Christ's own teachings, except dubious interpretations of the parable of the leaven and the mustard seed, to justify this interpretation of world history. In the whole of the New Testament, Gospels and Epistles alike, there is only one interpretation of world history. That pictures history as moving toward a climax in which both Christ and anti-Christ are revealed.

The New Testament does not, in other words, envisage a simple triumph of good over evil in history. It sees human history involved in the contradictions of sin to the end. That is why it sees no simple resolution of the problem of history. It believes that the Kingdom of God will finally resolve the contradictions of history; but for it the Kingdom of God is no simple historical possibility. The grace of God for man and the Kingdom of God for history are both divine realities and not human possibilities.

The Christian faith believes that the Atonement reveals God's mercy as an ultimate resource by which God alone overcomes the judgment which sin deserves. If this final truth of the Christian religion has no meaning to modern men, including modern Christians, that is because even the tragic character of contemporary history has not yet persuaded them to take the fact of human sinfulness seriously.

V

The contradiction between the law of love and the sinfulness of man raises not only the ultimate religious problem how men are to have peace if they do not overcome the contradiction, and how history will culminate if the contradiction remains on every level of historic achievement it also raises the immediate problem how men are to achieve a tolerable harmony of life with life, if human pride and selfishness prevent the realization of the law of love.

The pacifists are quite right in one emphasis. They are right in asserting that love is really the law of life. It is not some ultimate possibility which has nothing to do with human history. The freedom of man, his transcendence over the limitations of nature and over all historic and traditional social situations, makes any form of human community which falls short of the law of love less than the best. Only by a voluntary giving of life to life and a free interpenetration of personalities could man do justice both to the freedom of other personalities and the necessity of community between personalities. The law of love therefore remains a principle of criticism over all forms of community in which elements of coercion and conflict destroy the highest type of fellowship.

To look at human communities from the perspective of the Kingdom of God is to know that there is a sinful element in all the expedients which the political order uses to establish justice. That is why even the seemingly most stable justice degenerates periodically into either tyranny or anarchy. But it must also be recognized that it is not possible to eliminate the sinful element in the political expedients. They are, in the words of St. Augustine, both the consequence of, and the remedy for, sin. If they are the remedy for sin, the ideal of love is not merely a principle of indiscriminate criticism upon all approximations of justice. It is also a principle of discriminate criticism between forms of justice.

As a principle of indiscriminate criticism upon all forms of justice, the law of love reminds us that the injustice and tyranny against which we contend in the foe is partially the consequence of our own injustice, that the pathology of modern Germans is partially a consequence of the vindictiveness of the peace of Versailles, and that the ambition of a tyrannical imperialism is different only in degree and not in kind from the imperial impulse which characterizes all of human life.

The Christian faith ought to persuade us that political controversies are always conflicts between sinners and not between righteous men and sinners. It ought to mitigate the self-righteousness which is an inevitable concomitant of all human con-flict. The spirit of contrition is an important ingredient in the sense of justice. If it is powerful enough it may be able to restrain the impulse of vengeance sufficiently to al-low a decent justice to emerge. This is an important issue facing Europe in anticipation of the conclusion of the present war. It cannot be denied that the Christian conscience failed terribly in restraining vengeance after the last war. It is also quite obvious that the natural inclination to self-righteousness was the primary force of this vengeance (expressed particularly in the war guilt clause of the peace treaty). The pacifists draw the conclusion from the fact that justice is never free from vindictiveness, that we ought not for this reason ever to contend against a foe. This argument leaves out of account that capitulation to the foe might well subject us to a worse vindictiveness. It is as foolish to imagine that the foe is free of the sin which we deplore in ourselves as it is to regard ourselves as free of the sin which we deplore in the foe.

The fact that our own sin is always partly the cause of the sins against which we must contend is regarded by simple moral purists as proof that we have no right to contend against the foe. They regard the injunction "Let him who is without sin cast the first stone" as a simple alternative to the schemes of justice which society has devised and whereby it prevents the worst forms of anti-social conduct. This injunction of Christ ought to remind every judge and every juridical tribunal that the crime of the criminal is partly the conse-quence of the sins of society. But if pacifists are to be consistent they ought to advocate the abolition of the whole judicial process in society. It is perfectly true that national societies have more impartial instruments of justice than international society possesses to date. Nevertheless, no impartial court is as impartial as it pretends to be, and there is no judicial process which is completely free of vindictiveness. Yet we cannot dispense with it; and we will have to continue to put criminals into jail. There is a point where the final cause of the criminal's anti-social conduct becomes a fairly irrelevant issue in comparison with the task of preventing his conduct from injuring innocent fellows.

The ultimate principles of the Kingdom of God are never irrelevant to any problem of justice, and they hover over every social situation as an ideal possibility; but that does not mean that they can be made into simple alternatives for the present schemes of rela-tive justice. The thesis that the so-called democratic nations have no right to resist overt forms of tyranny, because their own history betrays imperialistic motives, would have meaning only if it were possible to achieve a perfect form of justice in any nation and to free national life completely of the imperialistic motive. This is impossible; for im-perialism is the collective expression of the sinful will-to-power which characterizes all human existence. The pacifist argument on this issue betrays how completely pacifism gives itself to illusions about the stuff with which it is dealing in human nature. These illusions deserve particular censure, because no one who knows his own heart very well ought to be given to such illusions.

The recognition of the law of love as an indiscriminate principle of criticism over all attempts at social and international justice is actually a resource of justice, for it prevents the pride, self-righteousness and vindictiveness of men from corrupting their efforts at justice. But it must be recognized that love is also a principle of discriminate criticism between various forms of community and various attempts at justice. The closest approximation to a love in which life supports life in voluntary community is a justice in which life is prevented from destroying life and the interests of the one are guarded against unjust claims by the other. Such justice is achieved when impartial tribunals of society prevent men "from being judges in their own cases," in the words of John Locke. But the tribunals of justice merely codify certain equilibria of power. Justice is basically dependent upon a balance of power. Whenever an individual or a group or a nation possesses undue power, and whenever this power is not checked by the possibility of criticizing and resisting it, it grows inordinate. The equilibrium of power upon which every structure of justice rests would degenerate into anarchy but for the organizing center which controls it. One reason why the balances of power, which prevent injustice in international relations, periodically degenerate into overt anarchy is because no way has yet been found to establish an adequate organizing center, a stable international judicatory, for this balance of power.

A balance of power is something different from, and inferior to, the harmony of love. It is a basic condition of justice, given the sinfulness of man. Such a balance of power does not exclude love. In fact, without love the frictions and tensions of a balance of power would become intolerable. But without the balance of power even the most loving relations may degenerate into unjust relations, and love may become the screen which hides the injustice. Family relations are instructive at this point. Women did not gain justice from men, despite the intimacy of family relations, until they secured sufficient economic power to challenge male autocracy. There are Christian "idealists" today who speak sentimentally of love as the only way to justice, whose family life might benefit from a more delicate "balance of power."

Naturally, the tensions of such a balance may become overt; and overt tensions may degenerate into conflict. The center of power, which has the function of preventing this anarchy of conflict, may also degenerate into tyranny. There is no perfectly adequate method of preventing either anarchy or tyranny. But obviously the justice established in the so-called democratic nations represents a high degree of achievement; and the achievement becomes the more impressive when it is compared with the tyranny into which alternative forms of society have fallen. The obvious evils of tyranny, however, will not inevitably persuade the victims of economic anarchy in democratic society to eschew tyranny. When men suffer from anarchy they may foolishly regard the evils of tyranny as the lesser evils. Yet the evils of tyranny in fascist and communist nations are so patent, that we may dare to hope that what is still left of democratic civilizations will not lightly sacrifice the virtues of democracy for the sake of escaping its defects.

We have a very vivid and conclusive evidence about the probable consequences of a tyrannical unification of Europe. The nature of the German rule in the conquered na-tions of Europe gives us the evidence. There are too many contingent factors in various national and international schemes of justice to justify any unqualified endorsement of even the most democratic structure of justice as "Christian." Yet it must be obvious that any social structure in which power has been made responsible, and in which an-archy has been overcome by methods of mutual accommodation, is preferable to either anarchy or tyranny. If it is not possible to express a moral preference for the justice achieved in democratic societies, in comparison with tyrannical societies, no historical preference has any meaning. This kind of justice approximates the harmony of love more than either anarchy or tyranny.

If we do not make discriminate judgments between social systems we weaken the resolution to defend and extend civilization. Pacifism either tempts us to make no judgments at all, or to give an undue preference to tyranny in comparison with the momentary anarchy which is necessary to overcome tyranny. It must be admitted that the anarchy of war which results from resistance to tyranny is not always creative that, at given periods of history, civilization may lack the resource to fashion a new and higher form of unity out of momentary anarchy. The defeat of Germany and the frustration of the Nazi effort to unify Europe in tyrannical terms is a negative task. It does not guarantee the emergence of a new Europe with a higher level of international cohesion and new organs of international justice. But it is a negative task which cannot be avoided. All schemes for avoiding this negative task rest upon illusions about human nature. Specifically, these illusions express themselves in the failure to understand the stubbornness and persistence of the tyrannical will, once it is fully conceived. It would not require great argumentative skill to prove that Nazi tyranny never could have reached such proportions as to be able to place the whole of Europe under its ban, if sentimental illusions about the character of the evil which Europe was facing had not been combined with less noble motives for tolerating Nazi aggression.

A simple Christian moralism is senseless and confusing. It is senseless when, as in the World War, it seeks uncritically to identify the cause of Christ with the cause of democracy without a religious reservation. It is just as senseless when it seeks to purge itself of this error by an uncritical refusal to make any distinctions between relative values in history. The fact is that we might as well dispense with the Christian faith entirely if it is our conviction that we can act in history only if we are guiltless. This means that we must either prove our guiltlessness in order to be able to act; or refuse to act because we cannot achieve guiltlessness. Self-righteousness or inaction are the alternatives of secular moralism. If they are also the only alternatives of Christian moralism, one rightly suspects that Christian faith has become diluted with secular perspectives.

In its profoundest insights the Christian faith sees the whole of human history as involved in guilt, and finds no release from guilt except in the grace of God. The Christian is freed by that grace to act in history; to give his devotion to the highest values he knows; to defend those citadels of civilization of which necessity and historic destiny have made him the defender; and he is persuaded by that grace to remember the ambiguity of even his best actions. If the providence of God does not enter the affairs of men to bring good out of evil, the evil in our good may easily destroy our most ambitious efforts and frustrate our highest hopes.

VI

Despite our conviction that most modern pacifism is too filled with secular and moralistic illusions to be of the highest value to the Christian community, we may be grateful for the fact that the Christian Church has learned, since the last war, to protect its pacifists and to appreciate their testimony. Even when this testimony is marred by self-righteousness, because it does not proceed from a sufficiently profound understanding of the tragedy of human history, it has its value.

It is a terrible thing to take human life. The conflict between man and man and nation and nation is tragic. If there are men who declare that no matter what the consequences, they cannot bring themselves to participate in this slaughter, the Church ought to be able to say to the general community: We quite understand this scruple and we respect it. It proceeds from the conviction that the true end of man is brotherhood, and that love is the law of life. We who allow ourselves to become engaged in war need this testimony of the absolutist against us, lest we accept the warfare of the world as normative, lest we become callous to the horror of war, and lest we forget the ambiguity of our own actions and motives and the risk we run of achieving no permanent good from this momentary anarchy in which we are involved.

But we have a right to remind the absolutists that their testimony against us would be more effective if it were not corrupted by self-righteousness and were not accompanied by the implicit or explicit accusation of apostasy. A pacifism which really springs from the Christian faith, without secular accretions and corruptions, could not be as certain as modern pacifism is that it possesses an alternative for the conflicts and tensions from which and through which the world must rescue a precarious justice.

A truly Christian pacifism would set each heart under the judgment of God to such a degree that even the pacifist idealist would know that knowledge of the will of God is no guarantee of his ability or willingness to obey it. The idealist would recognize to what degree he is himself involved in rebellion against God, and would know that this rebellion is too serious to be overcome by just one more sermon on love, and one more challenge to man to obey the law of Christ.

1 – 8

"Six Pillars of Peace"

JOHN FOSTER DULLES with commentaries by members of
the Federal Council's Commission on a Just and Durable Peace[1]

Introduction by John Foster Dulles

AS THIS WAR TURNS from a defensive to an offensive operation, as territory is regained and as peoples are liberated, the United Nations are brought face to face with grave problems that will imperil their unity. Already we see that threat. Russia and Poland have broken relations and opposing factions of French and of Yugoslavs compete for support from among the Allies. Developments such as these will compel the United Nations to make soon the basic decision of whether the future is to be one of international collaboration. If that is not to be, if as in the past each nation must depend upon itself alone, then the United Nations will surely begin to play power politics against each other. While the form of unity may temporarily be preserved, its soul will be extinct. The seeds of new war will be sown and, indeed, a decisive ending of this war may long elude us.

Of course no one nation can determine that the future shall be one of collaboration. That requires joint action. But peculiar responsibility rests upon the American people for it was they who, after the last war, unexpectedly elected to "go it alone." The shock of that was unforgettable. We cannot expect others now to take it for granted that this time it will be different. That is a great uncertainty which bedevils the present and beclouds the future. It is an uncertainty which only the American people can resolve.

Christian citizens should, in this matter, feel a great responsibility and see a great opportunity. They know that strength and safety do not come primarily from material things, but from things of the spirit. They know that true greatness is incompatible with narrow selfishness and that power, such as that our nation possesses, cannot be divorced from broad responsibility. They know that if we follow what may seem the easy path of self-sufficiency, the result will be internal decay, a mounting hostility of the rest of the world and a certain renewal of conflict.

---

1. Dulles et al., "The Six Pillars of Peace." John Foster Dulles wrote the introduction to this article, published as a series in 1943 by the Federal Council's Commission on a Just and Durable Peace with commentaries based upon the "Political Propositions" of each of the declaration's six pillars.

Those who believe these things, face now the time for action. Unless their beliefs are soon translated into realities, the opportunity to do so may not recur in our time. The pattern of the future is already in the making and before long it will have been irrevocably set.

In order to promote thinking and action along realistic lines, our Commission has formulated a Statement outlining six areas within which national interdependence is demonstrated, and where, accordingly, international collaboration needs to be organized. We call these the "Six Pillars of Peace."

A group of eminent Americans will discuss them in a series of articles to appear in this paper. . . . We hope that this will stimulate many others to follow their example. Only widespread discussion can produce a clear and dependable mandate to our Government from its citizens. Only if that mandate be to seek international collaboration can we expect a Just and Durable Peace.

The First Pillar by Harold W. Dodds

The peace must provide the political framework for a continuing collaboration
of the United Nations and, in due course, of neutral and enemy nations.

Unless we organize for peace we shall not have peace. It is through social and political institutions that ideas are made to march. Unless the idea of international collaboration is embodied in political institutions it will remain a polite platitude.

It is true that institutions root in the past and that we cannot suddenly change the political habits and attitudes of peoples. This limits what we can usefully now attempt. But the peoples of the United Nations are already becoming accustomed to collaboration through meetings of their leaders. Out of this, if we will it enough, can be built an institution which will serve our most pressing needs today and provide a basis for peaceful growth in years to come.

We should be able to generate the will power to do this, for it provides the only realistic possibility of durable peace. No nation can hope to be strong enough in the post-war world to guarantee its own peace. Nor is the "balance of power" method any longer reliable. A delicate balance of power may have discouraged some wars in the past, but it has always broken down in the end. Today, the developments of science and technology are such that any balance that might be achieved after this war would be too unstable to deserve the name.

Pillar I does not contemplate the impossible. It would begin modestly. It recognizes the existence of national loyalties. It does not propose an order so new and unfamiliar that men would be emotionally unprepared to participate in it. Obviously, if a more-than-national organization is to work, men's emotions, as well as their intellects, must be favorable to it. Therefore, as other parts of the Commission's statement make clear, they would now seek organized international collaboration primarily at the points at which world interdependence is strongest. Thus, much of this collaboration might be regional, e.g., European or Pan-American, and much of it might be topical, e.g., commercial and financial. But there would be an overall framework of political organization sufficiently broad and sufficiently flexible to develop to meet whatever the needs of the future might prove to be. The Commission's proposals are less sweeping than many being put forward. Their success will be due, in part, to the fact that they do not attempt too much.

In planning the framework of a world political organization, we must not exalt the legislative and judicial elements of government at the expense of the administrative. National legislatures and courts deal with the controversial. They are devices for settling arguments, not agencies for carrying into daily life results upon which all are agreed. The greater part of government has to do with day-by-day administration of necessary matters. There is a useful hint in this. I believe that the cause of peace will be best served by more attention to the acknowledged services that international administration can render, rather than by concentration in advance upon the structure and scope of legislative and judicial powers. The latter will evolve naturally as administrative functions are established.

The Second Pillar by Sumner Welles

> The Peace must make provision for bringing within the scope of international agreement those economic and financial acts of national governments which have widespread international repercussions.

This seems to me the plainest common sense. Friendship between peoples, and political collaboration between governments, cannot be achieved or successfully maintained if collaboration in economic matters fails. For the economic acts of governments affect the personal prosperity of individuals. The price of crops, the chance to get or hold a job, the supply and price of goods on merchants' shelves, the money to pay off the mortgage, these are the realities that lie behind and are affected by the wise or unwise acts and policies of governments. And when those acts of government, as has often been the case, reach out in their effects across the boundaries of States, and deprive human beings in near or distant lands abroad of work, or of a market, or of the materials they need for their livelihood, then it should not be surprising that their resentment shows itself in action. Real and lasting friendships between large groups of people depend in the long run on their being willing to cooperate in the fundamental business of earning a living.

The United Nations stand committed to a cooperative program. The Fourth point of the Atlantic Charter, which they have all subscribed, expresses their common desire "to further the enjoyment by all States, great or small, victor or vanquished, of access, on equal terms, to the trade and to the raw materials of the world which are needed for their economic prosperity" and the Fifth point bespeaks their common wish "to bring about the fullest collaboration between all nations in the economic field with the object of securing, for all, improved labor standards, economic advancement and social security." That collaboration started in practice with their alliance in the war, with combined efforts to utilize their pooled resources in the most effective ways to hasten complete victory over the Axis powers, and with mutual-aid agreements for this same purpose. In these agreements with a growing number of our Allies mutual pledges have been exchanged to seek, through agreed action, the attainment of all the economic objectives of the Atlantic

Charter, and specifically, "the expansion, by appropriate international and domestic measures, of production, employment, and the exchange and consumption of goods, which are the material foundations of the liberty and welfare of all peoples; . . . the elimination of all forms of discriminatory treatment in international commerce, and . . . the reduction of tariffs and other trade barriers." This war-time collaboration has moved forward to the problems of the peace with the conference on food and agriculture, the preparations for relief and reconstruction in the devastated areas, the discussions about stabilizing currencies, and the reciprocal trade-agreements program.

At this very moment, the Congress is considering legislation to extend the trade-agreements authority. As I recently stated: "The decision about the trade agreements authority is not the only choice, or the most difficult, that the people of the United States will have to make about the foundations of the peace. But it is fundamental, and it happens to come first in time. Our action on it will be an acid test of our intentions."

The general direction of international collaboration has been charted, and the work is underway. What remains, and it is a task for many men for many years in many lands, is so to remake our relations with each other, in loyal and cooperative effort, that the great productive forces which technology has brought within our sight may function freely for the prosperity and benefit of all. The active help of all men and women of good will is needed to make that effort a success. Only as it moves forward with gathering momentum can we begin to be assured that the great hopes of the future, freedom from want and fear, are more than empty words.

The Third Pillar by Arthur Hays Sulzberger

> The peace must make provision for an organization to adapt the treaty structure
> of the world to changing underlying conditions.

Change is an invariable law of nature. Nothing that lives is static. If we are to achieve the functioning, effective peace called for by the Federal Council of Churches then—in the language of the Council—we must provide the means periodically to adapt the treaty structure of the world to changing conditions.

Such provision is advisable as an act of common sense and self-protection. No one can foresee the future. Nor can we as a nation claim any great genius for anticipating events. We have never gone into war prepared. We have not even been able always to distinguish between our friends and our enemies. Often, in the past one hundred and fifty years, events beyond our control have impelled us to alter both our national and our international policy. Our independence was won in conflict with Great Britain; yet since then Great Britain has proved our most reliable ally. In the past three decades, Italy and Japan have been first our associates and are now our enemies; and Soviet Russia, with whom for years after the last war we did not have even diplomatic relations, has become a valiant companion in arms. The impossibility of determining the acts of other nations should of itself commend to us the desirability of reconsidering from time to time the structure of all treaties.

The advisability of such a course is suggested also by our Constitution. Our Founding Fathers not only provided the means of changing the Constitution, but themselves made use of that machinery to add the Bill of Rights to our basic law. The elasticity of the document they shaped accounts for its success and permanence.

The fate of the League of Nations indicates that it might be wise not only to provide machinery for changing the peace structure, but also to make it mandatory that all nations reconsider the treaties at definite intervals. This was the intention of Lord Robert Cecil who, on behalf of the British delegation to the last Peace Conference, proposed that Article 19 of the Covenant of the League should state that "the Body of Delegates *shall make provision* for the periodic revision of treaties which have become obsolete and of international conditions the continuance of which may endanger the peace of the world."

Under this clause the members of the League would have been obligated at specific periods to survey legal, economic and social factors—such factors as helped produce this war. They would have been obligated to consider in orderly manner and in reasonable atmosphere such questions as those of the mandates and colonies, of the Sudetenland, of Austria and Danzig. But the wording of Article 19 was changed so that instead of providing that the Assembly *"must* consider grievances," it read *"may* consider grievances." Then, when Bolivia and Chile sought to have the League settle their boundary dispute at the Second Assembly, it was eventually ruled that the League could not "of itself modify any treaty."

This time it should be recognized that the primary business of a peace system is to modify treaties when the necessity arises. More should be done than has ever been attempted heretofore to watch the development of disputes, grievances, conditions of any kind that are likely to cause trouble if not dealt with in time. To this end a permanent commission charged to study and report on the early symptoms of war might well be as organic a part of a peace structure as the international health section of the League. The Chile-Bolivia boundary case suggests that regional councils, if set up within an overall world organization, might form a first court of appeal for disputes within the region.

The main difficulty will be in making governments accept revisions and modifications of the status quo in interest of world peace. Therefore I suggest that the United States (which played an important part in changing the wording of Article 19 from *must* to *may*) should accept its full responsibility and join with other nations in helping to solve these international problems, and that this time we support Lord Robert Cecil's vital proposal.

Most wars are made in violation of treaties. Even benign governments have abrogated contracts with their citizenry when changing events have suggested that the public interest lay in other directions. If we are seeking a lasting peace, let us be prepared to adapt our agreements to realities.

Peace is no less dynamic than war. To win it and to preserve it require a degree of sacrifice as great almost as that of battle.

The Fourth Pillar by Francis B. Sayre

> The peace must proclaim the goal of autonomy for subject peoples, and it must establish international organization to assure and to supervise the realization of that end.

For the building of the coming peace one of the fundamental issues will be the problem of foreign rule over alien peoples. Shall the post-war world in Asia and in Africa be based upon nineteenth-century patterns or must we look for something different?

The answer is clear. We are coming to see that the only possible foundation upon which a peace that will last can be built is that of Christian brotherhood; and this is as applicable to alien peoples as to home folks. Brotherhood allows no room for the exploitation of one people by another for the sake of selfish gain; it is incompatible with racial or national intolerance.

Ultimate autonomy for every subject race is the goal. "It has been our purpose in the past and will remain our purpose in the future," declared Secretary Hull, "to use the full measure of our influence to support attainment of freedom by *all* peoples who, by their acts, show themselves worthy of it and ready for it."

Clearly the problem of alien rule allows of no easy and quick solution. The way of peace does not lie through the grant of immediate independence to every subject people. When the United States assumed the responsibility of sovereignty over the Filipino people in 1898, an overnight grant of freedom to them would not have advanced the cause of peace. Our undertaking instead required the slow and arduous and baffling task of preparing the Filipino people for ultimate autonomy. For over forty years Americans have labored at that task. Insofar as we have succeeded, American ideals of liberty and democracy have gained a foothold in Asia and, we hope, solid groundwork has been laid there for stability and peace in the years to come.

What are the concrete directions in which we must move in the coming peace treaty in dealing with the problem of alien rule?

In the first place, the twentieth-century method of approach must be fundamentally different from that of the past. The goal must be not exploitation for another country's profit, but the preparation of an underprivileged people for self-development and self-rule. This means a task infinitely more adventurous and more difficult than nineteenth-century methods of imperialism. It means not how to extract natural wealth and trading profits from a backward people but how to build shoulder to shoulder with them schools and hospitals and roads and water systems, how to improve their public sanitation and to reduce their death rate, how to raise their general standard of living, and, above all, how to stimulate and inspire in them the ability and the desire to build for themselves.

In the second place, those undertaking the responsibility for alien rule in areas not yet ripe for self-government must work out with leaders of the subject race a forward-looking program, marking by definite steps the advance toward autonomy, and this program must be publicly declared. This involves progressively handing over to the subject people the responsibilities of government in one field after another; for the difficult art of self-government can be learned in no other way except by trial and error, costly as that may be. The acid test of sincerity will be the implementation of such declarations by concrete action, which cannot be too long delayed. The peace of the world depends upon this implementation.

In the third place, this progress toward autonomy must be subjected to international control since the problem of alien rule is part of the problem of peace.

No single formula for international control can be worked out applicable to every area. Each presents a problem of its own. What we must achieve is an effective international control, exercised in such form as individual needs and conditions require.

In the fourth place, provision must be made at the coming peace conference for absolute equality of commercial opportunity in all areas subject to alien rule. Non-discrimination with respect to tariffs and all trade barriers would mean in the subject areas of the world the removal of fundamental causes of conflict and warfare. It would be an immense step forward. Accompanying these provisions looking toward economic freedom, steps should be taken to prevent economic strangleholds. Tariffs in subject areas must not be manipulated for the benefit of the ruling race. Neither must the winning of autonomy be frustrated by a growing economic dependence upon the ruling people. In conclusion, we must not expect the problem of alien rule, *which* has torn the world for more than three centuries, to be mastered overnight. Neither will it be solved by mere machinery or organization. Doubt less the solution will come only gradually and almost imperceptibly as part of the incoming tide of new world brotherhood. "The world is growing ready again for adventure."

The Fifth Pillar by Joseph H. Ball

The peace must establish procedures for controlling military establishments everywhere.

There are several basic and deep-rooted causes of war. But the immediate cause of all of the great wars of modern times has been either aggression or fear of aggression. The majority of Christian nations wanting peace have been forced into armament races by a few nations whose power-hungry leaders were arming for conquest. The result has been a powder keg of heavily armed nations waiting only for the match of a border incident or a shift in alliances to explode into war. Procedures and machinery to free all nations, great and small, from the constant fear of aggression are essential to a lasting peace.

A system of collective security as implied in the Fifth Pillar, functioning under the United Nations political organization of the First Pillar, is the keystone of the world peace structure. We must implement every one of the six pillars, but it would be futile to attempt the lengthy task of solving world economic problems, raising subject peoples to self-governing status and fostering education, intellectual and spiritual freedom throughout the world if it must be done in an international atmosphere of insecurity and fear, magnified by the terrifying and ever-increasing destructive force of modern war.

A workable system of international security is the first step toward permanent peace and is, furthermore, the only condition under which individual nations will even consider giving up the right to create unlimited armaments for national defense. Realistically, it is doubtful whether nations will give up that right until such a collective security system has proven that it can protect individual nations against aggression.

The overwhelming majority of individual citizens obey our laws without any coercion. Yet we recognize the need of policemen to control that minority who recognize no moral obligation to the community. Similarly, on the international level there must be some force to control those outlaw nations whose leaders recognize no moral obligation to the world community. No nation, however aggressive, will start a war against overwhelming odds. Therefore, a necessary corollary to real disarmament by nations must be the creation of an international military force sufficiently strong to stop aggression by such outlaw nations.

The United Nations should begin now organizing the peace. Disunity is already developing and as the day of victory nears and the pressure of immediate and common danger relaxes, that disunity is likely to in crease rather than decrease.

With these facts in mind, two Democratic and two Republican Senators have introduced Senate Resolution 114, which urges our country to take the lead in forming now a United Nations organization to establish machinery for peaceful settlement of international disputes and to provide for the assembly of a United Nations military force to be used for the sole purpose of stopping future attempts at military aggression.

The Sixth Pillar by Thomas E. Dewey

> The peace must establish in principle, and seek to achieve in practice, the right of individuals everywhere to religious and intellectual liberty.

All experience has shown that the best of laws can be rendered useless by poor administration but even poor laws can be made to work under good leadership and administration. The same will be true of the machinery to achieve a just and durable peace.

Thus, the most skillfully devised political machinery for peace will be no better than the purposes and capacities of the human beings who direct it. Police forces will serve to keep peace only so long as they are controlled by the forces of good will.

To achieve the basic objective we must recognize that, in the long run, peace rests on the implemented will of mankind. Essential to this will to peace are two fundamentals, first, spiritual faith which rests upon the dignity of the individual and equality among all human beings, and second, sufficient knowledge among peoples, to provide continuous support for an organized society which respects the right to individual freedom.

We have found the spiritual basis for peace within our own citizenry. Here Protestants, Catholics and Jews, while holding vital and distinctive faiths, feel no urge to master and oppress others. Internationally, we see peace promoted by the sharing of great faiths by many in different lands. On the other hand, war comes whenever, as in Germany and Japan, a nation and race are deified and mastery of others is taught as a divine duty.

As Americans, we must be prepared to insist that any organization for peace shall fully, frankly and boldly require of all participants a declaration establishing "in principle the right of individuals everywhere to religious and intellectual liberty." Our whole experience and the history of this war have taught us that this is a basic necessity. It is right. It is in accordance with the most fundamental of human impulses to seek God freely.

But, as the Sixth Pillar also says, it is not enough to establish these rights "in principle;" we must seek to achieve them in practice. I am convinced that the peace will be only as durable as our success in achieving generally, religious freedom in practice. This will require strong leadership and stout resistance to compromise. But only thus shall this war end in a result worthy of the name of victory.

Having learned from this war the truly interdependent relationship between peoples, we must also learn that sound relationships must be built upon respect and independence. The interdependence of peoples does not require a system of international charity. We cannot buy peace in that way. What is required is a code of conduct which promotes the interests of all because it leads people to act with a decent and intelligent regard for each other.

Both religious and intellectual liberty, being fundamental to the freedom on which peace must be based, it is clear that individual economic freedom must also be achieved. As we seek the ultimate we must not forget the only means by which the ultimate can be made a reality.

Just as surely as man does not have the free opportunity to work and to earn food, shelter and clothing, for himself and his family, he is not free. Inevitably those who control man's livelihood will use their power to control also his knowledge and beliefs. That is true whether the economic dictatorship be in Germany or in the United States and whether it be exercised by organizations of capital or labor or by those who bear the title of public office. Against all such absolutism everywhere, we must be constantly alert.

These freedoms, interdependent as they are, belong, of course, to all men regardless of race, creed or color. The struggle for freedom and equality will go on ceaselessly in a world in which they are not fully achieved. Whether that struggle is to be violent or evolutionary depends on the sincerity with which the peace to come is built. If we insist upon recognition of the principles of religious and intellectual freedom and seek to achieve them we may hope for a just and durable peace.

Part 2: **Cold War Christian Realists**

Cold War Christian Realists: An Introduction

THE SECOND PHASE OF Christian Realism corresponds roughly to the era of significant escalation in Vietnam through the end of the Cold War, roughly 1965–90. The former lieutenants of the Second World War had become the world's leaders—in the United States (Kennedy, Johnson, Nixon, and Reagan) and abroad (Mitterand, Helmut Schmidt, Jaruzelski). Especially in Washington, DC and London, leaders looked back to the lessons of appeasement, whether with the Nazis at Munich or soft-dealing with the Soviets in the 1930s and 1940s and decided on resolute courses of action for the U.S.-led West. Many of the issues of the time were framed by the bipolar world of communism vs. Western liberal democracy, but the underlying questions were familiar to Christian Realists, such as:

- What does Christianity say about politics, diplomacy, and war, not just for the leader, but for the citizen?

- How should we understand Vietnam geopolitically and morally?

- How should the responsible Christian respond to the new pacifism of the era, from anti-war protests to the nuclear-freeze movement?

- How should Christians think about weapons of mass destruction?

- How should Christians think about the interface of our government with international law and international organizations?

- How should Christians think about human rights and power politics?

Although some of the first generation of Christian Realists continued to be active into the 1960s, albeit dramatically slowing down due to health and retirement, their mantle passed to a new generation, most notably Princeton University ethicist Paul Ramsey (1913–88), foreign policy expert Ernest W. Lefever (1919–2009), and political scientist Kenneth W. Thompson (1921–2013). Ramsey's emphasis on Christian just war thinking, in the context of wars of national liberation, communist insurgencies, WMDs, and Vietnam inspired a generation of new just war thinking rooted in Christian tradition, most notably that of his student James Turner Johnson (b. 1938). Kenneth Thompson supported the work of Niebuhr and others from his position leading the Rockefeller Foundation's International Relations Program and then went on to publish dozens of books and monographs of his own, while at the University of Virginia, on the ethics of domestic and foreign policy. Some Catholics, most notably the young (b. 1951) George Weigel, rose to prominence making Augustinian and just war arguments about the Cold War: Weigel went to work at Lefever's Ethics and Public Policy Center. Jean Bethke Elshtain (1941–2013) increasingly cited the influence of Augustine and Niebuhr, whom she called the "greatest public theologian of our time."[1]

Morality and Moralism in the Cold War

Like Niebuhr and others, Ernest Lefever journeyed from pacifism to what he called "humane Realism." What changed him was seeing first-hand the Bergen-Belsen concentration camp. He famously kept, and displayed, a bone taken from the camp to demonstrate the depravity of the Holocaust. He went on to work as a world affairs expert for the National Council of Churches, Senator Hubert Humphrey, and the Brookings Institution before founding the Ethics and Public Policy Center in Washington, DC. Lefever's 1972 essay, "Morality and U.S. Foreign Policy," republished multiple times over the next three decades, contains a number of key themes that are timeless within the Christian Realist tradition. Using Niebuhr's terms, Lefever distinguishes between "rational idealism" and "historical idealism." The former emphasizes perfectibility and progress in history; the latter emphasizes "the moral limits of human nature and history and has its roots in Saint Augustine, John Calvin, Edmund Burke, James Madison . . . rejecting all forms of religious and secular utopianism." Lefever notes that neither perspective, in its extreme form, is useful. For instance, he criticizes a "lopsided Realism" that can result in a militant nationalism: "What is good for America is good for the rest of the world [and so we should] make other peoples over in our own image, by force if necessary." This is a question about the use of American power that recurs, from Niebuhr's 1952 *Irony of American History* to Mark Amstutz's 2005 examination of the Bush Doctrine. Lefever rightly notes that the strategy of remaking the world is also that of the revolutionary idealist,[2] hence "the extremists in both groups have more in common with each other than with the mainstream of their own tradition."

Lefever helps today's reader by distinguishing "morality" from an imposter: "moralism." The former is the ethics of right and wrong, whereas moralism is "sham morality . . . self-righteous rhetoric or manipulative symbols designed to justify, enlist, condemn or deceive rather than . . . serve the cause of justice." This distinction, between a deep commitment to ethical reflection on the one hand and foppish moralizing on the other, distinguishes Christian Realists from pundits and sophists.

When it comes to national security policy, Lefever condemns the "crusading impulse" to reform the world and argues that U.S. involvement and intervention should be focused on stability, because outsiders have "severely limited capacity . . . to influence

1. Elshtain's major books on war, politics, democracy, and sovereignty were all published after 1991, and for that reason, we include her among the Contemporary Christian Realists. On Niebuhr, see her chapter "Where Is the Legacy of Tillich and Niebuhr?" 106.

2. See, for example, resonances in Calvinist and proto-Kuyperian intellectuals like Groen Van Prinsterer in his essays in *Unbelief and Revolution*.

and reshape alien cultures," whether in Vietnam or in Afghanistan. When military or financial aid "serves the interests of both parties," such "presents few problems." Echoing Niebuhr and Butterfield, Lefever is proud of the ethical commitments of the West, rooted in Judeo-Christian teaching and affirming "the dignity of the individual and the necessity of the state. It is precisely because the individual is finite and inclined to pursue his selfish desires at the expense of neighbor that the structure of order and justice are needed." Lefever believed that "the great majority of the American people" of his day, "by temperament and their respect for law, are committed to a domestic order rooted in a prudent balance of justice and freedom, and to an international order that is safe for diversity and peaceful change." This moderate position is both practical and morally sound. He concludes, "our times call *for idealism without illusion* and *realism without despair*" [italics added].

Transcendent Foundations or Revolutionary Relativism?

Kenneth Thompson's essay, "The Transcendent and the Relative in Morality and Foreign Policy," was reissued numerous times over two decades due to the way that it sketched out, for politics and policy, what he called, "the debate over a *transcendent* as against a *relativist* ethics" [italics added].[3] Thompson, like earlier Christian Realists, begins with huge questions: Can a transcendent ethical system "provide principles which can serve as guides to action? What are the standards it seeks to establish? How viable and relevant to the social order is the set of principles it brings forward? What kind of ordering of priorities among ethical and political principles takes place within the ethical system? How does such ordering relate to mankind's most urgent problems?"[4] Thompson summarizes classical and Christian natural law thought and the modernist attacks on them, but then develops a more nuanced, Christian-rooted approach to questions of the individual, the community, and the "overarching moral and political order."[5]

Thompson argues that religion can, beyond just articulating restraint, provide a number of factors for foreign policy analysis. It can "help provide a proper background of ideas. It can assist men in straightening out notions about human motivations and the persistence of selfishness and sin. It can free men of the [utopian] belief that all of our problems could be solved" while at the same time providing hope.[6] On this point he quotes Butterfield, "perhaps the most Christian thing that could happen would be for one of the Great Powers (acting not out of weakness but out of strength) to risk something . . . involving a trust in human nature this time, even though we know how foolish it is to trust human nature. Something of that sort might be required, just as a marginal experiment, because it happens to be the only way out of the worst deadlock, the tightest of predicaments."[7]

3. Thompson, "Transcendent and the Relative in Morality and Foreign Policy," 107.

4. Thompson, *Morality and Foreign Policy*, 130.

5. Thompson, *Morality and Foreign Policy*, 141.

6. Thompson, "Transcendent and the Relative in Morality and Foreign Policy," 117.

7. Thompson, "Transcendent and the Relative in Morality and Foreign Policy," 118.

Throughout this period, Christian Realists argued that it was possible to have an ethically informed response to world events, keeping an eye on the machinations of Beijing and Moscow as well as the flurry of Third World coups, counter-coups, and revolutions. The world certainly appeared evil at times, especially from the viewpoint of the West. What was fresh on people's minds in the Vietnam era was that the Soviets sent in the tanks to crush dissent in Hungary (1956) and Czechoslovakia (1968) and kept up the old czarist practices of torture and banishment to the "gulag archipelago" (Siberia). Chairman Mao's Cultural Revolution (1966–76; twenty million deaths), following on the heels of the "Great Leap Forward," which resulted in thirty million famine-related deaths (1958–62). Other diabolical practices remained, from the concentration camps of North Korea, China, and Vietnam to the killing fields of Cambodia. All of this destabilization, death, and destruction in the Far East seemed to be part of a global communist conspiracy, labeled by Western strategists as the "domino theory." Just as the West appeased Hitler by allowing him to gobble up his neighbors, it appeared that there was a calculated strategy—by clandestine undermining or lurid bullying—to turn East Asian governments to communism, first in China (1949) and Korea (Korean War, 1951–54), and then in Cambodia, Laos, Vietnam, Malaysia, the Philippines, and Indonesia. Western resolve to not lose Vietnam was an attempt to arrest a chain reaction of communist victories ("falling dominos").

Unfortunately, today's student of history may not realize the moral vocabulary with which Christian Realists of that time interpreted these events. The brutal tactics of the communists were not just the politics of the Cold War geo-political rivalry: they were evil policies rooted in anti-Christian revolutionary ideologies. Just as Niebuhr and Wight had warned about demonic revolutionary ideologies, so too later Christian Realists understood that there was a totalitarian, secular religion in the Russian, Chinese, and other revolutions that followed the anti-religious and anti-human ideology of the French Revolution. The crushing of the human spirit, the unfettered *libido dominandi* of the Soviet and Chinese elite, the attempt to reset history to Year Zero in Cambodia, and the attempts at destabilizing law and order in pursuit of "the Revolution," whether in Latin America or Africa, were all examples of an anti-God philosophy.

As John C. Bennett discussed in his last foreign policy book (1966), despite the West's flaws, the West had a responsibility to a world order that was more just than what the communist East offered and more in tune with the realities of both sin and human potential. Hence, the second generation of Christian Realists typically supported policies of robust containment (containing and balancing global communism) in places such as Vietnam and East Berlin. The United States was willing to support authoritarian regimes, such as in Latin America, as a lesser evil when confronting the brutal tactics of totalitarian communists. The Christian Realists knew that case-by-case decisions on policy had to be made: Christians could not turn a blind eye to a world of tough choices and pretend a sanctimonious impartiality that left so much of the world in the shackles of global communism.

Christian Realism in Practice: Vietnam and
the Hot Wars of the Cold War

The second generation of Christian Realists, quite naturally, focused much of their attention on the United States and its policies. Whereas the U.S. had entered an existing coalition in the Second World War as the junior partner, and later led a grand multi-national coalition in Korea, by the mid-1950s the power of other Western powers was so far behind that of the United States that everyone recognized that America was the dominant Western actor. To be more specific, by the 1960s the French empire had crumbled, and French politics were in disarray; France's influence fell even further when it left NATO. Britain was just a shadow of its Churchillian self by the Vietnam era and withdrew entirely from "East of Suez" by 1972. Anglophone countries, such as Canada and Australia, as well as most of Western and Northern Europe, were important players when working in concert, but were tiny actors when it came to balancing the military might of the Warsaw Pact and China's million-man army.

In the 1960s the leaders of both the Republican and Democratic parties largely saw Vietnam as another Munich: if the United States backed down, it would signal to the entire world that the United States could not be counted on to assist against communist insurgencies. Indeed, most policymakers took heart from Western toughness, sanctioned by the United Nations, in Korea the previous decade. The Korean Conflict ended with an armistice, but South Korea was firmly in the West's orbit, much of the global community had supported the UN-sponsored intervention, and even by the mid-1960s one could see the obvious difference in economic opportunity and growth for South Koreans, despite a form of soft authoritarianism, as compared to the plight of people under the iron fist of Pyongyang. The same evidence of the difference between East and West could be found in central Europe, as Bonn presided over a rapidly growing economy with significant individual freedoms, whereas East Berlin's secret police kept the population under constant surveillance and fear.

We provide here snapshots of some of Thompson's writings on the Vietnam War, a region where the United States was involved for nearly two decades. Realists were divided over Vietnam, and not just in its later years. For instance, Thompson's mentor, Pragmatic Realist Hans J. Morgenthau, was skeptical of U.S. involvement in Indochina by the late 1950s because he believed that this was a localized civil war and not necessarily a falling domino.[8] Reinhold Niebuhr and others were early supporters of U.S. aid to Vietnam and a general containment strategy, although shifted their views over time as the war became increasingly expensive in human lives and other costs. A look at Thompson's evolving view of the conflict provides us with a lens for understanding how Christian Realists could speak to a dynamic, changing situation, from limited

8. The "domino theory" is a foreign policy heuristic based on events that occurred in Eastern Europe and Asia that led to the theory that if communism infiltrated and took over one country, it had a way of knocking down the governments of neighboring societies and hence create a "domino effect." Although mocked by some in the intelligentsia, the domino theory seems to have occurred under the Soviet thumb in Eastern Europe and then again in East Asia: China, North Korea, North Vietnam, and insurgencies in Laos, Cambodia, and elsewhere. Over time, the domino theory was applied also to containment in Latin America and Africa.

support to the South Vietnamese government early on to growing uneasiness about the destructiveness of carpet bombing.

The politics of intervention and the role of the West in foreign affairs came under dramatic scrutiny during the anti-war protests of the Vietnam era and continued all the way through the 1980s. Indeed, even when a small foreign state asked for assistance—as Israel did in 1973 and Grenada did in 1984—U.S. policy was castigated, especially by the Left, as imperialistic. The U.S. nuclear deterrent, which shielded Western Europe from Soviet missile attack, was derided as disrupting the peace. Calls for a nuclear freeze and even nuclear abolition in the West, regardless of the Soviet's massive stockpile of weapons, became the *cause celebre* on university campuses and on the Left. Following what appeared to be a gross politicization of the war effort by successive presidents and the failure to decisively win in Vietnam, the U.S. military went into a period of mourning, wondering if the American people would ever support it as they had during the two world wars. Add to all of this the oil "shocks," inflation, terrorism, and the global economic recession of the 1970s and the era of Nixon, Carter, and Ford looked increasingly bleak.

Atomic Ethics

The language of Christian Realists at the time, however, was not so bleak. They consistently pointed to the dire global situation and urged robust yet moderate, principled but canny, action by political leaders. Ramsey, Thompson, and others argued for a moral foreign policy and attacked the theological roots and political posturing of the neo-pacifists, most notably those of the anti-Vietnam and anti-nukes generation. Ramsey, in particular, articulated the ethics of nuclear deterrence, including key limits on how nuclear weapons might be used (e.g., on the opponents' military forces and installations, but never against cities).

When the United States dropped the atomic bombs on Japan in August 1945, none could imagine how quickly the destructive power of nuclear weapons would advance. The next two decades saw tremendous growth and sophistication in the raw destructive power of thermonuclear devices, the delivery mechanisms (e.g., nuclear submarines, intercontinental ballistic missiles), and game theoretic models of deterrence. We will see in the chapters that follow the key moral questions that Christian Realists asked, and answered, about nuclear weapons. Interestingly, most of the Christian Realists did not take a position disavowing nuclear deterrence because they recognized how important the deterrent was against the massive military investments of the communist bloc. Nevertheless, these authors, especially Paul Ramsey, dissected the morality of nuclear deterrence, from counter-force (the enemy's military) to counter-population (cities) warfare, and from tactical (battlefield) nuclear artillery shells to strategic nuclear weapons that could wipe out entire civilizations.

Human Rights for the Christian Realist

The Christian Realists also became proponents of the next generation of what today we call human rights. Just as the Holocaust and other depredations of the Second World War had shocked the world into producing not just the Tokyo and Nuremberg war crimes tribunals, but also the updated Geneva Protocols and Genocide Convention, the UN's lack of potency in addressing the human rights abuses of the East meant that the West must try another strategy. One important step was the 1972 Helsinki Accords, a diplomatic win based on a trade-off for both sides. The Soviet Union agreed to a certain set of human rights protocols and the West agreed to formally endorse the *de facto* Soviet borders of 1945 (which included land grabs in Eastern Europe). President Jimmy Carter, a former submarine officer and state governor who claimed Niebuhr as an important influence, promoted human rights in his foreign policy, and despite a number of miscalculations and failures (e.g., Iran), earned the Nobel Peace Prize for successfully bringing the Israelis and Egyptians to a cold peace at Camp David. More than anyone, Carter's successor, Ronald Reagan, consistently championed the rights and spirit of those imprisoned behind the Iron Curtain, from supporting the emigration of Soviet Jews to establishing the National Endowment for Democracy.

Christian Realists maintained multi-faceted views on human rights. For example, English diplomat and scholar Adam Watson, writing in an edited volume about Herbert Butterfield's work that was published by Kenneth W. Thompson, argued that the first political right, religious liberty, resulted from the exhaustion of Europe's wars of religion. European governments had to change course and embrace religious freedom or continue costly, never-ending warfare.[9] Such a "never again" approach also animated post-Holocaust human rights realism, approaches nested into larger, pragmatic approaches to foreign policy. Christian Realists supported various human rights proposals due to the moral worth of humanity and as a prudential approach to defining the West's identity and national interest.

In conclusion, a second generation of Christian Realists assumed the mantle of Reinhold Niebuhr and applied Christian Realist analyses to the foreign policy challenges of their day. Although not united as a formal school, this community of discourse continued to emphasize bedrock themes in their analyses: human sin, human potential, human limitation, transcendent truth and ultimate justice, political order, and approximate justice. They applied these themes to provide what Henry P. Van Dusen called "middle axioms" within policy guidance that was moral and prudential on key issues of the day such as containing communism, countering violent insurgency, resisting utopian pacifism, and stewarding national defense resources. As we will see later in the book, Ramsey, Thompson, Lefever, and others provide an intellectual bridge between the Niebuhrian era and the post-Cold War Christian Realists, influencing a burst of intelligent Christian Realist thinking beginning in the 1990s.

---

9. Watson, "Toleration in Religion and Politics."

2–1

"Morality and U.S. Foreign Policy"

ERNEST LEFEVER

IT IS TOO SIMPLE to attribute the pervasive moral confusion in America to our involvement in Vietnam, though that protracted trauma doubtless has brought to a head our growing weariness with the burdens of power and disenchantment with what Denis Brogan once called "the illusion of American omnipotence."

Even before Vietnam our earlier and more naive national self-confidence had been shattered by a series of disappointments and reverses—the "fall of China" in 1949, the inconclusive Korean War, the loss of Cuba to the Communist camp, and the divisiveness and conflict in the wake of decolonization. Most Americans have finally learned that even the mighty United States cannot shape the destiny of peoples in the larger world, at least not without violating our profound moral inhibitions against the exercise of unabashed force to aggrandize our power or nourish our vanity. Since Pearl Harbor, few spokesmen have advocated that we shed our cherished scruples in the quest for an American imperium.

Underlying the moral awakening and confusion has been a continuing struggle between two different ways of looking at history and politics, two streams of American thought that have vied for ascendancy, especially since the mid-nineteenth century. The late Reinhold Niebuhr called these inclinations "rational idealism" and "historical realism," each manifesting itself in diverging political attitudes, expectations, and behavior.

Rational idealism in essence is the child of the Enlightenment and in its pure form it affirms the perfectibility, or at least improvability, of man and the possibility, if not inevitability, of progress in history. The diverse schools within this approach are united in their ultimate faith in the nobler nature of man. The earlier idealists saw reason as the redemptive agent that would save man and politics and eventually inaugurate an era of universal peace and brotherhood—the socialist paradise or the Kingdom of God on earth. The natural goodness of man, they believed, can be translated into the structures of politics. Poverty, injustice and war can be eliminated. The rational idealists were supported by the views of men such as Tom Paine, Walt Whitman, and Walter Rauschenbusch, the articulate spokesman of the Protestant Social Gospel movement. Wilsonian idealism, the manifestation of rationalism in the international sphere, reached its zenith in 1928 with the signing of the Kellogg-Briand Pact outlawing war as an "instrument of national policy."

Historical realism, in contrast, emphasizes the moral limits of human nature and history and has its roots in St. Augustine, John Calvin, Edmund Burke, James Madison, and most other classical Western thinkers. Rejecting all forms of religious and secular utopianism—including fascism and Communism—the post-Versailles realists have included men as varied as Niebuhr, Carl L. Becker, Winston Churchill and Dean Acheson. Noting that the extravagant expectations of the Wilsonians were not ratified by subsequent events, the self-designated realists hold that all political achievements are limited by man's dogged resistance to drastic reconstruction. With this recognition of "original sin," they argue that perfect peace, justice, security, and freedom are not possible in his world, though approximations of these lofty goals are not beyond man's grasp. To the rational idealist, the "impossible ideal" is achievable because it is rationally conceivable. To the historical realist, the "impossible ideal" is relevant because it lends humility without despair and hope without illusion.

In the real world there are few wholly consistent adherents to either approach. Were Jefferson and Lincoln rational idealists or historical realists? Obviously, they were a combination of both—Jefferson leaning toward the idealist view, and Lincoln toward the realist. Like most Americans, they tended to be optimistic about the more distant future and at the same time practical and realistic about immediate problems and possibilities.

Rational idealism and historical realism are not complete moral systems, but two different perspectives coexisting uneasily within the Western commitment to a political order of justice and freedom. As approaches, they are subject to certain limitations and weaknesses. In one sense each tends to balance and correct the other. Most moral philosophers, political theorists and statesmen tend toward one view or the other. On the practical level, virtually all political leaders have been realists, regardless of how idealistic their rhetoric may have been. I believe that the historical realist approach is a more adequate reading of the Judeo-Christian tradition and a sounder guide to politics than its post-Enlightenment rival, but recognize that it, like rational idealism, is subject to corruption.

Idealists vs. Realists

Both of these respectable philosophical approaches have been demeaned and distorted by emphasizing certain of their virtues to the neglect or exclusion of other elements in the larger body of Western normative thought. Each is vulnerable in its own way to the vices of political aloofness on the one hand, and crusading arrogance on the other. Rational idealists, frustrated by stubborn political realities, sometimes degenerate into sentimentalists whose strident demand for perfection becomes a substitute for responsible behavior. When personal purity becomes more important than political effectiveness, the resulting aloofness is virtually indistinguishable from that of cynical Machiavellians who insist that might alone makes right. The historical realist becomes irresponsible when his preoccupation with man's baser nature cuts the taproot of social concern and permits him to become a defender of injustice or tyranny.

A lopsided realist can come to hold that what is good for America is good for the rest of the world and that it is our "manifest destiny" to make other peoples over in our own image, by force if necessary. An equally lopsided idealist can support efforts to reshape other societies by more subtle, but not necessarily less reprehensible, means. Members of each approach can degenerate into cynical isolationists or overbearing crusaders. Seen in this light, the extremists in both groups have more in common with each other than with the mainstream of their own tradition.

The corruption of realism or idealism can be called moralism—the most popular rival and impostor of genuine morality. Morality or ethics (the Greek derivative with the same meaning) has to do with right or wrong behavior in all spheres. It is the discipline of relating ends and means. However primitive or sophisticated, all moral systems define normative ends and acceptable rules for achieving them. Moralism, on the other hand, is a sham morality, a partial ethic. Often it is expressed in self-righteous rhetoric or manipulative symbols designed to justify, enlist, condemn, or deceive rather than to inform, inspire, or serve the cause of justice. The moralism of the naive and well-intentioned may be sincere. The moralism of the ambitious and sophisticated is likely to be dishonest. Intellectually flabby and morally undisciplined, moralism tends to focus on private interests rather than the public good, on the immediate at the expense of the future, and on sentiment rather than reason. Morality is a synonym for responsibility. Moralism is a conscious or unconscious escape from accountability.

Soft and Hard Moralism

The varieties of moralism flowing from the corruption of the two approaches always subvert honest political dialogue and responsible behavior, but at the present point in American history *soft moralism* of the sentimental idealists is a greater threat than *hard moralism* of the power realists. The views of the hard cynics—the extreme Machiavellis and gung-ho imperialists—find little hospitality in the university, the church, the mass press, or in the public generally. Few Americans call for the reconquest of the Philippines or the military "liberation" of Cuba or Eastern Europe. The small voice of the hard moralists is barely audible. In sharp contrast, the soft moralism of the rational idealists has had increasing appeal because many Americans are wearied by the burdens of power—the cost of nuclear deterrence and the perplexities of helping to keep the peace in distant places. Senator George McGovern in significant respects is a soft moralist, though his more extreme views have been chastened by his attempt during the 1972 presidential campaign to develop a broad base of support among the American people.

Today, the rational idealistic approach—in its religious and secular versions—and the various corruptions of this stance find wide acceptance among certain articulate leaders in the church and university, and are actively promoted by a segment of the mass media. Given the high level of moral turbulence and uncertainty, it is important to take critical note of this more pervasive manifestation of American moralism, acknowledging that some of its attributes are also similar to those of hard moralism.

Moralism, soft or hard, tends toward a single-factor approach to political problems, while mainstream Western morality emphasizes multiple causation, multiple ends, and multiple responsibilities. Many Americans have demanded peace (often simplistically defined as the absence of war) with insufficient regard for the other two great social ends, justice and freedom. Some have urged the United States to withdraw immediately and totally from Vietnam or to stop building nuclear arms without weighing the probable impact of their advice on the prospects for justice in Southeast Asia, freedom in Western Europe, or global stability. Others have insisted that U.S. involvement in the Third World has thwarted the march toward justice. If one of the valued goals—peace, justice, or freedom—becomes the supreme political end, the other two are bound to suffer. Peace (or order) without justice and freedom is tyranny. Justice without freedom is another form of tyranny.

The statesman has a mandate to use the resources at his command to maintain a tolerable balance among the competing claims of order, justice, and freedom, though in grave crises he may be compelled to sacrifice one temporarily to save the other two. Confronted with the infamy of Pearl Harbor, the American people sacrificed peace in the interests of security and were prepared to accept limitations on their freedom for the same end. Any political community must enjoy minimal security before it can develop the discipline of justice and the safeguards of freedom.

Preoccupation with a particular value, such as "the right of self-determination" (one expression of freedom), can have dire consequences. A single-minded emphasis on self-determination insured the Balkanization of Eastern Europe after World War I. In the 1960s, when the Katanga and Biafra lobbies marched under the same banner, the effect was to prolong conflict and suffering in the abortive secessionist attempts in the Congo and Nigeria. The pro-Biafra crusade, a dramatic example of the moral confusion of single-issue causes, was led by an improbable conglomeration of the New Left and Old Right, humanitarians and hirelings, churchmen and secularists, isolationists and interventionists.

The Sovereign State

The soft moralistic view tends to distrust the state, especially its coercive power, while Western ethical thought affirms the necessity of the state and insists on the responsible use of its power. Absolute power may corrupt absolutely, as Lord Acton asserted, but less-than-absolute power may or may not corrupt those who exercise it. There is little evidence that Lincoln, Churchill, or Truman were corrupted by power; they may even have been ennobled by it. Hitler, Stalin, and Mao were doubtless corrupted before they gained power. Power is amoral. It can be enlisted to liberate or enslave, to guarantee security or take it away. There is a vast difference between the Germany of Adolf Hitler and the Germany of Willy Brandt.

A state government must possess a monopoly on the legitimate use of violence within its domain. As the sovereign authority over a given territory—whether city, country, or empire—the government is the ultimate agency for resolving internal conflicts of power and interest. Were it not for the state, St. Augustine said, men would devour one another as fishes. Martin Luther asserted that the central task of the state was to protect the innocent by restraining evildoers. Of the modern democratic state, Reinhold Niebuhr wrote: "Man's capacity for justice makes democracy possible; but man's inclination to injustice makes democracy necessary." The problem is not to eliminate the state, the professed goal of Marxists and anarchists alike, but to make political power accountable to its citizens by a system that permits them peaceably to give or withhold consent and if necessary to throw the rascals out. If a government becomes tyrannical and all peaceful means for redressing grievances have been exhausted, the people, said Lincoln, have the right to rebel by violent means. The acceptance of Lincoln's view on the right of revolution does not negate the essential character of the responsible state. It is the fundamental agency for "insuring domestic tranquillity [sic], providing for the common defense, promoting the general welfare, and securing the blessings of liberty." In serving these central social objectives there is no substitute for the state, the sovereign political community. In a democratic and pluralistic society, however, other agencies, such as the university, the church, and economic organizations, have a positive role to play.

American Military Power

Soft moralism is highly critical of the exercise of American military power, except in self-defense, and even this is often narrowly defined. America has been criticized for throwing its weight around, and even for repressive policies toward the Third World, though solid evidence is seldom adduced to buttress these charges. On the other hand, a few hard zealots have called for a stronger exercise of power to impose an American order in one part of the world or another. Classical moralists reject both the arbitrary abstention from power and its unrestrained use, and insist that the United States has a responsibility for international peace and order commensurate with its capacity to affect external events. Our military power—as a deterrent, a threat, or an active force— should be limited to dealing with real and present dangers to world peace. A workable international order can only rest on a propitious balance of forces with each of the two superpowers inescapably playing a vital role. U.S. military might, including its nuclear arsenal, is an essential factor in preventing a shift in the balance of forces that could lead to war or the capitulation of friendly states to nuclear blackmail.

The international security system led by the United States—involving NATO, other mutual defense arrangements and military assistance—has gone a long way toward protecting the weak against the ambitions of the strong. What would have been the fate of Western Europe, Greece, Turkey, Iran, Thailand, Taiwan, South Korea, and Japan if the United States had not extended its protection? Since the balance sheet on Southeast Asia is not yet completed, it is not certain that U.S. involvement has set back the long-range prospects for stability, order, and freedom. American security assistance to some fifty Third World states in the past two decades has helped to maintain in many of them the minimal stability essential to constructive political and economic development.

To affirm an indispensable American burden for reinforcing peaceful change is not to define the specific disciplines of that role. How, when, and under what circumstances Washington should threaten or use how much coercion poses a perplexing political and moral question. It can be resolved only by statesmen who understand both the limits and possibilities of American power in situations where the United States has little control and an uncertain moral mandate. Because of these complexities and uncertainty about its own responsibilities, the United States has on occasion used too little or too much power or exercised it too early or too late. The Bay of Pigs comes to mind.

Intervention and Reform

Some soft American moralists actively call for interventionist foreign policies designed to reshape the internal customs and institutions of other states. At the same time, they often degrade or even deprecate the primary security role of foreign policy. This strange combination of reform-intervention and security-isolation turns foreign policy on its head. In the classical view, the first task of domestic policy is order and justice. The reform interventionists, soft or hard, blur the salient distinction between what can and ought to be done by a government for its own people, and what can and ought to be done in the vast external realm over which it has no legal jurisdiction and where its moral and political mandate is severely limited. The insistence that the U.S. government employ extraordinary and sometimes coercive means to reshape the internal political, economic or social structures in other sovereign communities is morally arrogant; it flies in the face of the most basic international law which, in the words of the UN Charter, prohibits intervention "in matters which are essentially within the domestic jurisdiction of any state."

Western morality respects the right of each political community to develop in its own way at its own pace, as long as it does not impinge coercively on other political communities. President Nixon's words in Rumania in 1969 were a refreshing restatement of this principle: "We seek normal relations with all countries, regardless of their domestic systems"; each state has the right to "preserve its national institutions." His trip to China underscored his words. Ignoring this self-constraint, moralistic voices keep urging the government to withhold security or economic aid in order to force domestic changes within Brazil, Greece, and other friendly states whose structure or policies do not accord with the critic's preferences.

This peculiar American penchant to export our virtue reached a highwater mark, at least in rhetoric, under President Kennedy and found belated legislative sanction in 1966 in Title IX of the Foreign Assistance Act. This act declared that all U.S. economic aid programs should encourage the development of "democratic private and local governmental institutions" in the recipient countries by using their "intellectual resources" to stimulate "economic and social progress" and by supporting "civic education and training skills required for effective participation in governmental and political processes essential to self-government." Still, this intrusive sally into other people's affairs, however naive or wrongheaded, does not compare to the breathtaking sweep or moral pretension of the Communist Manifesto with its strident call to the workers of the world (read self-appointed elect) to redeem societies everywhere without regard to state frontiers. Arrogance is the chief sin. Civilized human beings, observed Leopold Tyrmand, should "agree not to burden each other" with their "excessive humanity."

Viewing U.S. foreign policy as an instrument for reform rather than of stability is not only arrogant; it also overlooks the severely limited capacity of any external agency to influence and reshape alien cultures. Any government has the right to request American or Soviet technical assistance. By the same token, Washington and Moscow have the right to accept or turn down the request. The provision of economic or military aid that serves the interests of both parties presents few problems. It is wrong, however, for the donor government to give, withhold, or modify aid to force significant domestic changes unacceptable to the recipient regime and unrelated to the efficient use of the assistance.

The crusading impulse to reform should be clearly distinguished from the humanitarian motive that has prompted the U.S. government over the years to do more for the foreign victims of famine, earthquake, and war than any other government in history. Earthquake relief is not designed to restructure institutions, overthrow regimes, or promote "free elections."

The Weak and the Powerful

Soft moralism tends to associate virtue with weakness, just as it associates vice with power. Western morality affirms the fundamental worth of the poor and the weak and recognizes that they are less able to defend their rights than the rich and powerful. Further, under the rubric of noblesse oblige, men privileged by wealth or station are duty-bound to protect and assist the lowly. But this does not automatically endow the weak with innocence or virtue, whether they are deprived by nature, sloth, exploitation, or other circumstances.

The behavior of all states, great and small, must be judged by the same moral yardstick, recognizing that the degree of responsibility is commensurate with the capacity to act. "He who has much given to him will have much required of him." Yet, there is a widespread tendency among moralistic Americans to regard the fledgling new states with a kind of perverse paternalism that excuses childish, demanding and otherwise irresponsible behavior, such as that of the delegates who applauded the expulsion of Taiwan from the UN in 1971 or those who charged Washington and Brussels with "deliberate genocide" and "massive cannibalism" for rescuing more than 2,000 innocent foreign hostages of nineteen nationalities in the Congo in 1964.

Neither the weak nor the strong are immune from error or corruption. The celebrated and much confessed "arrogance of power" should not blind us to the arrogance of weakness, which may express itself in simple claims of virtue, insistence on unjustified "reparations," or demands for minority control, all calculated to exploit a pervasive sense of guilt in the American character. As Churchill pointed out, we Anglo-Saxons tend to feel guilty because we possess power. Prime Minister Nehru and other Third World spokesmen often assumed an air of moral superiority, insisting that they were uncorrupted by power and therefore possessed an innocence and humanity denied the leaders of the powerful, and hence guilty, states. In a UN speech in 1960, Premier Saeb Salaam of

Lebanon said: "We, the small, uncommitted nations, can perhaps take a more objective view of the world situation. We can judge international issues with comparatively greater detachment and impartiality; in a sense, the small uncommitted nations can be said to represent the unbiased conscience of humanity."

Recent official Swedish statements reflect this moralistic tendency. Though espousing neutrality, Swedish officials have been quick to condemn the behavior of the big powers, particularly the United States, and to take "moral" stands on a variety of international issues. Stockholm has supported Hanoi and the Viet Cong against America and has given moral and material aid to the Communist-assisted guerrilla fighters seeking to overthrow Western-oriented regimes in southern Africa. It is morally easy for politicians or religious leaders to cheer or condemn from the sidelines when they have no responsibility and are unwilling to become committed. With studied hyperbole John P. Roche makes the point: "Power corrupts. And the absence of power corrupts absolutely."

Preoccupation with the Present

The prevailing moralistic approach tends to be preoccupied with the present, neglectful of the past, and nonchalant about the future. Impatient with imperfection, the new romantics indulge in what Elton Trueblood has called the "sin of contemporaneity." It may be argued that enchantment with the chronological now represents a positive contribution drawn from the existential emphasis on the present tense imperative, but evidence suggests it is usually an escape from the eternal now that binds the past and future in an endless chain of responsibility. Man is a creature of history, a product of the past, an actor in the present, and an influence for the future. To reject the past, as so many radicals do, is to reject the fabric of human continuity that gives moral meaning to the present.

Many students today show no interest in the developments that had the most dramatic impact on the political outlook of their parents. If events like Pearl Harbor, the Korean War, and the Budapest uprising are not known or have no common meaning, how can the two generations communicate? The understanding of recent history is vital, even if earlier eras must be shortchanged. This suggests the advisability of teaching history backward, starting with today's newspaper and covering the past decade before moving to the more distant past.

Moral and Political Calculation

In their disdain for history, ancient and recent, and their insistence on achieving quick solutions, many romantic idealists sell the future short by neglecting the disciplines of moral and political calculation. The principal practical test of any political decision is not the intention of the actor or the means he uses, but its immediate and long-range consequences.

Moral choice demands calculation—an assessment of multiple causes, multiple alternatives, and multiple consequences. Many critics of U.S. defense policy condemned the announced underground nuclear test that was carried out in Alaska in November 1971.

Some said it would trigger a devastating earthquake or tidal wave or otherwise damage the natural environment. Other critics insisted that the test was a giant step in accelerating the strategic arms race. After careful calculation, President Nixon decided to go ahead, convinced that the natural risks had been exaggerated and that the probable consequences were on balance good for U.S. security and world peace. Following the test there was no indication of a radioactive leak and the damage to the environment appeared to be slight. It did demonstrate the feasibility of the Spartan warhead, an essential component in any viable ABM system designed to protect America's land-based Minuteman missiles, which in turn are designed to deter a nuclear attack against this country. Further, the test may well have strengthened the U.S. position at the Strategic Arms Limitation Talks with the Soviets, which produced agreements in May 1972 on nuclear weapons. These and many other factors were considered in the calculus preceding the president's decision. Critics do not bear the burden of decision, but are they not obligated to consider all the major issues at stake before they pronounce final moral judgment?

The Devil-Theory

Some of the more extreme American moralists, baffled by complexity and impatient with the untidy state of the world, sometimes adopt what amounts to a devil-theory of politics. They attempt to identify the central flaw, the fatal error, the demonic force underlying our present plight.

The earlier rational idealists discovered a series of plausible devils that, separately or in combination, were held responsible for war, injustice, poverty, and many other afflictions of mankind. Each was fatally vulnerable to its rational and righteous counterpart. The prince of darkness, capitalism, could be slain by socialism. The confusion of tongues, the cause of international misunderstanding and conflict, could be cured by education and Esperanto. Nationalism could be exorcised by internationalism and world government. The military and the "merchants of death" could be abolished by the renunciation of war. The idealists and their ideal solutions failed. The Wilsonians, it has been said, reached for utopia and gave us hell.

The targets of present-day devil-theorists bear a striking resemblance to those of earlier decades. Now it is the military-industrial complex, the establishment, the system, the corporate structure, technology, or greed. For many of the radical dissenters the chief demon is "decadent liberalism," a menacing Mephistopheles embracing all the vices of gradualism, reform, due process, and peaceful evolution—benign bourgeois beatitudes that blur the necessity to "destroy the system" and thus subvert revolutionary zeal. Some zealots prefer more personal devils, such as Lyndon Johnson, Dean Rusk, or Richard Nixon. By the same token, some have personal messiahs such as Mao, Ho, and Che.

The devil-theory approach lends itself to an apocalyptic interpretation of the political situation. The whole world is polarized and the golden mean, the vital center, and orderly change are thrown to the winds. The forces of good (read progressive or revolutionary) at home and abroad are arrayed against the forces of evil (read status quo or reactionary) and there is no compromise. The "establishment" will be crushed and "the people" will prevail. It is only a matter of time and dedication. Here one sees the rhetoric of the Maoists and Marxists being used loosely and without discipline by the soft romantics.

Limits of Moral Reasoning

Most American moralists have an inadequate understanding of the limits and possibilities of logic, rationality, and calculation. According to classical Western norms, moral reasoning is a possibility, indeed a necessity. Man is a reasoning creature. Within the limits of circumstance, he can plan, devise, calculate, though he can rarely control or determine events. Circumstances are too complex and intractable and human emotions too unpredictable to come up with full solutions. Precise prediction is impossible and risk is never absent.

To acknowledge the serious limits of rational calculation is not to deprecate reason, or the necessity to marshal relevant facts, or the desirability of projecting the probable consequences of competing lines of action. Politics is more an art than a science, but the scientific discipline of weighing evidence is a compelling moral obligation. To ignore evidence, to disdain logic, or to overlook empirical data is to retreat into blind emotion which spawns illusions. If the romantics fail to discipline their desires with data and persist in their illusions, they become almost indistinguishable from cynics or nihilistic troublemakers.

Just as the contemporary sentimentalists expect too little from reason, the earlier rational idealists expected too much. Reason provides the capacity to behave responsibly. Reason is not an independent human agency that transcends the self, but rather a servant of the self with all its pride and prejudice. A morally sensitive statesman can enlist reason in the pursuit of wise and prudent policies. A morally corrupt politician can likewise enlist reason for his ignoble ends. The old utopians believed that reason and goodwill, unaided by power, would transform politics, but the new romantics seem to despair of reason altogether.

Western morality, in sum, affirms the dignity of man and the necessity for the state. It is precisely because man is finite and inclined to pursue his selfish desires at the expense of his neighbor that structures of order and justice are needed. The responsible state alone is capable of insuring that basic human rights will not be trampled underfoot.

The great majority of American people, by temperament and their respect for law, are committed to a domestic order rooted in a prudent balance of justice and freedom, and to an international order that is safe for diversity and peaceful change. Movement toward these political goals at home and abroad requires a working combination of the "impossible ideal" and an appreciation of political limitations. A man's aim should exceed his grasp, but not by too much. Our times call for idealism without illusion and realism without despair.

2–2

"U.S. Policy in Vietnam: A Statement"

Kenneth W. Thompson[1]

United States policy in Vietnam has been increasingly questioned both in the Congress and by the public at large. The reason for this mounting criticism and massing of informed opinion is that we have not turned back the "aggression" from the North despite the fact that we have stepped up the war. Many men of insight doubt the wisdom of our policy.

Much of what we are doing in Vietnam has the opposite effect of what is intended— we may be destroying our chance to cooperate with the Soviet Union for peace in Asia, and we are likely to drive the North Vietnamese into the hands of the Chinese. Furthermore, by continuous bombing north of the 17th parallel we are risking a war between major powers that no one wants. In no case can we sanction the bombing of population centers in North Vietnam.

Those who are responsible for U.S. policy bear the unenviable burden of having to determine the next steps that may bring us into another and more tolerable situation, one that will enable both parts of Vietnam to develop resistance to the encroachment of China, that will provide some protection for the supporters of the various regimes in Saigon against reprisals from the Vietcong. Nevertheless, citizens who do not have the Government's information about details of the present political or military or diplomatic situation are still entitled to challenge what seem to be the presuppositions that underlie the present policy.

The most basic presupposition seems to be that we are opposing aggression in Southeast Asia because of what happened when we failed to stand up to aggression at Munich. But this analogy is not a good one. There are not only significant differences between National Socialism and communism but also between Europe and Asia.

Communism is capable of change and of evolution in a favorable direction. We can live with it as it develops in different ways from country to country. National Socialism,

---

1. This statement, written by Kenneth W. Thompson, was published in *Christianity and Crisis* on June 14, 1965 and signed by the Editorial Board, including Reinhold Niebuhr, Richard T. Baker, M. Searle Bates, John C. Bennett, Wald Beach, Robert McAffee Brown, Wayne H. Cowan, Harvey Cox, Tom F. Driver, F. Ernest Johnson, James Kuhn, Robert W. Lynn, Stephen C. Rose, Robert L. Shinn, Frances S. Sith, and Robert W. Spike.

on the other hand, was primarily a military threat, which is only secondarily the case with communism (though we recognize that the mere existence of military power is always a form of pressure that supports diplomatic and conspiratorial initiatives). Communism can be resisted only when nations can find constructive political and social alternatives. The President's recent speeches indicated awareness that Vietnam represents more than a military problem.

In Europe we were able to ward off the threat of Soviet communism because each of the Western European nations had in its own way developed political and economic institutions that were genuine and viable alternatives to communism and that rendered it immune against subversion. This is obviously not true of several nations in East and Southeast Asia. There our major task is to support every country that has some national substance and a will to be independent. They need our help to develop institutions that will enable them to solve their basic problems.

China's military and political influence is dominant and will remain so. Attempts to limit it will ultimately be useless unless we are able at the same time to develop alternatives to communism. This constructive effort seems now to be lost in the military maneuvers.

Nor is our policy gaining allies for us. On the contrary, Asians think as Asians, and the action that we take against one is felt to be an attack upon all. The Japanese, for instance, are for the first time since 1945 seriously questioning U.S. actions. Throughout the cold war era Japan was a steady ally against Russia; now we see indications of a shift away from the U.S.

We also believe that our policy needs to reflect awareness that the disorder in South Vietnam is in part an internal conflict and cannot be overcome merely by action taken from outside. The US must also clarify the apparent conflict between its offer of unconditional negotiations and its insistence on an independent South Vietnam as the outcome of negotiations. We favor, furthermore, direct negotiations between the hostile parties, including the National Liberation Front.

Finally, although we do not claim that these political judgments are the only ones compatible with Christian faith and ethic, we are guided by our faith and ethic to seek two things. The first is the prevention of general war and the holding down of violence at all stages. The other is relationships with the people of China, relationships that may lead to some forms of reconciliation. We should not expect too much, but we hope for some transcending of the absolute hostility on both sides.

2–3

"We Protest the National Policy in Vietnam"

Kenneth W. Thompson[1]

"The hardest strokes of heaven fall in history upon those who imagine that they can control things in a sovereign manner, as though they were kings of the earth, playing Providence not only for themselves but for the far future—reaching out into the future with the wrong kind of farsightedness, and gambling on a lot of risky calculations in which there must never be a single mistake."[2]—*Herbert Butterfield*

THE UNITED STATES INVOLVEMENT in Southeast Asia has become a case study in Herbert Butterfield's thesis. In the last decade *Christianity and Crisis* has frequently appealed for a change in American policies in Asia. Now we must register our emphatic protest against the policies and acts that are leading to increasingly portentous war.

Nobody planned this war. Neither brute malice nor innocent miscalculation brought it about. It is the result of a series of fateful decisions in which human fallibility, accentuated by moral insensitivity and pretension, turned a brush-fire war into a major conflict. In the process the nature of the initial U.S. commitments has changed beyond recognition.

Beneath all the immediate perplexities is the deep confusion in our Government's aims. Sometimes the stated policy is to prevent any gains for communism. At other times it is to give the people of Vietnam their free choice of a government—and that, everybody knows, may be a Communist government. Talk of unconditional readiness to negotiate is mixed with adamant unwillingness to concede anything. These contradictions may not be confusing the enemy, but they are certainly confusing the American public and our allies.

We would like to assume the best, although much that the Administration does make this difficult. Let us acknowledge that Washington has engaged in a dramatic peace offensive that has drawn scornful rebuffs. Let us grant that the national leaders have told

---

1. This editorial by Kenneth W. Thompson was published in *Christianity and Crisis* on March 7, 1966 and was signed by the Editorial Board, which included John C. Bennett, Richard T. Baker, M. Searle Bates, Waldo Beach, Robert McAfee Brown, Wayne H. Cowan, Harvey Cox, Tom Driver, Johannes C. Hoekendijk, James Kuhn, Robert W. Lynn, John D. Maguire, Stephen C. Rose, Roger L. Shinn, Frances S. Smith, and Robert W. Spike.

2. Butterfield, *Christianity and History,* 104.

the world and particularly the UN that we want a solution based on the Geneva accords of 1954; a solution that will offer self-determination to the people of Vietnam. Let us point out that we see slender clues of willingness to modify the refusals, previously adamant, to give the Vietcong a place in negotiations.

Even if this best possible case is made, the U.S. still finds itself engaged in a war that is destructive to the people whom we claim to be helping, to the peace of the world and to our best interests.

- The burning of villages, the killing and maiming of civilians, area bombing and the use of napalm and chemical destruction of crops inflict immediate human suffering that makes incredible the official promises of pacification and remote benefits. Repeatedly such tactics alienate and harm the very people we purport to save.

- The US is concentrating on one dubious battleground the brainpower and resources needed for meeting a world that bristles with unsolved problems. Constructive acts in Latin America, Africa and the Middle East get little attention because of the hypnotic preoccupation with East Asia.

- Contrary to the evidence of history and the wisdom learned in Europe, our leaders still treat Asian communism as a single enemy. Instead of promoting diversity within it, their acts drive Ho Chi Minh to greater dependence on China (despite the traditional feelings of his people). Thus American policy creates the monolithic Communist unity that it fears.

- The war in Asia aggravates irritations between the U.S. and the Soviet Union at a time when the two share more common purposes than in any period since World War II.

- Our nation is becoming increasingly lonely in the world, losing or embarrassing European, African, and Asian allies, and building a legacy of hatred and resentment for "neo-colonialism."

- The Government is neglecting or deferring its attacks upon urgent needs of American society, needs that the President has heretofore met with impressive resourcefulness.

- By continuing to isolate China from the world of nations, U.S. policy reinforces the Chinese paranoia and isolation that a wiser policy would seek to overcome. A look at a map of American bases near China makes obvious some reasons for Chinese fear and distrust.

- Our society is letting the specific struggle in Vietnam blind us to the nature of the world revolution, which calls for far greater understanding and appreciation than we have yet shown.

Thus we find the American nation deeply committed to a self-defeating course of action. Every intensification of the war makes the ultimate resolution more difficult.

We do not pretend that there are ideal solutions. Rather than look for painless ways out, we need to compare various possibilities with the present grim realities. For example:

- We are told that American prestige is at stake and that we cannot settle for anything less than victory. We answer that our country has shown in Korea that a strong people can afford to value peace above victory. We believe that a stubborn vanity, provoking continued hostility, is more damaging to prestige than is a wisdom that seeks peace.

- We are told that only our military power can protect our allies from vengeance at the hands of their enemies. We do not deny that all factions in Vietnam have a capacity for vengeance. Any settlement should make all possible provision for the protection of people. But we also know that our present policies inflict great cruelties on our friends as well as our enemies.

- We are told that any concession will start dominoes falling throughout Asia. We do not accept this simplistic theory, especially when, as in Vietnam, the US must both create and support the domino. (At the same time, we endorse effects to strengthen the viable governments and economics that afford alternatives to communism.) But we readily grant that a settlement in Vietnam will have consequences elsewhere. These must be compared with the evidence effects of the present perilous course.

Our Government has sufficient political, military and diplomatic ingenuity to work through these very real difficulties. What is lacking so far is the willingness to look at realities and the moral imagination to seek better methods than the present contradictory mixture of peaceful rhetoric and stubborn policy. If the President and the Secretary of State find the will and insight, they can devise the precise maneuvers that hold most hope.

Such maneuvers must show "a decent respect to the opinions of mankind"—to use a phrase from a more glorious time in our national history. They must involve a greater concern for the well-being of people than for ideological abstractions. They must include some sense of proportion in relating means to ends.

The shape of such a settlement may include a convening of the Geneva powers under the persuasion of the United Nations. More likely will be a series of steps of de-escalation, disengagement, multilateral diplomatic efforts and economic reconstruction. Alternatives can be found to the present bitter impasse, but only if policy-makers will give up the dogmatic illusions that lead to a fixation on rigid ends regardless of the costs.

Scripture warns that "where there is no vision the people perish." The failure of vision in our time is a blindness to realities no less than to ideals. The threat of this moment is a preoccupation with the enemy that destroys our society's power to understand itself or its foes. In such a time the greatest service to the society comes from those voices—in church, politics and press—that risk the displeasure of the powers that be in order to challenge dogmatisms that imperil ourselves and our world. To these voices we again add our own.

2–4

"Stopping the Bombing: Promise and Peril"

KENNETH W. THOMPSON

FOREIGN POLICY DECISIONS NEARLY always involve on-balance judgments that in moments of great emotion and tension require exacting moral and political discrimination. The statesman, in particular, must weigh the importance of military requirements, diplomatic possibilities, and moral and political considerations. He must consider questions of fact and national capacity, public support and prospects of success. It would seem that in judging the importance of bombing North Vietnam we have given due consideration to military necessity without always paying as much heed to diplomatic, moral and political factors. The time has come when these elements in our overall policy must be reevaluated and a new balance struck if prospects for opening up more hopeful diplomatic channels are to be tested fully.

The time may be rapidly approaching, as a . . . *Life* magazine statement argued, when stopping the bombing over North Vietnam is the wisest course of action. The choice to limit drastically the use of military options is, for any Chief Executive, an excruciatingly difficult one. Where lives of American soldiers may be still further endangered, the decision to restrict operation is fraught with serious implications. Moreover, the debate over the results of the bombing is not easily resolved between those who claim the adversary has been in no way deterred and those who point to the limitations placed on the North in its conduct of the war.

The decision to stop the bombing ultimately rests on profound moral and political issues that can no longer be ignored. North Vietnam through intermediaries, who, it must be said, appear somewhat vague on the terms of their mandate, has thrown down the gauntlet on peace: "Stop the bombing . . . and then we will talk." Pressures at home and anxieties abroad run sufficiently deep that this challenge cannot any longer be ignored.

Any Administration, and especially an embattled one, must test the prospects of peace, however skeptical it may be of the results. Presumably, it would retain limited power of interdiction, perhaps in the southern layer of North Vietnam's provinces—if the security of troops can be protected only in this way. The point is that the credibility of the other side must be tested. The price of not doing so will be further loss of understanding and support beyond the point that a representative government and a world leader cannot ignore.

More serious than any of these risks is the grave danger that if the pause were to fail, an Administration that has conducted a limited war, despite the hawks and doves, might lose control to hawks once and for all. Pressure for escalation might then be irresistible.

The prospects for the policy we propose are two-fold: it will either make gradual progress in bringing negotiations to the table and in taking a first step toward peaceful settlement, or, in the face of a failure, the pressure for all-out war may mount and carry us all toward a far more perilous course.

The first development could lead to the broadening of the peace constituency to include a wide spectrum from peace demonstrators to those who would base peace on power and the use of limited war. This might be the most hopeful event since the beginning of the war. Failing that, the situation could deteriorate, the rationale for drastic measures come into its own, and a far more dangerous East-West confrontation emerge. Even those of us who call for stopping the bombing must face up to the broad range of possible consequences.

2–5

"Tides and Traumas"

Kenneth W. Thompson[1]

For most of us, reviewing the 1960s, Viet Nam emerges as the source of greatest national trauma. It divided the generations, split political parties and turned family against family. It is already the longest in our history and the present Paris peace negotiations, which began May 10, 1968, have passed their 100th session with little progress and no end in sight. Yet when trauma occurs, deep-running tides in human affairs underlie the trauma. In our haste to deal with symptoms we run the risk of overlooking root causes.

No reader of this journal need be reminded that the United States as the leader of Western civilization confronted two great challenges, National Socialism and world-wide Communism. The nation that for 40 years had remained aloof from international conflicts became everywhere involved. Stung by the political consequences of its hasty withdrawal from the heart of Europe following World War II, the U.S. set out to redeem its innocence. Having met and defeated the mightiest military force in history, it took on some of its trappings and learned too well the lessons of military preparedness and international involvement.

By 1970 mounting defense budgets exceeded $70 billion; military assistance to other nations is variously estimated at $29 billion (the Defense Department) or $4.8 billion (Senator Proxmire). The tides of history reflect themselves in President Eisenhower's warning of the dangers of a military-industrial complex; in a headline, "Decision Power Ebbing at the State Department," in a recent *New York Times* series on American foreign policy; and in continuing reports of military judgments overriding political and diplomatic concerns in both the Kennedy-Johnson and the Nixon Administrations. Add to this reports of massive computerized data files on dissenters as well as the many more overt forms of oppression, and the picture is complete. A nation long plagued in international crises by its unpreparedness and isolationism seems threatened today by opposite trends; yet the debate over Viet Nam scarcely touches this fundamental issue.

More troubling still is the fact that popular reactions to this national trend, perhaps because they have been equally unsettling in their form and character, have evoked almost no significant response and have had little influence on the shape of policy.

1. Kenneth W. Thompson's essay, "Tides and Traumas," was published in *Christianity and Crisis* on April 5, 1971.

The remedy proposed for too many international commitments is no commitments; the substitute for too much military expenditure is unilateral disarmament; the answer to international conflicts around the globe is to proclaim they are nobody's business except the attacked and the attacker.

To say this so flatly and unequivocally is to ignore the lessons of modern history that increasingly we live in a tightly interdependent world and that from the Spanish Civil War to the present, external forces are as often a part of local conflicts as those who control or seek control of local territory, its people and resources. It is as utopian to pretend that a superpower can leave the rest of the world to others as it is to imagine that it can police the world.

This grievous problem is aggravated by the two contending philosophies that have dominated the great debate on the problem. The one is a simple-minded militarism that locates national security exclusively in overwhelming military superiority. The other arises from a curious inversion of the liberal strategies of the sixties, translating nonviolence into an international strategy and justifying varying forms and degrees of violence as national strategies. Yet only when nonviolence is practiced within free and open societies with established constitutional safeguards and channels for minorities to become majorities does it enjoy a fair chance.

It is an accident of history that those who had achieved some modicum of success in civil rights and social change domestically were thrown abruptly, thanks to Viet Nam, into the breach to challenge the excesses of a military approach to foreign policy. The complaints against military preoccupation are as valid as those against racism, but the context is more intractable to sudden change.

Could it be that the pacifist champions of nonviolence, bruised and battered by largely futile efforts to effect change in two national administrations, have reentered the domestic arena with new creeds and doctrines shaped by their international experience? Is it possible that some of them imported violence as an instrument of change from the realm in which it has been most ineradicable to the sphere in which it has proved most successful only exceptionally (as in the American Civil War and the labor wars of the first part of the 20th century)? Here the dedication and idealism of the radical and liberal young, which many see as America's best hope today, was temporarily merged with a curiously unrealistic stress on force and violence.

They are right in saying that many of the nation's problems stem from greed, selfishness and the corruption of power. In this criticism they touch a deep-running taproot of residual American idealism. Yet the route that is almost certainly calculated to separate them from the rich national legacy of institutional and legislative change is the route of violence. Two young Englishmen, Stephen Milligan and Anthony Speaight, surveying American intolerance in a *New York Times* article, wrote: "Extreme radicals told us that violence will lead to repression, which in turn will radicalize more and more people. Oh that they would study history! It was precisely such an attitude which prevailed among left-wing revolutionaries in prewar Germany. People forget how often repression is successful. All it can produce is more repression."

What is needed instead is patience, but patience coupled with persistence. The lesson of open societies is that yesterday's heresies have a way of becoming tomorrow's orthodoxies, provoking in turn new heresies. What gives this lesson such urgency today is that there is need in every realm for heretics who in this turbulent and troubled world seek change when survival demands it. Nationally and internationally, change must occur in context, and the credibility of reformers will be great only as they perceive this. Even in trauma, we should look for the tides of history and seek to control and shape them so as not to be ruled by them.

2–6

"Justice in War"

Paul Ramsey

Question: How do porcupines make love?

Answer: Carefully!

THIS IS A PARABLE of the nations in a multinational world. They can't get along with and they can't get along without one another. They make love and reach settlements, or they make war when they cannot reach or postpone settlements—all, carefully!

There is nothing more like a pacifist than a believer in massive deterrence: both think it possible to banish the use of force from human history before banishing the porcupine nation-states from off this planet. To them may be added what Walter Lippman called the "war *whoop*" party in this country, which thinks we won't ever need to use nuclear weapons if only we say loudly enough that we are going to. So do we as a people—whether by confidence in moral suasion and omnicompetence of negotiation or by confidence in our deterrence technology or by confidence in our superior bluffing ability—avoid facing up to the moral economy governing an actual use of the weapons we possess. With peace and the nation-state system as our premises, we have designed a war to end all war: God may let us have it.

Since, however, the porcupine-nations are unlikely soon to be banished, since they are armed with massive nuclear weapons, and since somewhere, sometime, a nation is likely to find itself so vitally challenged that it will believe that even in the atomic era war can be an instrument of its justice, we are today forced to reexamine an ancient set of teachings which many people thought was out of date. This is the doctrine of the "just war," or the morality governing a resort to arms which is only an elaboration of the morality governing the use of power generally.

One of the "tests'" in this body of teachings about the morality of warfare is the principle of "proportionate grave reason," or the justification of one good or evil effect only by weighing the greater good or lesser evil of the other effects let loose in the world. This is a test in terms of consequences, and this criterion has been the focus of significant developments in recent years both in Christian analysis, Protestant and Roman Catholic, and in the communist theory of "just war."

In this chapter, however, I want to deal with the origin and the meaning of another criterion for the morality of war's conduct. It is a more intrinsic one, having to do with the justice or injustice of an act of war, considered apart from its consequences. In the course of tracing its origin, the systematic meaning of "just conduct" in war will be exhibited. This is the distinction between legitimate and illegitimate military actions. This distinction cuts across all distinctions among weapons systems and applies to them all, even though it is nuclear weapons that have decisively raised the question whether there are just and unjust acts of war by raising the question whether these particular weapons can possibly be used in a just manner. To learn the meaning of "justice in war" (and its origin out of love-informed reason) will be to learn what it means to say, in connection with military policy, that the end does not justify the means and that it can never be right to do wrong for the sake of some real or supposed good.

The Western theory of the just war originated, not primarily from considerations of abstract or "natural" justice, but from the interior of the ethics of Christian love, or what John XXIII termed "social charity." It was a work of charity for the Good Samaritan to give help to the man who fell among thieves. But one step more, it may have been a work of charity for the innkeeper to hold himself ready to receive beaten and wounded men, and for him to have conducted his business so that he was solvent enough to extend credit to the Good Samaritan. By another step it would have been a work of charity, and not of justice alone, to maintain and serve in a police patrol on the Jericho road to prevent such things from happening. By yet another step, it might well be a work of charity to resist, by force of arms, any external aggression against the social order that maintains the police patrol along the road to Jericho. This means that, where the enforcement of an ordered community is not effectively present, it may be a work of justice and a work of social charity to resort to other available and effective means of resisting injustice: what do you think Jesus would have made the Samaritan do if he had come upon the scene while the robbers were still at their fell work?

Now, I am aware that this is no proper way to interpret a parable of Jesus. Yet, these several ways of retelling the parable of the Good Samaritan quickly exhibit something that is generally true about the teachings of Jesus—namely, that by deed and word he showed the individual the meaning of being perfectly ready to have the will of God reign and God's mercy shed abroad by his life and actions. These versions quickly exhibit how a social ethic emerged from Christian conscience formed by this revelation, and what the early Christians carried with them when they went out into the world to borrow, and subsequently to elevate and refine, Stoic concepts of natural justice.

While Jesus taught that a disciple in his own case should turn the other cheek, he did not enjoin that his disciples should lift up the face of another oppressed man for him to be struck again on his other cheek. It is no part of the work of charity to allow this to continue to happen. Instead, it is the work of love and mercy to deliver as many as possible of God's children from tyranny, and to protect from oppression, if one can, as many of those for whom Christ died as it may be possible to save. When choice must be made between the perpetrator of injustice and the many victims of it, the latter may and should be preferred—even if effectively to do so would require the use of armed force against some evil power.

This is what I mean by saying that the justice of sometimes resorting to armed conflict originated in the interior of the ethics of Christian love.

Thus Christian conscience shaped itself for effective action. It allowed even the enemy to be killed only because military personnel and targets stood objectively there at the point where intersect the needs and claims of many more of our fellow men. For their sakes, the bearer of hostile force may and should be repressed. Thus, participation in war (and before that, the use of any form of force or resistance) was justified as, in this world to date, an unavoidable necessity if we are not to omit to serve the needs of men in the only concrete way possible, and to maintain a just endurable order in which they may live.

There was another side to this coin. The justification of participation in conflict at the same time severely limited war's conduct. What justified also limited! Since it was for the sake of the innocent and helpless of earth that the Christian first thought himself obliged to make war against an enemy whose objective deeds had to be stopped, since only for their sakes does a Christian justify himself in resisting by any means even an enemy-neighbor, he could never proceed to kill equally innocent people as a means of getting at the enemy's forces. Thus was twin-born the justification of war and the limitation which surrounded noncombatants with moral immunity from direct attack. Thus was twin-born the distinction between combatant and noncombatant in all Christian reflection about the morality of warfare. This is the distinction between *legitimate* and *illegitimate* military objectives. The same considerations which justify killing the bearer of hostile force by the same stroke prohibits non-combatants from ever being directly attacked with deliberate intent.

This understanding of the moral economy in the just use of political violence contains, then, two elements: (1) a specific justification for sometimes killing another human being; and (2) severe and specific restrictions upon anyone who is under the hard necessity of doing so. Both are exhibited in the use of force proper to the domestic police power. It is never just for a policeman to forget the distinction between the bearer of hostile force who must be stopped and the "innocent" bystanders (no matter how mixed up they are). He may hit some innocent party accidentally, but it would never be right for him to "enlarge the target" and deliberately and directly kill any number in the crowd on Times Square as a means of preventing some criminal from injurious action. Nor do we allow the police the right to get a criminal's children into their power as hostages and threaten to kill them in order to "deter" him. Yet the source of the justification of such limited use of force is evidently to be found in "social charity." This is clear from the fact that a man, who in one situation could legitimately be killed if that were the only way to save other lives, would himself in another situation be saved at grave risk to the lives of the very same policemen—i.e., if that man alone is in need of rescue because he has gone off his rocker and is threatening to jump from the ledge of a building twenty stories up.

This is the moral economy which regulates the use of force within political communities, where it is both *morally* and *legally* binding. This same moral economy is morally if not legally binding upon the use of force between nations. It will become *both* legally and morally binding if ever there is world law and order abolishing the nation state system. War may *in fact* be more than an extension of politics in another form, but the *laws* or war are only an extension, where war is the only available means, of the rules governing any use of political power. We are not apt ever to "abolish war" if we keep on denying that there is a morality of war, which is only a concise summary of right and charitable reason in the simultaneous *justification* and the *limitation* of the use of power necessary to the political life of mankind.

To summarize the theory of just or civilized conduct in war as this was developed within Christendom: love for neighbors threatened by violence, by aggression, or tyranny, provided the grounds for admitting the legitimacy of the use of military force. Love for neighbors at the same time required that such force should be limited. The Christian is commanded to do anything a realistic love commands (and so sometimes he must fight). But this also prohibits him from doing anything for which such love can find no justification (and so he can never approve of unlimited attack upon any human life not closely cooperating in or directly engaged in the force that ought to be repelled).

This means that nuclear war against the civil centers of an enemy population, the A-bomb on Hiroshima, or obliteration bombing perpetrated by both sides in World War II were all alike immoral acts of war, and that Christians can support such actions only by dismissing the entire Western tradition of civilized warfare that was originally born in the interior of that supreme compassion which always seeks if possible to wound none whom by His wounds Christ died to save. This theory of just and severely limited conflict has guided action and served as the regulative norm for military conduct for nineteen centuries. If a man cannot irresponsibly forsake those who need to be saved from an oppressor, neither can he directly and indiscriminately attack innocent people in order to restrain that same oppressor. If to protect his own children he should resist an aggressor, that gives him no leave directly to intend and directly to do the death of the aggressor's children as a means of dissuading him from his evil deeds.

If the just war theory did not already exist, Christians would have to invent it. If in the fullness of God's time and the emptiness of ours, Christ came into our present world (instead of when he did), then would the just war theory still have to be produced. Then would Christian thought bring together the notions of justice lying around in the Renaissance and the Enlightenment (if you can imagine these periods without their Christian background), as St. Augustine and other great Christian thinkers brought together the notions of justice lying around in the Graeco-Roman world, galvanized them into action, elevated and firmed them up, illumined and sensitized the justices of men to produce severer restrictions upon the forms of human conflict which the Christian or any truly just man can ever believe justified. Had I the space I could derive the same moral restrictions upon the use of force from the ethical perspectives of the Old Testament. These would have been productive of a remarkably similar just war theory, had Judaism been the predominant influence in Western civilization.

I can only briefly indicate that this distinction between combatant and noncombatant never supposed that the latter were to be roped off like ladies at a medieval tournament. The fact of twilight, as Dr. Johnson said, does not mean you cannot tell day from night. So with noncombatant status, and the difference between discriminate and indiscriminate acts of war. Moreover, it was never supposed that noncombatants were immune from all damage but only from direct, intended attack. The range of indirect, unintended, collateral damage might be quite large. Moreover, closeness of civilian cooperation, in contrast to some degree of remoteness from the force used, was sufficient to bring the civilian under the category of "combatant." But these qualifications were never the same as "enlarging the target" to include the whole of civil society as a legitimate military objective, directly damaging whole peoples in order to get at their leaders and fighters. Translated into modern terminology, this means that just or limited warfare must be *forces*-counter-*forces* warfare, and that *people*-counter-*people* warfare is wholly unjust.

At stake in preserving this distinction is not only whether warfare can be kept barely civilized, but whether civilization can be kept from barbarism. Can civilization survive in the sense that we can continue in political and military affairs to act civilized, or must we accept total war on grounds that clearly indicate that we have already become totalitarian—by reducing everyone without discrimination and everyone to the whole extent of his being to a mere means of achieving political and military goals? Even if an enemy government says that is all its people are, a Christian or any truly just man cannot agree to this.

Now pacifism teaches people what massive deterrence is built on. It "teaches people to make no distinction between the shedding of innocent blood and the shedding of any human blood. And in this way pacifism has corrupted enormous numbers of people who will not act according to its tenets. They become convinced that a number of things are wicked which are not; hence, seeing no way of avoiding 'wickedness,' they set no limits to it."[1] That is to say, pacifism teaches people to believe that there is no significant moral difference, except in the ends sought, between murder and killing in war. It seems incredible to accept that anyone really seriously believes that soldiers are only "licensed murderers" and that murderers are only unlicensed soldiers. Yet, at the operational level where the thoughts of a multitude of human hearts shall today be revealed, this seems to be what it comes down to. The desperate attempt to maintain the current state of non-war by indiscriminately aiming weapons at people, and a fervent attempt to abolish war by declaring it in any shape to be a wickedness to which no moral limits can or should be applied, lie down peaceably together in the declaration by both parties that there is no moral economy that should or can govern the use of armed violence.

It has certainly to be admitted that all the wars of the past have been conducted more or less justly, more or less unjustly; but attacks on Civilian life have been peripheral even if often carried out. In former ages it simply took too much muscle to fight war unlimitedly. You will understand the point on which present-day politics squirms, and military strategy squirms, if you see that in the nuclear age the nations are trying to make unjust war the central war, and to base strategy on the deliberate aim of attacking cities. They will never succeed in basing politics or purposive military strategy on such an inherently irrational and immoral plan of way.

They will never succeed in making war "carefully" by such planned disregard for the moral economy governing the use of force as an extension of the moral economy governing any purposive use of political power. It seemed reasonable for President Kennedy to

---

1. Walter Stein, ed., *Nuclear Weapons and Christian Conscience*, 6.

say in his speech at Frankfurt, Germany, "The United States will risk its cities to defend yours because we need your freedom to protect ours."[2] This seems reasonable because the risks are still in the state of non-war. The *plus* in front of that policy statement is within a parenthesis preceded by a *minus* sign, as shall be revealed if we ever factor the equation. Then the pluses will all become minuses. For it cannot make sense for the President to say, "The United States is now, this moment, accepting the destruction of its cities in order to defend yours, which are also now being destroyed along with the Russian cities, because we need your freedom to protect ours." If one perseveres in thinking the thinkable (because it is the actual, present) state of non-war all the way through to an actual war conducted in the fashion apparently planned, he will have thought an unthinkable and a politically undoable action. He will have factored the massive deterrence—or retaliation—equation, and found that the pluses within the parenthesis all become minuses.

The traditional teaching about the conduct of war taught us that it is never right to intend or do wrong that good may come of it. Nuclear weapons have only added to this perennial truth a morally insignificant footnote: it can never do any good to intend or do wrong that good may come of it.[3]

---

2. *New York Times*, June 26, 1963.

3. Note: In chapter 11 of *The Just Wars*, "The Limits of Nuclear War," 248–58, I argue that deterrence sufficient to keep war limited and just need not rest on the intention to do murder. This is a significant correction of the treatment of the morality of deterrence in my book, *War and the Christian Conscience*. See chapter 2–8 in this book [i.e., *The Just War: Force and Political Responsibility*].

$$2-7$$

"The Limits of Nuclear War"

PAUL RAMSEY[1]

On the basis of just war concepts, Ramsey concluded that the use of nuclear weapons directly to attack noncombatants is strictly forbidden under any circumstances; thus, for example, no moral warrant existed for American attacks on Hiroshima and Nagasaki during World War II. But how should we assess a strategy of nuclear deterrence in which nuclear arsenals and accompanying threats to use them are employed to keep the peace among nations? Ramsey argued that a viable deterrent could be based on a morally legitimate war-fighting capacity, one that met the jus in bello conditions of discrimination and proportionality. The following excerpt shows Ramsey distinguishing his position from that of "nuclear pacifism." The subsequent letter to *Newsweek* withdraws his earlier endorsement of the "bluff," in which deterrence rests on the perceived but not actual threat to use nuclear weapons directly against a political adversary's noncombatant population.[2]

IN APPROACHING THE MORAL issues involved in appearing to be willing to do something that is wrong, I shall make use of a volume of essays by British Roman Catholics[3] who follow the anatomy of the just war doctrine to a conclusion altogether different from mine, namely, nuclear pacifism.

It is never right to do wrong that good may come of it. Nuclear weapons have only added to this perennial truth the footnote: it can never do *any good* to do wrong that good may come of it. Neither is it right to *intend* to do wrong that good may come of it. If deterrence rests upon genuinely intending massive retaliation, it is clearly wrong no matter how much peace results. If weapons systems deter city exchanges only because and so far as they are *intended* to be used against cities, then deterrence involves a "conditional willingness" to do evil, and evil on a massive scale. Granting that deterrence deters before or during the war, and that it supports peace or the control of war, that alone cannot justify it. It would be justified "if, and only if, in employing this threat, we were not involved in . . . *immoral hypothetical decisions*." The distinction between murder and killing in war, or between directly killing combatants and directly murdering

1. In Ramsey, *The Just War: Force and Political Responsibility*, 250–58.
2. Werpehowski and Crocco, eds., *The Essential Paul Ramsey: A Collection*, 96.
3. Stein, ed., *Nuclear Weapons and Christian Conscience*.

noncombatants, posits an ethico-political principle that can only be violated, never abrogated. "Nothing, not even the alleged interests of peace, can save murderousness from evil," and nothing, not even the alleged interest in deterrence during war for the control of war, can save the *intention* to commit murder from being evil. Does reliance on nuclear weapons for deterrence hypothetically commit us, here and now, to murder, there and then? If so, such deterrence is wrong, and can never be anything but wickedness. This conclusion would seem to follow from the comparatively simple moral truth that "if an action is morally wrong, it is wrong to intend to do it."[4]

This is surely a correct "finding" as to the moral law. The authors of these chapters, however, intermix with this a certain "finding of fact" which may be questioned. They assert that "deterrence rests, in the end, on the intention to use nuclear weapons," not that in some or many of its forms it *may* or *might* rest on either present murderous intention or on a "conditional willingness" to do murder. No wonder the conclusion follows: if this is the case, deterrence "cannot but be morally repugnant for the same ultimate reason as is the use of the weapon held in reserve."[5] The following statement of the case is a better one, and by accenting the first word the fact to be questioned can be stressed: "*If*, then, we find that 'having' nuclear weapons involves intending to explode them over predominantly civilian targets, no more need be said; this intention is criminal, just as the action is criminal."[6] This is the matter of fact that needs to be determined—whether it *is* so, and must or should remain so if it is now the case—before we can know how the moral prohibition of intending to do wrong is to be applied in an assessment of deterrence policy.

The authors of these essays systematically fail to show that there can be no deterrent effect where there is no actual intention to use nuclear weapons directly against cities. They underrate what is pejoratively called "the argument from bluff," while admitting that if this deterred and if this is what deters there would not be an implied "conditional commitment to total war." These essays are remarkably sophisticated, and at many points suggest their own answer. "Having an H-bomb" for example, is no simple matter. It is not only that "having an H-bomb" differs from having a gun "in respect to the nature of the object possessed." One can "have" one or both these instruments with subtly but significantly different ways of "having" them. There is then a considerable difference "in respect to the nature of the 'possession' of the object" that has to be taken into account.[7] The question is whether "possession" of massive nuclear weapons is reducible to the crime of planning to use them over civilian targets. The question is whether "having" or "possession" implies a criminal intention to use them murderously, or a conditional willingness to do so. These questions cannot be answered without first exploring a spectrum of "havings" that may be possible, and indeed desirable. This further exploration of the nature of the "possession"

---

4. Stein, ed., *Nuclear Weapons and Christian Conscience*, 23, 36 (italics mine), 125, 71.

5. Stein, ed., *Nuclear Weapons and Christian Conscience*, 78 (italics mine). This was the analysis of deterrence which I held in 1961 and set forth in the concluding chapters of my *War and the Christian Conscience*. The moral argument, I believe, remains irrefutable, but findings of fact are not to be deduced from this.

6. Stein, ed., *Nuclear Weapons and Christian Conscience*, 73–74 (italics mine).

7. Stein, ed., *Nuclear Weapons and Christian Conscience*, 32, 75.

of nuclear weapons which may be possible will determine whether deterrence by means of them before or during any war can ever be judged legitimate.

The technical possibility of deterrence before and during war can now be indicated, as can its compatibility with the moral prohibition of both the use and the intention to use nuclear (or any other) weapons in direct attacks on centers of population.

1. The collateral civilian damage that would result from counterforces warfare in its maximum form may itself be quite sufficient to deter either side from going so high and to preserve the rules and tacit agreements limiting conflict in a nuclear age. In that case, deterrence during the war and collateral civilian damage are both "indirect effects" of a plan and action of war which would be licit or permitted by the traditional rules of civilized conduct in war. To say that counterforce strikes over an enemy's own territory are licit or permitted is to say that one can morally intend and be "conditionally willing" to engage in such a war. Whether one positively should ever do so depends on the conditions. Collateral civilian damage is certainly an unavoidable indirect effect and, in the technical sense, an "unintended" result of something a nation may and should make itself conditionally willing and ready to do. The deterrent effect, of which we are now speaking, is then, as it were, an indirect effect of the foreseeable indirect effects of legitimate military conduct.[8]

   One can certainly "intend" to deter in this fashion, and oneself be similarly deterred. Not knowing the tyrannies future history may produce, one cannot say whether the one effect of successful resistance to them will justify the direct and the indirect costs. Still, we foreknow that these costs may be very great indeed. This is to say that, at least to a very great degree, perhaps a sufficient degree, nuclear warfare is a design for war that is inherently self-limiting upon rational decision makers without their having to intend to use these weapons directly to murder cities and civilians.

   This is not at all a matter of "double-think about double effect."[9] To justify "possession" for the sake of deterrence one does not have to invent possibly legitimate uses for nuclear weapons, such as their use against a ship at sea. Many a military installation in the nuclear age is fifty or more miles in diameter.

2. In respect to the nature of the weapons we possess, there are two possible uses which cannot be removed from them. The dual use the weapons themselves have—the fact that they may be used either against strategic forces or against centers of population—means that *apart from intention* their capacity to deter cannot

---

8. This was a quite inadequate, indeed, an unfortunate, formulation of this first step in defense of the justice of deterrence. I should not have described "collateral deterrence" as the "indirect effect of foreseeable indirect effects" of legitimately targeted nuclear strikes. Instead, this deterrent effect should have been described as a direct and a wanted effect of the unwanted, indirect, collateral consequences of even a just use of nuclear weapons. For me to revise the language of the text above and remove this mistake would be to attribute to myself a prescience and an aptitude for words that I did not have. This would also prevent the reader from being drawn into the argument over the justice of deterrence as it unfolds in subsequent chapters. Therefore, in what follows this misleading wording will continue to be used until I was forced to supplant it by better wording for the same thought.

9. Stein, *Nuclear Weapons*, 57.

be removed from them. This means that there may be sufficient deterrence in the subjectively unintended consequence of the mere possession of these weapons. No matter how often we declare, and quite sincerely declare, that our targets are an enemy's forces, he can never be quite certain that in the fury or in the fog of war his cities may not be destroyed.

This is so certainly the case that the problem of how to deter an enemy from striking our cities ought not for one moment to impede the shift to a counter-forces policy and to the actual intention to use nuclear weapons only against forces. We should declare again and again, and give evidence by what we do, that our targets are his forces rather than his cities. Since it is morally repugnant to wage war without renouncing morally repugnant means,[10] this should be speedily done, and communicated as effectively as possible to the enemy. Still, without any hesitation or ambiguity on our part, the weapons themselves will continue to have deterrent effect because they have ambiguous uses. They always *may* be used over cities; and no enemy can *know* that this will not be done. Was [Secretary of Defense Robert] McNamara's reserved use of massive nuclear weapons for retaliation in case Russia strikes our cities really necessary, or his declared policy of conditional willingness to do this? Was not this aspect of his [1962 commencement] speech [at the University of Michigan] mainly needed to reassure domestic public opinion which is still so far from supporting any steps toward a counter-force, strategy and away from pacifistic maximal deterrence?

Similar conclusions can be reached from an analysis of the "familiar spiral of reciprocal expectations," which is an important aspect of war in the nuclear age. This spiral not only threatens to be illimitable, but it serves as a built-in dampener, which no deliberate policy nor any intention can remove. This is the truth in T. C. Schelling's contention that in the nuclear age all forms of limited war raise the risk of general war, whether intended or not. The point here is not the "threat" of general war because of some technical or human failure or some mistaken calculation. The point is rather than in a nuclear age all war raises a risk of general war by an apparent *possibility* of a *politically irreversible trend*. War creates this risk which we share with the Russians. They can never "be confident that even the lack of resolution sometimes attributed to the United States could guarantee that general war would not result." "It is our sheet inability to predict the consequences of our actions and to keep things under control, and the enemy's similar inability [or our reciprocal doubt whether the other is in control], that can intimidate the enemy," and ourselves.

If war is no longer a matter of making no threat that does not depend on our ultimate willingness to choose general war, it is no longer a matter of having to put forth acts or threats that involve a conditional willingness to choose general war.[11] War being sufficiently threatening, a conclusive case can be made for the proposition that massive nuclear weapons should never be intended for use against societies. The nations of the world should and can devote all their attention and intention

10. Cf, Stein, *Nuclear Weapons*, 82.
11. See Schelling, "Nuclear Strategy in Europe," 421–24.

to making only just or counter-forces war possible. A single great power can and should do this since the other ominous possibility will always remain in the background as a shared and unintended threat.

3. Only now do we come again to the suggestion that the distinction between the *appearance* and the *actuality* of being partially or totally committed to go to city exchanges may have to be employed in deterrence policy. In that case, only the appearance should be cultivated. If the first two points above do not seem to the military analyst sufficiently *persuasive*, or *able to be made* so, then an *apparent* resolution to wage war irrationally or at least an ambiguity about our intentions may have to be our expressed policy. This is a matter, not of the nature of the weapons themselves, but of the manner in which we possess them—the "having" of them that might be necessary to sustain deterrence during justifiably conducted war.

The moralist can certainly say to the decision maker that it can never be right for him to do such a thing as attack an enemy's society, or for him actually to intend to do so, or under any conditions to be willing to match his resolution against that of the enemy by means of populated cities. He can point out to the statesman that it can never be right for him to contrive to "make" the undoable intention irrevocable, or to have the intention of doing so. He can even point out where the military analyst will be found saying the same thing about the irrationality of total committal to an irrational act of war, or even of appearing quite unambiguously to be totally and irreversibly committed.

But the moralist must be careful how he rushes in with his ethico-political principles mixed with an assortment of findings of fact and various arguments *ad horrendum*. He must be careful how he spells out his moral guidance for deterrence policy. For, on a sound solution of this problem the security of free societies may well depend in a nuclear age which is also an age of "megacorpses,"[12] "deracination from humanity,"[13] and "unparalleled moral landslide."[14] The moralist must be careful how he disparages the so-called argument from bluff to a morally licit form of deterrence; and he should examine whether the reasons *he* uses to dismiss this argument are telling *moral* ones or rather technical judgments he has gathered to fulfill a prejudice.

The crucial question for the moralist is whether deterrent effects that flow from a *specified kind* of studied ambiguity concerning the intention with which a nation holds nuclear weapons in reserve are *praeter intentionem* (besides or without the actual intention to attack cities) as surely as are the first two types of deterrent effects we have analyzed. To say and to act as if we might go to city exchanges is certainly a form of deception. But, if this can be done without intending to make irrational, immoral use of nuclear weapons, or even with the intention that our weapons be not so used and with the intention of revoking what had never even the appearance of total committal, such deception cannot be said to be based on the criminal intention or conditional willingness to do murder. The first thing

12. One million dead bodies.
13. Stein, *Nuclear Weapons*, 31.
14. Stein, *Nuclear Weapons*, 125–26.

to be said then, is that the intention to deceive is certainly a far cry from the intention to murder society, or to commit mutual homicide.

The second thing to be said is in connection with the moral problem of *deception* in politics and in wartime. A moralist need not slur over the fact that in all sorts of ways deception may be an evil, just as he need not slur over the fact that the killing of combatants is evil (though certainly not wicked). But having said this, it must then be pointed out that there are deceptions and deceptions. Or rather, the word *deception* ought perhaps to be reserved for any denial of the truth to someone to whom the truth is due, or permitting him to gather from you a false or inadequate impression concerning the exact truth which, in some sense, "belongs" to him. If this is a fair statement of the moral rule, then an experienced finding of fact must be that there are many situations in both private and public life when withholding the "truth" or even communicating an inadequate representation of the "truth" is not a lie. Relative to this, there is a teaching of long standing in the Western tradition about the virtues of a military commander, to the effect that there is nothing wrong with his having military secrets provided he does not pretend that he has none. It would be extremely difficult to support the judgment that an effective reservation about the use of the weapons we possess, or about our intention that they not be used over cities, in any sense belongs to an enemy, or that this information is due to be given him, if thereby deterrence will fail and war break out and go *whoosh*!

Finally a moralist must raise the question of whether this truth is not owed to the people of an enemy nation, if not to their military commanders. In answer to this, it goes to the point to say that this may be necessary to save *their* lives as well as those of our own civilians. Or (worse than their death from the point of view of an ethics that does not place supreme value in mere physical existence) it may be necessary in order to save them (and ourselves) from a measure of complicity in their government's conditional or actual willingness to save them by doing mass murder, or from the *tragedy* (not the *wickedness*) of actually being saved by murderous intention (if a wrongly willed deterrent worked) and some of them from the tragedy of living on in a world in which their lives have been spared in the midst of the greatest possible wrong*doing* by a government which in remote degrees of participation was still their own (if the shared intentional risk does not work). So the question resolves itself into the question whether it is ever right to withhold the truth in order to save life, to save from moral wrongdoing, to save from sheer tragedy. Does the truth that might well be "fatal" in all these senses "belong" to them? Is it "due" to be given if it can be[?] Do we "owe" them a true report that will unambiguously quiet their fears by effectively communicating to them (if this can ever be done) that we have no intention of engaging with their government in intersociety warfare under any circumstances? I am so far from believing that one ought readily to justify this deception that it seems to me that the first two types of deterrence must, if at all possible, be made to work. Still, if deterrence were based on a cultivated ambiguity about our real intentions, and if "deception" in an objectionable moral sense would thus in some measure be perpetrated, it would still be an intent to deceive and not an intent possibly to do murder.

Perhaps we should say that we ought to be conditionally willing to strive for this ingredient in deterrence, that is, on the condition that it is necessary to deter and to save life. I do not grant to a physician any right to withhold from a patient knowledge of his true condition; but then I also do not believe that learning the truth about his condition can be demonstrated to be so nearly fatal as, in our present supposition, it would be for an enemy government and population to learn that we do not intend to attack people. A better analogy might be the following one. If you were trying to save a man out on the ledge of a building, threatening to commit suicide and to take you with him, would you withhold from him, and have an obligation to withhold from him, any blandishments, including "daring" him to join you inside for a duel to the death by "Russian roulette" at three paces, with no intention of ever carrying out this dissuasive dare or threat?

The military and political analysts I have consulted do not reject as infeasible the sort of "possession" of nuclear weapons for deterrence which we are now discussing.[15] If it is thought to be infeasible now, then the "system" may have to be studied and perfected so that it can be done. For this may be one of those customarily "unthinkable" things which, the more you think about it, will prove to be technically and politically "doable." If needed, it should be developed in many a scenario. It is on balance, I believe, morally "doable," as city-busting is not, however much you think about it. Whether this ingredient in deterrence can be adopted and exercised by a democratic society is, of course, a serious question. It requires of a people a mature "ethic of restraint, limits and silence,"[16] not moral protest always, much less punitive fury or he-man morality; and it requires a reliance on the morality and rationality of their political leaders not to be expected or (on any policy decision not so crucial) desired in a free society. For this reason, if for no other, all our attention and intention should doubtless be directed toward adopting, declaring, and implementing a policy of counter-forces warfare, with the "collateral" deterrence that policy affords. This is the doctrine which should form the consciences of free men today; and if their consciences are thus formed, it may then be possible to add to the "graduated" deterrence of a counter-force policy this last type of non-murderous deterrence.

Then it may be possible to put, not nuclear weapons as such, but the intercity use of nuclear weapons into a category by itself, so that, while the capability still exists, the intention to attack cities will recede into the background so far as not to have actuality. Things as strange have happened before in the history of warfare. Tribes living close to death in the desert have fought cruel wars. They even used poisoned arrows, and certainly to a limited extent they fought one another by means of direct attack upon women and children. But they knew *not to poison wells*! That would have been a policy of mutual homicide, and a form of *society-contra-society* warfare that would have removed the possibility of any more bloody cruel wars, not to mention peacetime pursuits. In refraining from massive well poisoning, or in keeping that ambiguous, did these tribes, in any valid or censorable sense of the word, still "intend" to poison wells?

The following letter appeared in *Newsweek*, July 5, 1982:

> I am honored to have my name linked with that of Reinhold Niebuhr, America's greatest twentieth-century political analyst. However, I would like to make one

---

15. Halperin, *Limited War in the Nuclear Age*, for example, develops at length the distinction between "communication policy" and "action policy."

16. Cf. Thompson, "The Nuclear Dilemma—A Discussion."

important correction in your account of my views. I did once argue—in 1965—that it is morally permissible for a statesman to go so far as to "bluff" about his intention to use modern weapons deliberately aimed at an adversary's society if, but only if, that was judged necessary to deter the maximum war possible today. The "bluff" was withdrawn from my analysis of a possibly moral deterrence within the year, for two reasons: first, one's real intentions not to go to such use will be found out, and the bluff will fail to deter; and, second, even if our top political and military leaders were pure in heart, they must count on thousands of men in missile silos, planes and submarines to be conditionally willing under some circumstances, to become murderers. One should never occasion mortal sin in others, tempt them to it or enlist them for it. It is never right to do evil, or to intend to do evil, so that good may come.

2–8

Christian Vocation and Resistance

PAUL RAMSEY

If Christian love enjoins discovering the neighbor in every person, the question arises as to whether and how there may be a decision and preference among the needs of the many neighbors who cross one's path. In *Basic Christian Ethics* Ramsey argued that there are grounds in scripture and tradition for an ethic that prefers the victim rather than the perpetrator of injustice. Preference may even take the form of violent resistance. Ramsey relies in part on a distinction between a self-regarding use of resistance in self-defense and an other-regarding resistance on the neighbor's behalf and for his or her protection, but he even permits the possibility of a "vocational" defense of self-justified derivatively from agape. Here we would find, then, another example of agape's eminently free and uncompromising commitment to the neighbor.[1]

The Problem of Christocentric Vocation

THE PROTESTANT REFORMATION ABOLISHED the medieval Catholic distinction between special religious merit and dignity attached to the role of the clergy and the inferior, though altogether necessary, function of ordinary lay Christians in the world. All vocations, said the Reformers, rank the same with God, none more sacred, none more secular than others, no matter how they are ranked by men. Of course, some callings are socially more pivotal than others, in that the vocations of many other individuals are subsumed under them; but the difference between monk or magistrate and gardener or garbage collector is an "official" distinction only, implying no real difference in merit or dignity before God. Therefore no individual, whatever his work may be, has any necessity for forsaking the responsibilities of his calling to go off on a crusade or to enter a monastery out of bad conscience about what he is now doing and under the illusion that he can be more perfect somewhere else.

> The Lord commands every one of us, in all the actions of life to regard his vocation. . . . He has appointed to all their particular duties in different spheres of life. . . . Every individual's line of life . . . is, as it were, a post assigned him by the Lord, that he may not wander about in uncertainty all his days. . . . Our life, therefore, will then be best regulated, when it is directed to this mark; since no

1. Ramsey, *Basic Christian Ethics*, 153–57, 166–84.

one will be impelled by his own temerity to attempt more than is compatible with his calling, because he will know that it is unlawful to transgress the bounds assigned him. He that is in obscurity will lead a private life without discontent, so as not to desert the station in which God has placed him. It will also be no small alleviation of his cares, labours, troubles, and other burdens, when a man knows that in all these things he has God for his guide. The magistrate will execute his office with greater pleasure, the father of a family will confine himself to his duty with more satisfaction, and all, in their respective spheres of life, will bear and surmount the inconveniences, cares, disappointments, and anxieties which befall them, when they shall be persuaded that every individual has his burden laid upon him by God. Hence also will arise peculiar consolation, since there will be no employment so mean and sordid (provided we follow our vocation) as not to appear truly respectable, and be deemed highly important in the sight of God.[2]

Martin Luther likewise wanted everybody to be somebody in the eyes of God even though this meant that no one would be anybody by comparison with each other.

What you do in your house is worth as much as if you did it up in heaven for our Lord God. For what we do in our calling here on earth in accordance with His word and command He counts as if it were done in heaven for Him. . . . Therefore we should accustom ourselves to think of our position and work as sacred and well-pleasing to God, not on account of the position and the work, but on account of the word and the faith from which the obedience and the workflow. No Christian should despise his position and life if he is living in accordance with the word of God, but should say, "I believe in Jesus Christ, and do as the ten commandments teach, and pray that our dear Lord may help me thus to do." That is a right holy life, and cannot be made holier even if one fast himself to death. . . . It looks like a great thing when a monk renounces everything and goes into a cloister, carries on a life of asceticism, fasts, watches, prays, etc. . . . On the other hand, it looks like a small thing when a maid cooks and cleans and does other housework. But because God's command is there, even such a small work must be praised as a service to God far surpassing the holiness and asceticism of all monks and nuns. For here there is no command of God. But there God's command is fulfilled, that one should honour father and mother and help in the care of the home.[3]

All this is familiar. Less has been said so clearly of how a Christian's duty in some secular calling stands in relation to Christian love, which should be normative for everything he does. Granted that a theocentric or a law-/or decalogue-centered theory of vocation may very well be formulated, how can there be a Christocentric vocation without withdrawing an individual quite completely from actual tasks in the world?

Count Leo Tolstoy, Russian novelist, Christian idealist, and opponent of all government, understood to the full the essential meaning of non-resisting Christian love in the respect that such love has absolutely no selfish reason for preferring one person to another. He defined Christian love as "a preference for others over oneself," with the immediate

2. John Calvin, *Institutes of the Christian Religion*, Ill, x, 6, in Kerr, Jr., ed., *A Compendium of the Institutes of the Christian Religion*, 107.

3. Luther, *Works*, V, 102; IV, 341; V, 100. Quoted by McGiffert in *Protestant Thought before Kant*, 33.

implication that before a man can love he must "cease from preferring some people to others for his own personal welfare."[4] For a Christian the activity of love does not:

> . . . proceed in any definite order with the demands of his strongest love presenting themselves first, those of a feebler love next, and so on. The demands of love present themselves constantly and simultaneously and without any order. Here is a hungry old man for whom I have a little love and who has come to ask for food which I am keeping for the supper of my much-loved children: how am I to weigh the present demand of a feebler love against the future demand of a stronger?[5]

Tolstoy not only seems to comprehend clearly the essential nature of unclaiming, non-resisting, non-preferential love for neighbor, but also his deep suspicion of introducing any other sort of preferences into the activity of love sprang from considerations which Christian ethics must judge quite correct. Any sort of preference among neighbors so easily turns again into care for them only in the sequence and degree called for by self-love.

If I admit that a freezing child may remain unclothed because my children may someday need the clothes I am asked to give, then I may also resist other demands of love out of consideration for my future children . . .

> If a man may reject the present demands of a feebler love for the sake of the future demands of a greater love, is it not evident that such a man, even if he wished it with all his might, will never be able to judge to what extent he may reject present demands in favour of future demands, and therefore, not being able to decide that question, will always choose the manifestations of love which please him best—that is, he will yield not to the demands of love but to the demands of his personality. If a man decides that it is better for him to resist the demands of a present very feeble love for the sake of a future greater love he deceives himself and others and loves no one but himself. Future love does not exist. Love is a present activity only.[6]

Tolstoy's views are at many points actually a paraphrase of the Sermon on the Mount and other of Jesus' strenuous teachings which we have seen are an eschatological stimulus making us well acquainted with the pure and perfect will of God. Jesus said, "If anyone comes to me and does not hate his own father and mother and wife and children and brothers and sisters, yes, and even his own life, he cannot be my disciple" (Luke 14:26); and to a would-be disciple who wanted first to wait until his father was dead and buried, he laid down the condition, "Follow me, and leave the dead to bury their own dead" (Matt 8:22). What then becomes of vocational obligation to one's own family? How can non-preferential love prefer some persons to others so far as must be the case within the actual lines of any vocation? How can non-resisting love take upon itself any responsibility for public protection or in support of just social reform through the vocation of legislator, judge, sheriff, hangman, or soldier? How can the strenuous teachings of Jesus come into

---

4. Tolstoy, *On Life*, xxiv, trans. Maude, 103 (italics added).
5. Tolstoy, *On Life*, xxiii, trans. Maude, 97 (italics added).
6. Tolstoy, *On Life*, xxiii, trans. Maude, 97–98 (italics added).

actual practice? How can the ferment of ideal perfectionism in Christian ethics provide foundation for any actual calling except by outright or thinly disguised compromise? These questions have now to be answered . . . .

A Preferential Ethics of Protection and the Teachings of Jesus

Unless the instance in which Jesus fled from the territory of Herod Antipas in order to avoid arrest (Luke 13:33) was a case of his saving his life for a better accounting and a more promising opportunity for sacrifice in Jerusalem, an explicit manifestation of "duties to himself" can hardly be expected within the short closing period of Jesus' lifetime, to which our knowledge of him is largely limited. Nevertheless, neighbor-centered preferential love and a Christian ethic of protection do have their beginning in him, in spite of the effect of apocalypticism in expelling concern for the permanent organization of justice and making men well acquainted with the pure will of God in the case of a single neighbor.

To see this, we need not bandy proof-texts back and forth or engage in St. Augustine's hair-splitting exegesis on the saying "If anyone strikes you on the right cheek, turn to him the other also" (Matt 5:39). This teaching, Augustine reasoned, involved only a case of insult, not of assault; for, assuming a greater number of right-handed assailants in the world, their blows would normally be delivered to an opponent's left cheek. A blow upon the right cheek, which Jesus talked about, would most likely be struck by the back of the hand; this is as if a glove were thrown in the face; we need only conclude, then, that in case a Christian is insulted he turns the other cheek and avoids unnecessary conflict. This interpretation, or any other which seeks to moderate the extremity of Jesus' requirement, cannot be correct, because Jesus spoke this saying merely as an illustration of his strenuous teaching "Do not resist one who is evil," than which nothing could be more severe. In case of attack or insult from "one who is evil" turning the other cheek can be the only possible meaning of non-resisting love.

Nevertheless—and this is to understand, not to lessen, the requirement—Jesus deals only with the simplest moral situation in which blows may be struck, the case of one person in relation to but one other. He does not here undertake to say how men, who themselves ought not to resist at all or by any means whatever when they themselves alone receive the blows, ought to act in more complex cases where nonresistance would in practice mean turning another person's face to the blows of an oppressor. We are not at all uncertain what Jesus' ethic was in bilateral, two-party situations. When his life alone was concerned Jesus turned the other cheek, when smitten he smote not again, and he died quite without defending himself.

Yet without distorting the text, the beginnings of a multilateral ethics of protection, certainly a multilateral neighbor-centered preferential love, may be found in Jesus' own attitudes and example. On occasion he showed indignation, even wrath, over injustice, using vitriolic words as weapons against the devourers of widows' houses (Luke 20:47). He was unsparing in his condemnation of the complacency of Israel's religious leaders.

Indeed, a great Jewish scholar, while attributing real originality to the teachings of Jesus, raises serious objection against the consistency of Jesus' practice:

> I would not cavil with the view that Jesus is to be regarded as the first great Jewish teacher to frame such a sentence as: Love your enemies, do good to them who hate you, bless them that curse you, and pray for them who ill-treat you" (Luke 6:27,28). Yet how much more telling his injunction would have been if we had a single story about his doing good to, and praying for, a single Rabbi or Pharisee! One grain of practice is worth a pound of theory. . . . But no such deed is ascribed to Jesus in the Gospels. Towards his enemies, towards those who did not believe in him, whether individuals, groups, or cities (Matt 11:20–24), only denunciation and bitter words! The injunctions are beautiful, but how much more beautiful would have been a fulfillment of those injunctions by Jesus himself.[7]

Jesus' prayer on the cross that God forgive his executioners (Luke 23:24) might be cited in reply, and here and there a friendly conversation with an inquiring scribe, or the act of healing the daughter of Jairus, a ruler of the synagogue. Moreover, some responsibility for anti-Jewish sentiment in the gospels must be laid at the door of later controversy between Christians and Jews. Still, in the last analysis the only answer to the charge that Jesus did not always display an attitude toward his opponents consonant with the main body of his own teachings must grant the fact yet deny the interpretation given. When it was a question of injustice done to persons other than himself, especially when he confronted the huge burden of fossilized religion fastened upon the people of the land, Jesus did not remain at his ease lifting up their faces to additional blows or supporting by silence their compulsion to go a second mile. Although his words were, "Do not resist one who is evil," Jesus did not even draw out very explicitly the distinction between resisting *evil* yet not resisting the *evil-doer*, between condemning "the system" and denouncing people who support it, which Christians often insist was his meaning. The evil and the one who does it are in any actual situation bound so closely together that a person who, in one-one relationship to an enemy-neighbor, wishes not to resist the evildoer can find no way of resisting evil; and a person in multilateral relationships with more than one neighbor who wishes for their sakes to resist evil will be unable to avoid resisting the evildoer as well. With prophetic indignation, therefore, Jesus denounced those who were evil as well as impersonal forms of evil itself. This he did from neighbor-centered preferential love, although so far as his life alone was concerned he showed no preference for his own personal welfare and did not resist evildoers when evil fell upon him.

When the two perspectives, Jesus' personal ethic of nonresistance and the beginning in him of a preferential ethic of protection, are not kept quite separate the resulting blend is some form of nonviolent or passive resistance. This permits more concern for the self in relation to the single neighbor than by its nature non-resisting Christian love allows, and at the same time limits what such love may find needs to be done when weighing the claims of more neighbors than one and the actual ways they may be served. Whether the whip Jesus used in driving the money-changers out of the Temple was plaited of straw or of leather, whether he applied it to animals or to men, whether the decisive factor that day

---

7. C. G. Montefiore, *Rabbinic Literature and Gospel Teachings*, 103ff. Quoted by Major in Manson, and Wright, *The Mission and Message of Jesus*, 344.

was the force of his own powerful personality justifiably indignant on behalf of a righteous cause or the threatening multitude of people gathered in Jerusalem who forestalled the immediate use of the Temple police, in any case some form of resistance was raised that day not only against perverse practices but also against the men who engaged in them. Force does not become any less resistant because of its "spirituality," or resistance wrong to a greater degree because it takes material form. Circumstances similar to those which warranted a change from Jesus' announced ethic of nonresistance to any manner of resistance he may have used in cleansing the Temple may not only permit but even on occasion require Christian love to adopt physical methods of resistance.

A recent study of Christian attitudes toward war and peace puts the issue of a preferential ethic of protection in terms of Jesus' story of the Good Samaritan: And now arises one of the unanswerable "ifs" of literary history. What would Jesus have made the Samaritan do while the robbers were still at their fell work? In answering this question, the author, apparently without any hesitation, substitutes Jesus' personal ethic in relation to a single neighbor, and all his apocalyptically derived strenuous teachings having to do with this simple situation, for what might have been his ethic in multilateral relation to two or more neighbors. He writes, "The protection of one life would have seemed to Jesus no excuse at all for taking the life of another, even a robber." Surely the most that can be said is that quite plainly the protection of his own life did not seem to Jesus any excuse for ceasing to express non-resisting love for another. It may be "there is no evidence for the suggestion that Jesus would have had him wield his traveler's sword."[8] Still, in the rudiments of preferential ethics to be found in Jesus' attitude toward the perpetrators of injustice there is some suggestion that he might, at least no decisive evidence that he would *not*, have approved such action. We perhaps should not go to the other extreme so far as to say, "When I try to imagine what would have happened had Jesus come upon the scene a little earlier than the Good Samaritan, I find it more natural to suppose that he would have helped the traveler in his struggle with the thieves than that he would have waited until the man was injured and the thieves departed before coming to his aid."[9] To say the least this would have been a different ethical situation from the one pictured in the story or from an attack by thieves upon Jesus himself. The difference is precisely that non-resisting, unself-defensive love must determine its responsibility in the one case toward more than one neighbor, in the other simply toward the neighbor or "the enemy" when injurious consequences of the decision will fall upon the agent himself alone.

> To express love at all in some situations one must seem to deny it. Jesus said: "If any man smite you on one cheek turn the other also"; here the situation is relatively simple—you and your enemy. But Jesus did not say: "If any man smite one of your friends, lead him to another friend that he may smite him also." Not only is it clear that Jesus could have made no such statement, but also that he would have felt that the involvement of the interests of others (that is, others besides one's self and one's enemy) transformed the whole moral situation and placed our obligations with respect to it in a radically different light.[10]

8. Scott-Craig, *Christian Attitudes to War and Peace*, 43.

9. Garrard, *Duty and the Will of God*, 78.

10. John Knox's essay can be found in Van Dusen, ed., *The Christian Answer*, 173.

Jesus once told the parable of a servant whom a merciful kin released from debt to the fantastic amount of ten million dollars who nevertheless insisted that a fellow servant pay in full a debt of twenty dollars. "Then his lord summoned him and said to him, 'You wicked servant! I forgave you all that debt because you besought me; and should not you have had mercy on your fellow servant, as I had mercy on you?' And in anger his lord delivered him to the jailers, till he should pay all his debt" (Matt 18:32,33). From this story it is evident that love which for itself claims nothing may yet for the sake of another claim everything, that anyone who unhesitatingly and times without number renounces "what is due" when he himself alone bears the brunt of such a decision may nevertheless turn full circle and insist with utter severity upon full payment of what is due to others; and what is due to others is never simply just payment but full forgiveness "as I had mercy on you," never exact justice alone but Christian love. This may be called neighbor-centered rather than self-centered severity, forgiving love which pronounces judgment on all that is not love, an attitude which gives up judging men in terms of their conformity to some legal or moral code and yet insists that men are judged in terms of the demands of unconditional self-giving. "So also my heavenly Father will do to every one of you, if you do not forgive your brother from your heart" (Matt 18:35).

A Christian Ethic of Resistance

Whether or not so much preferential ethics of protection may be seen in Jesus himself, beyond question Christian ethics soon developed such a view, the primitive pacifism generally practiced by early Christians so long as they were in a minority giving way to what were judged more effective means for assuming responsibility for the whole of organized society. Although decades before their time individual Christians had begun to accept service in the Roman legions, often with the explicit approval of church authorities, St. Ambrose (A.D. 340–396) and his great convert St. Augustine (A.D. 354–430) were the first to give fully elaborated theoretical defense of Christian participation in armed conflict. Since Christian ethics is not a legalism concerned with external deeds only or even mainly, it would be a great mistake to regard Christianity's accommodation to Constantine's empire as necessarily a compromise of its genius or a "fall" from the pristine purity of its ethic. As a matter of fact, careful examination of the first literary defense of Christian participation in war gives striking evidence that underneath the obvious reversal of tactic, the general strategy of Christian love continued without abatement and without any alteration in its fundamental nature. While first formulating for Christian thought a theory of *justum bellum*, both St. Ambrose and St. Augustine continued to teach that when a man himself alone is concerned he ought never to resist "one who is evil." Both combine their justification of war because of a Christian's responsibility for public protection with an utter denial that under any circumstances he ever has any right of private self-defense. No Christian, they said, should save his own life at the expense of another; yet when other persons than himself are involved in the decision, no Christian ought to fail to resist evil by effective means which the state alone makes available to him. This combination of ideas, which seems strange to men today, is clear proof that non-resisting love was still the groundwork of all reasoning about Christian participation in conflict of arms; and indeed this continued to be true down to the "holy war" enthusiasm of the crusades, as can be seen in the requirement that a private soldier do penance for the evil he may have done or thought while participating even in just wars he *should* have joined.

Commenting on a passage from Cicero, St. Ambrose asked the question, Should a wise man in case of shipwreck take away a plank from an ignorant sailor? Leaving aside the consideration that an emaciated philosopher probably would not prove victor in struggle with an ignorant sailor, ought he try to save his own life at the expense of another? Ambrose answered this question in the negative, and likewise for all one-one neighbor situations.

> Some ask whether a wise man ought in case of a shipwreck to take away a plank from an ignorant sailor? Although it seems better for the common good that a wise man rather than a fool should escape from shipwreck, yet I do not think that a Christian, a just and wise man, ought to save his own life by the death of another; just as when he meets with an armed robber he cannot return his blows, *lest in defending his life he should stain his love toward his neighbor.* The verdict on this is plain and clear in the books of the Gospel. . . . What robber is more hateful than the persecutor who came to kill Christ? But Christ would not be defended by the wounds of the persecutor, for He willed to heal all by His wounds.[11]

A Christian ought never to value his own possessions so highly as to be willing, for his own sake, to take the life of another person, though from identically the same sort of neighbor-love he will value the possessions of another enough to resist, for his sake, a criminal attempt against them. This he will do not only occasionally but in the vacation of police or judge as well. When he alone is imperiled he will not presume to estimate the comparative worth of his own wisdom or righteousness and another man's lack of these qualities, though in the vocation of prince or soldier such judgments about relative justice must be made by a comparison of the righteousness of one conflicting side or party with another.

In the views of St. Augustine we can penetrate more deeply the reason for this strange combination of doctrines, why for Christian ethics generally self-defense is the worst of all possible excuses for war or for any other form of resistance or any sort of preference among other people. Augustine makes this distinction between public and private protection when considering the more general question "whether Libido dominates also in those things which we see too often done."

> For me the point to be considered first is whether an on-rushing enemy, or an assassin lying in wait may be killed with no wrongheaded desire (for the saving) of one's life, or for liberty or for purity. . . . How can I think that they act with no inordinate desire who fight for that (i.e., some creaturely good), which they can lose without desiring to lose it? . . . Therefore the law is not just which grants the power to a wayfarer to kill a highway robber, so that he may not be killed (by the robber); or which grants to anyone, man or woman, to slay an assailant attacking, if he can, before he or she is harmed. The soldier also is commanded by law to slay the enemy, for which slaying, if he objects, he will pay the penalty

11. Ambrose, "The Duties of the Clergy," in *Nicene and Post-Nicene Fathers,* iv, 27, (italics added).

by imperial order. Shall we then dare to say that these laws are unjust, or more, that they are not laws? For to me a law that is not just appears to be no law. . . . For that he be slain who lays plans to take the life of another is less hard (to bear) than the death of him who is defending his own life (against the plotter). And acting against the chaste life of a man in opposition to his own will is much more evidently wrong than the taking of the life of him who so does violence by that one against whom the violence is done. Then again the soldier in slaying the enemy is the agent of the law (in war), wherefore he does his duty easily with no wrong aim or purpose. . . . That law, therefore, which for the protection of citizens orders foreign force to be repulsed by the same force, can be obeyed without a wrong desire: and this same can be said of all officials who by right and by order are subject to any powers. But I see not how these men (who defend themselves privately), while not held guilty by law, can be without fault: for the law does not force them to kill, but leaves it in their power. It is free therefore for them to kill no one for those things (life or possessions) which they can lose against their own will, which things therefore they ought not to love. . . . Wherefore again I do not blame the law which permits such aggressors to be slain: but by what reason I can defend those who slay them I do not find. . . . How indeed are they free to sin before Providence, who for those things which ought to be held of less worth are defiled by the killing of a man?[12]

When a judge on the bench renders decision between two parties other than himself, it is universally agreed, he will likely be more impartial and clear-headed about justice than when he judges in his own case. Now, Augustine believed that the decision of a prince or a man acting in some public capacity might well be of this same sort. In multilateral relationships a man can weigh what is just and unjust without undue influence on account of his selfish partiality. In this way he may express decided preference, but from neighbor-regarding considerations, not simply on account of what pleases him best from the point of view of his own personal welfare. The contrary is true, he believed, in all cases of private self-defense, even instances which a third party would call entirely just. Every man is so centrally interested in his own preservation that, Augustine believed, private self-defense could only arouse or proceed from some degree of inordinate self-love or "wrong-headed desire." In defending himself a man's egoism either manifests or gains control over his action, and the passion of selfishness, concupiscence, or libido warps his moral judgment so far as to render him totally incapable of deciding rightly between himself and his neighbor. If he should happen to defend the right person in defending himself, if he should actually save the life of the person a third party would assist or protect, this would be only by chance; it would be because of egotism, not because of justice or love.

Now, Ambrose and Augustine doubtless need to be criticized for their rather unqualified acceptance of public protection and also for their complete rejection of private self-defense. They tend to undertake the danger that in conflict between nations collective egotism will be so aroused that the judgment of any individual member of the group will come rather fully under the sway of self-interest. Even in his vocation, where multilateral neighbor-relationships intersect, an individual finds himself drawn not by

12. Augustine, *De libero arbitrio*, Bk. I, chapter V, 25–29; trans. Tourscher. Cf. *Ep.* XLVIL, 6.

neighbor-love alone or by considerations of justice alone but by selfish preference or personal affinity, for these persons rather than those. In actual conflict situations he is already inextricably bound to one side or the other by geography or language or existing mutual interest. In short, he always judges his own case, and, though he is sinfully incompetent ever to judge in such a situation, he cannot, like a judge of some court, disqualify himself and let someone else decide the issue. Love for neighbor must necessarily be exercised from points of view which are never quite those of an impartial observer. Beyond question there takes place grave exaggeration of the claims to righteousness made on behalf of the relatively innocent individual or nation even by those who more or less "unselfishly" champion them.

On the other hand, Ambrose and Augustine were perhaps too extreme in excluding private self-defense as in every case unjustified for the Christian. Luther disagreed with them on this point, but he did so only after surrounding the exercise of any right of personal self-defense with extreme conditions:

> You ask, Why may I not use the sword for myself and for my own cause, with the intention by so doing not of seeking my own interest, but the punishment of evil? I answer, Such a miracle is not impossible, but quite unusual and hazardous. Where there is such affluence of the Spirit it may be done. . . . No one but a real Christian and one who is full of the Spirit will follow this example. If reason also should follow this example, it would indeed pretend not to be seeking its own, but this would be untrue. It cannot be done without grace. Therefore, first become like Samson, and then you can also do as Samson did.[13]

We must ask, What moral conditions will be effected by being full of the Spirit? The answer to this question should be given in light of the fact that Christian ethics always recognizes the Holy Spirit as the spirit of Christ. If from the motivating strategy of Christian love there can be vocational resistance and Christian vocations in society using protective coercion, may there not also be such a thing as vocational self-protection? A Christian does whatever love requires, and the possibility cannot be ruled out that on occasion defending himself may be a duty he owes to others. Whenever sacrificing himself, or in any degree failing to protect himself and his own, actually would involve greater burdens or injury to others, surely then a Christian should stick to his post whether he wants to or not. In such circumstances self-protection becomes a duty, a form of neighbor-regarding love, the protection of others performed first and most effectively upon oneself. Making use of the distinction between "self-defensive self-protection" and "neighbor-regarding self-protection," self-defense may be but an extreme instance of those "duties to the self" which are a part of Christian vocational obligation. This we can conclude without in any way ignoring the fact that Christian ethics from Ambrose to Tolstoy has always, quite correctly, looked upon self-defensiveness and any other form of selfish preferential love with profound suspicion. The Christian point of view, we should always remember, also surrounds an act of giving one's body to be burned with just as grave doubt.

During the height of the submarine warfare in the North Atlantic (during World War II), four chaplains gave over their lifebelts to four "ignorant sailors" and went down

---

13. Muhlenberg, ed., *Secular Authority: To What Extent It Should Be Obeyed*, 249–50.

with the ship. This was, so far as men may judge, a Christian act of self-sacrifice. Suppose the captain of the vessel, himself not involved in the case, had presumed to choose among these men, by his command saying whose life should be saved, whose lost. In order to make such a decision, the captain would have to take many factors into account; on the side of the sailors, their greater service to immediate military ends; against one of them, the fact that he had broken ship's rule by going to sleep without his lifebelt on, that he was unmarried and had few fixed responsibilities to others, that he was not so wise or well-trained or likely to serve humanity in more than ordinary ways; on the side of one of the chaplains, that he was married and the father of several children, moreover a "wise man" and a man of rare character and capacity for unusual service. Now arises the crucial question: In the absence of a third, impartial party responsible for the decision, should a wise man ever refuse to give up his lifebelt to an ignorant sailor? Ought ever an individual act in favor of himself, making the same choice between two lives, his own and his neighbor's, which everyone would regard as entirely just, even obligatory, when such a decision is rendered by some third person not himself involved in the issue?

Men, being evil, may nevertheless know how to give good gifts to their children (Matt 7:11). Just as selfish partiality is never completely absent from decisions about public protection, so also partiality for the interests of one's neighbors need not be completely excluded from decisions and actions which actually undertake to protect the self. Enlightened weighing of a person's responsibilities to others may not only permit saving one's life "for better accounting even if it means only a more promising opportunity for sacrifice" by the merely negative act of keeping possession of a lifebelt or failing to pause and help countless other refugees trekking out of Burma. Care for others for whom a person is vocationally responsible, closely and obviously bound in with protecting himself, may also require more positive action, actually taking away the lives of others, as can be seen in the following modern version of "taking away a plank from an ignorant sailor":

> Today Tom, one of our ambulance drivers of whom I have spoken, went to China. He wanted to go, and yet he did not want to go. The reason he did not want to go was that he found India pleasant, and besides this, he was attached to us as we were to him. The reason he wanted to go was this: When we were coming out of Burma, before we had to abandon our trucks and start walking, we came across a company of wounded Chinese soldiers near Katha. There must have been two hundred of them. My guess is that they had been evacuated from the battlefield to the south and had progressed to Katha. Here the railroad was hopelessly blocked with the tangle of fleeing traffic and the soldiers were thrown on their own to get away from the Japanese who were closing in on all of us. In the staggering heat of that day they saw our convoy of trucks rolling toward them on the dusty road. They must have said to themselves, "Here is perhaps a way of escape. We are desperate men." When our trucks, which had to proceed haltingly for all the traffic, dust, and crowds of evacuees thronging the road, drew opposite them, they hobbled out and swarmed all over the trucks, stopping us.
>
> I cannot find it in me to say a word of blame for what Tom did. I was spared this fearful problem by losing my truck in the muddy bottom of the last river we tried to cross by fording. We were under strict orders not to take on anybody else. To take anybody else would prejudice the hopes we held of

getting our already large, weary, half-sick crowd through safely. We had been without enough to eat, without much sleep for forty-eight hours, and the dust was a distressing coat on our eyelids.

With all these things, elemental, physiological, and spiritual in the setting, *Tom got out and pushed the wounded Chinese soldiers off his truck* as the only means of being able to carry on.—More than one night on the walk out and later in Assam he told me, "I owe the Chinese a debt." When he left today he went to pay it.[14]

The foregoing analysis, it should at once be granted, comes dangerously close to one of Raskolnikov's justifications for his "right to crime" in Dostoyevsky's *Crime and Punishment*.

I simply hinted that an "extraordinary" man has the . . . inner right to decide in his own conscience to overstep . . . certain obstacles, and only in case it is essential for the practical fulfillment of his idea (something, perhaps, of benefit to the whole of humanity). . . . I maintain that if the discoveries of Kepler and Newton could not have been made known except by sacrificing the lives of one, a dozen, a hundred or more men, Newton would have had the right, would indeed have been duty bound . . . to *eliminate* the dozen or the hundred for the sake of making his discoveries known to the whole of humanity. . . . But if such a one is forced for the sake of his idea to step over a corpse or wade through blood, he can, I maintain, find within himself, in his conscience, a sanction for wading through blood—that depends on the idea and its dimensions, of course.[15]

What, if anything, is the difference between this line of reasoning and a justifiably Christian ethic of protection? For one thing, the Christian does not suppose that he is "extraordinary," but that his duty is extraordinary, or in another sense ordinary, all too ordinary, human, all too human. For another, the Christian acts not for the sake of "the idea and its dimensions" or primarily for the sake of some abstract truth. He acts on behalf of his neighbors and their concrete needs which may have to be served on occasion by the employment of unpleasant means. Christian morality does not permit him even to disguise his private self-assertion under the rubric of abstract concern for "benefit to the whole of humanity." This Raskolnikov finally confesses was the true analysis of the nature of his crime. As for wanting to be an extraordinary man who really has the right to step over corpses, he says later:

Of course that's all nonsense, it's almost all talk! . . . I wanted *to have the daring* . . . I wanted to murder without casuistry, to murder for my own sake, for myself alone. . . . I didn't do the murder to gain wealth and power and to become a benefactor of mankind. Nonsense! I simply did it; I did the murder for myself, for myself alone. . . . I wanted to find then and quickly . . . whether I can step over barriers or not.[16]

Purified of such perverse self-concern, the Christian nevertheless must adjudicate and decide one way or another among the claims and needs of neighbors he is to serve.

14. Geren, *Burma Diary*, 55–56 (italics added).
15. Dostoyevsky, *Crime and Punishment*, Part 3, chapter 5, 247, 248.
16. Dostoyevsky, *Crime and Punishment*, Part 5, chapter 4, 392, 395.

In doing so, he at least omits to serve some, and in this sense he wades through blood and suffering. If such a one is forced for the sake of his neighbors visibly to step over a corpse, he can, I maintain, find within himself, in his Christian conscience, a sanction which depends on a proper reading of his actual situation, and the needs of neighbors determining his vocation. The only way of avoiding this conclusion is by recourse to "intuition" as the basis of obligation. This would be a form of "unenlightened unselfishness" which surely requires for justification more than the fact of man's proneness to sin in using his intelligence.

No doubt a man stands always in grave peril of choosing only the manifestation of love which pleases him best. He faces this same peril of deceiving himself and others and loving no one but himself even when he sacrifices himself and others. This . . . gives special relevance and validity to Christian love as a requirement in every action. Men who are always surrounded on every side by complex relationships delineating their vocational obligations, and whose moral decisions can never escape from these bonds, for this very reason have special need of a sense that they still "owe the Chinese a debt," they need some St. Francis to walk by their side troubling them. Since there is always more than one neighbor, men have special need of an ethic which defines with utter clarity and rigor their full duty toward any and every one of them. Whether Jesus intentionally or from his sense of apocalypse pictured the simplest possible moral situation, the result is undeniable: men may see in his strenuous teachings how they ought conscientiously to act toward every neighbor. Walking beside this unqualified disclosure of the pure will of God, measuring their lives in this mirror, Christians find repeated stimulus for remembering all their obligation, even though they are always surrounded by a vast network of neighbor-claims which converge and create for each of them some specific vocation. The essential meaning of Christian vocation, therefore, is not simply some worldly position interpreted in general religious fashion as God-given. Christian vocation means the secular occupation, the "station" and its full, often obnoxious duties, to which an individual feels himself assigned by Christian love or by the love of Christ controlling him.

The fundamental meaning of Christian ethics may be thrown into bolder relief by comparing the entire expulsion of legitimate private self-defense by Ambrose and Augustine with what has happened in much modern pacifism. Modern pacifists frequently revealed their non-Christian rootage by making quite the reverse combination of ideas from that which prevailed for centuries in Christian ethics. Early Christian thought, we have seen, was concerned to deny any analogy between private and public defense in order to say that a Christian, who might participate in armed and bloody conflict for the sake of public protection, would of course not resist even by mild or passive means any neighbor who might assault him when his own goods and life alone were threatened. In direct contrast, much modern pacifism also attempts to break down all analogy between private and public defense, but for purpose of establishing almost the reverse conclusion, namely, that of course individuals ought to resist by going to law if someone wishes to take away their coat and with possibly bloodless methods in case they individually (and certainly when their grandmothers) are violently attacked. We need have no great sympathy for the "grandmother argument" often presented by draft boards to "conscientious objectors" to military service. Nevertheless, it is clear that modern pacifists, in withdrawing completely from resistance on behalf of national defense, frequently make greater accommodation to the supposed natural necessity of self-defense (or some sort of multilateral ethic of defense limited to the private area where extreme violence need not be used) than ever occurred to the great thinkers who first forged a Christian theory of *justum bellum*. Searching for an explanation, we may be driven to reflect that both the pacifism of early Christians and their shift over to resistance in the light of increasing responsibility were basically grounded in Christian love, while in contrast a good deal of contemporary pacifism is grounded in horror and revulsion at the sight of violence or bloodshed and in an ethic which values life above everything else. Violence and bloodshed are no doubt horrifying, especially in destructive, total war, but the word unlovely has in Christian ethics a mainly spiritual, not a mainly physical, meaning, A selfish act is the most unlovely thing, and an unselfish motive may lead the Christian to perform necessary responsibilities which prove not so "nice" in terms of physical contamination, For a Christian outlook, sin came first into the world, death followed; sin, or the contrary of love, is the greatest evil from which men need to be delivered, death is only the last enemy of mankind which shall be destroyed, and the sting of death is in fact sin (1 Cor 15:26,56). For many pacifists, however, bloodshed and death are the worst evils, life a conditional or even the highest value which ought never to be violated. And as a consequence they are willing to approve resistance in those forms and under circumstances, in court or at fisticuffs or by aiming low, when a man may hope to stop short of bringing death to an opponent.

Such a view has more in common with dualistic pacifism in the ancient world or with otherworldly Indian religious ethics than with early Christian pacifism. As we have seen, Christian ethics first of all approved public protection and the defense of organized justice as the only means of loving the neighbor with all his concrete physical and social needs in *this* world, and judged that such action might be unselfish even if hopelessly bloody. Centuries later Christian ethics approved private self-defense, which doubtless is nicer but almost always more selfish.

Moreover, it is still true that emotional horror over physical evils may indicate stronger love for ourselves than for love for neighbor.

> Today we have to move the evacuee patients out of one hospital building into another. It was a filthy job because so many patients had dysentery. The man whom this foul disease clutches soon becomes unable to move or do anything for himself. He fouls his clothing, the bedding, the stretcher on which we have put him. There is no fresh clothing and bedding to change him. Piles of it lie all about the place all the day unwashed.
>
> It rains every day and no one has the resolution to start the cleansing job since he could never get the things dry. Patients, soiled bedding, soiled clothing all join to send up a reeking stench like a burnt offering to some perverse devil.
>
> Three of us stood surveying the preparations for moving: an American boy who had joined the British Army before we got into the war, his British soldier comrade and I. We saw that the patients had to be moved and that the sweepers who had been assigned to the task were not getting along very quickly with it. If the others were feeling what I felt, we were all dreading to get on any more

intimate terms with the stench and handle it. The American turned to his British comrade and said, "I am very glad at this moment that I am agnostic."

I do not know how seriously he intended this. However that is, the conclusion which he implied certainly held: Since he did not believe in the love of Christ he could leave the handling of these dysentery victims to the sweepers. Since his friend did believe in it, he was not free to stand by and watch. Nor was I. Get down in it! Pick the patients up! Soil yourself with the disease! St. Francis kissed the beggars' sores. However this ended in him, it must have begun as the practice of the only medicine he knew. There is no need to call this filthiness sweet, or to start enjoying it through a strange inversion. Only one thing is necessary: for love's sake it must be done.[17]

Participation in regrettable conflict falls among distasteful tasks which sometimes become imperative for Christian vocation. Only one thing is necessary: for love's sake, it must be done. All things now are lawful, all things are now permitted, yet everything is required which Christian love requires, everything without a single exception.

17. Geren, *Burma Diary*, 51–52.

2–9

"Lima or Amsterdam: Liberation or Disclosure?"

Nicholas Wolterstroff[1]

OUR MODERN SOCIAL WORLD is a world of striking triumphs. Many in this world have experienced that unprecedented expansion in range of choices of which we spoke in the preceding chapter. But this world of ours is also a world of deep sorrows.

There are, for one thing, the *sorrows of injustice*. Those who enjoy a vast range of choice coexist in our world-system with nearly a billion others who live in a state of perpetual poverty, and with hundreds of millions for whom political terror, torture, and tyranny are the ever-present context of their lives—their oppression often being perpetrated or supported by those very governments whose citizens enjoy great freedom.

There are also *sorrows of misplaced values*, as one might call them. The desires we choose to satisfy by our conquest of nature in our alteration of society are often profoundly perverse. Hundreds of billions of dollars are spent each year on armaments to terrorize and kill our fellow human beings. Tens of billions are stupidly spent each year by the well-to-do on outrageous luxuries.

In addition there are all those miseries that *result* from our social order—call them the *sorrows of undesired consequences*: the destruction of traditions, the loss of a sense of rooted support and belongingness resulting from the destruction of concrete communities, the agonies of indecision resulting from costly being confronted with the need to make choices concerning one's social rules and one's worldview, the boredom resulting from work utterly lacking in intrinsic satisfaction and performed merely as a means to acquire the money to support one's family, the loss of freedom resulting from the encroachment of bureaucracies, the elimination of environments expressive of our inner selves resulting from the pervasive rationalization of our lives.

This is not even to mention the threats, which we in the core area all acutely sense, to the maintenance and direction of the social system that we have created. The shared frameworks of belief whereby we interpret our experience and legitimate our actions, thus, to undergird our life together, are slipping away, often to be transformed into little else than chauvinistic nationalism. The limits of that natural world to revise the indispensable context for the social order are being severely depressed by pollution of

---

1. From Wolterstroff, *Until Justice & Peace Embrace*, 42–68.

the environment and exhaustion of resources. And through it all, our system acts in ways we are either do not understand or cannot control.

This is the world we have made for ourselves. It is a world with which only the privileged, and the imperceptive at that, could be satisfied. What we must now begin to consider is how Christians should act in this world, and how, as they see it, others should act as well. In a world such as this, what should be our *project*? As background to these considerations we shall also want to reflect on how the picture drawn of our society fits into the larger Christian vision of life and reality. How does it all hang together?

I propose that, rather than conducting these reflections from the ground up by ourselves, we see what we can learn from two of the most penetrating contemporary articulations of world formative Christianity: *liberation theology*, especially in South American, mainly Catholic form; and the *neo-Calvinism* which has its source in the Netherlands of late 19th and early 20th centuries. I picked these two because in both one finds a penetrating analysis of our contemporary social world combined with a comprehensive Christian vision of history and Society. All too often one finds either or both of these missing in the approach of contemporary Christians to social issues; their analysis is typically superficial, or their vision pitched. We shall see that there are some fundamental affinities between these two patterns of thought, but we shall also uncover some substantial disagreements. At several points we shall find ourselves forced to choose, and the decision-making process will help greatly in illuminating some of the profound issues at stake.

Since it is not my aim to give a comprehensive description of the social thought of these two movements, but rather to elicit from them patterns of Christian social thought, I propose that we concentrate our attention on representative spokesmen. For liberation theology I shall concentrate mainly on Gustavo Gutiérrez; for neo-Calvinism, on Herman Dooyeweerd and Bob Goudzwaard. In effect, we will be engaging in what Max Weber called "ideal-type" analysis; but rather than doing so in the abstract, we will look at the formulation of those who come as close as any to expressing the ideal type.

To grasp the thought of the liberation theologians, let us begin where they themselves begin: with the cries of suffering humanity for deliverance, or, more pointedly, with the cries of those whose misery is grounded in the social order. Liberation theologians are not indifferent to the suffering caused by disease, anxiety, or other pandemic maladies, but they're especially attuned to the poor, the hungry, the voiceless, the terrorized of the world. And since they live in the Third World, it is the cries of those in that part of our world-system that they hear most clearly.

Liberation theologians, who are urged to their reflections by the cries the wretched of the earth, begin having already come to certain conclusions as to the cause of their misery. Why are those with whom they identify so wretched when others in the world— some in their own country, and very many in the core areas of our world-system—are so wealthy and powerful? Of course they know the traditional answer—something within the structure of Third World societies causes lack of development—but they no longer accept it as the full truth. Says Gutiérrez, "there will be a true development for Latin America only through liberation from the domination by capitalist countries.

That implies, of course, a showdown with their natural allies: our national oligarchies."[2] In short, the liberation theologians have chosen decisively for the world-system interpretation of the underdevelopment of the Third World, an interpretation that considers underdevelopment to being in good measure rooted in the exploitative domination of the periphery of the world-system by the core.

They have seen the coming and going of development programs since the Second World War; none has alleviated the misery of their people. Their net result has always been greater development for the core areas along with luxury for the oligarchies of the Third World. The benefits of development do not trickle down to the masses. Hunger and poverty remain their daily ration. One of the most significant sources of the misery of the people is the fact that they belong to the periphery of the capitalist world-economy and in their exchange with the core areas find themselves constantly losers. The oppressive political structures of the periphery are among the mechanisms that ensure this. Voicelessness and terror join hands with hunger and poverty.

In short, the liberation theologians' analysis of the misery of their people leads them to the conclusion that those people are being wronged—they are being exploitatively dominated by the core areas of the world system and by the small but powerful oligarchies in the periphery. Their analysis leads the liberation theologians to take sides with those whose cries they hear, to stand against those who oppress them. They declare their solidarity with the people, and to implement that declaration they resolve to contribute as best they can to the relief of this oppression. There are theorizing is openly done on behalf of the miserable. They intend to give the wretched of the earth their voice. Their theorizing is a species of *praxis-oriented* theory. Their theology "does not stop with reflecting on the world but rather try to be part of the process through which the world is transformed."[3]

It is obvious now why such individuals are called *liberation* theologians (though we shall shortly see that the theme of liberation resonates yet more deeply in their theology than this). They have heard the cries of their people and perceived the deep root of their misery is oppression: the people are being wrong. In response, liberation theologians declare that the people must be liberated from oppression if they are to be released from their misery—and that liberation is their project. Says Gutiérrez, "to speak of a transformation of history from the perspective of dominated and exploited peoples, from the perspective of the poor of this world brings us to see it as a *liberating* praxis [which] acquired a *subversive* perspective. It is subversive of a social order in which the poor person, the 'other' of this society, scarcely begins to be heard."[4]

I've been describing the situation in which Liberation theologians do their theorizing: they intend their theorizing as a *reflection on* that situation and as *an instrument in* its alteration. But we are not yet done. The situation, as our theologians see it, includes more; it includes the spreading of a certain consciousness in the masses—mainly, an

2. Gutiérrez, "Notes for a Theology of Liberation," 249–50.

3. Gutiérrez, *A Theology of Liberation: History, Politics and Salvation*, 15. Subsequent references to this book (hereafter abbreviated *TL*) will be made parenthetically in the text.

4. Gutiérrez, *Liberation and Change*, 84–85.

awareness that a fundamental cause of their misery lies in their domination by the rich and powerful of the world. In other words, the liberation theologians' own analysis of the situation of their people is increasingly being shared by those very people.[5] "The poor countries," says Gutiérrez, ". . . are becoming ever more clearly aware that their underdevelopment is only the by-product of the development of other countries, because of the kind of relationship which exists between the rich and poor countries. Moreover, they are realizing that their own development will come about only with a struggle to break the domination of the rich countries" (*TL*, 26).[6]

It is important for us in the West to let these words sink in. Most of us are still in the thrall of development (modernization) theory. We believe that a bit of economic aid scattered here and there around the globe will get things moving, and we expect those to whom these crumbs are tossed to applaud our largesse. But those in the periphery of the world increasingly see us as predators rather than benefactors. The buildup of this discrepancy of perception is filled with explosive potential. From what I said in the preceding chapter, it will be evident that my own conviction is that the Third World is largely right on this issue and that we are wrong. (I shall have more to say on the matter in the next chapter.)

Of course the concepts of domination and exploitation are common tools of the trade for Marxists, and, as one might well expect, liberation theologians are regularly accused of being Marxists. The answer is that they are simply trying to understand what it is that perpetuates the social misery of their people. They find Marxist analysis, and its general contours, to provide the most plausible explanation of their situation. They're not committed to Marxism as an ideology by which to live and die; if someone offers them an alternative analysis, they will consider it. Furthermore, some such social analysis is unavoidable. The Christian gospel cannot be applied immediately to the issues in society. A mediating analysis is imperative.[7]

Gutiérrez and his colleagues argue that the spreading consciousness of domination, in the spreading the termination to throw off the shackles of that domination, must be set in the yet larger context of an alteration taking place in the consciousness of mankind generally. "A historical vision in which mankind assumes control of it [*sic*] on destiny" is emerging, suggests Gutiérrez; ". . . the social praxis of contemporary man has begun to reach maturity. It is the behavior of man ever more conscious of being an active subject in history; he's ever more articulate in the face of social injustice in all repressive forces would

---

5. For illustrations of the spread of this new consciousness, see Part 5 of Gunder Frank's *Crisis: In the World Economy*.

6. See also *TL*, 84; and Gutiérrez, *Liberation and Change*, 76–77.

7. The liberationists' interaction with Marxism goes beyond the basic social analysis they share: they are committed, remember, to working substantively for the liberation of their people, and many Marxists are committed to working for the same goal. Thus the liberationist shares with the Marxist the *praxis* of liberation as well as the analysis of social dynamics. One senses that it is here, at the level of praxis, that the relation of these two becomes more problematic: although their background ideologies are profoundly different, their short-term goals are similar. What then is the advisability of cooperation? The Argentinian theologian José Míguez-Bonino examines this issue with care in his book *Christians and Marxists*.

stand in the way of his fulfillment; he is ever more determined to participate both in the transformation of social structures and in effective political action" (*TL*, 25, 46).

The spreading consciousness of man as "an active subject of history" is taking the form, says Gutierrez, of an increasing commitment to liberation from all that binds and enthralls: "A broad and deep aspiration for liberation inflames the history of mankind in our day, liberation from all that limits or keeps man from self-fulfillment, liberation from all impediments to the exercise of his freedom. Proof of this is awareness of new and subtle forms of oppression in the heart of advanced industrial societies . . ." (*TL*, 27). The point here is so important that it is worth citing one of Gutiérrez's liberation colleagues as well; J. Severino Croatto puts it this way:

> The struggle of so many oppressed peoples who are seeking to "say their word" who desire to "be" what now they know they can be and must be, is perhaps the characteristic phenomenon of our time. There is no value placed on freedom. . . . The massive cry of humankind, which suddenly feels itself groaning under the human-made yoke of "being-of-another" now attains an unprecedented volume thanks to the new method of "conscientization" orchestrated by the social sciences in the mass media. The degree of maturity achieved by the people of our century does not permit them to attribute their ills to *fate* . . . .[8]

Thus Gutiérrez and his colleagues do not merely reflect on that longing for political and economic liberation which is now so pervasive among the miserable of the Third World; they reflect as well on this broader and deeper "liberation consciousness": "At a deeper level, *liberation* can be applied to an understanding of history. Man is seen as assuming conscious responsibility for his own destiny. . . . In this perspective the unfolding of all man's dimensions is demanded—a man who makes himself throughout his life and throughout history. The gradual conquest of true freedom leads to the creation of a new man and a qualitatively different society. This vision provides, therefore, a better understanding of what in fact is at stake in our times" (*TL*, 36–37). For the liberation theologian, history both is, and is increasingly seen to be, "a process of the liberation of man"; and the liberation in question is "a historical conquest": "the stuff from an abstract to a real freedom is not taken without a struggle against all the forces that oppress man. . . . The goal is not only better living conditions, a radical change of structures, a social revolution; it is much more: the continuous creation, never ending, of new ways of a man, a *permanent cultural revolution*" (*TL*, 32).

It is here that I find one of the most unsatisfactory points in Gutiérrez's thought. What exactly is this liberation that he sees as taking place in history by virtue (in good measure) of man's *determination* to be free? What, for him, is liberation in its comprehensive sense? That it *includes* liberation from exploitative domination is clear, but that it goes beyond this is also clear. Often Gutiérrez makes the point that comprehensive liberation includes liberation from sin—that is, from the hostility among men and between man and God. And he insistently adds that sin must not be seen as something *in addition* to social oppressions; to the contrary, structures of unjust domination and exploitation are *manifestations* of sin:

8. Croatto, *Exodus*, 5.

> In the liberation approach sin is not considered as an individual, private, or merely interior reality.... Sin is regarded as a social, historical fact, the absence of brotherhood and love in relationships among men, the breach of friendship with God and with other men, and therefore, an interior, personal fracture. When it is considered in this way, the collective dimensions of sin are rediscovered. ... Sin is evident in oppressive structures, in the exploitation of man by man, in the domination and slavery of peoples, races, and social classes. Sin appears, therefore, as the fundamental alienation, the root of a situation of injustice and exploitation. It cannot be encountered in itself, but only in concrete instances, in particular alienations. It is impossible to understand the concrete manifestations without understanding the underlying basis and vice versa. (*TL*, 175–176)[9, 10]

But does Gutiérrez wish to say that *all* liberation is liberation from sin? As we shall shortly see, it does seem that sin constitutes for him the key link between liberation and salvation; yet, is it at all plausible to read history as an increasing liberation from sin? And does Gutiérrez not also have in mind, when he speaks of "liberation," certain processes not connected with sin, such as improvement in living conditions? My own guess is that when he describes our own actual history as a growth in liberation, he is in fact describing the process I outlined earlier as the unprecedented expansion in the range of choice that has come to many in the modern world-system as a result of our expansion of mastery over nature and corresponding alterations of social structure. Yet when Gutiérrez gives his *theological* interpretation of history as the history of liberation, he tends to have something different in mind: liberation from *sin* and its effects—particularly its social-structural effects.

Apart from these last critical comments, I have thus far been describing what Gutiérrez sees as our present situation and what his commitments are within that situation. He considers his task as Christian theologian to be that of reflecting critically on this situation in the light of the Word of God; Christian theology in general, as he sees it, is "a critical reflection in and on historical praxis in confrontation with the word of the Lord lived and accepted in the faith."[11] Mainly, says Gutiérrez, he will reflect on the relation "between salvation and historical process of the liberation of man," or in other words, on the relation "between the Kingdom of God and the building up of the world" (*TL*, 45).[12]

9. See also Gutiérrez, *TL*, 35, and *Liberation and Change*, 84.

10. I would add that it seems to be doubtful that all injustice has its roots in sin, if we are understanding sin as hostility; some injustices, for example, are committed through ignorance.

11. Gutiérrez, "The Hope of Liberation," 67. Elsewhere Gutiérrez similarly speaks of his project as "a reflection on the theological meaning of the process of the liberation of man throughout history" (*TL*, x); and he also speaks of "the function of theology as critical reflection on Christian praxis in the light of the Word" (*TL*, 13) and of "reflect[ing] critically on the praxis of liberation," (*TL*, 14), etc.

12. I have described Gutiérrez's approach as if his social-theoretical *interpretation* of his situation and his *project* in that situation are givens so far as the Word of God and the task of the theologians are concerned, and that the business of the theologian is simply to interpret these givens in the light of the Word of God. Though this is usually the picture Gutiérrez draws, I do not think that he entirely means it thus. In any case, I would insist that the following points must also be kept in mind: (1) the Word of God comes as critique of, and guide and dynamic for, our praxis (project); (2) the Word of God ought to inform our social-theoretical analysis of our situation (this point is further developed in chapter VIII of this text and also in my *Reason within the Bounds of Religion*); and (3) we should also reflect on the Word of God itself, and, in so doing, we should see that it speaks of more than just social praxis.

Two principles are fundamental here, he says. First, "there are not two histories, one profane and one sacred, 'juxtaposed' or 'closely linked.'" There is not a history of the world and then in addition a history of the church, with only the latter being of abiding significance. Our history is the history of the world with a church in it: "there is only one human destiny, irreversibly assumed by Christ, the Lord of history" (*TL*, 153). Second, this history has a salvific significance; or, better, this history is the *scene* of salvation. It is not the case that salvation is to be found only at the end of history, with all that preceded it having been nothing more than a preparation; it is, as Gutiérrez states, "an intra-historical reality." After all, the sin from which we are saved is not only an impediment to salvation in the afterlife. Insofar as it constitutes a break with God, sin as historical reality. . . . One looks then to this world, and now sees in the world beyond not the "true life" but rather the transformation and fulfillment of the present life. The absolute value of salvation—far from devaluing this world—gives it its own autonomy, because salvation is already latent there. . . . The history of salvation is the very heart of human history. . . . The salvific action of God underlies all human existence. The historical destiny of humanity must be placed definitively in the salvific horizon. Only thus will its true dimensions emerge and its deepest meaning be apparent. (*TL*, 152–53)

If we grant that history is in essence the history of liberation, then we must conclude that Gutiérrez is suggesting that the liberation of mankind and salvation of mankind are not two separate things, but one and the same. Salvation is the total liberation of humanity in all dimensions of its existence, achieved by Christ: "the liberating action of Christ—made man in this history and not in history marginal to the real life of man—is at the heart of the historical currency of humanity . . ." (*TL*, 168). But what exactly is the link here between liberation and salvation? Far and away the dominant thrust of Gutiérrez's discussion is that the link is sin: the salvation of Christ secures is salvation from sin, and liberation at its deepest level is also liberation from sin. "Christ the Savior liberates man from sin, which is the ultimate root of all disruptions of friendship and of all injustice and oppression. Christ makes man truly free, that is to say, he enables man to live in communion with him; and that is the basis for all human brotherhood" (*TL*, 37).

But despite his insistence that salvation from sin constitutes the essence of liberation, one senses in Gutiérrez a hesitant awareness of the point I made earlier: that much and what he wants the word *liberation* to denote within the context of history as the history of liberation has been achieved not by the conquest of sin but by the master of nature. In the extended consideration of the relation between creation and salvation (*TL*, 153–60), Gutiérrez takes notes of the teaching of Genesis 1 that, as he puts it, "man is the crown and center of the work of creation and is called to continue it through his labor" (*TL*, 158). No doubt a development of this point could go a long way toward providing the missing link. Yet in this same passage he devotes most of his efforts to arguing that God (and, correspondingly, man's) creative activity must itself be seen as salvific. The evidence that he presents for this conclusion is the fact that when Israel confessed God as creator, it spoke of the God whom it already knew as liberator, and furthermore that it never ceased to link its confession of God as creator with its confession of God as savior. In short, what we see in Gutiérrez is an example of that regular practice among contemporary theologians of treating creation as an act of salvation—without ever being able to say what creation saves us from—rather than setting salvation within the context of (a disrupted) creation. As a result, salvation and history, in spite of the deepest motivations on the part of Gutiérrez, remain unlinked. If we understand liberation in such a way as to make it possible to read history as the history of liberation, then there is no plausible direct link between liberation on the one hand and salvation from sin on the other. But if we understand liberation in such a way that is directly linked to salvation from sin, then it becomes impossible to read history as the history of liberation.

But let us return to Gutiérrez's argument. If salvation is ultimately liberation from sin, and if sin manifests itself in oppressive social structures, then it follows that the struggle to eliminate those structures has salvific significance. Although "the liberation of Christ cannot be equated with political liberation," still "it takes place in historical and political liberating acts. It is not possible to avoid these mediations," he asserts.[13] "All struggle against exploitation and alienation . . . is an attempt to vanquish selfishness, the negation of love. This is the reason why any effort to build a just society is liberation. . . . It is salvific work, although it is not all of salvation" (*TL*, 176–77).

On the other hand, "the process of liberation will not have conquered the very roots of oppression and the exploitation of man by man without the coming of the Kingdom, which is above all a gift." Although "the historical, political liberating event *is* the growth of the Kingdom and *is* a salvific event, . . . it is not *the* coming of the Kingdom, not *all* of salvation" (*TL*, 177). "Radical liberation is the gift which Christ offers us. By his death and resurrection he redeems man from sin and all its consequences . . ." (*TL*, 176).

In short, the movement of history toward *freedom*, whereby man shapes his own destiny, is the movement toward God's *salvation* of mankind, and political and economic liberation is an indispensable component in this process; consequently,

> when we assert that man fulfills himself by continuing the work of creation by means of his labor, we are saying that he places himself, by this very fact, within an all-embracing salvific process. To work, to transform this world, is to become a man and to build the human community; it is also to save. Likewise, the struggle against misery and exploitation and to build a just society is already to be part of the saving action, which is moving toward its complete fulfillment. All this means that building the temporal city is not simply a stage of "humanization" for "pre-evangelization" as was held in theology up until a few years ago. Rather it is to become part of a saving process which embraces the whole of man and all human history. (*TL*, 159–60)

To conclude our presentation of Gutiérrez's views, let us circle back and bring to light one last feature of the situation in which he sees himself as doing his theologizing. Not only is there a growing longing in humankind for comprehensive liberation, of which the growing awareness of oppression among the miserable of the Third World (along with their growing determination to throw off the bonds of that oppression) is a reflection; there is also a growing conviction among *Christians* of the Third World that it is their evangelical calling to participate in these revolutionary movements. Gutiérrez

13. Gutiérrez, *Liberation and Change*, 85–86.

sees himself as giving expression to, and reflecting on, this new Christian consciousness. "From this viewpoint of faith," he writes, "the motive which in the last instance moves Christians to participate in the liberation of oppressed peoples and exploited social classes is the conviction of the radical incompatibility of evangelical demands with an unjust and alienating society" (*TL*, 145). More and more this conviction is spreading throughout the Christians of the Third World:

> The different sector of the People of God are gradually committing themselves in different ways to the process of liberation. They are becoming aware that this liberation implies a break with the status quo, that it calls for social revolution. In relation to the entire Latin American Christian community it must be acknowledged that the number of persons involved is small. But the numbers are growing and active and every day they are acquiring a larger hearing both inside and outside the church. (*TL*, 102)[14]

It is here that I wish to pose my last question to Gutiérrez, a question intimately connected with the preceding ones: What exactly is the historical project in which he sees the Christian as called to work? Toward what goal do we devote our efforts and call others to devote theirs as well? Liberation is a process, a movement *from* something *toward* something. In choosing the word *liberation* our theologian wishes, among other things, to emphasize that often this process is a *conflictual struggle*. But what are we to move from what are we to move toward? After liberation, what?

Often the answer to this question given by liberation theologians is "freedom." After liberation, freedom. Freedom is the end-state toward which we aim. Consider, for example, these words of Croatto: "we discover ourselves as 'called to freedom'"; at the same time, we "become conscious that we do not possess it—whether as individuals or as people. In the face of both the danger of frustration and the attraction of that vocation, we initiate a *process* of liberation. Hence the important goal is not liberation, but freedom. The former is a process 'toward' the latter, which is the ontological 'locus' wherein human beings can be fulfilled."[15] But what are we to understand by *freedom* here? The answer to that question does not become clear; or rather, insofar as it becomes clear, it becomes equally clear that *freedom* is a poor word for the end-state envisaged. It sometimes appears that Croatto has in mind what he calls *creativity*.

Similar difficulties haunt Gutiérrez's discussion. In one important passage he cites Descartes, Kant, Hegel, Marx, Freud, and Marcuse as the great "freedom thinkers," though indeed he also makes it clear that he does not "endorse without question every aspect of this development of ideas" (*TL*, 28–32). Now, for Hegel, Marx, Freud, and Marcuse, I think it is indeed accurate to say that the goal they envisage for liberation is simply *freedom*, for in their view the great evil from which we must be saved is that of being shaped by influences external to ourselves, whether those influences take the

14. Speaking of the "client states" of the United States, Noam Chomsky and Edward S. Herman say that "as in Europe in the 1930s, only the church has survived as a potential protector of the majority"; and, speaking of Latin America, they say that "the churches fight a lonely battle as the last institutional protection of the mass of the population" (*The Washington Connection and Third World Fascism*, Vol. 1, in *The Political Economy of Human Rights*, 11, 262).

15. Croatto, *Exodus*, 5.

form of external formation or of internal inhibition; correspondingly, the goal is self-determination, autonomy, maturation.

It is my own view that this vision of our goal is deeply unsatisfactory. In the first place, it is psychologically untenable. We are all shaped in countless ways by the people who surround us, unavoidably so. Nobody is and nobody could be self-determining.[16] Everybody is "dominated." The relevant question is not how to eliminate influence on the self, but instead the normative question as to which forms of influence are desirable and which not—and, in particular, which forms of influence constitute oppression.

In the second place, we all know from experience that when each of us is given a voice in the direction of society, we say different things, and clearly we cannot all have our way. Some can, some cannot. I know of course that to solve this dilemma there have been attempts to distinguish the voice of the "real self" from the voice of the "unreal self," the assumption being that all true selves speak with one voice. I also know that the ideology which sometimes lies behind the so-called "dictatorship of the proletariat" is that the Party knows what the real self of the proletariat is saying, and that that voice is in turn the voice of the real self of all members of the society.[17] The metaphysics of real and unreal selves is as implausible as the oppression is tangible among those in the contemporary world who find themselves saddled with these dictators who tell them what their true selves are saying.[18]

There is yet a third reason for finding it unacceptable to say that freedom, understood as self-determination, is the overarching goal of our social endeavors. We human beings are a mixture of good impulses and bad, amongst these latter being even, on occasion, the impulse to do what one knows one should not do. The Christian reads these impulses of having, at bottom, the character of sin: hostility toward God and one's fellows. But if this is true, then obviously the goal for each cannot be self-determination, maturation, removal of all external influence and all internal inhibition. Our sinful impulses are not to be satisfied but to be conquered, inhibited—dominated, if you will. To acknowledge the presence of sin in our existence is to acknowledge that we have no choice but to engage in the difficult task of *normative reflection*, asking, among other questions, which impulses of the self are to be satisfied and which suppressed.

As I have already indicated, Gutiérrez also sees sin as a profound factor in the human self. Consequently, although the direction of Enlightenment thought clearly has some allure for him, his awareness of sin prevents that line of thought from being dominant in his thinking. Never does he link his understanding of salvation with his reading of history by proposing that Christ saves us for autonomy and self-determination. Christ saves us from sin. But once again, for what? "For love" is the answer most prominent in Gutiérrez: after liberation, love. "Liberation from sin and communion with God in solidarity with all men" is the end-state (*TL*, p. 238). He does indeed say such things as that "the utopia of liberation [is] the creation . . . definitively, of freedom," but immediately

16. I shall not at this point stop to consider Kant's strategy of dividing us up into a transcendent self which is self-determining and an empirical self which is not. For an extended treatment of the whole issue of human self-determination, see my book, *Educating for Responsible Action*.

17. See Lukács, *History and Class Consciousness: Studies in Marxist Dialectics*.

18. See Berlin, "Two Concepts of Liberty."

he makes it clear that by "freedom" he has in mind "the communion of all men with God. This communion implies liberation from sin, the ultimate root of all injustice, all exploitation, all dissidence among men" (*TL*, p. 237).

Surely this is better than positing that illusory state of self-determination as the goal of our human project. But now our old question returns to haunt us. Love pertains to the relation among human persons, and between them and God. How does our mastery of nature fit into this image of the goal of our human project? Once again the failure of linkage between salvation and history becomes manifest—though what never comes undone in Gutiérrez is the link between salvation from sin and liberation from oppression.

The paradigmatic biblical event for the liberation theologians is the Exodus. Yet the hexateuch does not use *freedom* to describe the end-state of this great liberation. Characteristically when it wants a single word to describe that rich and complex reality which Israel found in the promised land, that word is *rest*. Is there a clue in that? And contrary to Croatto's interpretation, Genesis does not say that mankind's uniqueness lies in our call to freedom; it lies in our being responsible, in our being created for responsible actions: to be human is to be *called*. Is there also a clue in that?

Let us move on to see whether some of the questions we have posed are answered in the neo-Calvinist vision—hanging on, however, to the core the liberation theologian's message: that the Gospel calls us to struggle for the liberation of the oppressed.

Turning from liberation theology to neo-Calvinism as expressed in Herman Dooyeweerd, one is struck first by the differences. Here the cries of the wretched of the earth are not given voice. Here there is little talk of oppression, and consequently little of liberation from oppression; the talk is more of "authority structures." And here there are no reflections on violence (which, incidentally, makes neo-Calvinism significantly different also from early Calvinism). There is indeed talk of conflict in society, but it is the religious conflict between believer and idolater and not the social conflict between oppressor and oppressed that is discussed.

It must frankly be said that in this respect the second generation of the neo-Calvinist movement, of which Dooyeweerd is representation, is different from the first generation. The movement began at the end of the nineteenth century by listening to the cries of certain oppressed people—the *kleine luyden* (little people) of nineteenth-century Holland.[19] Victimized economically by agricultural crises and industrialization, they felt themselves even more profoundly threatened in matters of both church and state by the liberalism of the regnant bourgeoisie. Their religious convictions were being trampled on, alien ideologies were being forced on them and their children, and all voice in the political-social and ecclesiastical shaping of Dutch society was being denied them. The neo-Calvinist movement arose out of commitment to the cause of these people. It was a struggle for their liberation—mainly successful, it may be added.

There can be no doubt that the social theory of the movement today continues to reflect its origins—as, for example, in its perception of the basic conflict in society as the Augustinian conflict between the City of God and the City of the world. And in general,

19. See Kuiper, *De Voormannen: Een Sociaal-Wetenschappelijke Studie over Ideologie, Konflikt en Kerngroepvorming binnen de Gereformeerde Wereld in Nederland tussen 1820 en 1930*. See also Kuiper, "Historical and Sociological Development of ARP and CDA."

the themes the Dooyeweerd developed were present in embryonic form in the movement at its beginning, but at that stage they were balanced by other themes as well—such as, importantly, those of oppression and liberation.

Basic to the neo-Calvinist analysis of society is the perception of history as fundamentally the interaction of two deep dynamics. One of these is the dynamic just mentioned—call it the dynamic of *faith/idolatry*. The other is the dynamic of *differentiation*. In the discussion that follows, our interest will not so much be in attaining a thoroughgoing understanding of these dynamics as such; rather, we will attempt an analysis of contemporary society in terms of these dynamics using the insights of Bob Goudzwaard contained in his book *Capitalism and Progress*. Nevertheless, if we are to understand Goudzwaard's thought, it will be essential first to say a bit about the dynamics of differentiation.

The foundation of human history, says Dooyeweerd, lies in a particular form of human activity which may be called *cultural* activity. Though cultural activity always does and always must occur in the context of tradition, yet in its essence it is in conflict with tradition, since it "always consists in giving form to material in free control over material. It consists in giving form according to a free design."[20, 21] Culture activity consists in breaking from tradition so as to attain mastery of the natural world—and presumably over the social world and oneself as well. And insofar as culture activity occurs, we are in the presence of a genuine human history.

Dooyeweerd observes that cultural activity, thus identified, is indissolubly linked to the exercise of power. "Free control," he says, "reveals itself in the formation of *power*" (*RWC*, 66). Thus, in his view power lies at the very foundation of history—the power of forming one's world. Cultural activity involves *mastering*. Likewise, he sees social conflict as a pervasive component in history. "All historical formation," he says, "requires power. Formation thus never takes place without a struggle. The progressive wheel of the moulder of history invariably clashes with the power of tradition, which, as the power of conservation, for this every attempt to break with the past" (*RWC*, 70).

Already we are confronted with an important normative issue: are the mastery and conflict that lie the very foundation of genuine human history to be seen as good or bad? Is history, as such, progress or decline? Dooyeweerd's answer is emphatic: mastery good; only its misuse is bad. Power "is rooted in creation and it contains nothing demonic. Jesus Christ explicitly called himself the ruler of the kings of the earth. . . . Only sin can place power in the service of the demonic. But this holds for every good gift of God. . . . Power is a great motor of cultural development. The decisive question concerns the *direction* in which power is applied" (*RWC*, 67). Similarly, the conflictive struggle against tradition is, as such, good. Granted, there could be no human society, and so there could be no cultural

---

20. Dooyeweerd, *Roots of Western Culture*, 64. Subsequent references to this book (hereafter abbreviated *RWC*) will be made parenthetically in the text. For a more detailed discussion of these matters, see Dooyeweerd, *Critique of Theoretical Thought*, 181–330.

21. It is clear that cultural activity, as Dooyeweerd understands it, is a version of what in Chapter II, following Weber's lead, I called *rationalized activity*. What makes it a version of this, rather than identical with it, is Dooyeweerd's stipulation of cultural activity as involving *control* over *material*. But perhaps we are to understand this stipulation rather freely.

development, without tradition. Nonetheless, "truly historical development also demands that a culture not vegetate upon the past but unfold itself" (*RWC*, 71).

The ultimate ground of the neo-Calvinist's conviction that the cultural activity that underlies history is good is the conviction that such activity is God's will, and thereby, normative for humanity. God at creation gave to humanity a cultural mandate. The obligation to act culturally, and thereby to set loose the dynamics of history, belongs to the very essence of what it is to be human; it is indigenous to our creatureliness:

> The story of creation itself indicates that the cultural mode of formative activity is grounded in God's creation order. God immediately gave man the great cultural mandate: subdue the earth and have dominion over it. God placed this cultural command in the midst of the other creational ordinances. It touches only the historical aspect of creation. Through this aspect, creation itself is subject to cultural development. (*RWC*, 64–65)

It is the calling of humanity to bring to realization the potentials stored in creation. I think we should see in this neo-Calvinist vision an advance over that of liberation theology, which indeed was struggling toward the same point, but was hindered from attaining it by its acceptance of the contemporary theological dictum that God's creation is of merely salvific significance.

As we have already seen, the pursuit of mastery and the social conflict which together constitute the essence of cultural activity, and which thus lie at the foundation of the emergence from the bonds of tradition into genuine history, can both be misused. So of course the question arises: What constitutes their proper use? In short, what constitutes genuine progress in history as opposed to nonprogressive alteration? The beginning of Dooyeweerd's answer is that *differentiation* is the norm for history. Cultural activity, and thereby history itself, ought to move in the direction of increasing differentiation. Insofar as cultural activity does not do so, it is regressive and thereby disobedient, for differentiation is at the heart of the realization of creation's potentials. Dooyeweerd himself saw Hitler's Germany as an example of historical regression inspired by romantic nationalism.

What does the neo-Calvinist mean when he speaks of "differentiation"? Well, after saying that the norm for history is *the opening or disclosure of culture*, Dooyeweerd states that "this norm requires the differentiation of culture into spheres that possess their own unique nature. Cultural differentiation is necessary so that the creational ordinance, which calls for the disclosure or unfolding of everything in accordance with its inner nature, may be realized also in historical development" (*RWC*, 74).[22] "This

22. It should perhaps be noted that Dooyeweerd views historical-cultural differentiation as part of a whole *cosmic* pattern of differentiation: "Historical development is nothing but the cultural aspect of the great process of becoming which must continue in all the aspects of temporal reality in order that the wealth of the creational structures be concretized in time. . . . In all its aspects, the process of becoming develops, in conformity to law, from an undifferentiated phase to a differentiated phase. The organic development of life beings from the still undifferentiated germ cell, out of which the separate organs gradually differentiate. The emotional life of a newborn child is completely undifferentiated, but gradually it unfolds into a differentiation of sensuous feeling, logical feeling, lingual feeling, artistic feeling, juridical feeling, and so forth. The course of human societal development is no different" (*RWC*, 79). In an important way, God too is caught up in this pattern of differentiation. In spite of his emphasis on God's difference from creation, Dooyeweerd speaks of the unity of God's being as expressed in the

differentiation," he continues, "occurs . . . by means of a 'branching out' of culture into the intrinsically different power spheres of science, art, the state, the church, industry, trade, the school, voluntary organization, etc." (*RWC*, 79). In traditional undifferentiated societies "there was as yet no room for the formation of life spheres characterized by their own inner nature" (*RWC*, 74). "Only in the differentiation of culture can the unique nature of each creational structure reveal itself fully. . . . Undifferentiated forms gradually differentiate into the various societal structures through a lengthy process of historical development" (*RWC*, 79).[23]

How is differentiation, thus understood, related to the differentiation of which I spoke in the preceding chapter when I discussed some of the characteristic microstructural features of our modern world-order? It is the same phenomenon. There I explained differentiation as having two aspects: differentiation of social rules and differentiation of social formations (institutions and organizations). The neo-Calvinist's eye is mainly on the latter: in the course of history, political formations differentiate themselves from economic formations, from educational formations, from family formations, from ecclesiastical formations, and so on. Of course this sort of differentiation is inevitably accompanied by a differentiation of social roles as well.[24] The neo-Calvinists add an additional note, however. They do not merely observe and approve this process of social differentiation; they give it an ontological interpretation, albeit a highly controversial and problematic one: they hold that there are certain irreducibly different abiding *types* of social formations—the State, the Family, the School, the Production Enterprise, etc.—and that originally (most of) these types were not exemplified. In traditional societies, one could not pick out any distinct formations that were their schools, their governments, etc. But as differentiation gradually and fitfully takes place in the course of human history, these types are exemplified in distinct institutions. And so neo-Calvinists interpret our fundamental cultural-historical obligation as the obligation toward God of working from the exemplification of these social types (structures) in order to "open up" creation's potentials.

I shall have more to say about this shortly, but first let me remark here that what I find seriously lacking in Dooyeweerd (as indeed in Parsons) at this point is any serious consideration of what has *caused* this increase in differentiation and its cognates in our modern world. Why has this radical increase in differentiation taken place in the

---

cohering diversity of creation. In this respect, there is a striking similarity between his thought and that of Plotinus, who saw the diversity of reality as emanating in stages from the simplicity and unity of God.

23. It is clear that Dooyeweerd is using the term *differentiation* to denote a process of social structuration. It is striking, then, that in his answer to the question of what norm our progressive mastery of the natural and social worlds should follow, he says nothing at all about how *nature* should be treated, but only about how *society* should be structured.

24. Talcott Parsons, you will recall, also cited the importance of an increase in differentiation in his list of the four basic traits of the evolution of human society—the others being increases in inclusion, adaptive upgrading, and value generalization. Regarding these latter three traits, we would note that Dooyeweerd considered *integration* (a trait essentially equivalent to Parsons's *inclusion*) to be necessary counterpart of differentiation; he considered adaptive upgrading to be the most fundamental of all of the processes, since it accounts for our breaking from tradition in order to increase our mastery over nature and society; and he failed to take any explicit note of value generalization as a significant feature in the process (ignoring the factor of a decrease in ascriptivism as well).

modern Western world (and spread out from there into the whole world), when most of the world's societies remained statically traditional? In the preceding chapters I made clear that in my own judgment the question can only be answered by studying the rise of our own capitalist world-economy. This is the energizer of differentiation and its cognates. Dooyeweerd's failure to see this—his failure, in fact, even to consider the question of causation seriously—implies that his thought is really a version of modernization theory. What may be added is that inasmuch as one cannot adopt the world-system approach without recognizing the pervasive role of domination—and exploitative domination at that—in the "development" of our world, a recognition of this factor in historical development has no place in Dooyeweerd's thought.

We were speaking of the neo-Calvinists' ontological understanding of differentiation as the gradual manifestation in history of abiding types: the State, the Productive Enterprise, etc. What must now be added is that they see each of these types as having a nature—specifically, a *normative* nature. Just as we may consider what constitutes the well-formed lion, so in a similar way we may consider what constitutes the well-formed state, the well-formed school, the well-formed family, and so forth. In short, there are abiding norms for the State, for the School, and all the other categorically distinct social structures.

With this in mind, Dooyeweerd suggests that the cultural-historical project of humanity should focus on achieving the following three goals in a differentiated society:[25]

1. We should see to it that each social formation realizes the normative nature of its particular type, or structure. Political institutions must follow the norm for the State, economics organizations, for the Productive Enterprise, etc. In that way, life within each sphere must unfold and flower in its own unique but normed way.

2. As a direct corollary to this, we should see to it that the institutions belonging to one sphere do not dominate those belonging to another, because when one sphere is dominated by another, life in the former is distorted and cannot flower in its own unique normed manner. We are to work for the *sovereignty of the spheres*: "A process

25. If these goals are indeed the whole of the matter, then the idea communicated is that our human social obligation amounts to no more than an obligation to God to see to it that each sphere unfolds in accord with its proper nature. It would also imply that human misery is a *symptom* of something having gone wrong in the unfolding of the spheres rather than something that is itself wrong. Accordingly, the implication would be that one ought not to set out to combat misery as such; instead, one should try to bring about a proper unfolding of the spheres, in which case misery would be relieved as an incidental (though no doubt desirable) by-product. And, indeed, the modern Afrikaner, who has often made use of Dooyeweerd's thought, insists that we must not really pay much attention to social misery, since in the long run if we just see to it that structures are unfolded properly, misery will vanish. In my judgment that is "cultural mandate" thinking gone to seed. I think Dooyeweerd himself is not entirely without blame here. Too often he gives the impression that mankind was created to unfold social structures, rather than that social structures *have no justification* unless they serve mankind Fortunately, Goudzwaard is clear on this point, stating, among other things, that "the purpose of norms is to bring us to life in its fullness by pointing us to paths which safely lead us there. Norms are not straight-jackets that squeeze the life out of us" (*Capitalism and Progress*, 242–43). It is the *fullness of human life* that is the decisive test, not the proper realization of each sphere's inner nature. On the whole, Goudzwaard does a good job of staying clear of that mankind-for-the-sake-of-structures way of thinking by emphasizing his third goal for humanity's cultural-historical project—*disclosure*—far more than Dooyeweerd himself does.

of over-extension in culture . . . conflicts with the norms that God established for differentiation in his creation order. Every extreme expansion of the historical power sphere for a specific life sphere occurs at the expense of other life spheres, for it retards their unfolding in an unhealthy way" (*RWC*, 80–81).

3. We must seek what may be called *disclosure*. Life within each sphere of activity, though it must find its own fulfillment free from domination by other spheres, must at the same time be *open to* the norms of the other spheres. Economic activity, for example, is never exclusively economic in its significance: it has moral significance, it involves the use of language, and so forth; accordingly, it must be faithful not only to economic, but to moral, linguistic, and all other norms.

All of this is extraordinarily general and abstract. Nonetheless it is this pattern of thought that is contained in the critique of modern society found in Goudzwaard's *Capitalism and Progress*, to which I now turn. I choose Goudzwaard because of the imaginative and penetrating use he makes of this pattern of thought—a use, I may add, which points in a thoroughly progressive, even radical, direction.[26]

What is the root of what has gone wrong in Western society? That is Goudzwaard's guiding question. That something has gone wrong, *profoundly* wrong, he has no doubt. He presents as evidence for this judgment many of the same phenomena I cited at the beginning of this chapter.

Goudzwaard's suggestion, supported with great richness of example, is that the fundamental root of what has gone wrong is that we in the West have accepted economic growth and technological advance as the ultimate social good. In the private sphere we subordinate everything to the production of ever more surplus by making profit the sole decisive goal of our enterprises and then using this profit to obtain more capital goods—which are then used to produce yet more surplus, and so on. On the national level we subordinate everything to growth in the Gross National Product. Economic growth, technological innovation, and scientific advance supersede all other values, and are in turn raised above all normative appraisals; they have, in fact,

> . . . attached themselves to our society as forward-moving forces which are *their own justification*, as sources of progress which are good in themselves, and therefore in principle need not be subjected to any critical assessment. Technical innovations are by definition considered desirable, all scientific findings are positive contributions, and in economics it is self-evident that bigger is always better. . . . The forces of economic growth, technical innovation, and scientific aggrandizement have established themselves securely in our society

26. It ought to be noted that Dooyeweerd's thought has regularly been used by social conservatives to undergird their position: they use his stress on the importance of resisting the expansion of government outside its sphere to justify their indifference to—and, indeed, their practice of—economic exploitation; they use his stress on the importance of recognizing governmental authority within its own sphere to justify their opposition to all who preach or practice resistance to government dictates; and so forth. Dooyeweerd's thought is one more example in that long line of "creation ordinance" theologians and philosophies that have been used to support conservative positions. We might well suspect that, as Karl Barth insisted, there is an affinity here to which we must be constantly alert. Some will argue that only by misinterpreting Dooyeweerd can the conservative find support among his ideas, but I am not persuaded of that. It seems to me that at the very least they contain certain ambiguities.

as *ultimate standards*. They need not measure up to society, but society must measure up to them.[27]

The result is that we have created what Goudzwaard aptly called a "tunnel society."

The structural manifestation of this overriding commitment to the production of ever more surplus are threefold. In the first place, the economic sphere has come to dominate all others: our society has become economized. Government education—everything is bent to the demands of the economy. Our social order throughout has been overwhelmingly shaped by production for profit on the market. Like a cancerous growth, the economy has violated the "sovereignty of the spheres."

Secondly, economic life itself has not followed its own appropriate norms. Goudzwaard's conviction is that the concept of *stewardship* best captures the norm for life in the economic sphere. But we have not been guided by the norm of stewardship; we have instead been guided by the goal of increasing production. He makes the point interestingly and forcefully:

> In classical antiquity two distinct Greek works were used to describe human economic activity: *oikonomia* and *chrematistike*. *Oikonomia* (the origin of our word *economics*) designated the behavior of the steward whose task it was to manage the estate entrusted to him in such a way that it would continue to bear fruit and thus provide a living for everyone who lived and worked on it. Central to this concept, therefore, was the maintenance of productive possessions on behalf of everyone involved. *Chrematistike*, however, meant something quite different. This word expressed the pursuit of self-enrichment, for ever greater monetary possessions, if need be at the expense of others. It is remarkable to observe that in western civilization the meaning of the word *economics* has increasingly become synonymous with *chrematistike*, while progressively it lost the meaning of *oikonomia*, the careful maintenance as steward on behalf of others of all that is entrusted to man.
>
> A business is not run economically if it is efficient merely in a monetary sense. *It is economically responsible only if it possesses the ability to render a net economic fruit*. In terms of normative-economic cost-benefit analysis, many financially viable businesses may be called economic fiascos, whereas the opposite might be true of a number of businesses which are losing money. As an example of the first we might cite producers of goods which can actually be marketed only by means of intensive advertising campaigns, but which pollute the environment (either during production or consumption), are energy-intensive, and use up the world's dwelling supply of non-renewable resources. Another example would be those firms which damage the health of their laborers during the process of production (health, too, is an economic good!), fail to utilize their workers; mental capacities, or even brutalize them by overdoses of mechanical and deadening drudgery. Corporations can also fail economically—despite great apparent success from a financial point of view—in their operations in developing countries. . . .

27. Goudzwaard, *Capitalism and Progress*, 191. Subsequent references to this book (hereafter abbreviated *CP*) will be made parenthetically in the text.

> Business enterprises, in other words, should be generally economic organizations, that is, institutions of stewardship. That is the key norm by which they should be judged, without neglect of market factors. (*CP*, 211–12)

Thirdly and it is especially this last point that Goudzwaard emphasizes—we have not allowed the economic sphere to be generally open to the norms of the other spheres. We have prevented "disclosure." We have not insisted that economic activity has to be morally responsible, technologically responsible, and so on. We have not pursued "simultaneous" realization of norms:

> A certain fixed sequence arises in which questions are asked and problems are solved. The first question concerns how we can ensure sufficient economic, scientific, and technological growth. Only thereafter is it asked to what extent we were able to counteract whatever harmful effects may result from such growth; for example, its effects on the environment, on the working conditions of laborers, on the economic status of the poor nations of the world, on the decreasing world reserves of energy and natural resources, on the freedom of consumers, and on interpersonal relationships in society. In a tunnel society such an order of priorities is self-evident. . . . A society with a measure of disclosure will be characterized by a conscious effort to reverse the sequence of posing questions. Its first concerns will be man's responsibility to protect and respect nature, the meaning of human labor, and human dignity of the consumer, and the opportunities for development of the poor nations; and to preserve for posterity sufficient energy and other natural resources. (*CP*, 194)

Earlier we saw that Dooyeweerd outlined three ways in which the development of the spheres can go wrong once they have differentiated from each other. I think we all sense that Goudzwaard's analysis, which is clearly conducted in terms of these three types of misadventure, is a profoundly insightful one. But for most of us that sense of illumination is combined with the uneasy question: To what extent must one accept the background ontology of Dooyeweerd in order to go along with the essentials of Goudzwaard's analysis? Must we hold that there are such categorically distinct types as a State and the Business Enterprise, each with its distinct normative nature; that these gradually become exemplified as societal differentiation takes place; and that we owe it to God to see to it that the inner nature of each of these types is opened up? In a word, *no*. We do *not* have to accept this ontology in order to preserve the core of Goudzwaard's contribution. Let me briefly sketch out an alternative picture.

> Every society consists in a certain array of institutions (or *formations* if you prefer a more neutral word). Our own society exhibits a dizzyingly complex array of them. We owe it to God and to our fellow human beings to see to it that our society's array of institutions adequately serves the life of its members—that they serve the cause of justice and *shalom*. (I shall speak of *shalom* shortly.) In our assessment of our society's institutions, it is our obligation to engage in normative reflection; we must not allow certain institutions and goals to be placed above all normative assessment. And as we conduct our normative reflections, we must be especially sensitive to the stultification of human life that occurs when one institution (or type of institution) dominates all others: it is our obligation to promote pluralism. Likewise, we must be especially sensitive to the stultification

of human life that occurs when, in tunnel-vision fashion, the need for "simultaneous realization" of norms is forgotten.

The institutions in every society or perform certain functions. We must ask whether the functions that they perform in our society are being performed well, whether there are some that are not to be performed at all, and whether there are others not presently being performed by any institution that ought to be performed. And we must ask how the functions performed are best parcelled out among the institutions of society: which should be assigned different institutions, and which to the same. When we look at the various societies to be found in the course of history, we find certain basic functions regularly performed, but we find them parceled out among institutions in all sorts of different ways. Functions that we assign to one institution may in other societies be assigned to different one, and functions that we assign to different institutions may in other societies be assigned to the same one. In societies quite different from ours we can still pick out institutions that are recognizably schools, state, and so on (though we cannot do so in all). But the assignment of functions to these is often quite different from what it is in our society. Is our assignment a good one *for us*? That must be our question.

In considering which functions are to be performed in our society, and which institutions should be assigned to perform them, we should keep in mind the guiding principle I mentioned earlier: what serves best the cause of justice and *shalom*. And our considerations must always be "situated" concrete. We must ask what *this* institution in *this* institutional array ought to be doing, or what redistribution of function ought to occur in *this* array. We must not ask what *the* State should be doing, as if what are recognizably states should in all times and all places have the same assignment of functions. We do not owe it to God to realize the inner state of the State; rather, we owe it to God that our own institutional array, including our state, serves humanity.

Dooyeweerd argues that *the* task of *the* State is the administration of justice. My own government, and most others in the world as well, provide certain services that enhance our life together: it builds roads, runs a post office, offers fire protection, and so on. This is not the administration of justice, as Dooyeweerd understands it; nonetheless, it is important that these functions be performed, and perhaps it is best in our situation that these functions be performed by the same institution that administers justice. In another institutional array, it might not be wise, but that case would have to be argued not by reference to the inner nature of the State, but by reference to the lives of human beings.[28]

We can still classify the functions performed by our social institutions into types. So too we can classify obligations in the types: ecological responsibilities, intellectual responsibilities, more responsibilities, aesthetic responsibilities, etc. And of course we can classify institutions into types. But the matching up of functions (and their correlative responsibilities) to institutions is not to be done by asking what *the* State and

28. It is true, of course, that an institution could scarcely be considered a state unless, among other things, it saw to the administration of justice in that society. But it does not by any means follow from this that the administration of justice is the *sole* appropriate function of the state. In some instances this may be the case, but it is not universally so.

the Business Enterprise ought to do, but by considering what *our* states in *our* business enterprises ought to do in *our* situation.

But let us return to Goudzwaard, for he has one more important point to make. How, he asks, are we to understand this pursuit of economic growth which is so profoundly shaped not only our economy but our entire social order? Perhaps it is best to see ourselves as dealing here with *religious* dynamics; perhaps we are dealing here with a "faith": "Insofar as a western man attributes divine stature to the forces of progress, we might well be confronted with a situation parallel to that of idol worship in primitive cultures. These forces are given divine prerogatives as soon as man puts an unconditional *trust* in them; that is, as soon as economic and technological progress are depended on as a guide to the good life and as mediators of our happiness" (*CP*, 152).

We have here touched on the second of the fundamental dynamics that the neo-Calvinists see as operative in history—the dynamic of idolatry and of its struggle with authentic faith. Goudzwaard's suggestion is our practice of giving decisive consideration to economic growth should be seen as an example of idolatry: something of *some* worth is being treated as if it were of *ultimate* worth. Like idols generally, this idol not only distorts life but eventually enslaves the very person who trusts it. We are enslaved by the very technology and bureaucracy which are among our principal agents of economic growth:

> As in primitive cultures, powers that are regarded as gods and saviors can gain a dominant influence over our lives from which we cannot readily extricate ourselves. . . . One cannot choose one's own masters in life without accepting the status of servant. It appears therefore that the sense of powerlessness present in western culture may well be closely connected with the *faith dimension* of the progress motive. Powerlessness results when one's own power is delegated; but it is precisely a *faith* (in progress) that can elicit such a delegation of power. (*CP*, 152)

But there's more involved here than simply the *practice* of treating economic growth as a social good of autonomous and ultimate worth. A whole ideology—a framework of justifying belief—has arisen within the society shaped by this practice, and this too must be seen as a component of our idolatry. The meaning of history lies for us and human progress, and we consider increasing the production of goods to be the decisive instrument of that progress; *we have faith in progress.* Our society has rewarded us with goods beyond comparison. Therein we see its justification. We assume that whatever problems arise along the way will be solved by technological advance and economic growth.

Goudzwaard realizes that we do not eliminate this ideology from our lives simply by renouncing its constituent ideology and by intellectually repudiating growth as a good of ultimate value—for the heart of this idolatry is a *practice*, the practice of taking growth as a good of unquestioned and ultimate worth. It is this *practice* that must be rooted out of our lives. We can do so only by adopting alternative practices in which growth is no longer treated thus. Furthermore, Goudzwaard is fully aware that this practice is at the very heart of what we know as capitalism. Once we no longer follow the practice, capitalism will be altered beyond recognition. It must be added, though, that this very same practice shapes life in the "socialist" countries. They, too, in their own way—indeed, often the same way—are in the grip of the idol of growth.

To release ourselves from this idol (without succumbing to another) we must once again bring normative considerations to bear on economic life, no longer letting ourselves be tyrannized by something placed above all normative appraisals. We must retract our abdication from normative reflection and decision. And as we begin once again to engage in such reflection, we must be constantly alert to the dangers of "tunnel vision," constantly open to the rich diversity of norms for our lives, in that way working for "the disclosure of society."[29]

In the preceding chapter I suggested that capitalism was a blend of certain legal arrangements and practices. Goudzwaard's discussion leads us now to see those practices in the new light. All together they amount to a "faith," a "social idolatry." I myself think that what we find of fundamental worth in our modern world-system is less accurately described as *increased production* than as *increased mastery of nature and society so as to satisfy our desires* (since, for example, the prolongation of life, which surely we regard as one of the good things which our system yielded, is not directly a matter of more goods available for use and consumption). I also think that the ideology accompanying the emergence of our world-order is somewhat less academic in its origins than Goudzwaard's discussion would suggest; as I see it, academics gave expression to an ideology which had already gained currency—though, indeed, by so doing they reinforced the grip of that ideology. But these are minor disagreements.

I have noted several points of difference between the neo-Calvinist analysis of our society and the liberationist analysis in the course of this discussion; there remains one more that I would like to address. It is also important, however, to take note of some of the deep affinities between these two patterns of thought, affinities that tend to be obscured by the obvious and substantial differences. Let me attend to that first, stressing affinities with which I am myself in agreement.

Liberation theology and neo-Calvinism have similarities that extend beyond the fact that they are both contemporary versions of world-formative Christianity. Both express, for example, a significant concern for the *victims* of modern society (though it is true that they differ in their specific definitions of which groups constitute the victims of a given society). In addition both express concern for the victims in essentially the same manner: not by applying bandages, but by searching out what it was that inflicted the wounds, seeking to effect change in that quarter. Both find the culprit in the structure of modern society and the dynamics underlying that structure rather than in acts of individual waywardness. Both offer architectonic analyses of the ills of modern society, and both locate the crucial dynamic in the economic sphere—and in the political sphere insofar as it supports the economic.

Furthermore, both the liberationist and the neo-Calvinist perceive the processes afoot in the modern world not as incidental to the ultimate fulfillment of human destiny, but as foundational to it. The neo-Calvinist interprets the grand sweep of history as the development of the potentials implicit in creation, with art eventually coming into its

---

29. "Taking norms seriously is the essence of every genuine process of disclosure." Goudzwaard, *CP*, 248.

own, science coming into its own, and so on.[30] The liberationist sees the grand sweep of history as the attainment of freedom (while remaining somewhat ambiguous concerning what exactly constitutes this freedom). Thus, both receive progress in history, though by no means a smooth, uninterrupted progress. Neither objects in principle to the growth of technology, nor indeed to bureaucratic organization, but both object to the *direction* in which these developments have been turned in the modern world. In neither is there any of the regressive romanticism of the late Frankfurt School (which, in despair over the invasion of modern society by what is called *instrumental reason*, eventually turned to art for salvation, because it came to believe that art was the one remaining area of life in which such reason did not yet hold sway, in which life was still characterized by wholeness and expressiveness and concreteness).

In addition, both consider the making of humanity in history to be intrinsic to the coming of the Kingdom of God—while at the same time both see the Kingdom in its fullness as a gift and not as an accomplishment; neither etherealizes human destiny. Life in history is incorporated into our destiny. Correlatively, both are so bold as to suggest that we human beings play a role in the coming of the Kingdom. Our relation to the Kingdom is not only obedient waiting, but active contribution. Whether one interprets history as a fitful movement toward differentiation or as a fitful movement of Liberation, it remains something that we contribute to, not merely something inflicted upon us.

There are indeed more affinities than these, but let us in conclusion move on to the most important of the differences not yet considered. Liberationists focus on domination and exploitation, which they see as age-old manifestations of the age-old phenomenon of sin—resistance love; neo-Calvinists, on the other hand, focus on the widespread faith in economic growth, which they see as a modern form of the age-old phenomenon of idolatry. For one the category of sin is prominent; for the other the category of idolatry is prominent.

It ought here to be recognized that although these interpretations are different, they are not mutually exclusive: it is possible, and advisable, to incorporate both into a larger perspective. We do in fact live in a world-system in which the core dominates the periphery, characteristically out of greed and lust for power. What is that but sin? We do in fact live in a world-system shaped by the practice of treating economic growth as an autonomous and ultimate good. What is that but idolatry?

The liberation theologians typically concluded from their analysis of the predicament of their people that they must work the formation of a socialist society in which there is no longer private appropriation of the surplus of production. Goudzwaard also decries the arrangement whereby only the owner of capital and not the worker has voice in the operation of, and title to the proceeds from, the enterprise to which they jointly contribute; but his analysis makes clear that the members of a socialist society—whether defined as a society in which private ownership of the means of production has been abolished or a society in which labor and capital have co-responsibility in the enterprise—can also treat growth as an autonomous and ultimate good, with results scarcely better than what we witness under capitalism. Our ills are deeper than such restructuring can cure.

30. For more on this, see Kuyper, *Calvinism: Six Stone Lectures.*

On the other hand, the liberationist analysis corrects an important deficiency in the neo-Calvinist analysis: our situation is not merely that we are all dominated by the idol of growth; it is also certain that groups of *persons* are exploitatively dominated by the other groups of *persons*. The neo-Calvinists scarcely take note of this *conflictual* aspect of our social order. Of course they are aware of *certain* conflicts—they recognize the differences of opinion people have as to the norms we ought to follow and the policies we ought to adopt, for example—but they pass by that conflict of wills between those have power in the system and those who lack it. Accordingly, though they suggest strategies for freeing ourselves from the idol of growth, they say nothing about groups of people struggling to *liberate* themselves from oppression and exploitation. But the truth is surely that there is no disclosure without liberation.

It would be pleasant if we could stop with this *both/and*: each division has insights that we should incorporate into a larger picture and each has limitations that the other helps to correct. But when it comes to practice, and to reflection that guides practice, we cannot stop with a *both/and*. The sorrows produced by our world-system are many. Among them is a domination of some by others which the system encourages. And, as one would expect, when one party dominates another, it customarily also takes advantage of the other and exploits it. In such a situation one cannot simply say that we all suffer from the idolatry of growth. One cannot just say that we are all in this boat together. One has to say that one human being is being wronged by another, and to say that is to take sides with the former. It is to declare solidarity with him or her in opposition to the oppressor. It is to take sides on a struggle occurring *within* the boat. And if one's declaration of solidarity is serious, the actions of liberation will flow forth. On all of this the liberation theologian is right.

Moreover, not only will Christians thus *take sides* as they concern themselves with the miseries of contemporary mankind, but this taking sides will be a priority for them. The exploitative domination experienced by many threatens their very livelihood, their very sustenance. The elimination of starvation, and the alleviation of the tyranny that supports it, has priority over, say, relieving the boredom of the well-to-do in a society devoted to growth.

This taking of sides will of course produce conflict (of which there was much already). The powerful will try to hang on to their positions. One will not be able to avoid reflecting seriously on the place of violence in that conflict. Sad to say, it is not a conflict in which the church is to be found exclusively on the side of the exploited. *Christ* was there, and is there, but his "body," the church, is not—not all of it in any case. So in taking the side of the exploited, Christians will find themselves in opposition to some of those who confess the same Lord. That, for them, is yet another of the great sorrows of our world.

Part 3: **Contemporary Christian Realists**

Contemporary Christian Realists:
An Introduction

ONE OF THE TRENDS in Christian Realism over time is the increasing theological conservatism of its principal representatives. The most notable first-generation Christian Realists (e.g., Niebuhr, Bennett) and many of the people they associated with (e.g., Henry P. Van Dusen, Harry Emerson Fosdick) were theological (and political) liberals. The theological liberals ambiguously applied certain orthodox concepts, such as sin and the law of love, to matters of politics and international security. In the 1940s and 1950s Niebuhr, Bennett, and others typically spoke in terms of biblical "motifs," "symbols," and what we would today call "narratives," but avoided terms like "truth" and "doctrine."

In contrast, over time, self-identifying Christian Realists have been more Augustinian, more theologically conservative, and more committed to the orthodoxy of Scripture and their theological traditions than Niebuhr and his Union Seminary friends ever were. Does this matter? Many of today's Christian Realists think so. For instance, Keith Pavlischek's essay provides an insightful critique of Niebuhr's thinking. Pavlischek argued that the idealist-turned-Realist Niebuhr never fully lost that idealism, and it corrupted Niebuhr's approach to war and security, allowing him to justify terrible things—such as the firebombing of Dresden—as "lesser evils" because Niebuhr lacked the discipline imposed by the Augustinian just war criteria of "proportionality" and "discrimination."[1]

Today, the theological conservative trend has meant a far more disciplined approach to matters of war and peace framed by Augustinian just war thinking, and thus a much more critical stance toward pacifism and the shoddy thinking that cannot tell the difference between non-violent direct action within a democracy (such as Martin Luther King, Jr.'s marches and sit-ins), terrorism and insurgency, or justified collective self-defense (war). Contemporary Christian Realism is also characterized by a friendly conversation between like-minded Catholics (Weigel, Capizzi) and conservative Protestants (Patterson, Charles, Pavlischek). Contemporary Christian Realism, with its Augustinian roots and moral-historical methodology, already had some overlaps with the English School of international relations theory, from Adam Watson to Scott Thomas. As Robert Joustra observes, Christian Realism has also found new international expressions in Reformed

1. Pavlischek, "Reinhold Niebuhr, Christian Realism, and Just War Theory."

circles, with a growing appreciation of Dutch theologian-statesmen such as Abraham Kuyper and Hermann Bavinck as early influencers of a nascent "Amsterdam School."[2]

Unravelling Blocs and Power Politics

The end of the Cold War, which began with the unraveling of the Warsaw Pact and peaceful revolts against communist regimes in 1989 and saw the entire Soviet bloc— including the Soviet Union itself—melt away in 1991, was the end of a historic era and a stable balance of power system. At the time, some trumpeted "the end of history" or pointed to the progressive possibilities of globalization, liberal democracy, and associated free market economics.[3] Truly, there was no ideological competitor on the global stage to Western political and economic liberalism. Others, however, worried we were entering a far less stable era of clashing cultures, or civilizations, due to the lack of superintending superpowers or the disjuncture between modernity's McWorld and backward tribalism.[4] As Yugoslavia and Rwanda imploded, and dozens of other insurgencies and civil wars ignited, the issue of armed humanitarian intervention, whether to stop genocide or the catastrophes of famine and disease, became a major issue on the international agenda. The outputs of these debates resulted in the Rome Statute and International Criminal Court in 1999 and the "Responsibility to Protect" concept, which was ultimately supported, tepidly, by the UN General Assembly. Although Christian Realists often thought that intervention to preserve international order—such as against Iraq in 1991–92, or to stop genocide in unique cases—was justified, they were far more reluctant to make idealistic commitments to impose Western political norms or reconstruct foreign societies after war.

The first challenge to the new world order of law and cooperation came with Iraq's 1991 invasion of Kuwait. Iraq was notorious for attacking three of its neighbors (Israel, Iran, Kuwait) and for financially supporting terrorists and suicide bombers. In two books and a number of essays, Jean Bethke Elshtain, James Turner Johnson, and George Weigel supported the global coalition, led by the United States, to liberate Kuwait in 1992 for reasons of international law and order.[5] If the international community allowed one state to gobble up its neighbor, it seemed we were back to the politics of appeasing bullies as in the 1930s. Reclaiming Kuwait was about international order and justice. Pushing back against such lawlessness is the responsibility of governments.

Just after the first Persian Gulf War, graphic television images of emaciated figures in concentration camps and images of grotesque butchery began to air from the former Yugoslavia and Rwanda. What about armed humanitarian intervention in the case of state collapse or a savage civil war? Elshtain, for one, suggested an ethic of "equal regard"

2. The best compendium on the Amsterdam School is by Polinder and Bujis. A new dissertation by Polinder should be published in 2022.

3. Fukuyama, *The End of History*. Thomas Friedman's many books look at the many goods, and some ills, of globalization, starting with *The Lexus and the Olive Tree*.

4. Huntington, *The Clash of Civilizations*; Barber, *Jihad vs. McWorld*.

5. Elshtain, Walzer, Weigel, et al., *Reflections on the Morality of the Persian Gulf War*; Johnson and Weigel, *Just War and the Gulf War*.

toward the suffering of others.[6] "Equal Regard" was not a foreign policy doctrine demanding that presidents and prime ministers throw military force at every global crisis, but rather that governments adopt a posture of recognizing the human dignity of every person around the globe and seriously consider what steps, within limits, could reasonably be taken to prevent or ameliorate human suffering. J. Daryl Charles, reflecting on the growing calls for such intervention (Kuwait [1991], Somalia [1992], Rwanda [1994], Yugoslavia [1995], Democratic Republic of Congo [1996], Kosovo [1999], East Timor [1999], Darfur [2003], etc.), argued in typical Christian Realist fashion that although some armed humanitarian intervention is appropriate to stop grotesque human suffering, we must observe limits in such conflicts, in part because so often there are resulting unintended consequences that are beyond our control.[7]

The War on Terror

During this time, another issue was foremost on the mind of the West's national security agencies: Islamist terrorism. Increasingly, attacks were being made on Western targets and in Western countries. For instance, the Shia group Hezbollah is believed to have been involved in the Khobar Towers bombing (in Saudi Arabia), the hijacking of TWA 847 (Egypt), the 1994 bombing of a Jewish Center in Buenos Aires (Argentina), and attacks on diplomatic posts in Georgia, India, and Bulgaria in 2012.

Separately, Sunni radicals that developed into al Qaeda and its children, such as ISIS (Islamic State), included the 1993 attack on the World Trade Center (NYC), U.S. embassies in Kenya and Tanzania (1998), the *USS Cole* (2000), and, ultimately, the September 11, 2001 attacks on New York and Washington, DC. The *mujahidin* of the 1980s, who liberated Afghanistan from the Soviet Union, with backing from the United States and Pakistan, fanned out across the greater Middle East, causing disorder and being expelled from Saudi Arabia and, subsequently, from Sudan. Al Qaeda-influenced terrorists went on to attack unsuspecting civilians in France, Spain, Tunisia, the United Kingdom, and elsewhere while different Islamist groups with similar ideologies attacked soft targets and massacred civilians across Southeast Asia and in Russia.[8] Not surprisingly, across the globe, average Muslim citizens bore the brunt of attacks at the hands of violent Islamists, especially in North Africa and Asia.

All of this led to vigorous U.S.-led intervention under the banner of a "global war on terrorism," first with an attack on Afghanistan, whose Taliban-dominated government would not hand over the Osama bin Laden and the terrorist plotters of 9/11. Eighteen months later Coalition forces took down the ever-destabilizing regime of Saddam Hussein, a long-time supporter of terrorism (although not of al Qaeda) who blustered

6. Elshtain, "Just War and the Ethics of Responsibility."

7. It is noteworthy that during the Cold War there were very few UN-authorized interventions: Korea and Congo were the two rare cases in point over forty years. After the demise of the Soviet Union in 1991, there were a dozen calls for UN-authorized intervention in just a short time: Rwanda, Yugoslavia, Somalia, Kosovo, East Timor, etc.

8. See Reuters/Jane's World, "TIMELINE: Major Attacks by al Qaeda," available online at https://www.reuters.com/article/idINIndia-56711920110502.

that he had massive stockpiles of chemical and biological weapons. Hussein's bluff was so widely believed that all of his own generals and family members believed it to be true, and it induced President George W. Bush to widen the war on terrorism to regimes sponsoring terrorism as well as lawless regions that were havens for terrorism, such as ungoverned spaces in Central Asia and Yemen. President Obama continued this approach with covert military engagement in Asia and Africa.

We will see some of these arguments about restraint, international order, and justice play out in essays by Capizzi, Strand, and others who were evaluating the global war on terrorism, from Afghanistan to Iraq and beyond, in real time.

All of this led to a number of practical foreign policy and moral questions. On the one hand are the questions associated with *jus ad bellum*, or the ethics of going to war. Can governments go to war with non-state actors? Is this an unlimited mandate? Is there a difference between throttling "outlaws and barbarians," traditional military action, and police work?[9] Is there a difference between how to fight against unlawful combatants and lawful combatants? Do the Geneva Conventions apply? What was the West's motivation: *vindication* of justice and a reestablishment of law and order, or raw *vengeance*?[10]

At the same time, this sort of warfare demonstrated how little sovereignty some governments exercised over their territory (such as Osama bin Laden living in hiding just down the road from a police station and military academy in Pakistan) and recognized the primary enemies to be non-state actors with lethal firepower at their disposal. This state of affairs created a set of *jus in bello* issues, from violations of state borders to the use of enhanced interrogation techniques, including torture. One of the great dichotomies of the time was the popularity of the "rough justice" of Hollywood's Jack Bauer and London's James Bond, while the political Left and many media elites decried such actions as immoral. What was the moral basis for utilizing or avoiding torture? James Turner Johnson provides a critical perspective on how Christian just war thinking, a form of Augustinian Realism, could be applied to the specific tactics of enhanced interrogation and torture.

War, Order, and Peace

The objective of war is, or should be, peace. But how does one get there? These authors continue as key voices in shaping debates about international order, justice, and security. Eric Patterson, for instance, has written at length about how a robust foundation of order is necessary before the implementation of post-war justice.[11] He and others, such as Elshtain, have argued that order and justice, over time, may lay the foundation for conciliation: "coming to terms with the past in order to imagine a shared future."[12] University of Notre Dame scholar Daniel Philpott, who has worked on reconciliation in

9. An evaluation of the Bush Administration's differentiation between lawful and unlawful combatants, rooted in customary international legal distinctions (e.g., pirates, brigands) can be found in Patterson and Puryear, "Outlaws and Barbarians," 199–211.

10. A major reference work of three dozen essays on the latest trends in military ethics is Johnson and Patterson, eds. *Ashgate Research Companion on Military Ethics.*

11. Patterson, *Ending Wars Well.*

12. Elshtain, "Just War and the Ethics of Responsibility," 98.

places such as Kashmir, calls for an ethic of reconciliation as one way to move beyond perennial conflicts that seem to have no solution.

The issue of weapons of mass destruction (WMD) continued to be a major issue in this period as a deep concern spread globally about the safety of Cold War-era stockpiles of nuclear material falling into the hands of terrorists. WMD experts remained vigilant about the possibilities of a nuclear exchange between India and its enemies (Pakistan, China) as well as an arms race in the Middle East, particularly between Israel and its neighbors. Nuclear pacifists continued to make arguments in favor of unilateral disarmament, even getting Pope Francis to challenge historic just war teaching by publicly denouncing WMDs.[13] Contemporary Christian Realists, such as Rebecca Heinrichs, continued to debate nuclear pacifists and others on the importance of great power deterrence as well as on the practical strategies necessary to make the world as safe as possible from chemical, biological, or radiological attack.

Christian Realists also continue to debate issues of the international system and international law. Niebuhr and his contemporaries saw international law and organizations as a network of power balancing, not as a utopian global order. Today's debates about whether there is a liberal international order and its relationship to global peace remain important to Christian Realists. Patterson, writing shortly after 9/11 and the failure of the international community to blunt terrorism, stop genocide, or thwart proliferation, argues that the arguments for multilateralism are typically utopian (when made by those far from power) or self-serving (when made by those in power). For the former, who have little perspective on how power politics actually works, multilateralism sounds like some sort of worldwide village where people take care of their neighbors. This is just not the case. Elites often use the language of multilateralism as a screen for avoiding responsible action unless a consensus forms, thereby limiting their own exposure to the costs associated with responsible action: this is what many say happened in the case of Rwanda. These trends make genocide and other state failures more, rather than less, likely.

However, *multilateralism* is not a dead word in Christian Realism. *Functionalist multilateralism* has been alive and well in the Christian Realist tradition, argues Robert Joustra, from pragmatically aligning state policy on ocean acidification to airline transponders. That there are limits to this multilateralism, and that such diplomacy hardly invalidates national interest nor power politics, goes without saying in the Realist imagination. But that such institutions, if they did not exist, would need to be invented, also goes without saying. Coordination and cooperation, on the basis of shared commitments, are hallmarks of an Augustinian Commonwealth—regimes aligned by common loves, by common virtues and values. It may be, as some like Joustra have argued, that such alignments are best found practically in the day to day of politics, and patched together to form things like international law and international treaties, rather than idealistically imagined top-down, smothering rather than leveraging sovereignty.

Christian Realism, in its widest sense, is in a period of growth and development. The primary reason for this is the need felt by many Christians, in and out of government, for

13. The papal encyclical, *Fratelli Tutti,* was released on October 3, 2020 and is available at http:// www.vatican.va/content/francesco/en/encyclicals/documents/papa-francesco_20201003_enciclica-fratelli-tutti.html.

more explicit Christian thinking linking public service vocations to doctrinally informed public policy arguments. Christian Realism does not have a technocratic answer for every narrow policy question, but rooted in biblical and Augustinian notions of sin, human potential, order, and justice, Christian Realism has a theological basis for providing Van Dusen's "middle axioms" for policy. We see this today in the revival of classical Christian just war thinking as well as in new streams, such as the evaluation of recently translated work by Kuyper and Bavinck (the Amsterdam School). Conservative Catholic and evangelical thinkers are in greater partnership than ever before, both on domestic issues (life, family) as well as in Christian Realist approaches to war, peace, and security. We also see a trend toward establishing institutions taking a Christian approach to policy seriously, such as graduate schools of government at Regent and Liberty Universities and Reformed Theological Seminary's recent establishment of the Institute for Theology in Public Life. Because the publications where Niebuhr and others published, such as *Christianity and Crisis* and *The Christian Century,* lost their moral compass, a new generation of periodicals have become places for Christian Realism, including the pages of the venerable *First Things,* at times in *Review of Faith and International Affairs,* and especially in the unabashed Augustinianism of the Institute on Religion and Democracy's *Providence: A Journal of Christianity and American Foreign Policy.*

In conclusion, the latest Christian Realist writing is focused on many of the same trends that Niebuhr and the first generation of Christian Realists faced: utopian pacifism in the face of deadly civilizational perils; wishful thinking among Christians who do not take seriously enough the tragedy of human sin and its political consequences; the fashion of avoiding or denouncing praiseworthy public service (e.g., military, police) as at best a "lesser evil"; and an irresponsibility that results in indecision or inaction when order and justice must be defended. Today's Christian Realists remain motivated not by pessimistic resolve or power politics, but instead, as portrayed in the writings of Niebuhr, Elshtain, and others, by "hope."

3–1

"Proportionality in Warfare"

Keith Pavlischek[1]

THE LAST TWO TIMES Israel went to war, international commentators criticized the country's use of force as "disproportionate." During the Israel-Hezbollah war in 2006, officials from the United Nations, the European Union,[2] and several countries used that word to describe Israel's military actions in Lebanon. Coverage in the press was similar—one newspaper columnist, for example, criticized the "utterly disproportionate carnage."[3] Two and a half years later, during the Gaza War of 2008–09, the same charge was leveled against Israel by some of the same institutions and individuals; it also appeared throughout the controversial U.N. report about the conflict (the "Goldstone Report"[4]).

This criticism reveals an important moral misunderstanding. In everyday usage, the word "proportional" implies numerical comparability, and that seems to be what most of Israel's critics have in mind: the ethics of war, they suggest, requires something like a tit-for-tat response. So if the number of losses suffered by Hezbollah or Hamas greatly exceeds the number of casualties among the Israel Defense Forces (IDF), then Israel is morally and perhaps legally culpable for the "disproportionate" casualties.

But these critics seemed largely unaware that "proportionality" has a technical meaning connected to the ethics of war. The long tradition of just war theory distinguishes between the principles governing the justice of going to war (*jus ad bellum*) and those governing just conduct in warfare (*jus in bello*). There are two main *jus in bello* criteria. The criterion of *discrimination* prohibits direct and intentional attacks on noncombatants, although neither international law nor the just war tradition that has morally informed it requires that a legitimate military target must be spared from attack simply because its destruction may unintentionally injure or kill noncombatants or damage civilian property and infrastructure. International law and just war theory only

1. Pavlischek's essay appeared in *The New Atlantis* in Spring 2010 and is available online at https://www.thenewatlantis.com/publications/proportionality-in-warfare.

2. http://www.ctv.ca/servlet/ArticleNews/story/CTVNews/20060713/eud_Mideast_060713/200607 13?hub=World.

3. http://www.washingtonpost.com/wp-dyn/content/article/2006/07/24/AR2006072400 810_pf.html.

4. https://www2.ohchr.org/english/bodies/hrcouncil/docs/12session/A-HRC-12-48.pdf.

insist that the anticipated collateral damage—the "merely foreseen" secondary effects—must be "proportionate" to the military advantage sought in attacking the legitimate military target. This sense of *proportionality* is the second *jus in bello* criterion; it has to do almost entirely with the foreseen but unintended harm done to noncombatants and to noncombatant infrastructure.

Paul Ramsey, the great twentieth-century ethicist, summarized the meaning and relation of these two criteria with characteristic bluntness in his book *The Just War* (1968):

> One does not calculate a prudent number of babies to be murdered (directly killed) for the sake of any good consequences (such as getting at the government); but one may and must calculate the prudent number that will and may be killed as an unavoidable side or collateral effect of military operations targeted upon the force to be repelled and whose goal and other consequence is expected to be the saving of many more from slaughter or from an oppressive tyranny, or in order to preserve in the international system accepted patterns in the actions of states on which grave consequences depend. Direct attacks on a civil population can never be justified; but unfortunately—in this world to date—a good many incidental deaths and extensive collateral damage to civil society may still be knowingly done lest worse befall.[5]

All the loose talk about proportionality during the last two Israeli wars provoked the prominent just war theorist and political philosopher Michael Walzer to jump into the fray. In an essay in *Parameters*, the professional journal of the U.S. Army, he noted the "anger over the ratio of deaths in the recent Gaza war—100 to one, Gazan to Israeli, according to figures accepted by the *New York Times*." If those deaths "were all soldiers (fighters or militants) on either side," Walzer wrote, "a ratio like that would simply be a sign of military victory, the deaths regrettable but probably not immoral."[6]

Walzer was perhaps being too charitable. The notion that a lopsided casualty ratio between the IDF and Hezbollah or Hamas militants is sufficient evidence of some moral failing on the part of the IDF so radically departs from any recognizable understanding of the requirements of proportionality and so evidences a lack of moral seriousness that one cannot help but wonder whether something even more pernicious was involved. Even some liberal political pundits were led to question the critics' motivations. In the *Washington Post*, for example, columnist Richard Cohen argued that the critics' appeals to proportionality were little more than "a fig leaf for anti-Israel sentiment in general."[7] Lanny Davis, the liberal lawyer and pro-Israel activist, called the appeal to proportionality a "double standard that is hypocritically applied to Israel."[8]

5. Ramsey, *The Just War*, 429–30.

6. Walzer, "Responsibility and Proportionality in State and Nonstate Wars," 41.

7. http://www.washingtonpost.com/wp-dyn/content/article/2006/07/24/AR2006072400808.html.

8. http://www.washingtontimes.com/news/2009/jan/26/israel-gaza-and-the-double-standard/.

Proportionality and the Combatant

Although the *jus in bello* principle of proportionality has to do almost entirely with the foreseen but unintended harm to noncombatants, there is one exception—although even that exception does not give Israel's critics a leg to stand on. Scholarly discussions of proportionality often mention the avoidance of *gratuitous harm*. For example, Sheldon M. Cohen notes in his book *Arms and Judgment* (1989) that the law of war requires that gratuitous harm against enemy combatants be avoided. This principle, explains Cohen, rests on the fundamental premise that "it is not the destruction of enemy forces, but the imposition of the nation's will on the enemy that is the ultimate goal in warfare, and this can sometimes be accomplished by neutralizing enemy forces without destroying them."

However, two points must be emphasized with regard to the avoidance of gratuitous harm to enemy combatants. First, to avoid causing gratuitous harm a combatant merely needs to stipulate that there is some military gain to be attained by the harm directed at enemy forces. That there should be no *gratuitous* harm does not specify the *proportion* between the military objective and the harm, much less a prescribed ratio between opposing combatants. Second, in some cases it may be possible for a combatant to avoid gratuitous harm by striving to achieve an objective without imposing significant casualties—for example, by isolating, ignoring, or bypassing an enemy defensive position or fortification. But, as Cohen is quick to add, "the law of war does not require this gentility." It is not, Cohen writes, "morally incumbent upon the attacker to pursue these alternatives (and it is never legally incumbent on the attacker to do so)."

Why should we be wary of insisting that combatants have a moral obligation to isolate, ignore, or bypass an attack on an enemy position or stronghold, even though an attack may appear gratuitous? How can there be no moral obligation on the part of an attacker to pursue tactics that might decrease the number of enemy combatant casualties? Put simply, the law defers to the decision of competent military authority, since only someone in the command position is capable of making the requisite complex and interrelated strategic, tactical, and moral judgments.

Suppose, Cohen asks, that a combatant is contemplating an attack on a town where the enemy's present position is hopeless. If attacked, it would certainly fall. Abstractly considered, one might think that a combatant has a moral obligation to avoid the gratuitous harm that an attack on the position would occasion, and offer terms of surrender. But then again, "in the time it would take to get a response to a request for surrender the town could be reinforced, or perhaps it is vital that the objective be secured in short order. It is thus not morally incumbent on the attacker to offer terms to the defender, even if the defender's position is hopeless." The same line of reasoning would apply to bypassing or isolating rather than destroying a military target. Enemy soldiers occupying a bypassed or isolated target may live to fight another day. For these reasons, with regard to legitimate military targets, the law (always) and morality (almost always) defers to the tactical and strategic judgment of military commanders.

The War Against Just War

So the genuine legal and moral question of proportionality relates to noncombatants, a fact that was badly muddied by the critics of Israel's military actions in 2006 and 2009. For example, consider the comments made by Kofi Annan, then Secretary General of the United Nations, in July 2006. Briefing the U.N. Security Council, Annan began by conceding that Israel had a right to defend itself, that it had been attacked and so was fighting a just war. But in short order Annan proclaimed that Israel's response had been "disproportionate" and "excessive" so that Israel was not fighting justly. However, as Michael Walzer notes in his *Parameters* article, "Annan never provided a measure for proportionality or gave any indication of what number of dead civilians would not have been disproportionate and excessive—presumably, the number in his mind was very low."

Ten days later, Annan acknowledged[9] that Hezbollah was firing rockets into northern Israel "from positions apparently located in the midst of the civilian population." A few days after that, Annan dropped the qualifying term "apparently." So, comments Walzer,

> Hezbollah was itself putting large numbers of civilians at risk. Did Annan consider those numbers to be disproportionate and excessive? He did not say. His politic position—that Israel had a right to fight, but only within the limits of an undefined proportionality—demonstrates the dilemma of justice in war very clearly, but not very helpfully. What is the appropriate measure? And once we know the answer to that question, how many deaths would it allow? What number of civilian deaths is "not disproportionate to" the value of destroying, say, a Hezbollah base in Lebanon, a Taliban base in Afghanistan, or a Hamas missile launching site?[10]

Walzer's remarks here raise two distinct issues. The first has to do with the ultimate source of the appeal to an undefined "proportionality." While anti-Israel sentiment surely accounts for some of the criticism, the abuse of the concept of proportionality has deeper intellectual roots. Walzer notes that when we argue about aggression, military intervention, and the conduct of battle, we now regularly use the language of just war; in 2002, he called this the "triumph of just war theory."[11] His critics responded by insisting that this did nothing more than provide new ways to justify war, to which Walzer now replies (in his *Parameters* article) that just war theory has more often than not been used the way it should be used: "to call for military action in a particular case and to reject military action in other cases." Those who have followed the debate over just war and pacifism for the past several decades will recognize the pattern. But then Walzer gets to the crux of the matter:

> Many clerics, journalists, and professors, however, have invented a wholly different interpretation and use, making the theory more and more stringent, particularly with regard to civilian deaths. In fact, they have reinterpreted it to a point where it is pretty much impossible to find a war or conflict that

9. http://www.un.org/News/Press/docs/2006/sgsm10580.doc.htm.

10. Walzer, "Responsibility and Proportionality in State and Nonstate Wars," 45–46.

11. Walzer, "The Triumph of Just War Theory (and the Dangers of Success)."

can be justified. Historically, just war theory was meant to be an alternative to Christian pacifism; now, for some of its advocates, it is pacifism's functional equivalent—a kind of cover for people who are not prepared to admit that there are no wars they will support.[12]

Walzer is not the first to notice what has variously been called a "crypto-pacifist" or "functional pacifist" reinterpretation of just war theory. As early as the 1960s, Paul Ramsey identified the problem, labeling it a *bellum contra bellum justum* (war against just war). Its fundamental line of reasoning is that all modern warfare—supposedly unlike pre-modern warfare—is inherently both indiscriminate and disproportionate. Therefore, since no war can meet the *jus in bello* tests of discrimination and proportionality, no war can be fought justly. And if no war can be fought justly, then the only moral option for a vast cohort of "clerics, journalists, and professors" has been pacifism—less the principled theological pacifism of the so-called "peace churches" than a modern "functional" pacifism. Among the most important and influential contemporary critics of this revisionist view of the just war tradition are James Turner Johnson of Rutgers University, who has conclusively demonstrated that such functional pacifism and moral confusion have no place within the just war tradition, and George Weigel of the Ethics and Public Policy Center, who for the past two decades has challenged such revisionist interpretations of the tradition among American Roman Catholics in particular.

While Walzer's remarks on the tendency toward functional pacifism are not particularly novel, it is nonetheless important for two reasons. For one thing, Walzer is arguably the most influential public intellectual in the fields of military ethics and just war theory. His *Just and Unjust Wars* (1977) is rightly considered a classic not merely in academia, but also throughout the U.S. military's formal education system, including the military academies, the command and staff colleges, and the war colleges. Second, Walzer is most decidedly a man of the left, so his reflections on this particular point cannot be dismissed as special pleading for conservative or neoconservative ends. He is an editor of the political quarterly *Dissent*, he is a contributing editor to *The New Republic*, and he regularly writes for that magazine as well as the *New York Review of Books* and other prominent outlets. It is not insignificant that Walzer, as an eminent left-wing academic, has acknowledged this fundamental distortion of the just war tradition and that he explicitly locates the recent charges of Israeli "disproportionality" within the context of that more fundamental controversy over how to understand the just war tradition. Indeed, Walzer acknowledges that the tendency toward thinking of the just war tradition as functional pacifism "is especially strong on the left," adding that this is why "it is stronger in Europe than in the United States."

Neglecting Responsibility and Discrimination

Walzer's question for Annan—did the Secretary General, who was so quick to charge the IDF with disproportionality, also consider Hezbollah's endangerment of civilians to be "disproportionate" and "excessive"?—could be put even more pointedly. Why didn't

12. Walzer, "The Triumph of Just War Theory," 938.

Annan and the other critics who claimed that Israel's actions were not proportionate explicitly condemn with at least as much vigor Hezbollah's systematic endangerment of civilians? Or do Annan and company believe that the hostage-shield tactics of terrorists and insurgents are required by "military necessity"?

Walzer is right to suggest that before discussing issues of proportionality we should ask questions about responsibility; the matter of just who put noncombatants at risk in the first place is logically and morally prior to questions of proportionality. That is just another way of saying that any morally informed discussion of the *jus in bello* proportionality criterion must first be considered in proper relation to the principle of discrimination. Walzer notes, for instance, that when Hamas or Hezbollah fighters choose to fire rockets from heavily populated areas, when they deliberately choose to make a response to their rocket attacks morally difficult by hiding among civilians, or seek to ensure that a response will be condemned throughout the world, or decide to use civilians as human shields, "the primary responsibility for [civilian] deaths then falls on the Hezbollah or Hamas militants who were using them."

Yet in any discussion of civilian deaths in warfare—not just in Lebanon and Gaza, but also in the U.S. operations in Afghanistan and elsewhere—the argument from proportionality is nowadays given priority over the argument from discrimination and responsibility. As Walzer puts it, "given our natural aversion to civilian deaths, it makes for an easy critique." Claims of disproportionality are "simple and compelling," Walzer writes, explaining that:

> proportionality without responsibility makes it possible for critics to condemn the military force that *causes* civilian deaths, whether or not it is *responsible* for them. When non-state organizations fight against state-organized armies, responsibility may lie on either side, probably on both sides, but it is almost always the army that will cause the greater number of deaths. Proportionality arguments are, therefore, favorable to the non-state actor, while responsibility arguments are necessarily discriminating. [13][Emphasis added.]

The idea that there is a bias against non-state actors has long been a complaint of leftist critics of the just war tradition and of the laws of war. This bias need not take the most extreme and explicit terrorist-justifying rejection of the idea of just war, as reflected in this 1970 statement by George Habash, then leader of the Popular Front for the Liberation of Palestine: "There can be no geographical or political boundaries or moral limits to the operations of the people's camp. In today's world no one is 'innocent,' and no one is a 'neutral.'" The more politically palatable and common version of this complaint is somewhat subtler: Because it would be a serious military liability for irregular forces—guerrillas and insurgents—to abide by the laws of war, particularly the civilian-protective requirement that combatants wear uniforms to distinguish them from noncombatants, it is licit for them to flout those legal requirements of the Geneva Conventions. Hence, Sheldon Cohen finds leftist academics like Princeton's Richard A. Falk arguing that the Geneva requirements "seem to be weighed heavily in favor of the constituted powers of government and to carry over into the laws of war the statist bias of the overall system

---

13. Walzer, "Responsibility and Proportionality in State and Nonstate Wars," 45.

of the world order." The first thing to go is the "dress requirement" (as Cohen calls it) because it reflects a bias favoring regular troops, or, as Walzer puts it, a bias for "state-organized armies" over non-state actors. This insistence on clearly distinguishing between combatants and noncombatants, the argument goes, is unfair to guerrillas, insurgents, and non-state actors generally.

This challenge to the laws of war on behalf of irregulars connects back to the issue of proportionality. The same argument that "military necessity" permits irregulars to eschew uniforms can be extended to operational behavior; perhaps it also allows irregulars to use babies and noncombatants as shields. By this topsy-turvy reasoning, a non-state actor would escape moral censure even though he completely disregards the principle of discrimination, but a military force that abides by the principle of discrimination both in refusing to target civilians and in refusing to use civilians as hostage shields would be subject to censure because its collateral damage is deemed disproportional. As Cohen remarked two decades ago,

> It is one of the striking oddities of contemporary politics and values that military necessity, so indignantly and unanimously rejected when it is brought in to justify the behavior of regular troops, should be so timidly readmitted through the back door when it is guerrillas who have come to call.[14]

Walzer's New Doctrine

At first glance, Michael Walzer would seem to have little sympathy for such justificatory gymnastics. Earlier we saw that he rather quickly disposes of the notion that a lopsided ratio of combatant deaths—even "100 to one, Gazan to Israeli"—is inherently immoral. He notes, quite correctly, that even if many of the victims were civilians, "to take this asymmetry as proof of a crime is not a serious moral engagement with these wars. When non-state fighters and militants hide among civilians, they may well bear a greater responsibility for civilian deaths."

If this were all that Walzer has had to say about proportionality and noncombatant casualties it would comport quite well with traditional just war theory. But at least since the publication of *Just and Unjust Wars*, Walzer has proposed a modification to the traditional understanding of discrimination and proportionality. Traditionally, the two *jus in bello* principles of discrimination and proportionality are understood to be related through the doctrine of *double effect*: An attack that harms civilians can be morally licit so long as, first, harming civilians is neither the goal nor the means of the attack but a side effect (that is, a "double effect"), and second, the harm done is not disproportionate to the good sought through the attack. The proportionality principle governs the extent to which collateral damage is permissible.

But Walzer argued in 1977 and he continues to maintain that the traditional doctrine of double effect is too lenient. The traditional doctrine of proportionality "makes

14. Cohen, *Arms and Judgment*, 158.

things too easy for the attackers," he writes in his *Parameters* article. "For the most part," proportionality has been a "darkly permissive principle."

As a corrective, Walzer has proposed a revision that has been called the doctrine of *double intention*. It is not enough, he argues, for a belligerent to merely not intend to strike noncombatants; the belligerent must also positively intend to reduce the risk of harm to noncombatants. There must be, as Walzer writes in *Just and Unjust Wars*, "a positive commitment to save civilian lives," reducing the foreseeable evil "as far as possible." To put it another way, not only should combatants *not attempt* to harm civilians; combatants should *attempt not* to harm them. An attacker has a moral obligation to "take positive measures to avoid or minimize injury to civilians in the target area," he argues in *Parameters*, "even if it appears likely that the number of deaths caused by the attack would not be 'disproportionate to' whatever the relevant measure might be." It is not enough to warn noncombatants in a combat zone that an attack is imminent, or to plead with them to leave. In Walzer's view, soldiers have a moral obligation to place themselves at an increased risk of harm even for the sake of enemy noncombatants.

Walzer's proposed doctrine of double intention has been criticized by adherents of the more traditional understanding of double effect. Cohen, for instance, in *Arms and Judgment* defends the traditional view as reflected in the moral reasoning behind the 1907 Hague Conventions. "The law of war implies that soldiers are not obligated to raise their already high stakes to even higher levels in order to lower further the risk to innocents in combat zones. This seems particularly reasonable in tactical combat, where civilians are usually free to leave the combat zone." Cohen suggested that a simple moral guideline was the basis for the traditional understanding, namely "that the attacker may, given the presence of innocents in a combat zone, do anything that it would be permissible to do if there were no innocents there—subject to the restrictions entailed by the principle of proportionality."

J. G. Fleury, a colonel in the Canadian military, also defended the traditional understanding in a 1998 research paper written for the Canadian Forces College.[15] Fleury argues that Walzer's conviction that combatants should assume greater risk "conflicts with military logic and the psychology of command." The traditional principle of double effect, Fleury writes, "provides the moral guidance necessary in such circumstances." What's more, "soldiers do not have the same positive duty to protect innocents among the enemy population, as they have to protect their own population, although they have an obligation not to harm innocents intentionally regardless of their nationality."

Rising to defend Walzer's revised doctrine, Steven Lee, a professor at Hobart and William Smith Colleges, claims that Fleury's arguments wrongly assume "that the moral status of civilians results from their being *enemy* civilians. Rather, their moral status, their right not to be attacked, results from their status as human beings, irrespective of their nationality."[16] Lee here cites Walzer's own justification from *Just and Unjust Wars*: "The structure of rights stands independently of political allegiance; it establishes

---

15. http://www.cfc.forces.gc.ca/papers/amsc/amsc1/fleury2.htm.

16. http://www.usafa.edu/isme/JSCOPE04/Lee04.html.

obligations that are owed, so to speak, to humanity itself and to particular human be-ings and not merely to one's fellow citizens."

Well, yes, of course the traditional doctrine of double effect does not deny that there are universal human rights; indeed, it asserts that enemy civilians and friendly civilians alike have the right not to be attacked *intentionally*. In the traditional view, the moral status of enemy civilians already does derive from "their status as human beings, irrespective of their nationality" (to use Lee's words). What the traditional view tends to resist is Walzer's suggestion that a soldier's obligation to put himself at greater risk for enemy civilians is identical to his obligation to his fellow citizens or to his civilian allies in a time of war.

Walzer is notoriously ambiguous on just how much additional risk a soldier must assume to prevent unintended harm to civilians and just how much the risk to civil-ians should be reduced. Even his defender Lee notes that Walzer's original formula-tion ("the foreseeable evil [must] be reduced as far as possible") is simply unworkable because "reducing the risk to civilians as far as possible would involve an open-ended increase in the risk to combatants or an abandonment of the military objective." This problem is not remedied in Walzer's *Parameters* article. He argues, for instance, that the Israelis must do "*everything they can*, including putting their own soldiers at risk" to avoid hitting innocent civilians in apartments when attacking a rocket launcher and its operators. Those responsible for selecting the target "*need to do the best they can* to discover how many civilians are in the building." Even if it appears that the number of civilian deaths would not be "disproportionate to" whatever the relevant measure might be, says Walzer, the attacking force "must protect civilians as *best they can*—period." (Emphases added throughout.)

The Perversity of "Double Intention"

Walzer's proposed new doctrine is not merely a matter of academic dispute, as evi-denced by a 2009 exchange in the *New York Review of Books* between, on one hand, Walzer and his Institute for Advanced Study colleague Avishai Margalit, and on the other, Tel Aviv University professor Asa Kasher and IDF Major General Amos Yadlin. In a previous academic article,[17] Kasher and Yadlin had noted that "a highly important and sensitive issue is what priority should be given to the duty to minimize casual-ties among the combatants of the state when they are engaged in combat acts against terror?" In puzzling through this problem, Kasher and Yadlin insist that the fact that terrorists "reside and act in the vicinity of persons not involved in terror is not a reason for jeopardizing the combatant's life in their pursuit. . . . The terrorists shoulder the responsibility for their encounter with the combatant and should therefore bear the consequences." And they add: "Where the state does not have effective control of the vicinity, it does not have to shoulder responsibility for the fact that persons who are involved in terror operate in the vicinity of persons who are not."

17. http://dx.doi.org/10.1353/sais.2005.0011.

Walzer and Margalit completely reject this argument. They offer instead this guideline:[18] "Conduct your war in the presence of noncombatants on the other side with the same care *as if* your citizens were the noncombatants" (emphasis in original). Walzer and Margalit invite us to consider four distinct hypothetical scenarios in which Hezbollah might attack and take over a kibbutz in northern Israel:

1. Hezbollah captured Manara and held all its members, Israeli citizens, as hostages. Hezbollah combatants mingle with the kibbutz members so as to be shielded by them from any counterattack.

2. Hezbollah captured only the outskirts of Manara, and a group of pro-Israeli, noncombatant volunteers from outside Israel—not Israeli citizens—who worked in Manara and lived near the border were seized and used as human shields.

3. Instead of well-wishing volunteers as in scenario 2, we now have a group of protesters from abroad, who traveled to the northern border of Israel to raise their voices against Israel's policy toward Lebanon. As it happened, Hezbollah did not pay much attention to their protest, but seized and used them as its human shields.

4. Before Hezbollah captured Manara, the kibbutz was evacuated, and now Hezbollah brings in civilian villagers from South Lebanon, in order to claim that the kibbutz land belongs to them, but also to use them as human shields.

"We claim," say Walzer and Margalit, that "Israel is morally required to behave in all those cases the way it would behave in the first case, when its citizens are held by Hezbollah in 'a mixed vicinity.'"

The radicalism of Walzer and Margalit's proposed guideline is evident in their insistence that it should apply even when noncombatants voluntarily intermingle with the terrorists. For the sake of argument, let us concede that the IDF (or any other military in an analogous situation) has a moral obligation to behave in the same way in the first three scenarios. But what about the fourth scenario? Are we really to say that whatever personal risks Israeli soldiers assume in the first scenario, they must also assume in the fourth scenario—even if the noncombatants *voluntarily* intermingle with the Hezbollah combatants, and even if other positive measures short of increased risk to the lives of IDF soldiers have been pursued? Here, Walzer and his coauthor reiterate his longstanding critique of the traditional principle of double effect. Israeli soldiers, he writes, are:

> . . . fighting against enemies who try to kill Israeli civilians and intentionally put civilians at risk by using them as cover. Israel condemns those practices; at the same time, however, it kills far more civilians than its enemies do, though without intending the deaths as a matter of policy. . . . But merely "not intending" the civilian deaths, while knowing that they will occur, is not a position that can be vindicated by Israel's condemnation of terrorism. So how can Israel prove its opposition to the practices of its enemies? Its soldiers must, by contrast with its enemies, *intend not* to kill civilians, and that active intention can be made manifest only through the risks the soldiers themselves accept in order to reduce the risks to civilians.

18. http://www.nybooks.com/articles/22664.

Walzer and Margalit's intentions are admirable. They rightly insist that "the crucial means for limiting the scope of warfare is to draw a sharp line between combatants and noncombatants." They rightly observe that terrorism is "a concerted effort to blur this distinction so as to turn civilians into legitimate targets." And they rightly say that "when fighting against terrorism, we should not imitate it."

But Walzer and Margalit are plainly wrong to claim that the only way to demonstrate opposition to terrorist tactics is "through the risks the soldiers themselves accept in order to reduce the risks to civilians." Israel or any other country's opposition to terrorist tactics can be vindicated by not engaging in terrorism. It can be vindicated by condemning without equivocation those who do. It can be vindicated by not using civilians as shields.

Moreover, Israel's intentions not to harm civilians can be manifest by other efforts to minimize collateral damage. As Kasher and Yadlin mention in their *New York Review* reply,[19] Israel's military actions in Gaza were preceded by "widely distributed warning leaflets, more than 150,000 warning phone calls to terrorists' neighbors, and nonlethal warning fire—unprecedented efforts in every respect."

Walzer and Margalit, in their final rejoinder,[20] complain that these efforts are morally insufficient. It is not enough, they say, to warn civilians; an army must "try to find out whether civilians have in fact left—and any effort to collect that kind of information will probably put soldiers at risk." But it is radical, indeed morally perverse, to claim that an army that strives to forewarn civilians fails, like terrorists hiding behind civilians, to behave morally.

There is an obvious practical downside to the Walzer position. Kasher and Yadlin mistakenly impute to Walzer and Margalit the claim that collateral damage is "never morally acceptable." They don't quite go that far: their actual claim is that responsibility for collateral damage is transferred from regular combatants to irregular combatants only when the regulars significantly put themselves at risk to decrease the collateral damage. Still, Kasher and Yadlin are correct to assert that by supplanting the doctrine of double effect with the doctrine of double intention, Walzer "encourages and enhances terrorism" in a practical sense by insisting that moral state actors assume new operational obligations to protect civilians, by providing a greater incentive for terrorists and insurgents to hide among civilians, and by even providing an incentive for terrorist sympathizers to offer themselves up as hostage shields.

All this is not to suggest that counterinsurgency and counterterrorist military forces should *not* put their soldiers at greater risk in order to minimize collateral damage. In many counterinsurgency efforts, such risk-taking and heightened standards of civilian protection will be an essential part of a larger strategy to win the trust of the local population and to separate civilians from insurgents. But that increased risk stems from strategic calculation—from the fact that counterinsurgency operations require boots on the ground instead of just precision-guided munitions—not from a moral or legal obligation. *Pace* Michael Walzer, the moral and legal obligation to enemy civilians, including those who willingly offer themselves to terrorists and insurgents as human

19. http://www.nybooks.com/articles/22761.

20. http://www.nybooks.com/articles/22761.

shields, remains exactly where the traditional doctrine of double effect locates it: Never attack them directly. Never attack them as [a] means to get at the enemy. And limit the unintended harm likely to fall upon them to that which is proportional to the just tactical and strategic objective. For the law of war to seek more than this is to incentivize what Paul Ramsey called the "wickedness" of using noncombatants as shields—and even the wickedness of terrorism itself.

"The Bush Doctrine: A Niebuhrian Assessment"

Mark R. Amstutz[1]

THE TERRORIST ATTACKS ON 9/11 mark a turning point in the Bush administration's foreign policy. The shift became apparent early on in the tone, content, and moral clarity of the President's rhetoric, evidenced in his major speeches following the attacks. Building on the themes and principles articulated earlier, the Bush administration released in September 2002 a new "National Security Strategy" (NSS), representing a codification of the post-9/11 foreign policy of the United States. This new orientation, which subsequently came to be called the Bush doctrine, has received significant criticism both domestically and internationally, especially for integrating moral language with security concerns.

This essay assesses the Bush foreign policy of muscular idealism from a Christian realist perspective. In carrying out this task, I focus on the Bush doctrine and use the political ethics of Reinhold Niebuhr to assess that doctrine. I argue that the Bush foreign policy approach and Niebuhr's political ethics share a number of common traits. At the same time, a number of significant differences exist between the optimism and forward-looking nature of the Bush doctrine and Niebuhrian thought. The aim here is not to evaluate the doctrine's efficacy but rather to assess its moral legitimacy from Niebuhr's Christian realist perspective.

Niebuhr's Christian Realism

Niebuhr is important because as founder of the Christian realist perspective he provided a sophisticated integration of power and morality in the context of global affairs.[2] The foundation of Niebuhr's political ethics was his conception of human nature.[3] Following

1. This article originally appeared in *The Review of Faith & International Affairs* 5.4 (2007) 25–33 and is reprinted with permission of *The Review*.

2. According to Bundy, Reinhold Niebuhr was "probably the single most influential mind in the development of American attitudes which combine moral purpose with a sense of political reality." See Bundy, "Foreign Policy."

3. For an overview of Niebuhr's views of sin and human nature, see Reinhold Niebuhr, *The Nature and Destiny of Man*—Vol. I *On Human Nature* and Vol. II *On Human Destiny*.

Augustine, Niebuhr regarded sin as universal and comprehensive, affecting all persons and every aspect of human life. Nobody was exempt from sin and no human action could successfully overcome self-interest. Since reason itself could be tainted by sin, reliance on moral principles could provide only a proximate guide to ethical action. At the same time, since humans were created in the image of God, Niebuhr assumed that they had the capacity to love others, to pursue the common good, and to advance justice. Niebuhr's idea of human nature thus consisted of two dimensions—one leading to selfless love and the other leading to self-interest. As a result, people were both creatures and creators, sinful yet capable of self-giving love. Niebuhr expressed this paradoxical, dialectical perspective of persons in his widely quoted aphorism: "Man's capacity for justice makes democracy possible; but man's inclination to injustice makes democracy necessary."[4]

Four features characterize Niebuhr's political ethics: the priority of power, the moral limits of political action, the need for humility, and the need for responsible political action. For Niebuhr, power was essential in maintaining global order because there was no common authority to resolve interstate disputes. Although he respected believers who sought to model Jesus' ethic of love, he opposed those who used this approach as a political tactic. He was especially critical of those who considered non-violence morally superior and more efficacious in confronting the problems of aggression and tyranny. According to Niebuhr, Christian idealists who are so concerned with avoiding violence were likely to end up supporting "the peace of tyranny as if it were nearer to the peace of the Kingdom of God than war."[5]

A second Niebuhrian principle was the inherent limitations of political action. Because of the universality of sin, all political initiatives would necessarily involve partiality and self-interest. While the quest for the common good was often impaired by insufficient knowledge, the primary reason for the moral shortcomings of collective action, according to Niebuhr, was the inability to apply moral ideals wholeheartedly and dispassionately. History was ironic because the pursuit of moral ideals often fostered injustice—not so much because plans were flawed but because of the arrogance and selfishness of leaders. Indeed, Niebuhr argued that evil was most likely to arise when people forgot that they were "creatures" and assumed that they had virtue, wisdom, and power that was beyond their competence.[6] Pretension, not wrong action or improper judgment, was therefore the chief source of injustice.[7]

A third Niebuhrian political norm was the need for humility in public affairs. Since understanding was always partial and human action was always tainted by sin, government leaders should avoid triumphalism. Moralistic language, and in particular Manichean dualism, should be avoided. "The Christian faith ought to persuade us," wrote Niebuhr, "that political controversies are always conflicts between sinners and not

---

4. Niebuhr, *The Children of Light and the Children of Darkness*, xiii.

5. Niebuhr, "Why the Christian Church Is Not Pacifist," 111.

6. Niebuhr, *The Structure of Nations and Empires*, 298.

7. In his short study of American history, Niebuhr develops this perspective, arguing that American history is ironic precisely because the hopes and ideals are unconsciously betrayed by the collective behavior of its people and government. See Niebuhr, *The Irony of American History*.

between righteous men and sinners."[8] Niebuhr also cautioned against reducing political ethics to a single moral value. According to Kenneth Thompson, Niebuhr was conspicuous among theologians by insisting that there was no single overarching norm for judging international affairs. He refused to see freedom, security, or justice as the controlling objective of American foreign policy. He agreed with Justice Holmes' claim: "[P]eople are always extolling the man of principle but the superior man is the one who knows he must find his way in the maze of principles."[9]

A fourth distinctive feature of Niebuhrian ethics was the call for responsible political action. While Niebuhr cautioned against overambitious, self-righteous political initiatives, he was equally concerned with the dangers of inaction resulting from an ethic of perfectionism. Some moralists were so concerned with their own moral purity that they refused to confront injustice and tyranny because such action would result in compromising the ideal of love. But Niebuhr, following Augustine, argued that the only way that a stable and partially humane world could be sustained was by harnessing power in the service of public justice. Accordingly, Niebuhr was a strong advocate of political action, personally demonstrating vigorous public engagement throughout his life. Through his sermons, speeches, and writings, he repeatedly and courageously sought to advance measures that he thought would foster a more stable and humane global order. For Niebuhr, the great danger was not erroneous action but simply inaction. This is why he observed at the outset of World War II that the fundamental source of immorality was "the evasion or denial of moral responsibility."[10]

The Bush Doctrine

After the 9/11 attacks, the U.S. government adopted a new national security strategy. The core ideas of this new paradigm, known as the Bush Doctrine (BD), were first expressed in the President's declarations and speeches and then amplified in the September 2002 "National Security Strategy of the United States" (NSS). The new NSS is noteworthy for its emphasis on promoting human dignity and democracy, maintaining military supremacy, responding to unconventional threats with preemptive force, and the willingness to act unilaterally. Following the issuance of the 2002 NSS, President Bush continued emphasizing the BD's core themes by highlighting a strategy rooted in power and morality that contributed to "a balance of power favoring freedom." Two of the most important subsequent expressions of the doctrine were the Second Inaugural Address on January 20, 2005 and the revised NSS, released in March 2006.

Scholars differ on which elements constitute the BD. Some thinkers view the doctrine chiefly in terms of power and security, while others regard it as an exercise in

---

8. Niebuhr, "Why the Christian Church Is Not Pacifist," 114.

9. Thompson, "The Political Philosophy of Reinhold Niebuhr," 249.

10. Niebuhr, "Repeal the Neutrality Act!" 177–78.

Wilsonian idealism.[11] Still others emphasize the unique relationship of the United States to Israel.[12] In this essay I characterize the doctrine as having four features:

- belief that unipolarity is conducive to peace and that a preponderance of American power can contribute to a peaceful and prosperous world order;

- belief in the need for multilateralism to advance peace, freedom, and security, but a willingness to act unilaterally when necessary;

- belief that the United States must be willing to use pre-emptive and preventive force to confront terrorist groups and rogue states with weapons of mass destruction (WMD); and

- belief in the need for the United States to champion human rights and help foster political democracy.

Of the doctrine's four elements, the first three are based on power and are concerned with security, world order, and the international management of power. The fourth element, by contrast, is based on political morality and is chiefly concerned with fostering human dignity through the expansion of free societies. The doctrine's dimensions of power and morality, realism and idealism, are thus integrated in the conviction that democracies are inherently pacific and "have common interests in building a benign international environment that is congenial to American interests and ideals."[13]

Most of the criticism of the BD has focused on the doctrine's unilateralism and pre-emptive use of force.[14] But much of this critique has exaggerated the extent of these alleged changes. Both the 2002 and 2006 NSS, for example, emphasize the need for coalition building and call for unilateral action only as a last resort. Moreover, the idea that preemption is a new doctrine is without foundation, for states have always possessed an inherent right of anticipatory self-defense. What is clear is that the emergence of international terrorism, especially when coupled with access to WMD, poses an unprecedented security threat. Given the widespread criticism precipitated by the claim of preemption, the NSS 2006 introduced the following qualification: "The United States will not resort to force in all cases to preempt emerging threats. Our preference is that nonmilitary actions succeed. And no country should ever use preemption as a pretext for aggression."[15]

Although most of the opposition to the BD has focused on its military dimensions, the most noteworthy feature of the BD is its emphasis on moral values. Indeed, Norman

---

11. For other definitions of the BD, see Jervis, "Understanding the Bush Doctrine," 365–88, and Singer, *The President of Good & Evil*, 144–55.

12. Podhoretz, "In Praise of the Bush Doctrine," 28.

13. Jervis, "Why the Bush Doctrine Cannot be Sustained," 351–77.

14. Ironically, the Bush administration has conflated preemptive force with preventive force. Preemption involves the use when clear evidence exists of an imminent attack; preventive force, by contrast, is the use of coercive power to eliminate danger before a threat can emerge. The war with Iraq was an example of preventive military action.

15. George W. Bush, *National Security Strategy of the United States* (2002), section 5. Available at https://georgewbush-whitehouse.archives.gov/nsc/nss/2006/sectionV.html. Accessed July 1, 2021.

Podhoretz claims that the power of the BD is its "incandescent moral clarity."[16] Political morality is used not only to champion human dignity and self-government but also to justify the cause of freedom. In the 2002 NSS, for example, the term freedom is used at least 46 times, while the notions of democracy and liberty appear, respectively, 13 and 11 times. Nowhere is the role of political morality more evident than in the President's Second Inaugural Address. In that noteworthy speech, Bush states the moral basis of American foreign policy as follows:

> From the day of our founding, we have proclaimed that every man and woman on this earth has rights, and dignity, and matchless value, because they bear the image of the maker of heaven and earth. Across the generations, we have proclaimed the imperative of self-government because no one is fit to be a master and no one deserves to be a slave. Advancing these ideals is the mission that created our nation. It is the honorable achievement of our fathers. Now it is the urgent requirement of our nation's security and the calling of our time. So it is the policy of the United States to seek and support the growth of democratic movements and institutions in every nation and culture, with the ultimate goal of ending tyranny in the world.

Historically, foreign policy has been regarded as the pursuit of vital interests, with moral values playing a subsidiary role, if at all. Challenging this traditional conception of foreign policy, the President boldly announces, "America's vital interests and our deepest beliefs are now one." Historian John Lewis Gaddis regards this conflation of ideals and interests as a major shift in the Bush strategy. No longer is freedom simply the aim and aspiration of American foreign policy, but it is now the strategy itself.[17]

Of course, the emphasis on right and wrong, good and evil, can be deeply disturbing not only to those who do not share a belief in transcendent morality but also to those who differ with the claimed normative judgments.[18] Moreover, since reliance on moral norms presents a direct challenge to the prevailing moral relativism common in contemporary discourse, it is not surprising that numerous foreign policy pundits found Bush's strategic perspective grounded in morality to be presumptuous and disconcerting.[19] Philip Zelikow observed that Bush's political ethics were likely to be especially troubling to "leftist moralists" who would prefer isolation rather than engaging foreign injustice.[20] For other critics, including religious officials of mainline Protestant denominations, focusing on America's shortcomings was preferable to confronting oppression, injustice, and egregious human rights abuses in other countries.

16. Podhoretz, "In Praise of the Bush Doctrine," 22.

17. Gaddis, "Past and Future of American Grand Strategy," Charles S. Grant Lecture, Middlebury College, April 21, 2005.

18. For a stinging critique of Bush's ethics, see Singer, *The President of Good & Evil*.

19. For an overview of some of these critics, see Podhoretz, "In Praise of the Bush Doctrine," 20.

20. See, for example, Zelikow, "The Transformation of National Security: Five Redefinitions," 17–28.

A Niebuhrian Assessment of the Bush Doctrine

What are we to make of the BD? What would Niebuhr think? In this section I assess the BD by highlighting similarities and differences between the doctrine and Niebuhr's political ethics.

Similarities

The most important similarity between Niebuhr's thought and President Bush's principled realism is their reliance on a common approach that integrates morality and power. Niebuhr held that because of excessive self-interest, the law of love could never be fulfilled in temporal communities. Only an imperfect peace could be realized in political society. But because humans bear the image of God, they nevertheless have a responsibility to pursue proximate justice and an imperfect common good, knowing that the conception and implementation of political justice will always be compromised by human finiteness and partiality.

Like Niebuhr's political ethics, the Bush foreign policy also relies on the integration of moral ideals and power politics. In his 2003 address at Whitehall Palace in London, Bush describes the Anglo-American approach as "our alliance of conviction and might." After observing that the British and the American people have "an alliance of values," the President declares: "The deepest beliefs of our nations set the direction of our foreign policy. We value our own civil rights, so we stand for the human rights of others. We affirm the God-given dignity of every person, so we are moved to action by poverty and oppression and famine and disease." President Bush's Second Inaugural as well as the NSS 2006 similarly expresses the principled realism of the BD. Although the doctrine is never explained or justified in theological or philosophical terms, its fundamental assertion is premised on an alliance of moral values and political power. In his covering letter to the NSS 2006, the President declares that idealism will inform the national goals of American foreign policy while realism will provide the means to pursue them.

A second shared feature of the BD and Niebuhrian ethics is the belief in the necessity of power. As noted earlier, a distinctive feature of Niebuhr's realism is the belief that evil in politics could only be contained through countervailing power. Unlike the religious idealists of his day, Niebuhr did not think that Hitler's threat to world order could be mitigated through rational dialogue or economic engagement. Rather, it had to be confronted with power.

The Bush administration foreign policy shares with Niebuhrian realism the conviction that a humane global order can only be sustained through the management of power. Accordingly, the central premise of the BD is to create "a balance of power favoring freedom." Since democracies are inherently more peaceful than autocracies, the BD integrates the quest for national and international security by seeking to expand democratic governance in the world. Although the administration leaders recognize that democracies can only develop from indigenous values and institutions, the BD assumes that the United States, collaborating with other major free societies, can create an environment that is conducive to the expansion of humane, participatory regimes, while simultaneously challenging the power of rogue states and terrorist networks with its own considerable power.

A third common feature of Niebuhr's political ethics and the BD is the shared conception of a human nature that emphasizes both the dignity and the sinfulness of persons. For Niebuhr, the foundation of this approach is a Christian view of persons and history. As noted earlier, Niebuhr assumed that a Biblical anthropology was dualistic and paradoxical in that it was based on both the glory and sinfulness of persons. Because humans were created in the image of God, they had the capacity to be creators; but because their nature was corrupted by sin, they misused their freedom by forgetting that they were finite and imperfect. As a result, Niebuhr's paradoxical anthropology leads to political action characterized by tentativeness and circumspection.

Bush, a staunch evangelical, also bases his political perspectives and judgments on a Christian view of human nature. Like Niebuhr, he regards humans as capable of great good when freedom is used responsibly and also capable of great injustice when evil is triumphant over the good. Although he frequently acknowledges the moral frailty of humans and the suffering arising from political injustice, the President repeatedly celebrates the inherent dignity of all persons, claiming that human rights are God's gift to all persons, not just rights defined by the state. Moral language is therefore used to set forth ideals rather than to chart dangers.

Finally, both Niebuhr and Bush are deeply committed to liberty and political democracy. Niebuhr claimed that freedom was indispensable in order for humans to use their gifts and abilities to carry out creative labor. He also argued that democracy was the most effective system to balance the demands of freedom and order. "It happens," he wrote, "that democracy is probably that form of society in which both freedom and order are brought most successfully in support of each other."[21] At the same time, Niebuhr cautioned against those who would regard democracy as a perfect resolution to the problem of community. Although democracy was the best, it was not, and could not be, the final fulfillment of life given the inherent moral limitations of all political initiatives. Indeed, religious faith played an important role in illuminating the tragic character of all human struggles, thereby contributing to a more balanced perspective about politics in general and democracy in particular. Niebuhr claimed that biblical faith not only reminded believers of the limitations of all temporal institutions and initiatives but also encouraged people to call on the mercy of God in their quest to develop and sustain "proximate solutions for insoluble problems."[22]

A central premise of the BD is the need to expand democratic government. The expansion of free societies is necessary, according to the President, not only because such regimes are more effective in promoting international peace but also because freedom is necessary for people to realize their full creative potential. In his Second Inaugural the President declares that human dignity will be the central guide of American foreign policy: "We will persistently clarify the choice before every ruler and every nation. The moral choice between oppression, which is always wrong, and freedom, which is eternally right." Lest

21. Quoted in Rasmussen, ed., *Reinhold Niebuhr*, 256.
22. Niebuhr, *The Children of Light and the Children of Darkness*, 118.

the inaugural is viewed simply as the product of zealous and expansive speechwriting, the global campaign for freedom is restated again a year later in the 2006 NSS. The revised NSS declares that the United States must "defend liberty and justice because these principles are right and true for all people everywhere" and then declares that it will do so by "leading an international effort to end tyranny and to promote effective democracy."

Bush readily acknowledges that the quest for freedom will take time ("it is the concentrated work of generations") and will be expressed in different ways in different societies. The United States, he argues, will not impose our version of democracy on other countries. Rather, the aim of U.S. foreign policy is "to help others find their own voice, attain their own freedom and make their own way."

Thus, both Niebuhr and Bush call for democracy and freedom, but they do so with different levels of confidence and triumphalism. For Niebuhr, democratic government is the best regime to provide human beings with both community and freedom. But such a regime provides no simple resolution to the problems of world order or the ongoing challenges of finding a proximate balance between social order and individual freedom. For Bush, by contrast, freedom is the road to political development, providing the foundation for a humane domestic political society and a stable and peaceful international society.

Differences

One important difference between the BD and Niebuhrian ethics lies in the scope of political reform. Since Niebuhr regarded sin as pervasive and inevitable in all of life, political action was always tainted by excessive self-interest. Modest reform was therefore preferable to grandiose projects. Moreover, since sin had even more deleterious effects in the anarchic international community than in domestic society, Niebuhr tended to be pessimistic about improving the human condition through radical reforms. This skepticism was evidenced by his strong opposition to solving the problem of war through world federalism. Given his preference for limited and modest political initiatives, the campaign for democratic expansion would no doubt have baffled him. Not only would he have regarded the goal of ending tyranny in the world as overambitious, but he also would have considered the campaign for democratic expansion as excessively simplistic. Even in the Cold War years, when the major superpower conflict pitted totalitarian communism against democratic capitalism, Niebuhr thought it unwise to view democracy in ideological or religious terms. Promoting a free society was desirable, but it should be done with modesty and based on a Christian view of persons.[23]

The Bush initiative to expand freedom is an ambitious, all-encompassing global project. The campaign for freedom—to end tyranny by helping to replace oppressive regimes with democracies—is a truly expansive initiative. In a historic address on liberty in November 2003, Bush stated:

23. The central aim of Niebuhr's book on democracy—*The Children of Light and the Children of Darkness*—was to provide a better defense of such government. He argued that a Christian anthropology was an appropriate basis for such a government because such a perspective provided both hope and caution.

> The advance of freedom is the calling of our time; it is the calling of our country. . . . We believe that liberty is the design of nature; we believe that liberty is the direction of history. We believe that human fulfillment and excellence come in the responsible exercise of liberty. We believe that freedom—the freedom we prize—is not for us alone; it is the right and the capacity of all mankind.

Thus, whereas Bush is confident in proclaiming the need for democratic expansion, Niebuhr is more cautious and circumspect in advocating political change.

A second point of tension between the BD and Niebuhrian ethics is found in the doctrine's optimistic, progressive nature. Niebuhr was a staunch critic of the religious, moralistic thought of the 1920s and 1930s. He regarded progressive ideologies as based on illusory and sentimental aspirations. Given the power and pervasive influence of sin, there could be no such confidence in the improvement of the human condition. As he noted in his study *The Irony of American History*,

> The illusions about the possibility of managing historical destiny from any particular standpoint in history, always involve . . . miscalculations about both the power and the wisdom of the managers and of the weakness and the manageability of the historical "stuff" which is to be managed.[24]

Since the course of history was unknown, and because leaders could never devise strategies to achieve a just peace on earth, political reforms needed to be modest and circumspect. Moreover, there could be no confidence in human progress. History would always remain inconclusive and indeterminate.

In contrast to the Niebuhrian uncertainties about historical change, Bush exudes confidence about the future, especially the cause of freedom. While acknowledging the uncertainties of life and the indeterminate nature of history, his moral rhetoric in his post 9/11 speeches is confident, if not triumphalistic. In describing the threat posed by "terrorist networks" in his address to Congress immediately after the 9/11 attacks, the President expressed this confidence as follows: "The course of this conflict [war on terror] is not known, yet its outcome is certain. Freedom and fear, justice and cruelty, have always been at war, and we know that God is not neutral between them." Bush's optimistic vision is perhaps best expressed in his Second Inaugural address, which ends on the following note:

> We go forward with complete confidence in the eventual triumph of freedom. Not because history runs on the wheels of inevitability; it is human choices that move events. Not because we consider ourselves a chosen nation; God moves and chooses as He wills. We have confidence because freedom is the permanent hope of mankind, the hunger in dark places, the longing of the soul.

A third difference between Niebuhrian ethics and the BD lies in the latter's use of expansive moral rhetoric. Although Niebuhr sought to integrate moral values and power, he was reluctant to frame political issues solely in moral or religious terms. Rather, he relied on a dialectical and at times paradoxical ethical framework that maintained

---

24. Niebuhr, *The Irony of American History*, 72.

competing moral values in tension. For Niebuhr, simple moral verdicts were not possible in politics.

By contrast, President Bush has been far more prone to apply moral values to public affairs and to reduce complex issues to simple moral verdicts. In particular, he has been eager to highlight the divine source of human dignity and freedom, claiming, for example, that the liberty the United States has sought to advance in the world "is not America's gift to the world, it is God's gift to humanity." Moreover, unlike Niebuhr's paradoxical ethics, Bush has tended to frame foreign policy concerns using dichotomous categories of justice and injustice, good and evil. The tendency to reduce to simple moral categories is illustrated in his 2002 West Point commencement address:

> Some worry that it is somehow undiplomatic or impolite to speak the language of right and wrong. I disagree. Different circumstances require different methods, but no different moralities. Moral truth is the same in every culture, in every time, and in every place. . . . We are in a conflict between good and evil, and America will call evil by its name.[25]

Undoubtedly, the boldest simple moral judgment made by the President was his description of Iraq, Iran, and North Korea as "the axis of evil." According to philosopher Peter Singer, in the first two and a half years of his presidency, Bush spoke of evil in 319 speeches, using the word as a noun far more often than as an adjective.[26]

Finally, the BD and Niebuhr part company on the issue of self-confidence. Niebuhr would have been troubled by the alleged self-confident and self-righteous nature of the Bush foreign policy. Niebuhr greatly admired Abraham Lincoln because he combined a moral resolve with a profound religious perspective about human beings and historical change. According to Niebuhr, Lincoln exhibited the "almost perfect model of the difficult but not impossible task of remaining loyal and responsible toward the moral treasures of a free civilization on the one hand while yet having some religious vantage point over the struggle."[27] For Niebuhr, bringing a religious dimension to political conflict was essential in maintaining a balanced moral perspective—one that acknowledged the limitations of human initiatives while providing direction and inspiration for political action. Such a perspective is important because it can nurture both moral confidence necessary to choose among alternatives as well as modesty and humility in carrying out actions.

The perception that the BD is excessively self-confident and self-righteous is no doubt due partly to the dominance of American power and the unilateralism of American foreign policy. It can also be attributed to the President's repeated claim of the universality of human dignity and freedom—a claim that some have interpreted as an assertion of American political ideology. Additionally, some have charged that the BD denies the role of national self-interest and unnecessarily regards American power only as a benevolent force in global society. The confident integration of moral purpose and American power is expressed in the 2002 NSS: "Freedom is the non-negotiable demand of human dignity; the birthright of every person—in every civilization. . . . Today, humanity holds in its

25. Bush, "Graduation Speech," United States Military Academy at West Point, June 1, 2002.
26. Singer, *The President of Good & Evil*, 2.
27. Niebuhr, *The Irony of American History*, 172.

hands the opportunity to further freedom's triumph over all these foes. The United States welcomes our responsibility to lead in this great mission."[28]

It needs to be stressed that the differences between Niebuhrian thought and the BD arise in part from the different styles of thought and contexts in which ideas are expressed. As a preacher and teacher, Niebuhr sought to influence political affairs by bringing biblical and theological perspectives to bear on the concrete political and social issues of his time. George W. Bush, by contrast, is a decision maker. As President, he is responsible for guiding and inspiring collective action—a task that is best achieved in simple, direct language. Whereas thinkers and analysts have the luxury of presenting different perspectives and interpretations along with multiple policy alternatives, leaders must decide, frequently having to do so by compromising ideals.

Conclusion

Both Niebuhr and Bush affirm a politics based on realism and idealism. To a significant degree, their shared perspective of principled realism is rooted in the Christian faith and, more particularly, a Christian anthropology that serves as a source of both hope and caution. Although Niebuhrian ethics and the BD represent different ways of conceiving political action, they share a principled moral discourse that seeks to advance a more peaceful and just world order through persuasion reinforced by the threat of force.

At the same time, Niebuhrian political ethics challenge some of the claims and methodology of the BD. In particular, Niebuhrian realism, with its keen sensitivity to the ubiquity and persistence of sin, is at odds with the doctrine's optimistic assumptions about democratization and beliefs in progressive social change. Given its profound appreciation for the limiting character of all human initiatives, the Niebuhrian perspective provides a useful reminder of the challenges and difficulties involved in all political efforts to advance human dignity and justice. Above all, Niebuhr reminds us that injustice occurs not simply because leaders intentionally pursue evil but because leaders fail to recognize the limited nature of their power, wisdom, and virtue. "Man is an ironic creature," wrote Niebuhr, "because he forgets that he is not simply a creator but also a creature."[29] Justice can be advanced, but only when leaders recognize that their perceptions of the good are incomplete and their pursuit of moral ideals is clouded by self-interest and partiality.

28. NSS 2002, Introduction.

29. Niebuhr, *The Irony of American History*, 156.

"We Have an Expectation Problem in Afghanistan"

Daniel Strand[1]

In the wake of the *Washington Post*'s big document dump of secret government and military communications about the war in Afghanistan, a fresh wave of calls for pulling out of Afghanistan is sounding across the media. I have no intention of trying to defend the government's strategy in Afghanistan nor its attempts to spin its policies or fudge its numbers. Officials deserve the criticisms that are coming their way on that score.

But really, is anybody that shocked? It does not take a genius to realize that the Afghanistan strategy lacked clarity and frustrated generals for years. That was all public knowledge. The aimlessness and half-heartedness of previous administrations were visible for all to see. The spin was not convincing to anyone, let alone the military. It was clear to anybody with two eyes that the Taliban was coming back. Talk to any American military personnel who spent time in Afghanistan, and they will regale you with tales of corruption and dysfunction. The Afghans are not the Finns and will not be anytime soon.

This is not some big massive coverup that everybody is surprised by. In fact, I suspect most people who spend any time paying attention to Afghanistan will see this as a confirmation of what we already knew.

The Bush and Obama administrations deserve a majority of the blame for the failure to have a clear strategy and an end state. Bush took his eye off of Afghanistan, and Obama told the Taliban he was going to leave. Afghanistan is a country America did not understand and may never fully understand.

Will it become a liberal democracy? No. Will it be a bastion of women's rights? No. The best realistic outcome we could hope for is a stable country that is not a breeding ground for terrorists. President Trump . . . restarted talks with the Taliban, which is a good thing. U.S. forces in Afghanistan are not large (roughly 14,000), and the amount of money we spend now in Afghanistan is substantially less than it was under previous administrations. Though we have stumbled along in Afghanistan, as is evidenced by the recently exposed lies and spin, we have held the Taliban at bay and helped the Afghan government to survive and become relatively stable.

---

1. This article originally appeared in *Providence Magazine* online at: https://providencemag.com/2019/12/expectation-problem-afghanistan/.

The Afghans will be reliant on the U.S. for the foreseeable future, but the expenditure in terms of resources is well worth the return, as it denies terrorists a haven from which to launch attacks. The "forever war" meme is just that, a meme. It says more about modern American impatience than it does about the wars themselves.

The American public expects wars to be quick, efficient, and have low casualties. This is ridiculous and seriously distorted. Whoever is to blame for these unrealistic expectations for easy, low-risk warfare should take a lesson from our own history about the time and money needed to bring stability and prosperity to a country.

Look at South Korea. The Korean War has never officially ended, but hostilities ceased in 1953. The U.S. has had bases and soldiers in Korea ever since. Today we have about 24,000 troops stationed there. Since the end of World War II, the U.S. has had bases and military personnel stationed in Japan. There are approximately 40,000 American military personnel stationed in there today. We have 320,000 military personnel in Europe.

The lesson in each of these cases is that we have taken the long-view approach to these conflicts, and we have reaped the rewards. Japan, Germany, and South Korea are prosperous, democratic societies who are close allies. They contribute to the stability of the world and share our fundamental values of freedom and human dignity. But we must remember this took decades to bring about. Not years. And we still have a military presence in those nations.

Afghanistan may never become South Korea, but it does not need to be. It just needs to be a relatively stable government that can deny the Taliban and its allies a place to regroup to launch attacks against us or our allies.

For a long time, we heard similar criticisms about American policy in Colombia— it's a failed war, it's wasting money, America is sticking its nose where it should not be, etc. With Colombia now a stable democracy that is bringing an end to its long civil war, the long-view policy of the American government looks prescient, even if imperfect.

The real story is the American people's loss of trust in the U.S. foreign policy establishment. The reason America could invest time, money, and resources into these other countries around the globe is that the American people fundamentally believed the government was competent and trustworthy. With trust in our federal government hitting record lows, perhaps deservedly so, the trust necessary for these large-scale and long-term endeavors has dried up. And when trust is in low supply, the ability to carry out long-term policies will be impossible.

"Just War and End Game Objectives in Iraq"

Joseph E. Capizzi[1]

BEFORE ANY SHOTS WERE fired in Iraq or Afghanistan, right political thinking required aligning the causes of the conflict with the goals war sought to attain. Both the causes of war and the goals it seeks are required to think rightly about the decision to go to war. For centuries, just war theory taught statesmen the importance of aligning causes to goals, and we're being reminded daily of the relationship of cause and goal in Iraq.

The just war theory is a politico-moral doctrine governing the responsible use of armed force.[2] As a politico-moral doctrine, the just war theory connects politics and the use of military force. It implies a continuity of movement in the political uses of power, from power without military force all the way to power joined to military force and back again. Whatever the cause, wars always seek to reorganize or preserve some current unstable or threatened organization of power. Decisions to go to war, then, always entail commitments to a more just and ordered reorganization of the political system. In other words, decisions for war result from the judgment that the current organization of international power must be changed (or preserved against threat) and that war is an apt instrument for that change. The criteria of the just war theory place all this before the statesman: the justifying rationale for war, the vision of the subsequent reorganization of power, and the conduct appropriate to achieving that vision. For the just war theory is an instrument for the civilizing of power; an instrument, in other words, that reminds statesmen that war serves political goals and as such remains bound by the same basic means as politics generally. The decision to go to war, to turn to this particular means of the pursuit of political goals, ought always to have in mind those political goals shaping the conduct of war and helping to determine the conditions or in the language of the day, "benchmarks" of success.

Since just war theory emerges as a means of civilizing power, war then pursues the same goods as politics does generally. These goods typically are understood by the just war tradition under the heading of "peace" and within the theory are designated by the *ius ad bellum* criterion of "right" or "just" intention. As with all political acts, war aims

---

1. Joseph E. Capizzi's essay, "Just War and End Game Objectives in Iraq," was published by The Heritage Foundation on December 13, 2007.

2. Ramsey, "The Uses of Power," in *The Just War*.

for peace understood as a particular organization of power.[3] This claim that war serves or aims at peace trips up many people who regard it as either disingenuous or paradoxical. War cannot possibly aim at peace, they believe. By its nature, they claim, war opposes peace. The height of dishonesty consists, they believe, in claiming war might serve peace. History and reason counsel otherwise.

History shows instead that the judicious use of war has righted wrongs, has defended against aggression, has spread freedom, and by reorganizing power has created the conditions for a better, if imperfect, peace than existed before war. In other words, wars like those against Germany, Japan, and Communist forces in Latin America and Asia have attained the political goals aimed at by statesmen. Such wars have conduced to the creation of a better peace, peace understood as a balance of political order and justice within which people can pursue their individual goods.

In addition, history shows as well precisely the kind of civilizing of power just war theory requires and enables. History shows the effectiveness of just war theory in restraining war's aims within political bounds. One of the great misjudgments of the twentieth century was the notion, shared by many in politics and religion, that technology and democracy had totalized war beyond usefulness; technology because of the devastating capabilities of modern weapons and democracy because democracies make all citizens responsible for their nations' wars. This misjudgment animated claims that war could never again be a useful instrument of politics; that all wars were bad wars because all wars must be total wars. Few claims have proven more utterly false more quickly than claims such as these. We see this in at least two ways; first by simple observation of the trend in wars since the beginning of the twentieth century. One of the fascinating phenomena of the two Gulf Wars and of the intervention in Kosovo and the war in Afghanistan was the universal concern about military targeting or what just war theory calls discrimination between legitimate and illegitimate targets of attack. Discrimination has become a virtually unquestioned assumption of American and NATO war tactics, built into its strategy and its weapons development. The contrast between concern for military targets in recent wars and the wars of the early twentieth century utterly invalidates the claim that modern wars are total wars.

A second bit of evidence in favor of civilizing war comes from a comparison of just war theory to its alternative. Simply, the alternative to viewing war as serving political ends is to believe war a means of serving objectives beyond politics. Allowing war to be separated from political objectives is a disaster as political goals alone are the means by which war is restrained. All non-political uses of war are unjust, as their justifications are inscrutable and their means without restraint. Non-political goals (call them religious or ideological) admit of no distinctions between combatant and noncombatant, or even friend and foe. Anything and anyone can be sacrificed to these ultimate goods. The West saw this in its wars against Nazism and Communism, and we're seeing it again today against an enemy that sacrifices its own and other people's children to purposes it takes to surpass political ones.

---

3. Weber, "Vengeance Denied, Politics Affirmed," 173.

Moreover, the assertion that war be placed in the service of political objectives requires that the course of war be continually reassessed with reference to the political goals with which it began. If war indeed be required by a politics of peace, then every activity within war must be scrutinized by its capacity for creating peace. As an example, this will involve critical attention to the role of forgiveness and reconciliation in politics, much as Hannah Arendt suggested in *The Human Condition*.[4] More attention to setting up the conditions for post-bellum peace in Iraq might have helped avert many of the problems associated with a de-Baathification program that quickly converted from reconciliation into vengeance-seeking. Robust analysis should attend, then, not only to questions about whether war is justified, but also to broader political questions about the dynamics that lead to war and strategies for reducing war.

The application of just war principles, then, must draw from a wider scope of political engagement than the most recent event or it will fail to offer guidance in pursuit of the goals of a genuine and effective politics. Too often the just war theory is treated as a crisis "ethic" that emerges only after some international catastrophe. This places war outside the operation of politics and thus also beyond the reach of morality.

The just war ethic, then, keeps war within the service of the political goals of justice and order. Justice and order are the ends of all politics. Just wars, then, will be those wars that are limited by and attentive to these goals. Military aims and goals will constantly be aligned with the precipitating causes of the war and with changed political realities. The contending parties will also be required to conceptualize and work towards the post-bellum reorganization of power. The post-bellum reorganization of power will thus chasten and control the military execution of war.

In Iraq the utter absence of peace (a balance between justice and order) became the basis for the just cause against it. We knew this already in 1991 when an alliance of nations repelled Iraq's invasion of Kuwait, but we knew then as well that merely repelling Iraq from Kuwait was not a sufficient reorganization of power in the region. Astute statesmanship knew, in other words, that politics would require more than we achieved.[5] That war's exit strategy, informed by the Powell Doctrine, involved achieving a very discrete aim—the removal of Iraq from Kuwait—followed up by the immediate and total removal of the American military from Iraq. It restored the region's organization of power to one that prevailed prior to Iraq's invasion of Kuwait, a good end certainly, but chose not to address the major cause of the region's instability. One wonders whether that strategy contributed to the need to reintroduce the American military ten years later.

In the public and in our politics, isolationism, war fatigue, discouraging reports in the press and other factors converged to pressure the American government to form an immediate "exit strategy" from the current war in Iraq. In September the media and many in Congress placed a great deal of emphasis on the apparent failure of the Iraqi government

4. Arendt, *The Human Condition*, 238: "The discoverer of the role of forgiveness in the realm of human affairs was Jesus of Nazareth. The fact that he made this discovery in a religious context and articulated it in religious language is no reason to take it any less seriously in a strictly secular sense."

5. Which was evident to all the time; thus, the U.S.'s encouragement of Kurdish and Shiite insurgents to rise up and overthrow Saddam, and thus as well the subsequent creation and enforcement of "no-fly" zones in southern and northern Iraq.

to meet more than nine of eighteen "benchmarks" measuring the progress of Iraqi government. But the benchmarks must be understood as merely a means of measuring political and military success in Iraq. That is, they are a means of following the just war theory's lead in aligning political and military goals. In a sense, something like the benchmarks is an apt and necessary reflection on the achievement and alignment of military and political goals; in another and more important sense, however, we should not confuse the means of doing so with the ends of attaining those goals. It's clear that many understand the benchmarks as a way to leverage the U.S. out of Iraq; the just war theory suggests using benchmarks this way would be a politico-moral disaster.

The decision to go to war in Iraq and to reorganize power by removing and replacing Saddam's regime committed us morally and politically to a more just and stable organization of power than existed in Iraq under Saddam. Once the cause involved "regime change" mere removal of Saddam was not enough politically and morally. To use the benchmarks to leverage U.S. forces out of Iraq prior to the attainment of our political goals would run counter to the ends necessary to peace. Rigidly following the benchmarks (for instance, on the distribution of "hydrocarbon resources") is not a sufficient political reflection on the conditions of a more peaceful reorganization of power. To remove our forces before establishing the necessary conditions of a better reorganization of power would be to remove a stabilizing force (the U.S. military) necessary to the achievement of a goal required by prudent politics. Whatever one thought of the initial move into Iraq, just war theory counsels now that peace would be undermined by premature departure from Iraq.

The Bush Administration has rightly resisted that pressure. When, in October of the past year President Bush refused to commit to consequences of missing benchmark targets, he was engaging then in the kind of political thinking suggested by the just war theory.[6] By our entry into Iraq and the subsequent removal of Saddam, we wed our national interests—our political good—to the Iraqi people and the stabilization of their political order. The cause of war in Iraq, the replacement of a dictator by another regime, requires the creation of conditions permitting a relatively stable political order. There is no way of getting around the lengthy military commitment that involves. Saying this is not to waive away legitimate concerns about the progress of Iraq's government, or the attainment of military goals, or the human and economic costs of the war, but simply to remind us—as the just war theory does—that the achievement of political order and justice is an exercise in prudential judgment and is not reducible to quantitative assessment of goals set by our legislature. The benchmarks require interpretation within the broader context of politics. Were this a math test, certainly failure to meet more than nine of eighteen goals would be a failing mark; but as an exercise in the political reorganization of power and judging the current policy of remaining in Iraq and increasing internal security against its alternative—summary withdrawal—the current course has much to recommend it. Indeed, since September when calls for withdrawal may have been at their loudest, nearly all the trends in Iraq have been positive; even if we must grant that as trends they remain unstable.

6. Cf. Ricks, "Bush's Proposal of 'Benchmarks' for Iraq Sounds Familiar."

The calls for withdrawal we've heard since 2003 are symptomatic of political thinking tempted to regard military conflict as always at odds with peace, but let's be clear about what the just war theory suggests: to withdraw American troops now is to commit other young American men and women at some point in the near future. The just war theory reminds us that peace is a principle of order, and order in international politics is the result of the organization of power. Therefore, peace itself depends on responsible politics. Aside from our clear moral obligations to Iraqi citizens, their political goals and ours do not currently permit us to withdraw. The current reorganization of power does not yet permit us to conclude we have as yet achieved something more stable than what we replaced; more just, yes, but more stable, no. Since the surge, conditions in Iraq have been moving in the direction of a more just order, but despite the claims of its advocates withdrawal is not a movement toward peace, but towards more war and violence now and in the foreseeable future.

3 – 5

"Torture: A Just War Perspective"

James Turner Johnson[1]

I HAVE BEEN ASKED to bring a just war perspective to the contemporary debate over torture. I do not believe I have seen any effort to do this in the various sorts of discussions of the problem of torture I have read over the past several years. Rather, the discourse has been framed largely in terms of the "war on terrorism"—arguments over how to combat terrorism, how to protect the lives of those threatened by terrorist attacks, how to preserve United States national security in the face of the threat posed by terrorism, and so on. More specifically, what I have seen—in abundance—is various forms of consequentialist argumentation, including the balancing of lesser and greater evils and debates over whether torture actually works or not to produce useful intelligence.

By contrast, the classic just war tradition is not, *pace* so many contemporary philosophers and ethicists, rooted in consequentialist reasoning. *Pace* also the United States Conference of Catholic Bishops, whose spokesmen since the bishops' adoption of a revised, untraditional form of just war theory in *The Challenge of Peace* in 1983, have regularly given priority to the consequentialist criteria of last resort, proportionality, and reasonable hope of success. These have figured prominently in all their public statements against the use of armed force by the United States.

The classic form of just war reasoning found in the historical tradition is something quite different. All the consequentialist criteria just mentioned have been added to just war reasoning quite recently, dating back no more than about forty years. This is not to say that they do not have their uses in moral argument, only that they are not part of the idea of just war found in the classic just war tradition, as this took shape from the twelfth- and thirteenth-century canonists through Aquinas, theorists of the Chivalric Code, and later theologians like Vitoria, Suarez, Grotius, and the English Puritan William Ames. This classic conception remained intact in the moral tradition until recently and, in a development tracing to Grotius, also provides the moral base for the law of armed conflict in international law. Properly to bring a just war perspective to the problem of torture means looking back into the formal provisions of the classic idea of just war and the moral logic underlying it, then asking what moral wisdom can be drawn from this for thinking about torture.

1. This essay was first published in *The Review of Faith & International Affair* 2 (2007).

Formally, the just war idea by the beginning of the modern period included requirements defining both when resort to force is just and imposing limits on how force might be used—the two aspects of just war reasoning later called the *jus ad bellum* and the *jus in bello*. The former included the requirements that use of force be undertaken only on sovereign authority (that is, by a person or persons with final responsibility for the common good of a political community); that it be undertaken only for a just cause (punishing evil-doing, retaking things wrongly taken by others, or in other ways defending the common good of the community in question); and that it be undertaken only with a right intention (understood negatively as avoidance of certain specified wrong intentions, positively as the intention of establishing or reestablishing peace). The limits on how force might be used were defined in two ways: by lists of classes of persons (and their property) not to be made the object of direct, intended attack, and by prohibitions against certain types of weapons and uses of weapons deemed *mala in se*. These formal provisions were conceived deontologically; that is, they established binding moral duties on those involved in the decisions about whether to use force and how to use it, if the former decision were that force is justified in the case at issue.

But underlying this deontological structure of the formal just war rules lay a conception of the moral agent in terms of a virtue theory of ethics. The sovereign, for example, was not conceived simply as whoever happened to be head of a political community, but as one who needed to possess the virtues necessary to exercise political leadership and serve the common good. Similarly, the soldier was not simply anyone who happened to carry arms but one who had had the virtues of the profession of arms inculcated in him. These two forms of moral logic supported each other: a ruler who misused the armed power at his command was understood as a tyrant, not a sovereign, and a soldier was reminded of what his professional virtue required by the just war lists of wrong intentions, illicit targets, and wrongful means.

To my knowledge none of the major theorists and jurists who gave shape to just war tradition in its classic form ever discussed torture. But they never discussed counter-city bombing or the use of poison gas, or many other specific matters, either. One may work forward from what they did say, and the moral logics behind that, to issues before us today. What we know as terrorism can never be just, by classic just war standards, because the people who authorize terrorist attacks do not have the moral right to do so and because the direct, intended objects of those attacks are noncombatants. Similarly, a response to a terrorist attack, even if undertaken in the name of sovereign responsibility for the common good, can never morally involve an attack on whole populations of persons among whom terrorists live and take shelter. Such judgments follow straightforwardly and simply from understanding the meaning embodied in classic just war thinking.

For the case of torture two elements of the classic idea of just war apply, and perhaps three: what the tradition says on wrong intention, what it says on those not to be directly and intentionally attacked, and perhaps also the limits on morally permissible means.

First to the matter of wrong intention. For classic just war thinkers this was defined by a passage from Augustine they often quoted:

> What is evil in war? It is not the deaths of some who will soon die anyway. The passion for inflicting harm, the cruel thirst for vengeance, an unpacific and relentless spirit, the fever of revolt, the lust of power, and such like things; all these are rightly condemned in war.[2]

For an extended period in the eleventh and twelfth centuries a series of church councils in western Europe imposed penances on warriors who had taken part in battle, assuming that in the heat of combat they might likely have been motivated by one or more of these wrong intentions and giving them the opportunity to repent and seek to atone for this. For the case of torture, this concept of wrong intention bears directly on any person or persons who inflict it: can they do so without one or more of the wrong intentions Augustine listed, or other similarly wrong intentions? Unless such persons have no moral sense at all (in criminal cases they are understood as psychopathic personalities), I think not, for torture not only harms the person who is its object, but it corrupts and damages the person who does it as well. In itself this is a strong reason why we should not, as a society, endorse torture.

Second, what about the matter of doing no direct, intended harm to noncombatants? Traditional just war thought, as well as the law of armed conflict in international law, approaches this matter by listing classes of persons who normally do not take a direct part in the fighting or in close support of those who do, and prohibiting direct, intended harm to them. The earliest lists include classes of people who normally did not bear arms: women, children, the aged and infirm, clergy and monks, peasants working their land, merchants and pilgrims on the road, ordinary townspeople. In the latter part of the Middle Ages this list expanded to include warriors who had been captured or rendered incapable of fighting by wounds. The most recent formulation in the law of armed conflicts renders all the former—and more—under the term "civilians," while specifically naming prisoners of war and the wounded as not to be made the object of further attack. This limitation applies to all persons involved in armed conflict of any kind, including those involving terrorism.

As to the matter of means, the classic prohibition of certain means as *mala in se* serves as a reminder that some means simply ought not to be used in war. The lists that could be compiled of weapons bans and limits in both the moral and international legal traditions quite obviously do not include every single means that ought not to be used. Sometimes the moral repugnance of a given means is itself reason not to have to name it explicitly as wrong to employ. I suggest the distinctive means of torture are of this sort: they are so morally repugnant no second thought should be needed to know that they ought not to be used.

In sum, reflecting on just war tradition yields two very basic and important pieces of moral wisdom, corresponding to the deontological and virtue-ethics aspects of the tradition, respectively. First, there are some things that are never to be done; the rules prohibiting direct, intended attacks on those not taking part in the use of force extend to the prohibition of torture of prisoners. Second, there are some things that a good person may never do; torturing involves intentions that are directly contrary to what it means

---

2 Augustine, *Contra Faustum*, xxii.74.

to be a good human person. Torture is wrong in both these ways. In addition, the means distinctive to torture violate both these concerns. Together, these implications of just war tradition tell us that torture should never be morally allowed.

3–6

"Christian Realism and Utopian Multilateralism"

Eric Patterson[1]

Two GENERATIONS AGO VOICES on either side of the Atlantic called isolationist America and pacifist mainline Anglo-American churches to accept responsibility for resisting evil by fighting against Nazi and later Communist tyranny. At the root of this clarion was the debunking of the utopian claims made by idealists that the West could rely on diplomacy and moral suasion manifested as international treaties, organizations, and law to keep the peace. Unfortunately it took *blitzkrieg* and Pearl Harbor to shatter the idealists' illusions that the Axis Powers were interested in consensus and accommodation.

The dissenting voices were the Christian realists such as Reinhold Niebuhr, John Foster Dulles, Herbert Butterfield, and their contemporaries. Their worldview was grounded in orthodox Christian faith and sought to apply that ethos to the real-world political dilemmas of their day. Classical Christian realism was Christian and realistic in its evaluation of human sin and human potential, both in the individual and corporate realms. This school of thought never had a doctrinaire set of positions, but was associated with principles of political responsibility, international security, and justice.[2] This chapter suggests that there is a renewed utopianism in international affairs, and that one important element of this worldview is an ideology of multilateralism: the faith that trans- and supra-national institutions and international law are morally superior to state-centric international "power politics." This chapter disagrees with the idealism of

1. A draft of this chapter was presented at the annual meeting of the American Political Science Association in Philadelphia, Pennsylvania on September 2, 2006. I am grateful to the panel discussant Jean Bethke Elshtain as well as members of the audience for their comments on the original draft.

2. There is no contemporary school of Christian realism led by a charismatic individual like Reinhold Niebuhr, indeed, Roger Epp ("The 'Augustinian Moment' in International Politics") has suggested that with the passing of Niebuhr and the fragmentation of the movement over the Vietnam War, Christian realism lost its coherency. Some of the novel and strange applications or comparisons of Christian realism bear out this loss of coherency: feminism and Christian realism (Hinze, "The Bonds of Freedom"), communitarianism and Christian realism (Dorrien, "Communitarianism, Christian Realism, and the Crisis of Progressive Christianity"), liberation theology and Christian realism (McCann, *Christian Realism and Liberatio Theology*), process theology and Christian realism (Bennett, "Process Theology, Christian Realism, and Liberation Theology"). Niebuhr himself has been contrasted with everyone from John Dewey (Rice, *Reinhold Niebuhr and John Dewy*) to Emmanuel Levinas (Flescher, "Love and Justice in Reinhold Niebuhr's Prophetic Chrusrian Realism and Emmanuel Levinas's Ethics of Responsibility").

PART 3: CONTEMPORARY CHRISTIAN REALISTS

contemporary multilateralism, arguing that political realism should be the foundation for efforts at international cooperation.

The Original Debate: Classical Christian Realism vs. Idealism

Liberal Idealism in the Interwar Period

Classical Christian realism—that associated with Niebuhr and his contemporaries in the 1930s–1950s—was a reaction to the liberal idealism of the interwar era that included a strong faith in multilateralism. This idealism informed many academic and political elites in the interwar era because many in the West blamed the First World War on the *realpolitik* of national and imperial governments in the years preceding August 1914. In international politics the aversion to such Machiavellian realism resulted in "liberalism," or political idealism, and this school of thought is most identified with Woodrow Wilson's legacy and the faith in international law (Washington Conference System, Kellogg-Briand Pact) and organizations (League of Nations, Geneva Disarmament Conference, World Court) to banish war from international life. Perhaps the most notorious example of this faith in negotiation and accommodation was Neville Chamberlain's short-lived diplomatic "success" at Munich.

The gist of Wilsonian idealism is that conflict in international life is not caused by human sin manifesting itself through individuals and groups as competitiveness, egoism, and greed. Instead, idealists felt that war was caused by a poorly managed international system that allowed imperialist exploitation, exacerbated misunderstanding through secret diplomacy and poor information flows, aggravated competition through trade barriers and arms races, flouted international law, and was unresponsive to domestic public opinion.

The failure of domestic and international mechanisms to check World War I led to a variety of liberal policy prescriptions. Wilson, modeling Kant, Locke, and Bentham, argued for transparent multilateralism based on international law and organizations to manage the peace.[3] Wilson's famous "fourteen points" called for "open covenants . . . openly arrived at" (no secret diplomacy), freedom of the seas and free trade, massive disarmament, national sovereignty and "the freest opportunity to autonomous development" (self-determination), and "a general association of nations . . . affording mutual guarantees of political independence and territorial integrity" for all states.[4] In short, Wilsonian liberals put a great deal of trust in multilateral arrangements to commit states to peace and hoped that commerce and democratic institutions would make war unlikely. Unfortunately, this utopian multilateralism did little to thwart the threats of the 1930s.

---

3. For an overview of the liberal tradition that includes Immanuel Kant's *Perpetual Peace* and Bentham's work by the same name; also see Doyle's *Ways of War and Peace*, chapters 6–8.

4. For a comprehensive discussion of Wilson's Fourteen Points speech, see Knock, *To End All Wars: Woodrow Wilson and the Quest for a New International Order*.

The Christian Realist Riposte

The Christian realists attacked the idealism of the 1920s and 1930s, disparaging it as utopian, sentimental, hyper-moralistic, and even mawkish. They rejected the liberal optimism in societal evolution to restrain the use of force in favor of law, negotiation, and arbitration. The Christian realists called this vision utopian because it failed to take into account the sinful nature of individuals and their communities.

Niebuhr recognized that there were multiple variants of liberalism, such as Joseph Schumpeter's free trade liberalism, Woodrow Wilson's vision of self-determination and transparent diplomacy, John Dewey's rationalism and focus on education, the Social Gospel, mainline Protestant pacifism, and the like. Niebuhr argued that various liberalisms shared a creed:

- That injustice is caused by ignorance and will yield to education and greater intelligence.

- That civilization is becoming gradually more moral and that it is a sin to challenge either the inevitability or the efficacy of gradualness.

- That appeals to love, justice, good-will, and brotherhood are bound to be efficacious in the end. If they have not been so to date we must have more appeals to love, justice, good-will, and brotherhood.

- efficacious in the end. If they have not been so to date we must have more appeals to love, justice, good-will, and brotherhood.

- That wars are stupid and can therefore only because by people who are more stupid than those who recognize the stupidity of war.[5]

Niebuhr concluded that "liberalism is in short a kind of blindness." He and other realists charged that this blindness resulted in a fallacious view of international politics, proceeding from the illusion that human nature was essentially rational and good. Thus, liberals believed that "enlightened" mass publics and their elected officials would realize that it was morally wrong to go to war and that multilateral commitment would keep the peace. Realists countered that not only were individuals egoistic, but that their collectives were even more so—motivated by nationalism, prejudice, and competition, operated primarily on the basis of self-interest. Furthermore, because Christian realists did not agree with liberal optimists that enlightened self-interest would lead nations to eschew war, they were certain that the liberal international order of law and organizations was powerless to stand against the determined behavior of a predatory state unless states believed that it was in their interest to act. With the rise of fascism in the 1930s and Communism in the late 1940s, Christian realists argued that liberal idealism made the West unprepared to fight against tyranny. Christian realists did not disparage the existence of international organizations such as the League of Nations, but were

---

5. Niebuhr, "The Blindness of Liberalism," 4. Niebuhr's list was even longer than the four points enumerated here.

disappointed that states neglected their moral responsibility and long-term interests by not fulfilling their obligations to collective security.[6]

Contemporary Utopian Multilateralism

In the past two generations the world which Wilson and Niebuhr knew has changed in many ways. However, both the idealists and the realists would quickly recognize the essence of contemporary debates regarding international law, the authority of the United Nations (UN), and multilateralism. Christian realism contributes to the debate by critiquing the weak philosophical underpinnings of utopian multilateralism and articulating a more realistic view of international politics, including a defense of the appropriate role of multilateralism in international affairs.

The Ideology of Utopian Multilateralism

Multilateralism is a term bandied about much of late, but which few scholars have attempted to demarcate with any precision. John Gerard Ruggie considers multilateralism to be an idea of "an architectural form" organizing international life.[7] In a famous article a decade ago political scientist James Caporaso asked, "why is multilateralism neglected in international relations theory?" Caporaso suggests a "distinction between multilateral institutions and the institution of multilateralism." The former refers to formal organizations with addresses and secretariats, the latter "appeals to the less formal, less codified habits, practices, ideas, and norms of international society."[8] Caporaso goes on to say that "multilateral" can refer to an organization or activity but that "multilateralism" "is a belief that activities ought to be organized on a universal basis. . . . As such, multilateralism is an ideology 'designed' to promote multilateral activity. It combines normative principles with advocacy and existential beliefs."[9] Caporaso concludes that multilateralism is not merely a means to a political end, but for many actors and activists it is an end unto itself.[10]

Multilateralism is an ideology. "Utopian multilateralism" is the perspective that a twenty-first-century world epitomized by international law, multilateral organizations, and transnational movements is practically and morally superior to the power politics of past millennia. Such postmodern politics are said to be practically superior because they are better equipped to deal with the global nature of contemporary issues.[11] Utopian multilateralism is morally superior in that it recognizes some harmony of human interests across borders and employs dialogue and consensus to achieve its aims as opposed

---

6. Niebuhr, *The Irony of American History*, 116.

7. Ruggie, "Multilateralism: The Anatomy of an Institution," 568.

8. Caporaso, "International Relations Theory and Multilateralism," 602.

9. Caporaso, "International Relations Theory and Multilateralism," 603.

10. Caporaso, "International Relations Theory and Multilateralism," 603–4.

11. The mammoth opus that suggests the nature and ramifications of these changes is David Held et al., *Global Transformations*. A more accessible version by Held et al. is *Globalization*.

to coercion. Often this multilateralism has shades of economic neoliberalism which believes that economic interests dominate all political questions, but it nonetheless remains utopian in its faith in overcoming individual interests and creating situations of mutual gain. As one author writes, European multilateralism in the form of Kyoto, Ottawa, and the International Criminal Court "shows the ability of the Europeans not only to reach consensus but to reflect the aspirations more widely shared at the global level for a more egalitarian international society with greater respect for the law."[12]

In contrast, unilateralist state action is morally suspect because it is selfish and self-interested, resulting in, at the least, diplomatic competition and, at the worst, out-right confrontation, including the use of military force. Furthermore, utopian multilateralists hold that authentic multilateralism takes place in formal settings governed by rules, procedures, and memberships. Thus, only structured institutional arrangements really meet the conditions of multilateralism, and ad hoc alliances, such as the recent "coalition of the willing" that toppled Saddam Hussein, are illegitimate. As Kofi Annan recently opined, "'the legitimate interests of all countries' must be accommodated for multilateralism to work."[13] Utopian multilateralism calls for structured multilateralism on nearly all issues from trade to international security, regardless of efficiencies or domestic political factors. In practice, the assumption of equal states with harmonious interests in pursuit of universal goods, such as collective security, cooperating and compromising via diplomacy is the essential foundation of utopian multilateralism.

Rethinking the State and Collective Security

Much of the inspiration for multilateralism comes from the perceived flaws inherent in the state system. Indeed, many utopian multilateralists tend to be critical of the nation-state itself as a historical artifact outdated due to contemporary global dilemmas or as the epicenter of national problems rather than a font of national solutions. From a historical perspective, the purpose of the nation-state since Westphalia was to be the fundamental unit of security for a group of people living in a defined territory. However, states were often characterized by a handful of thuggish elites, or at best, the parochial interests of the citizenry, which in either case tended to be exclusivist, self-absorbed, and competitive in international affairs. Local and regional identity politics based on creed or race were often the cause of local repression and international aggression, justifying discriminatory strife and even ethnic cleansing.

Moreover, utopian multilateralists argue, national governments continue to be barriers to people achieving their aspirations or engaging in transnational organizations and culture. Kofi Annan recently denigrated state sovereignty in favor of what he calls "individual sovereignty . . . the human rights and fundamental freedoms enshrined in our Charter" which the UN has an obligation to defend "from the peoples, not the governments, of the

---

12. Boniface, "Reflections on America as a World Power," 15.
13. "Annan Plays to Harvard Crowd with Bush Jab," 22.

United Nations."[14] In sum, if the state itself causes human insecurity, utopian multilateralism argues, then we should do something to mitigate its power.

A second charge leveled against the contemporary nation-state in favor of robust multilateralism is that globalization has incapacitated states in dealing with "postmodern" threats to security which are said to "transcend" national borders: environmental degradation, diseases from AIDS to avian influenza, international terrorism, and the like.[15] Utopian multilateralists rightly point out that such phenomena cross borders and therefore require flexibility and creative action to deal with. Vaclav Havel writes, "in the next century I believe that most states will begin to change from cult-like entities charged with emotion into far simpler, less powerful . . . administrative units" while power will be abdicated "upward to regional, transnational, and global organizations."[16] However, utopian multilateralists often assert that such transnational issues divine a deeper truth—the emancipation of humanity from the old limitations of parochial power politics and the advance of a new pacific millennium characterized by a cosmopolitan citizenry. Utopian multilateralists are most derisive in their characterization of modern and pre-modern relations among states as "power politics." Utopian multilateralists deplore Vegetius' admonition, "*si vis pacem, para bellum*."[17] The old model associated with paleolithic warriors from Julius Caesar to Ronald Reagan of unilateral "peace through strength" is simply dangerous, rooted in a Hobbesian (or Waltzian) view of international affairs characterized by security- or power-seeking states in conditions of anarchy. That go-it-alone, Wild West, competitive world of unilateral states motivated by nationalism and militarism is precisely what utopian multilateralism wants to do away with. In short, power politics are evil because they are competitive and self-interested.

In contrast, utopian multilateralism assumes that systems of rules, exhaustive diplomacy, overlapping institutions, and moralistic political declarations demonstrate the moral resoluteness of effective multilateralism and can result in collective security to throttle threats. Potential wars can be averted by diplomacy because increased dialogue will ultimately achieve some form of compromise short of violence. French President Jacque Chirac recently asserted, "There is no alternative to the United Nations,"[18] and went on to argue, "no one can act alone in the name of all and no one can accept the anarchy of a society without rules."[19] Most importantly, utopian multilateralism suggests that when states stand shoulder to shoulder in support of collective security, the world is safer because aggressor states will back down in the face of the overwhelming moral, political, economic, and military superiority of the collective (e.g., apartheid South Africa).[20]

14. Quoted in Thiessen, "Out with the New," 64.

15. Cha, "Globalization and the Study of International Security," 391.

16. Thiessen, "Out with the New," 64.

17. "If You Want Peace, Prepare for War."

18. "It's Time to Choose the UN's Future Path Says Secretary-General," 8.

19. "The Future of World Politics," 15.

20. Although it is true that international pressure played a major role in bringing down apartheid, it is nonetheless remarkable that South Africa so frequently shows us as the exemplar of collective action in international life when there was no war being fought there. Better recent examples, of failure or success, would seem to be Gulf War I, Bosnia, Rwanda, Zaire/Congo, Chechnya, Kosovo, Sudan, Macedonia,

Hence, utopian multilateralism is optimistic that we can reform power politics by diluting the sovereignty of individual states through embedding them in international institutions within a new world order.[21] Multilateral approaches may take many forms, be it inter-agency cooperation across borders (e.g., INTERPOL), treaties to address cross-border initiatives (e.g., the Kyoto Protocol), international bodies like the Organization for Security and Cooperation in Europe and African Union (OSCE, AU),[22] or inviting non-governmental organizations "to the table" as political players in international fora such as the UN.[23] Perhaps the most evolved of such international entities is the European Union, which has taken decisive steps to implement integrative regulations, and procedures that are distinctive and beyond the ken of national parliaments or public referenda. Furthermore, there are those who long for an entirely new world order—a global parliament or world government or terrestrial federation—that would abolish great power politics and usher in a chiasm of peace. As one former U.S. official stated, "Within the next hundred years, nationhood as we know it will be obsolete; all states will recognize a single global authority."[24]

Christian Realism and Utopian Multilateralism: Power, Responsibility, and Morality

Power Politics and the State

Christian realism does not dispute that cooperation is often a good means of international politics, but as noted below, Christian realism does call into question the philosophical assumptions of utopian multilateralism. Christian realism also needs not take a strong position on whether or not the state should give way to a new form of authority and governance, but many are skeptical that nation-states are a relic that will quickly be superseded by some new form of government that is morally and practically superior. In addition, Christian realism is certainly concerned about issues that cross borders and is critical of those national elites who oppress their citizens and neighbors.

A Christian realist analysis of international affairs recognizes that power is central to international politics—it is still power politics out there. Power is the fundamental currency of security. Domestic and international structures may evolve from tribes to empires to democracies, but the fundamental need for order and security has not changed. Furthermore, the nature of the specific threat as well as the unique means employed to defend oneself or one's collective from that threat may change, but the reality of human history is that power—understood fungibly—is the critical element for security.[25]

Nagorno-Karebekh, and Gulf War II. In successful cases, diplomacy was back by military power.

21. See Cooper, *The Postmodern State and the New World Order*.

22. Leonard, "Soybeans and Security," 67–68.

23. Edwards, *NGO Rights and Responsibilities*.

24. Strobe Talbott, quoted in Thiessen, "Out with the New," 64.

25. There has been vociferous debate in recent years on the nature of security and security studies. For more, see: Baldwin, "Security Studies and the End of the Cold War"; Baldwin, "The Concept of Security"; Barry Buzan et al., *Security: A New Framework for Analysis*; Glieck, "Water and Conflict"; Krause

Thus, it is a fallacy to believe that states are subordinating their national interests in favor of global interests, or that postmodern states have given up on power politics.[26] In contemporary international affairs states continue to be self-interested and seek to promote their interests within the international playing field which is available to them.[27] For a variety of reasons, many states have decided to pursue their national agendas—economic, security, political—through multilateral institutions rather than unilaterally. One obvious reason for such behavior is the desire by smaller states to utilize the mechanisms of multilateral organizations to promote their individual interests, such as by free-riding on the coattails of larger states. As Chris Patten, External Relations Commissioner for the European Commission, observed in 2004,

> Militarily weaker by choice and by taxpayer demand, we Europeans recoil from using arms to solve problems except as a last resort. Our appetite for negotiation, for soft not hard power, and our contention that this approach is morally superior to the Americans, is a flight from responsibility, only available as a political option because we can always count on Uncle Sam to keep us safe and to bear the civilized world's burden.[28]

A second reason that states self-interestedly promote multilateralism is as a tool for weaker states to constrain the strong. Although it is often said that the EU transcends power politics, the simple truth is that the EU aspires to be an international economic and political counterweight to the US, and certainly there remain internal disputes over power. More importantly, one of the foundations of the EU is the attempt by weaker states like France and the Benelux countries to tie down colossal Germany within a framework that will limit Germany and strengthen them. Christian realism recognizes these facts and demands that we deal with the world as it is, rather than lying to ourselves that contemporary international affairs is morally superior to the politics of the last century.

Power Politics and Responsibility

At the heart of utopian multilateralism is the idealistic faith that dialogue can always achieve compromise or consensus. Hence, success in the operation of international organizations, such as the UN, is the achievement of consensus, not necessarily action on some initiative. Consensus means that every party's equities were taken into account and that the outcome document, statement, or initiative has the approval of all involved. Consensus

---

and Williams, "Broadening the Agenda of Security Studies"; and Roland, "Human Security: Paradigm Shift or Hot Air?"

26. There is a lengthy and profound literature in the rational choice and collective action areas that discusses how actors will cooperate because they see it to be in their interests. See Hardin, *Collective Action*; Axelrod, "The Emergence of Cooperation Among Egoists"; and Taylor, *The Possibility of Cooperation.*

27. On the debate regarding the competition between global governance and state sovereignty in the US, see the roundtable "Trends in Global Governance: Do They Threaten American Sovereignty?"

28. Patten, "Europe and American—Has the Transatlantic Relationship Run Out of Road?" Available at http://ec.europa.eu/comm/external_relations/news/patten/spo4_77.htm.

need not result in action, for the achievement of even a modest consensus is a diplomatic triumph in and of itself, regardless of whether or not concrete action is taken.

Christian realism realizes that consensus is a morally problematic form of decision-making. If it is necessary to get all or most actors to agree on a given document, be it in the area of arms control, human rights, or environmental policy, it is likely that a consensus decision or treaty will be at the lowest common denominator, not the highest. As Australia's foreign minister recently quipped, "[multilateralism] is a synonym for an ineffective and unfocused policy involving internationalism of the lowest common denominator."[29] Christian realism does not descry political consensus; rather, it expects it as the reality of real-world politics. Indeed, we should be hopeful that modest, least common denominator steps in the right direction can lead to real solutions for concrete political and social problems. However if action is taken, it is taken because states see it in their interest to act.

The fundamental problem with the "multilateralism is moral" school of thought is that consensus can dissolve the notion of responsibility. States may be abdicating their responsibility for individual moral action by excusing themselves under the guise of "no international consensus." As one writer says, "multilateral action is clearly preferable. There is only one problem with this conclusion: experience has shown that multilateral action is frequently impossible . . . even with causes on which there is broad international agreement."[30] The genocides of the 1990s are cases in point. No European state was willing to intervene individually in the Bosnian bloodbath, and they absolved themselves by pointing at the lack of consensus and political will both at the EU and the UN to stop the genocide.[31] Similarly, African governments, both individually and collectively via the Organization of African Unity, refused to intervene to stop the bloodbath in Rwanda (and elsewhere).[32] Again, states obfuscated their real reasons for choosing inactivity by hiding behind the cover of "no international consensus in our organization" to keep from taking moral action.

Christian realism recognizes that responsibility is a key feature of political decision-making for individuals and for collectives. A political ethic of state responsibility recognizes that a certain level of self-interest, such as self-defense, is a moral response to threats. The Golden Rule also informs an ethic of responsibility in political affairs in the protection of the weak as well as the punishment of wrongdoing.[33] Unfortunately, consensus-based utopian multilateralism does not necessarily have the moral resources to justify political action or intervention on moral grounds—it must wait and abide by the consensus. If the

29. Gratton, "The World According to Howard," A2.

30. Gordon, "The Pitfalls of Multilateralism," 15.

31. One scholar observes that governments are relinquishing their involvement in such affairs by hiring private security firms, such as the U.S.-based MPRI to train the Croatian military in the early 1990s or the use of Bahamas-based Sandline, Inc. to provide security in Sierra Leone. The same is true with the out-sourcing of humanitarian and quasi-military services such as landmine abatement, security, and refugee services to NGOs and private companies. See Krahman, "The Privatization of Security Governance."

32. Patterson, "Rewinding Rwanda: What If?"

33. This point is part of the classical Just War tradition associated with Augustine and Aquinas. See James Turner Johnson's "Just War, as It Was, and Is," 14–24.

vote is "no, there is no genocide in Darfur," or, "something is happening in Darfur, but we are not going to act," then for the multilateralist, "that is that."[34] For the Christian realist, such inaction may be imprudent, or, it may be sin.

Of course, responsibility does not mean that one can or must do everything. It is ludicrous to think that the US or the UN has the capacity to solve every humanitarian, political, and social crisis around the globe. Responsibility is about the freedom to take some action, when possible, to ameliorate the tragic conditions of insecurity in human affairs.[35] Nonetheless, in contemporary international life it is still states that have the legitimate monopoly on the use of force and are the repository of collective morality for the citizens whom they represent. Action, or inaction, has moral content in international affairs, but the alleged demise of the nation-state suggests increasing lack of ethical accountability and an unwillingness to respond to specific crises beyond passing resolutions. Moreover, utopian multilateralists optimism that international law and organizations are changing international life fails to consider, or is cleverly disingenuous, that individual states have a moral responsibility to utilize the various types of power at their disposal as appropriate.

Neutrality and Moral Equivalence

Perhaps the fundamental moral crisis for utopian multilateralism is that all of its hopes for a world of amity require shared values. The present crisis in international affairs suggests the opposite—that there is no such cosmopolitanism. For multilateralists, perhaps the only alternative is the relativism of postmodernity. Such relativism sees the intractable conflicts of political life as problems to be solved mechanistically rather than imbued with the moral significance of good and evil.

This relativism makes the political equality of states at international organizations possible—regardless of size, regime type, or human rights record. Of course, it is not called relativism at international fora, but rather trumpeted as the principles of "collective equality" and "political neutrality." Such neutrality is very different from the ethic of political responsibility discussed above.

If the UN or other international instrument can only approach the aggressor and the victim as equal parties, such as the "equal" application of an arms embargo on both the sophisticated Serbian military and barely armed Bosnian Muslims, there is a lack of moral insight. Jean Bethke Elshtain calls this "moral equivalency." Her example is the choice by many Western religious and academic elites to not distinguish between Al Qaeda's barbarism directed at unsuspecting civilians and America's conventional military response

34. An oft-quoted story originating from the Rwanda debacle is that the UN Secretary-General felt that he simply could not "use the G-word" in trying to motivate action. The text of the "Convention on the Prevention and Punishment of Crime of Genocide" deals primarily with punishing genocide after the fact. Only Article 8 deals with prevention: "Any Contracting Party may call upon the competent organs of the United Nations to take such action under the Charter of the United Nations as they consider appropriate for the prevention and suppression of acts of genocide . . . ."

35. Robin Lovin's excellent article on freedom and responsibility, "The Limits of Freedom and the Possibilities of Politics: A Christian Realist Account of Political Responsibility," deals with this dilemma.

in Afghanistan as categorically different uses of violence.[36] The classical Christian realists also railed against this moral equivalency. In Niebuhr's day, many in the church and academy argued that the United Kingdom was an empire, as was the Third Reich, and as both were sinful, there could be no justice on the British side. Niebuhr countered that all political systems have an element of sinfulness in them, but that the British Empire was a far lesser evil than the satanic Nazis and therefore should be supported.

Christian realists recognize that the claim to "neutrality" by international institutions often masks something else. For example, it is routinely in the interest of the African Union to turn a blind eye to genocide in its bailiwick, because identifying the killing fields of Rwanda, Congo, or Sudan as "genocide" would prompt action by state parties. Or, perhaps international organizations like the UN claim neutrality because they realize their own real impotence in most cases of conflict. Again, the argument of moral neutrality is a thin veneer trying hiding the much larger questions of power politics and responsibility in international life.

Christian Realism and International/Multilateralism

The fact that utopianism underlies much contemporary internationalist and multilateralist programs do not mean that such political means should be condemned out of hand. Christian realism disagrees with the idealistic presuppositions that are based in liberal philosophy, but affirms many aspects of international law and organizations.

For instance, Christian realism rejects the assertions of neorealists and neoliberals (institutionalists) that international relations can only be understood at the "third level of analysis."[37] Christian realists, along with classical scholars of politics, refuse to rule out the centrality of individual human beings and human nature, both individually and collectively, in influencing international affairs.

Of course, Christian realists accept the existence of universal values, such as the value of individual human life, but reject the international legal paradigm which asserts that such values arise out of the consensus of nations, or the constructivist account that we are experiencing a "norms cascade" based on the heavy lifting of norm entrepreneurs who promoted a change in societal values that is belatedly taking root in current history. Instead, Christian realists affirm the dignity of individual human beings as children of God and refer to divine or natural law as the origin of all moral systems. This further judges the exclusive claims of some national and state groups as idolatrous.

Therefore, the universalization of some norms that have achieved prominence in international life, such as discriminating between combatants and non-combatants, the genocide convention, and human rights, is positive. But, such gains in the international political realm were the consequence, in part, of a curious mixture of state interests, backroom dealing, good intentions, face-saving, moral suasion, power politics, and a measure of deceit. Furthermore, the statement of such values, such as in the Universal Declaration of Human Rights, are substantively more than the consensus of legal scholars or

36. Elshtain, *Just War Against Terror*, chaps. 2 and 7.
37. Waltz, *Man, the State, and War.*

governments; they are rooted in universal morals valuing individual human beings as children of God. However, Christian realism is pragmatic and willing to work with others from a plurality of traditions to promote these goods, as well as introspective in recognizing the failings in our own civilization. In the end we must be practical—for such values to have force, they must be vitiated by political power.

There is a spiritual dimension to politics disdained by the positivists and post-positivists alike—the existence of evil in the world. Much of the social scientific world has dispensed with the idea of evil, unless one means "structural" forms of evil or violence, such as ignorance and poverty. Christian realism returns to the classical notion of evil in human affairs—that individuals are moral agents capable of good and evil and that the actions of citizens and their leaders, whether locally or internationally, have immediate and long-term moral consequences. *Ergo*, multilateral cooperation that provides security to the insecure, such as through a peacekeeping mission in the wake of civil war, has positive moral content. Similarly, the choice by national leaders to sign onto, but not abide by, an international covenant such as the Convention on Torture, is an immoral act of hypocrisy.

A related point is that Christian realists respect the manifold creativity of individuals and collectives to seek solutions to many of humankind's historical dilemmas. International institutions that manifest this positive creativity toward ameliorating the conditions of a fallen world, be it the International Committee of the Red Cross, the World Health Organization, or UNICEF demonstrate the universal Law of Love as well as God's unique gift to humankind—free will to choose to do good.

As often as not interests are involved in philanthropic or humanitarian action. Christian realists are not naïve in thinking that moral principles alone will goad states into right action. Instead, Christian realism recognizes the nexus of values and interests in every collective endeavor, and realizes that this is the natural order of politics.[38] For instance, the Geneva Conventions do not only limit the actions of our state, they also theoretically protect our soldiers captured by the enemy. This *quid pro quo* does not rob the Geneva Conventions of their moral worth; rather, it roots them in the *terra firma* of human experience.

Therefore, we should be wary of the claims of utopian multilateralists that international and supranational organizations are more moral than self-interested states. The same claim has been made regarding the alleged moral superiority of governments over individuals and interest groups. It is true that there is great potential for organizations and international law to do some work in promoting goodwill and seeking solutions to the thorny knots of international security, but we should also recognize that collectives tend to be less morally sensitive than individuals. This is because groups, from mobs to labor unions to governments, may face less immediate moral restraint on their activities than do individuals, because groups tend to compromise among their members to achieve consensus—regardless of the fact that this often results in a lowest common denominator morality. Furthermore, collectives tend to enhance group egoisms at the subnational, national, and regional levels, manifested as ideology (e.g., Communism) or

---

38. One liberal institutionalist account of this is Martin, "Interests, Power, and Multilateralism."

nationalism: "society merely cumulates the egoism of individuals and transmutes their individual altruism into collective egoism so that the egoism of the group has double force. For this reason no group acts from purely unselfish or even mutual interest, and politics is therefore bound to be a contest of power."[39]

This does not mean that Christian realists reject international law, treaties, or organizations. Instead, Christian realism reminds us that the pitfalls attendant to all human collectives likewise exist at the international level. Moreover, Christian realists traditionally have pointed to the concepts of power and interests as critical to understanding domestic and international politics. In the discourse of utopian multilateralism, power and interests are often forgotten. However, in truth multilateralism and international institutions are often designed to promote the interests of some members. Certainly the UN Security Council is a case in point. France's constant calls for multilateralism are grounded less in a philosophy of consensus but in France's interests in remaining a player, albeit an increasingly weak one, in international life.

In short, the case for multilateralism in all of its forms must rest on a realistic appraisal of the continuing centrality of power in international life. State and non-state actors seek power and influence in international life. The value of international institutions is to bind states together in ways that they can pursue their own interests and accommodate others' without the resort to war. A goal of multilateral efforts is the division of labor and costs in international life. Most importantly, the value of collective security arrangements, such as Chapter VII of the UN Charter, as well as regional alliances like NATO and international instruments such as the Geneva Conventions, is to create checks and balances on power in international life.

Finally, this discussion reminds us that Christian realism differs from other some other Christian perspectives, such as pacifism or monasticism, in articulating a collective notion of responsibility. Monks and some pacifists withdraw from society because they understand their individual devotion to trump obligations associated with society at large. However, individuals—be they day-laborers or presidents—are moral agents both as individuals and as part of their community. Similarly, governments and international organizations are complex moral agents constituted of individual and group interests. Such institutions do have some moral responsibility based on their identity or charter, and therefore their action (e.g., to save Kosovar civilians from genocide) or inaction (e.g., to neglect Bosnian civilians facing genocide) does have moral content. This notion of morality and responsibility should commission international organizations which have clearly defined moral imperatives to go beyond reflection to action.

Conclusion

Christian realism was not really a new phenomenon in the 1930s—it is heir to a historic tradition spanning the author of the epistle to the Romans, Augustine, Aquinas, Calvin, the Puritans, and others, and which continues to be the thoughtful, practical, hopeful, and sometimes anxious attempt to engage real-world political dilemmas with

---

39. Niebuhr quoted in Thompson, "Moral Reasoning in American Thought in War and Peace."

feet rooted in the soil of a fallen world but hearts seeking the City of God. Christian realists have typically been frustrated by the utopian claims of those who prescribe solutions rooted in idealistic worldviews to the tragedies of politics. In contrast, Christian realism articulates a conception of political responsibility for action to engage evil, recognizes the ubiquity of power politics in world affairs, and suggests pragmatic solutions for matching power with power in order to find proximate solutions to the issues of competition and struggle in social relations.

This chapter suggests that the worldview underlying much of the contemporary rhetoric regarding multilateralism is utopian, for it lacks a realistic consideration of the inherency of power to politics and often fails to consider responsibility in cases of moral tragedy. Christian realism provides an alternative conception of international politics that reminds us of the centrality of power to any notion of international law and organizations and the necessity of backing up the rhetoric of security and human rights with the political force necessary to protect them.

"The International Institutionalism We Need Now"

Robert J. Joustra[1]

THE LOFTY PHRASE "GLOBAL governance" has often been met with suspicion, if not outright alarm, in the evangelical world. Global governance sounds vaguely like one-world-government on the one hand, or the hegemony of a misbalanced capitalism on the other. And evangelicals are hardly alone in their reaction. The conventional wisdom about global governance, writes Daniel Drezner in *The System Worked: How the World Stopped Another Great Depression*,[2] resembles an old Woody Allen joke: the quality is terrible—and yet such small portions!

I want to make three arguments about this pessimistic picture of global governance—that set of formal and informal rules that regulate international order and the collection of authority relationships that extend, coordinate, monitor, and enforce them. (1) Suspicion of international institutions, including the United Nations, is endemic to contemporary political culture in America; (2) evangelicals are a lot like everybody else in this respect, but an evangelical political theology gives *good reason* to be different; (3) and finally, there is also good reason to be optimistic about international institutions, and Christians in particular should be at the forefront of this optimism.

Seeing Only the Bad in Global Governance

Kathryn Yarlett asked at the beginning of May if the United Nations was still an institution worth engaging.[3] Her answer, which I heartily second, is that it certainly is. But I'm less encouraged by the data she cites on American attitudes. She cites a Gallup poll in which 66 percent of Americans believe the UN has a necessary role in global affairs, but only 35 percent think it's actually *having* a positive role in global affairs. This means that one third of Americans believe that the United Nations should never have even opened its doors, and only 35 percent think even after opening its doors that it has done "a good

---

1. This article originally appeared in *Public Justice Review* in June 2015.
2. https://global.oup.com/academic/product/the-system-worked-9780195373844?cc=us&lang=en&.
3. Yarlett, https://cpjustice.org/public/capital_commentary/article/7.

job in trying to solve the problems it has had to face." The figure of 35 percent is actually slightly up from a historic low of 26 percent in 2009, right after the global financial crisis.

These numbers are consistent with what Drezner says has been a general trend downward on polled attitudes toward multilateral institutions. Why?

There are the usual suspects to blame. "Trashing global economic governance seemed to be a prerequisite for writing for *The Financial Times*," Drezner jokes in his opening chapter, and again in his closing chapter, "in the world of international affairs punditry, pessimism sells." But cathartic as it is to finger point at sensationalist media, a certain degree of navel gazing is also to blame. Since 2009, he writes, the top five journals in international relations and international political economy published a combined total of more than one hundred articles on global economic governance. Authors based in the United States and Europe were responsible for approximately 93 percent of those articles.[4] In the four years following the 2008 financial crisis, even the United Nations' *own* journal *Global Governance* had 88 percent of its articles authored by Western scholars and practitioners. This matters because financial recovery in the West, especially in America, was much slower than in other parts of the world. While Germany's economy stood on the brink of retraction and Greece's debt-financed economy essentially collapsed, Sub-Saharan Africa was posting growth rates of 6 percent. Writing from Detroit, the end of the global capitalism as we knew it was nigh. But that's not what they were writing in Delhi and Jakarta.

This matters because it reinforced two biases: the already soft bias against international institutions in developed countries, especially in the United States, and the bias after 2008 that multilateral institutions were failing because economic recovery was lethargic in the United States. This is a bit like polling the Germans after successive Greek bailouts on whether the E.U. was working; they may have proved rightly skeptical in the moment. In brief, "global governance had a bad reputation at the start of the twenty-first century, and it has only gotten worse."[5]

Finding the Good in Global Governance

And yet on institutions themselves, we've seen an attempt at a minor renaissance of institutional thinking. Jonathan Chaplin wrote a moving manifesto on "Loving Faithful Institutions" as the "building blocks of a just global society."[6] James K. A. Smith[7] and *Comment* magazine dedicated a whole issue to their belief in institutions.[8] Gary Haugen and Victor Boutros in *The Locust Effect* make powerfully persuasive arguments about systemic justice and institutions, using practical cases to demonstrate how

---

4. Drezner, *The System Worked*, 68.

5. Drezner, *The System Worked*, 14.

6. https://www.cardus.ca/comment/article/loving-faithful-institutions-building-blocks-of-a-just-global-society/.

7. http://www.cardus.ca/comment/article/4039/editorial-we-believe-in-institutions/.

8. http://www.cardus.ca/comment/print_issues/4026/.

well-functioning systems of justice are *necessary* to development.[9] All of this has footnotes in style, if not in substance, to people like James Davison Hunter in *To Change the World*, and Andy Crouch in *Playing God* and *Culture Making*, an attempt to build off the consensus that individual "hearts and minds" are necessary, but not sufficient, to the call of the Gospel. We must evangelize the culture too, even down to its institutions, its systems of justice, of commerce, and of industry.

These have been hard lessons to put into practice, in part because a theology of institution building is also a theology which *necessarily* puts Christians shoulder-to-the-wheel with non-Christians. It presumes, in other words, making peace with proximate justice.[10] "Looking for perfection in global governance," writes Drezner, "is the enemy of finding the good in global governance."[11] But there are at least two powerfully important reasons for Christians to find that good.

The first is very pragmatic: these institutions exist because *we need them*. The twentieth century witnessed the expansion of globalization at a breakneck pace, which meant we suddenly had a whole range of ways of relating to each other that we simply didn't have before. The International Civil Aviation Organization, a United Nations Specialized Agency, simply was not needed before the Second World War. Neither was the International Atomic Energy Agency. These marvelous smart phones that beam me the latest Katy Perry news all rely on a backbone of internet infrastructure that is buried under oceans and governed by international conventions. Even the most skeptical, small government-minded pundits have to admit that the scale and pace of our world simply mean that multinational treaties and organizations are now a necessary feature of global affairs. No single state can manage the rules and regulations that make commerce, communication, travel, and more possible around the globe. If we didn't have these institutions, we'd need to invent them.

This is the basic premise behind something called *functionalism*, which emerged as a way to think about international connectedness in the twentieth century. Although its roots stretch back to people like Kant and Woodrow Wilson, its simplicity is not confined to that tradition. That states will find common interests and needs and that they will "pool their sovereignty" to produce better integrated, and better managed, global systems is in some ways obvious. This is not a world government. Functionalism doesn't even deny real, heated argument over the limits of that connectedness, it simply says that where governments can realize real benefits from coordinating certain functions together, they should, and they will.

There has always been something vaguely subsidiary-like that I have appreciated about this, something that tracks with the tradition of Christian political thought and practice. Authority should be given to the lowest unit possible, but in some cases, multilateral treaties and institutions will be the necessary authorities. And those authorities

---

9. http://www.thelocusteffect.com/.

10. http://www.cardus.ca/comment/article/932/finding-our-way-to-great-work-even-in-politics-making-peace-with-proximate-justice/.

11. Drezner, *The System Worked*, 15.

are not only essential for "better global governance," they are essential for the thing we call justice, the peaceful conciliation of diversity.

Which means, second, that the institutions of global governance are also ways we love our neighbors. That they are broken, maybe even that they need to be rebuilt, is fair enough to argue. That we need something like them is not. The World Trade Organization, with its almost comic history of abuse and inaction, is instructive here. It took *decades* for the world to turn the Breton Woods' General Agreement on Trades and Tariffs (G.A.T.T.) into an actual organization, which remains a disappointment to almost everyone. But some mechanism that monitors and enforces trading regimes is surely indispensable. Could it be that even the nearly universally vilified International Monetary Fund has a *functional* task that only something like the I.M.F. could actually accomplish? If we accept the argument of Chaplin, Smith, Boutros, Haugen, and others, then we know that justice needs to be scalable, and part of that scale is global.

Christian Engagement in Global Governance

Finally, the story also isn't as bad as we've been told. In his book, Drezner spends a lot of time trying to settle the record on just how bad these international financial institutions actually are. His conclusion is not that "all is well" but that compared to stress tests in the past, "the system" performed passably well. In the middle of the Great Recession, the World Bank reported that the first Millennium Development goal of halving the 1990 levels of extreme poverty had been achieved ahead of schedule. The UN Development Programme reported that, despite the crisis, there had been more rapid improvement in human development since 2001 than during the 1990s. The poor had greater access to global markets, and growth rates in developing economies, with some significant exceptions, were stable or growing. The crisis itself spurred no major reversal of globalization, and China and the United States, for all of their rhetoric and genuine disagreement, collaborated together with the rest of the world's largest economies to create a package of coherent political-economic responses.

This is not the same as saying all is well. All is not well. But this is *why* we need our best and brightest at the World Bank and in the United Nations, serving in NATO and on the array of treaties and organizations that continue to coordinate the rules and regimes that make globalization possible. Genuine progress can and is being made, and that progress is being made not only *despite*, but in some cases *because* of international institutions. Evangelicals should be at the front of that line, because our call to an evangelical politics, one which preaches and practices justice and mercy, necessarily dovetails with the scale, capacity, and longevity of these organizations. It is proximate work, to be sure, filled with the kind of faithful compromise that the diversity of something like global governance presumes, but it is also *good* work.

I cannot imagine something more transgressive and less hip than studying to be an economist for the International Monetary Fund today. But that is right where the Christians should be, treating our (global) politics, like our theology, with a robust dose of *semper reformanda*.

"The Ethics of Humanitarian Intervention and the Just War Tradition: Rethinking the Implications of Neighbor-Love in the 21st Century"

J. DARYL CHARLES

No authority on earth can withdraw from "social charity" and "social justice" their intrinsic and justifiable tendencies to rescue from dereliction and oppression all whom it is possible to rescue. . . . This justification can never be withdrawn; it can only be limited, supplanted, or put in abeyance.—Paul Ramsey[1]

1. Introduction

IN THE AFTERMATH OF the Rwandan tragedy, just war historian James Turner Johnson rightly observed that, with the end of the Cold War, policy-makers were ill-prepared to deal with geopolitical crises that have arisen since, not to mention the fact that it exposed an utter lack of moral discourse regarding international affairs.[2] Adding insult to injury, those who might have viewed Cold War tensions as the fruit of defects in the international order, and thus envisioned a post-Cold War increase in the United Nations' prestige, surely have had their hopes dashed. The truth of one Burmese human rights activist is patent: "There are no countries in the world which have gained liberation through the help of the United Nations."[3]

The question before us: how might those in relatively free nations who are responsible for political and military policy propose to deal with the scale of humanitarian need in our day that is massive and frequently the result of unstable regimes?[4] Specifically, what moral and political resources might inform our response to what has been called

1. Ramsey, *The Just War*, 35–36.

2. Johnson, "Humanitarian Intervention, Christian Ethical Reasoning, and the Just War Idea," 127.

3. Ludu Sein Win is a veteran Burmese (and Rangoon-based) journalist, cited in *Irrawaddy*, April 2008, p. 5 (the *Irrawaddy* online website has since been removed).

4. This instability might be characteristic of new states, failed states, or those states on the verge of collapse.

"complex humanitarian emergencies"[5]—situations that fall short of formal war *per se* but which require some measure of military force?[6]

My paper attempts to address this question by marshalling the neglected—if not often misunderstood—resources of the just war tradition—resources that are permanent and applicable to the humanitarian dilemma. Herewith I am assuming that moral "neutrality" in life is impossible and thus untenable. Most mainstream debates about foreign policy and humanitarian intervention proceed from questionable—and contestable—assumptions about state sovereignty, human rights, and cultural relativism that, alas, are anything but "neutral." I wish to argue that the just war idea, because of its moral framework, is the *only* legitimate means of attempting to think responsibly about the dilemma of humanitarian intervention.[7]

Writing on the ethics of intervention two generations ago, ethicist Paul Ramsey set forth the argument that military intervention for the sake of justice and charity remains both a right and a duty.[8] In Ramsey's view, the failure of relatively free nations to intervene in humanitarian emergencies would be "tragically to fail to undertake responsibilities that . . . are not likely to be accomplished by other political actors."[9] Responding to the common objection that intervention can be unjust and illicit, Ramsey acknowledged both possibilities—unjust as well as just causes. But the mere *possibility* of unjust causes, Ramsey insisted, does not release political actors—and the "extended hands" of the military—from their moral responsibility. Not intervening can also be unjust; hence, one's obligations are the fruit of charity toward one's neighbor.[10]

5. We may define humanitarian intervention as "the proportionate international use or threat of military force, undertaken in principle by a liberal government or alliance, aiming at ending tyranny or anarchy, welcomed by the victims, and consistent with the doctrine of double effect" (Fernando R. Tesón, "The Liberal Case for Humanitarian Intervention," 94). Characteristic of "complex humanitarian emergencies" are several factors: they are crises that are (1) multi-dimensional (involving a wide array of disasters such as war, widespread violence and human rights violations, famine and disease, widespread suffering, social-political disorder, mass displacements of people-groups, etc., resulting in massive death rates), (2) man-made (and thus not "natural disasters"), and (3) essentially political and politicizing. See Klugman, *Social and Economic Policies to Prevent Complex Humanitarian Emergencies*, 1–2.

6. Indeed, the sheer number and intensity of geopolitical horrors since the Cold War—from Bosnia and Kosovo, Rwanda, Sudan, Sierra Leone, and Liberia to East Timor, Iraq, Syria and the Central African Republic—force us to reconsider the *necessity* of military force in "humanitarian intervention." The tragic lesson of genocide in Rwanda and ethnic cleansing in the Balkans is that large-scale violations of human rights may be *impossible* to prevent or punish *without* military intervention. And where the problems are internal, that is, where they are rooted in particular social structures, a particular political culture, a collapsed infrastructure, or a mindset that gives rise to ethnic hatred, resentment and violence, the conundrum of humanitarian intervention requires us to ponder the costs of nation-building. I shall argue in this paper that states in faraway places do indeed have an obligation to intervene, where they have the wherewithal and when the costs are not unreasonable. Politically, I assume that stable states in particular have this obligation, given that they have a stake in global security. From a moral standpoint, I assume stewardship based on the principle that to whom much is given, much will be required.

7. Elsewhere I have argued similarly in "The Ethics of Humanitarian Intervention," 145–69.

8. More recently, Michael Walzer has also made a similar argument in chapter 5 "The Politics of Rescue," 67–81. His essay originally appeared in the journal *Dissent* (Winter 1995) 35–41.

9. Ramsey, *The Just War*, 23.

10. In his writings on social ethics, war and force, Ramsey shares the Augustinian conviction that charity must motivate all that we do, inclusive of restraining social-political evil. On charity as a

The viewpoint assumed in this paper is that humanitarian intervention is justified in *some*, not all, cases. The reason for this is that the purpose of government is to protect and secure basic human rights of all persons by virtue of human personhood, worth, and dignity. Those regimes which violate these basic rights in the end forfeit their own right to be protected by international law. State sovereignty is not an intrinsic value, as is human personhood. Sovereignty must serve human ends.[11] In respecting those basic human rights, we are hence obligated to assist and rescue others at reasonable cost to ourselves, and, where possible, assist in the social-political reconstruction of those victims' lives. We do unto other as we wish that they do unto us.

1. Humanitarian Concern and Making Moral Judgments

Challenges in Contemporary Humanitarian Thinking

To intervene or not intervene? should always be a difficult question. Few have expressed this hesitation more potently than Michael Walzer in his essay "The Politics of Rescue." The need for extreme caution in such matters, of course, is uncontroversial. The problem, however, is that many governments and politicians prefer the "easy" solution to the humanitarian dilemma: *not* getting involved, given the "costs" to their political standing at home, which will be affected by the public's perception of costs to their own soldiers.[12]

The diversity of "humanitarian" operations in our day spans a mind-boggling array of scenarios that are both civilian and military in nature, with the two *always intertwined*. This multiplicity has caused one analyst to speak of "the fog of peacekeeping"[13] to describe the imprecision and ambiguity of guidelines surrounding the humanitarian task. And given the veritable explosion of new states or quasi-states since the Cold War era[14] as well as the collapse, fragmentation or disintegration of the same, "chaos has replaced tyranny," in the words of one analyst, as the new challenge to human rights in the 21st century.[15]

Although the presumption against intervention must remain very strong, it must be said that non-intervention is not an absolute moral rule; it is a pragmatic policy.[16] While there is no higher moral law that *requires* non-intervention, the same cannot be said of intervention. While no higher moral principle requires that we *always and everywhere*

---

governing motive of going to war or intervention, see as well Hugo Grotius, *The Rights War and Peace* 2.1.9; 2.17.9; 2.25.3, 9; 3.1.4; 3.2.6; and 3.13.4. Multiple times in this work Grotius refers to the "rules of charity" as they relate to—and support—formal justice.

11. Tesón, "The Liberal Case for Humanitarian Intervention," 93–129.

12. Walzer, *Arguing about War*, 67.

13. Blocq, "The Fog of UN Peacekeeping: Ethical Issues regarding the Use of Force to Protect Civilians in UN Operations," 201–13. In his 1992 report *An Agenda for Peace*, then UN Secretary-General Boutros Boutros-Ghali identified four different kinds of "peace" intervention: pre-crisis deployment, peace-making (ending a conflict), peace-keeping (securing and maintaining peace), and peace-building (from truce to permanence).

14. Much of this corresponds with what Samuel Huntington has described as the "third wave" of democracy in the 1990s. See Huntington, *The Third Wave: Democratization in the Late Twentieth Century*.

15. Ignatieff, "State Failure and Nation-Building," 299.

16. Walzer, *Arguing about War*, 69.

intervene, there *is* a higher moral principle requiring that, in *extraordinary and tragic* situations, we have a duty to intervene. Hugo Grotius anchors this obligation in the natural law. He writes that those in political authority have a right to defend not only against injuries done to their own subjects but those injuries that *are excessive* and *do not directly affect them.*[17] In fact, Grotius insists, it is "much more honourable" to avenge other people's injuries than our own.[18]

My intention, however, is not to attempt a "how to" guide to humanitarian intervention. It is, rather, to highlight the moral wisdom of the just war tradition as it applies to this challenge, to which we shall now turn.

Moral-Philosophical Assumptions That Inform "Neighbor-Love" and the Just War Idea

All human action is subject to moral evaluation, and it needs emphasizing in our day—a day of post-consensus, post-everything nihilism—that such evaluation is *not* arbitrary. No one is a pure moral relativist, for as soon as someone begins to use the language of "should" and "should not," he exposes his real nature, believing indeed that there *are* moral reference points. In point of fact, all people will draw the line between "acceptable" and "unacceptable"; the difference, of course, is *where* people decide to draw the moral line. But make no mistake: all people *do* draw the line; *all* people use the language of "should" and "should not."

And because society—any society—collapses without common standards (insofar as morality mirrors a community's values and priorities), moral diversity cannot be "total," even when there is moral-cultural particularity. The very notion of "justice" is sufficient to illustrate. Very few people believe that justice is different for Kansans, Cambodians, Canadians, and Kazakhstanis.[19] And where justice *does* seem different, we call this a "travesty" or "miscarriage" of justice. In this way, then, we arrive at the realization of universal human rights.

But our understanding of human nature, which undergirds any conception of "human rights," is critically important—an understanding that is rooted in a moral realism.[20] This moral realism lies at the heart of just war thinking. By virtue of their common humanity, human beings have moral duties—duties that are intuited through reason and

17. Grotius, *The Law of War and Peace* 2.20.40, emphasis added. Here I am relying on the translation provided by Kelsey in ibid., 504.

18. Grotius, *The Law of War and Peace,* 504. Elsewhere, in addressing the question of whether we have a just cause to intervene in order to relieve the suffering of people who are being oppressed by a ruler, Grotius answers that this "right of human society" may not be excluded, where the injustice is "visible" and the prince "disturbs and molests" his own country (ibid., 2.25.8).

19. That a common morality and a culturally specific morality co-exist needs no major philosophical justification. What needs emphasis is that the common—i.e., the over-arching—defines how that community relates to the outside world.

20. In his important book *A Conflict of Visions: Ideological Origins of Political Struggles,* Thomas Sowell contrasts two competing visions of human nature in our world today—what he calls the "constrained" and "unconstrained" visions. The difference between the two understandings cannot be over-stated. Sowell's great service is to point out the ethical, social, and political consequences of the latter while arguing for a more modest and, ultimately, realistic or "constrained" understanding of human nature.

understood to be universal and immutable. These duties, moreover, are not limited to family, ethnicity or politics; they extend to our "neighbor," which is to say, *whoever stands in need*. Such duties, then, are "pre-political," anchored in an awareness of a higher law, the natural law, from which any form of civil or positive law must derive.[21] The moral is supra-legal. Only in this way are we able to posit any sort of grounding for "universal human rights." If that were not so, then "Nuremburg was nothing but victors' vengeance dressed up in a fiction of 'justice,'" in the words of one just war theorist.[22]

Just war thinking, then, allows us to conceptualize the assistance of a "neighbor" in need, through its morally justified application of limited force. This is because of its fundamental moral-philosophical commitment to desire the highest, the best, for fellow human beings.

2. Just War Moral Reasoning: A Closer Look

The Logic and Unity of Just War Moral Criteria

The just war concept, as I've suggested, is not just about war; it is a way of thinking about broader political life. For this reason, it has been described as an "ethic of responsibility."[23] After all, as Martin Luther famously quipped, if the lion and lamb are expected to lie down together in the present life, then the lamb will need constant replacing.

This just war "ethic of responsibility" concretizes human duties in the direction of those who stand in dire need, seeking to restore a justly-ordered peace. Hence, the ethic is not some "dirty hands" conception of armed force that utilizes some "lesser evil" to

21. Hugo Grotius observes that the natural law "remains still in Force where there are no Courts of Justice" (*The Rights of War and Peace* II.20.8, art. 5). I am here using the version edited by Richard Tuck.

22. Biggar, *In Defence of War*, 214. Although the political development of "human rights" is more recent, our cultural tradition's understanding of human respect—and hence basic "rights"—has deep roots, anchored in the Judeo-Christian emphasis of human dignity and intrinsic worth and issuing from the conviction of human beings being fashioned in the "image of God." This "natural-law" understanding of human nature, wherein human beings are understood to be morally "free" agents (and hence morally responsible), has been coupled with the Judeo-Christian belief in a transcendent moral order, has contributed to a social-cultural environment in which the very notion of human "rights" and human flourishing has been bred. Since 1948, major international declarations have borrowed and assumed these essential truths, even when such declarations have been clothed in secular language. The problem with cultural relativism, for those who would deny or question the notion of a fundamental human "nature" and inherent human "rights," is that if cultural relativism and moral pluralism are true, then nations could never pass judgments—indeed, *any* judgments—on "crimes against humanity." If, however, there is such a thing as "universal human rights," then preventing genocide, mass murder, ethnic cleansing, and the like must be a part of our foreign policy. And although historically such abuses have been due to dictatorial regimes, the reality is that in our day these atrocities more often than not occur in failed or collapsing states. This burden, in 2001, led the International Commission on Intervention and State Sovereignty (ICISS) to argue for a "re-conceiving" of the notion of sovereignty in its report "The Responsibility to Protect (R2P)" which was endorsed with strong support again at the 2005 United Nations World Summit. Whether "R2P" has been effectual is, of course, another matter.

23. Elshtain, "Just War and an Ethics of Responsibility," in Patterson, ed., *Ethics beyond War's End*, 123. This, of course, places just war thinking at odds with pacifism, which rejects the essence and significance of political activity *qua* politics. Because it ignores questions of power, pacifism can offer little in terms of authentic peace-building in a fallen world, despite its claims.

achieve some good or remove some greater evil. It is rather a necessary, though limited, means by which to bring about a *good* result, based on a *good* intention, just as criminal justice is designed to achieve a *good* result—an ordered peace in which people can flourish—in domestic life.[24] The just war ethic is rooted in civic virtue.[25]

At the most basic level, the tradition presupposes certain moral truths that not infrequently are ignored or forgotten by contemporary theorists, strategists, and political pundits—for example:

- That human nature is such that both individual persons and governments can do intolerable things to human beings—things that must not be (humanly) tolerated; and because injustice and evil may be politically and legally entrenched, the moral act is *never only* strictly legal or contractual.[26]

- That both natural and religious (or theological) sanctions inform the tradition, through which human beings can reason toward a normative understanding of human nature and human moral obligation (hence the significance of the natural law).

- That a moral distinction between relative guilt and innocence *can* be discerned, in spite of unbridled nationalism, political complexities, and non-state actors.

- That "war" and "peace" are not two discontinuous and distinct realms,[27] each with its own set of rules.

- That "peace" does not merely mean the absence of hostilities; rather, authentic peace must be justly ordered, since the mafia, pirates, dictators, and terrorists maintain an orbit of "peace" in which they operate.[28]

- That coercive force is both permissible and limitable, thereby avoiding the two extreme positions of pacifism and political realism, resisting both cynical relativism and despairing withdrawal.[29]

- That both conventional and non-conventional military operations will be necessary in the affairs of nations.

---

24. Grotius insists that the laws governing the ethics of war and peace are anchored in the same principles of justice that hold together all domains of civil society (*The Rights of War and Peace*, prol. no. 24; cf. also 2.1.9–11). In the same vein, Augustine writes that it is good—and charitable—to resist, prevent, or subdue a wrongdoer; we do him a service by expressing a "benevolent harshness" (*Epistle* 138 ["To Marcellinus"]).

25. Elshtain, "Epilogue: Continuing Implications of the Just War Tradition," in Elshtain, ed., *Just War Theory*.

26. This in no way is to deny the moral logic that requires military interventions to receive international support.

27. See especially Murray, *We Hold These Truths*, 12–13.

28. As Augustine famously quipped, "Without justice, what are kingdoms but great robber bands?" (*City of God* 4.4). That is to say, the legitimacy of a state rests on justice. Here I am relying on the translation found in E. L. Fortin and D. Kries, eds., *Augustine: Political Writings*, 30.

29. While this "mediating" has always been lodged at the heart of just war reasoning, it is succinctly stated by Grotius in the Prolegomena (no. 30) of *The Rights of War and Peace*.

- That a hierarchy of moral values must guide military and humanitarian intervention—not a mere utilitarian estimate of material damage but the realization of human suffering and death caused by coercive operations.

- And that a moral continuity exists between ends and means, between *ius ad bellum* and *ius in bello*, based on the justness of a cause for intervening and the right intention that governs both ends and means; thus, even if the cause of interventionary action is justified by legitimate political authority, the means or execution of that intervention can be unjust.[30]

By just war reasoning, intervention must always be commensurate with the degree of human suffering where it is occurring and oriented toward a greater good, based on the natural law, which proceeds on the assumption of self-evident truths accessible to all—namely, do good and avoid doing evil. These "self-evident truths" are implicit in the so-called "Golden Rule" ethic by both Plato and Jesus, which places upon us both positive and negative moral obligations. Positively, we are to do to others as we would want others to do to us; negatively, we must not permit to be done to others what *we ourselves* would not want done to us. The implications here for humanitarian action are clear. Quite properly the just war idea has been called a "citizenship model" for international justice, because it insists that "no unbridgeable conceptual and political divide be opened up between domestic and international politics."[31]

What needs emphasis in just war thinking is the coherence as well as both formal and logical unity existing among the various criteria. All conditions need to be met as they interlock with and illuminate one another. So, for example, among the primary *ad bellum* criteria,[32] just cause is *necessary but not sufficient* to intervention; it needs the confirming or "verifying" light of right intention, which can unmask imperial pretensions or wrongful designs. Moreover, ends and means, aims and execution, must be interlocking and proportionate to the victims' suffering.[33] Morally calibrated means have the effect of "verifying" the justness or appropriateness of an interventionary cause.[34]

---

30. Aquinas (*S.T.* II-II Q. 40, a. 1) writes that "it is necessary that those waging war should have a rightful intention, so that they intend the advancement of good, or the avoidance of evil. . . . For it may happen that the war is declared by the legitimate authority, and for a just cause, and yet be rendered illicit through a vile intention." Here I am utilizing the translation found in Reichberg, Syse, and Begby, eds., *The Ethics of War*, 177.

31. Boyle, "Traditional Just War Theory and Humanitarian Theory," 66.

32. Here I follow those just war theorists who distinguish between "primary" and "secondary" just war criteria. The primary *ad bellum* considerations, following Aquinas (*S.T.* II-II Q. 40) are just cause, legitimate authority, and right intention; *in bello* criteria are chiefly twofold: considerations of discrimination and proportionality. The designation "secondary" does not suggest that these moral considerations are insignificant; it is only to emphasize that they are prudential considerations and owing their moral character to the primary criteria. Thus, we do not begin moral deliberation with "last resort"; "last resort" is only meaningful as it mirrors our deliberations over the justness of a cause.

33. Proportionality, in just war moral reasoning, is not foremost the reckoning of *more versus less force* used but rather a calculation of *harm versus good* done.

34. See Ramsey, *War and the Christian Conscience*, 8. In the words of Grotius, the means employed in pursuit of any object "must, in a great degree, derive the complexion of their moral character from the nature of the end" (*The Rights of War and Peace* 3.1.2).

Regardless of our disagreements about the specifics of interventionary activity, moral wisdom does not call us to be indifferent toward the suffering of others in the face of atrocity.[35]

This leads us to a recognition of an important moral-philosophical underpinning in the just war tradition: the symbiosis of justice and charity, which creates a continuity between ends and means and elucidates the very essence of right intention.

The Conjoining of Justice and Charity in Just War Reasoning

Even when "humanitarian intervention" finds little support in modern international law, an older tradition, anchored in just war thinking, justifies force not only to correct wrongs but to protect the innocent. It is this "tradition" that best explains—and "re-locates"[36]—humanitarian intervention, and at the heart of this "tradition" is the conjoining of justice and charity.

To divorce justice and charity is to do irreparable damage to the character of both virtues as well as to alter the very moral foundation upon which just-war thinking rests. Both justice and charity are non-fluid in character. As quintessential *human* virtues, they are deemed universally binding, and hence, are "owed" all people. As already noted, evidence of this universality is the transcultural "Golden Rule" ethic surfacing in the teaching of both Plato and Jesus. And in the Christian moral tradition, this ethic, wherein justice and charity embrace, gives embodiment to the natural law and finds powerful expression in the parable of the "Good Samaritan."

Charity, as Augustine conceives of it, must motivate all that we do, including the application of coercive force. Not the external act but our internal motivation determines the morality of our deeds.[37] As a social force, this "rightly ordered love"[38] is foremost concerned with what is good—good for the perpetrator of criminal acts, good for victims of criminal acts, good for society which is watching, and good for future/potential offenders.

To read Thomas Aquinas' treatment of both charity and justice in the *Summa Theologica* is instructive. Therein he examines the nature of charity, its moral dimensions, and its consequences. Charity, according to Aquinas, must be developed *through habit* and thus is "a principle of action."[39] Moreover, what is noteworthy is the fact that *war* is contextualized in the middle of Aquinas' discussion of charity (Q. 40 of II-II). In Thomistic thought, charity and justice meet and guide us in applying coercive force. Because "justice directs a man in his relations with others,"[40] justice and love meld in Thomistic thought.

---

35. See Seybolt, "The Myth of Neutrality," 521–27; Betts, "The Delusion of Impartial Intervention," 2–33; and Weiss, "Principles, Politics, and Humanitarian Action."

36. Nardin, "The Moral Basis of Humanitarian Intervention," 57–58.

37. Augustine, *The City of God* 14.9.

38. All that was created is "good," for Augustine; however, when our loves are not rightly ordered, the ultimate good is violated (See *City of God* 15.22).

39. *S.T.* II-II Q. 23–46, 58; cf. also *Commentary on Nicomachean Ethics*, Lectures IV-VI.

40. Because "justice directs a man in his relations with others" (*S.T.* II-II Q. 58, a. 9, r. 3), justice and love meld in Thomistic thought.

Two innovative, early-modern thinkers in the just war tradition who saw the symbiosis of justice and charity applying in distinctly "humanitarian" situations of their day were Francisco de Vitoria and Francisco Suárez. Their context—Spanish "New World" discovery—is important, for it placed them at odds with conventional thinking of the day. Vitoria's task in particular was to challenge Spanish imperial pretensions and the unjust treatment of native Americans. "The barbarians are all our neighbors," he wrote, "and therefore anyone, especially princes, may defend them from . . . tyranny and oppression."[41] Spanish intervention could *not* mean *conquest*, based on the natural law and the natives' innocence, even when their customs might seem strange. Recall Vitoria's context: he advances just war reasoning on behalf of *those outside his cultural world*, that is, those who technically were not his "neighbors."

Like Vitoria before him, Suárez taught at a leading university of his day. Trained both as a lawyer and a theologian, he addressed the subject of war as did Augustine and Aquinas—as a duty of charity. This element, coupled with the belief that moral principles based on the natural law must guide the use of coercive force in war, formed the main argument of his treatise *On the Three Theological Virtues, Faith, Hope, and Charity*.[42] Following Aquinas, Suárez argued that not merely natural justice[43] but also the norm of charity constitutes the proper motivation for war and coercive force.

Two Christian thinkers closer to our time share this commitment to prevent love and justice from being disengaged, though in differing ways. Reinhold Niebuhr, as clouds were forming on the European horizon in the 1930s, grew impatient with standard Protestant ethics of his day. In the end, Niebuhr rejected the divorce of love and justice (even when his theological reasoning must be viewed as deficient).[44] The divorce of love and justice, he believed, is tragic: we end up abetting *injustice*.[45] Hence, with sarcasm he lampoons Protestants' WW2-era naïveté: "if Britain had only been fortunate enough to have produced 30 percent instead of two percent conscientious objectors to military service, [then] Hitler's heart would have been softened and he would not have dared attack Poland."[46]

---

41. Francisco de Vitoria, "On the American Indians," reproduced in Anthony Pagden and Jeremy Lawrance, eds., *Vitoria: Political Writings*, 288.

42. This was published posthumously in 1621.

43. Cf. in this regard Aristotle, *Politics* 1333b–1334a. Suárez rejects the Aristotelian assumption of a natural moral "elite" within society who through their superior knowledge intuit justice over injustice and right over wrong.

44. Here I refer to his now famous words, the "impossible possibility," to describe Jesus' love ethic. See Niebuhr, *Christianity and Power Politics*, 3. In *An Interpretation of Christian Ethics*, 134, Niebuhr writes, "The ideal possibility is really an impossibility." What Niebuhr called "Christian idealism" creates an illusion; what is needed, rather, is a "Christian realism" (Robertson, ed., *Love and Justice*, 41–43). A useful corrective to Niebuhr's deficient theology is offered by Paul Ramsey in "Love and Law," and more recently, in Corey and Charles, *The Just War Tradition*, 207–26.

45. Niebuhr, *An Interpretation of Christian Ethics* 136.

46. Niebuhr, *Christianity and Power Politics*, 6.

A generation closer to us, the noted Princeton ethicist and just war theorist Paul Ramsey cautioned that "a Christian, impelled by love," simply "cannot remain aloof . . . toward the neighbor."[47] Love, Ramsey insisted, originates in justice.[48]

Neighbor-love is the primary feature of Ramsey's construal of love because it is cognizant of the dignity and worth of others. For this reason Ramsey could speak of a "preferential ethics of protection"[49] that has the innocent neighbor or third party in view.[50] "[N]o authority on earth," he writes, can withdraw from charity or justice their inclination to "rescue from dereliction and oppression all whom it is possible to rescue."[51] To his great credit, Ramsey's theological orientation always had responsible policy in view.[52]

Just war thinkers, then, from Augustine to Ramsey and beyond illustrate why, particularly in *our* day, charity will need to be redefined once more.

Right Intention as "Verification" of Justness

Thus far I have argued that the symbiosis of justice and charity lies at the heart of just war reasoning. Specifically, it underpins right intention. Without right intention, there can be no continuity between ends and means, and hence, no justification for intervention.[53] Without right intention, the link between one's action and one's justification for the action can be—and often is—severed, which means that "just cause" might be serving as a pretext for other ulterior motives. In the just war ethic, the criterion which explicitly directs of the use of force in the task of building or restoring peace is right intention.[54]

---

47. Ramsey, *Basic Christian Ethics*, 345–46.

48. Ramsey, *Basic Christian Ethics*, 367.

49. Ramsey, *Basic Christian Ethics*, 166–71.

50. In this vein, Ramsey takes Jesus' teaching on "turning the other cheek" in the Sermon on the Mount and extrapolates, noting that Jesus does not say, *If someone strikes your neighbor on the right cheek, turn to his aggressor the other as well* (*Basic Christian Ethics*, 170–71).

51. Ramsey, *The Just War*, 35–36.

52. Despite the volume's sensitivity to the divorce—theoretically and practically—of justice and charity, Nicholas Woltertorff's *Justice in Love* is remarkable for its inattention to the work of Ramsey. An additional fundamental weakness of Wolterstorff's volume is its deficient understanding of the relationship between punishment and forgiveness and its rejection of retributive justice and restitution, which Wolterstorff fails to distinguish from revenge. I have evaluated Wolterstorff's book at length in the review essay "Toward Restoring a Good Marriage: Reflections on the Contemporary Divorce of Love and Justice and Its Cultural Implications," 367–83.

53. Here I depart from Walzer's otherwise insightful exposition of just war reasoning in *Just and Unjust Wars: A Moral Argument with Historical Illustrations*, 21, 228–32, 251–5. Walzer believes that *ad bellum* and *in bello* criteria are independent, even existing in a tension or possible opposition, in the end tempting him in the case of "supreme emergencies" to set aside moral principle. Paul Christopher follows Walzer in this regard, asserting that "questions of *jus ad bellum* are not relevant to *jus in bello* proscriptions" (*The Ethics of War and Peace*, 91).

54. This function has been described with exceeding clarity by H. David Baer, *Recovering Christian Realism: Just War Theory as a Political Ethic*, especially chapter 4 ("The Criterion of Just Intention").

Intention in humanitarian emergency as well as in war is both forward- and backward-looking.[55] It is forward-looking in the sense that our stated aims should be evidenced through our actions, and it is backward-looking in the reverse sense: actions will confirm or conflict with the originally stated aims. Formally, we may argue that right intention consists of two components: (1) avoiding wrong intention, which harms and does not assist, and (2) facilitating a justly-ordered peace.[56] Right intention is help-fully illuminated by the character of its opposite, wrong intention, which would include imperialism, unbridled state nationalism, vengeance, blood-thirst, lust for domination, or territorial expansion.[57] This anatomy demonstrates that just war reasoning is not ex-trinsic to or removed from civic life; rather, it is an extension of community, responsible government, and our most basic values.

In the end, we might reasonably argue that right intention—strategically—is *the most important* of all the just war criteria,[58] inasmuch as without an appropriate moral disposition, without the ability to ask a myriad of *why* questions about *motive*, the other criteria can become distorted or inoperable.[59] And it is right intention that will guide—via *public acts*—the restraining *in bello* principles of discrimination and proportional-ity. (An important component herein is the moral distinction between retribution and revenge. While time does not permit me to develop this important distinction, perhaps we can discuss this in the Q&A.[60])

55. See Cole, "War and Intention," 188.

56. This is the *tranquillitas ordinis* described by Augustine in *City of God* 19.13.

57. *Against Faustus* 22.72. To these I would even add the spread of democracy, insofar as not every state or sovereignty in the world is necessarily suited to democratic form of governance as the West has known and practiced it.

58. Coates, "Is the Independent Application of *Jus in Bello* the Way to Limit War?" 191.

59. These "why" questions entail—but are by no means limited to—the following: What is the threshold for violating a state's "sacred borders"? By what authority do agencies, actors, or collations in-tervene? What are the motives of intervening actors? What do charity and good will require? How long do potential intervening actors wait before intervening? What measures are needed for a "successful" intervention? What goal represents a "better peace"? To what extent are the host governing authorities responsible/accountable for victims of injustice and suffering? What level or degree of force is needed to protect victims and supply aid? How long will retaining or peacekeeping force be needed to restore order? What is the "common good" as it applies to a broken, failing, or oppressive state? What response and actions are proportionate to the country's need? How are innocents/citizens properly protected during the interventionary process? And what will be needed for long-term healing?

60. At its core, *right intention* in just war thinking distinguishes between revenge and retribution. If a categorical moral distinction cannot be made—and preserved—between the criminal act and the retributive act (a moral qualification that distinguishes not only right from wrongful intention but legiti-mate from illegitimate political authority), then it follows that a culture, society, or community cannot be considered "civil" and just. At its base, the moral outrage that expresses itself through retributive justice is first and foremost rooted in moral principle and not hatred, prejudice or uncontrolled passion. For this reason Augustine can speak of retribution in terms of "benevolent harshness." Conceptually, revenge and retribution are worlds apart. Whereas revenge (i.e., vengeance or retaliation) strikes out at real or perceived injury, retribution speaks to an objective wrong. Because of its retaliatory mode, revenge will target both the offending party and those perceived to be akin. Retribution, by contrast, is targeted yet impersonal and impartial, thereby distinguishing itself from "vigilante justice." It is for this reason that "Lady Justice" is depicted as blindfolded. Moreover, whereas revenge is wild, insatiable, and not subject to limitations or moral constraints, retribution acknowledges both upper and lower limits

3. Concluding Reflections

The Costs and Character of Non-Intervention

Assuming that all moral conditions for intervention have been met, charity and human decency compel us to conclude that we have not only a right but a responsibility to intervene where atrocity is afoot. And *who* should do the rescuing? Our answer must be: those states that are (a) best placed and (b) able to assist. While agreement on specifics of those options may elude us, *that* human beings are morally obligated to intervene and come to the aid of victims of gross injustice, where possible, should be beyond controversy.[61]

A word of caution: current unpopularity among the American public and American policy-makers regarding humanitarian intervention *may or may not* represent moral principle. While no nation on earth *can or should* "police the world," and while no outcomes are guaranteed, a general attitude of moral detachment *may* in fact serve as a smokescreen for our inability to make moral judgments and engage social-political evil head-on.

The Morality of National Interest: Responding to Charges of Inconsistency

But *what about humanitarian interventions where we have no national interests?* This is a legitimate question. While acknowledging our responsibilities at home, these do not preclude responsibilities abroad. They simply remind us that there are finite limits on the responsibilities that we owe others. And these responsibilities abroad, of course, will vary according to the situation.[62]

---

as well as the moral repugnance of both draconian punishment for petty crimes and light punishment for heinous crimes. Vengeance, by its very nature, has a thirst for injury, delighting in bringing further evil upon the offending party. The avenger will not only kill but rape, torture, plunder, and burn what is left, deriving satisfaction from the victim's direct or indirect suffering. Augustine condemns this "lust for revenge" (*City of God* 4.6 and 14.28), a propensity prompting C. S. Lewis—who served as a soldier in World War I—to observe: "We may kill if necessary, but we may never hate and enjoy hating. We may punish if necessary, but we must not enjoy it. In other words, something inside us, the feeling of resentment, the feeling that wants to get one's own back, must be simply killed. . . . It is hard work, but the attempt is not impossible" (*Mere Christianity*, 109). The impulse toward retribution, it needs emphasizing, is not some lower or primitive instinct, even when many social scientists and social psychologist in our day hold this view. It is rather to dignify fellow human beings by treating them as responsible moral agents. Civilized human beings will not tolerate murder and mayhem at any level; the uncivilized will. Correlatively, civilized humanity will exercise moral restraint in responding to moral evil—a commitment that is rooted in neighbor-love and an awareness of the dignity of all human beings. The particular character of this response is chiefly twofold in its expression during interventionary action: it is both discriminating and proportionate in its application of coercive force.

61. Among those "first-order" priorities that inform the ultimate justification for intervening are the following: (1) embodied justice as it affects the people who stand in need, (2) creating order out of chaos in social-political terms, and (3) seeking the common good of those in need, and (4) seeking the international common good as it is affected by the crisis (thus Ramsey, *The Just War*, 28–33).

62. These realities are argued with great clarity in James Turner Johnson, "Moral Responsibility after Conflict."

"National interest" as it concerns security issues is not merely "selfish"; it is inevitably tied to the security of *other* nations. Granted, it is *not* unreasonable to ask, *Why should we be bearing the burden of military intervention in remote parts of the world?* And it is *not* unreasonable to ask, *Why should our soldiers in particular be bearing that burden?* But national interest, in the end, need not vitiate the motivation to assist other nations where the need is dire. And should we be accused of hypocrisy or a double standard regarding intervention, as is inevitable, it is "better to be inconsistently responsible than consistently irresponsible."[63]

Second Thoughts on "Last Resort"

A final source of frequent misunderstanding invites our consideration. If we insist on viewing "last resort" as the *mathematical last* in a serial line of possible actions or strategies, there will *always* be one more alternative to try. And in our day, intervention is more likely to be late than pre-mature. Hence, we must qualify possibilities constituting "last resort" with the word "reasonable," and for two reasons. First, all who oppose coercive force in principle will *never* acknowledge that diplomatic maneuvering is ever exhausted. Second, last resort might be immoral—and destructive—when and where it stalls and becomes too late to defend the suffering innocent. Quite properly, Michael Walzer has written: "Taken literally . . . 'last resort' would make war [indeed, any forceful intervention] morally impossible. For we can never reach *lastness*, or we can never know that we have reached it. There is always something else to do: another diplomatic note, another . . . resolution, another meeting . . . ."[64]

Delay for the sake of delay, however, is not the intent of last resort in classical just war thinking. For if there is some great evil that must be prevented or stopped, we are not morally permitted to wait on every possibility. Delay at some point becomes immoral, inhumane and complicit with the crime or crimes needing interdiction—a *critically important* consideration as it applies to the question of "humanitarian intervention." (After all, economic sanctions will not deter terrorists or tyrants.) For this reason, "last resort" is anchored in considerations of just cause, not vice versa.[65]

Human Solidarity and Neighbor-Love

In an important address in 1997 at the U.S. Holocaust Museum, South African Justice Richard Goldstone, who had previously been chief prosecutor of the International Criminal Tribunals for the former Yugoslavia and Rwanda, had this to say:

> The one thing that I have learned in my travels to the former Yugoslavia and in Rwanda and in my own country is that where there have been egregious human rights violations that have been unaccounted for, where there has been no justice, where the victims have not received any acknowledgement, where they

63. Biggar, *In Defence of War*, 233.

64 Walzer, *Arguing about War*, 88.

65. Again, this suggests the need for prioritizing "primary" and "secondary" criteria (see note 339).

have been forgotten, where there's been a national amnesia, the effect is a cancer in the society. It is the reason that explains, in my respectful opinion, spirals of violence in the former Yugoslavia for centuries and in Rwanda for decades . . . .[66]

Goldstone's remarks, fresh on the heels of unprecedented genocidal violence, serve to remind us that Paul Ramsey was right. No authority on earth can withdraw from "social charity" and "social justice" their intrinsic and justifiable tendency to rescue from dereliction and oppression all whom it is possible to rescue. That justification can never be withdrawn; it can only be limited, supplanted, or suspended temporarily.

It has been said that people will not cherish their own freedom if they are unwilling to intervene on behalf of others in need. Ancient proverbial wisdom beckons people of principle, irrespective of their location in life, to act on behalf of the traumatized. Such a call bears repeating, especially in a post-consensus cultural climate and at a moment when nations suffer from "humanitarian fatigue":

> If you faint in the day of adversity,
>
> How small is your strength.
>
> Rescue those who are being led away toward death,
>
> Hold back those stumbling toward the slaughter.
>
> If you say, "But we knew nothing about this,"
>
> Does not He who weighs the heart consider it?
>
> Does not He who guards your life
>
> Not know it?
>
> And will not He repay each person
>
> According to what that person has done?[67]

---

66. The transcript of this address appeared in the *Washington Post*, February 2, 1997, C4. In this speech, Goldstone recommended doing four things for the sake of those who have suffered: (1) exposing the truth of specific guilt and avoiding general guilt; (2) recording the truth of moral atrocity for the historical record in order to counter attempts by the guilty to avoid guilt; (3) publicly acknowledging the loss of the victims, who, as terrified people, need justice; and (4) applying the deterrent of criminal justice, since human nature tends to be deterred from criminal behavior by the fear of punishment.

67. Prov 24:10–12 (Berean Study Bible).

"Why U.S. Foreign Policy in Iraq Needs an Ethic of Political Reconciliation and How Religion Can Supply It"

Daniel Philpott[1]

SINCE THE END OF the Cold War, U.S. foreign policy has encountered its thorniest troubles in its efforts to build peace in societies sundered by conflict. The problem has proved far more difficult than military victory itself. The Clinton administration's worst foreign policy disaster—in Somalia—came not in securing the delivery of relief supplies but in seeking to build state institutions afterwards. The knottiest dilemmas of President George W. Bush arose in trying to secure order after formal military victories in Iraq and Afghanistan. It is fitting, then, that in late 2005 the Department of Defense raised post-conflict reconstruction operations to a "core mission," and that the State Department, the Agency for International Development, the World Bank, and the United Nations have performed similar elevations. The global struggle against terrorism lends peacebuilding still more urgency as policymakers conclude that riven societies are terror's most fertile incubators.

Are the problems of peacebuilding ones for which religious ethics can provide guidance? In the United States, Christian and Jewish ethicists had far more to say about the justice of the war in Iraq that defeated Saddam Hussein—as they did about interventions in Bosnia and Kosovo—than they have had to say about the far more difficult aftermath of these conflicts—unsurprisingly. After all, when it comes to going to war, ethicists have at their disposal the centuries-old just-war tradition. But this tradition has much less to say about the dilemmas faced when the formal part of a war is over but a just and stable peace is still distant What obligations do outside intervening states have to build stable and just institutions? May perpetrators of war crimes receive amnesty? What about mere combatants? Or does justice require trials and punishment? If so, again, for whom? Should members of an unjust regime be debarred from holding office? Which ones? Can apologies and forgiveness be appropriate political practices? If so, who should practice them, and under what circumstances? What is the most just way to acknowledge and remember victims and their wounds? Should victims receive

---

1. Daniel Philpott's article originally appeared in Chaplin and Joustra, eds., *God and Global Order: The Power of Religion in American Foreign Policy*, 171–86.

reparations? If so, which ones? What about living representatives of the dead? These questions beg for a development of the tradition for moral reasoning about a new set of dilemmas. Such a development could advance the project of generating what in this book is called a "Christian perspective on International Relations." That question will not be explicitly addressed here, but what is clear is that the development will certainly contribute to making "faith-based diplomacy" an effective reality.

Here I propose and outline the broad contours of an ethic of peace building. Its unifying concept is reconciliation. The ethic shares the just-war tradition's foundations: the Bible and philosophical sources. It incorporates, too, a core proposition of St. Augustine and St. Thomas Aquinas, two of the just-war tradition's pioneers: that the purpose of a just war is a just peace. But it addresses a problem that presidents have faced since the end of the Cold War: that a just peace requires more than going to war and fighting it well. It requires also an effort to build peace after the war is over. I will then deploy the ethic of reconciliation to Iraq, the site where peacebuilding dilemmas are now at their most difficult. Reconciliation has indeed risen to prominence in the parlance of policymakers and other influential voices in the United States as well as in Iraq. It is a buzzword, a focal point, an organizing concept, proffered as a solution yet debated in its meaning. Most commonly, it means some combination of political measures meant to heal communal rifts in the Iraqi political order: amnesties, a reversal of de-Ba'athification measures, changes in the constitution, the sharing of oil revenue, and the like. But the ethic that I propose calls for more. Stability and a modicum of justice—Augustine's *tranquillitas ordinis*—themselves require a broader range of activities conducted by a broader range of actors in a wider range of social spheres, all aimed at healing the munificent wounds bequeathed by Iraq's past.

An Ethic Of Reconciliation

It is not only the United States that has faced the problem of peacebuilding. Confronting the dilemmas of past injustices in order to construct a stable liberal democracy has been the central challenge of at least forty societies that have emerged from dictatorship amidst the "third wave of democratization" over the past generation and of a concentration of societies that have settled their civil wars since the end of the Cold War.[2] These efforts have involved international peacekeeping and peacebuilding forces, economic aid from the World Bank, the European Union, the U.S. Agency for International Development, and other international institutions, as well as truth commissions, election

2. The exact number of countries that have become democracies since the "third wave" began in 1974 is not clear. In his *The Third Wave: Democratization in the Late Twentieth Century*, Samuel P. Huntington documents thirty transitions between 1974 and 1989. Freedom House reports that the number of "free" countries increased by thirteen from 1989 to 2004. See Freedom House, "Russian Downgraded to 'Not Free'" press release, 2004; and Freedom House, *Freedom in the World 2005: The Annual Survey of Political Rights and Civil Liberties.* Democracy theorist Larry Diamond estimates that between 1974 and 1996, between thirty-six and seventy-seven states became democracies, depending on how one counts democratization exactly. See Diamond, "Is the Third Wave of Democratization Over? An Empirical Assessment."

monitoring, trials, reparations schemes, official apologies, dramatic statements of forgiveness, and many other measures.

These efforts, and broadly the U.S. effort to reconstruct Iraq, generally follow the moral logic of the "liberal peace," the paradigm that predominates in the world's most powerful institutions.[3] It can be described through seven tenets. First, armed conflict must come to a halt through a ceasefire or a more enduring settlement. Second, human rights, democracy, the rule of law, and free market economic institutions are to be established. Third, prominent among the actors who build peace in societies that have suffered massive violence and other injustices are international organizations like the United Nations and the World Bank as well as powerful liberal democracies like the United States and Germany. The next three tenets, though not always included in descriptions of the liberal peace, prescribe responses to past injustices that resonate with liberalism's philosophical commitments. The fourth tenet is punishment for violators of human rights—trials, imprisonment, sometimes (though controversially among liberals) execution, and often "vetting" procedures that debar past perpetrators from holding certain jobs—measures justified either through Kantian retributivist arguments, consequentialist appeals for the importance of accountability in establishing new regimes based on the rule of law, or a combination of the two. The fifth tenet is reparations for victims. The sixth is a wariness toward the political promotion of personal and spiritual healing, the transformation of emotions, and interpersonal reconciliation—phenomena properly relegated to the private realm, liberals say.[4] Seventh, included in the liberal peace is a commitment to expressing rationales through secular language.[5] It is because of their promotion of values like rights, democracy, constitutionalism, and certain rationales for punishment that are found in the thought of Locke, Kant, and their philosophical descendants, most notably John Rawls, that these tenets can be called collectively "the liberal peace."

At least one other paradigm for peacebuilding has sprung up across the globe in recent years, though, one that is rooted in religious traditions, that sets forth a vision of peacebuilding that differs distinctly from (though it also overlaps with) the liberal peace, and that can be best called reconciliation. It is found in the leadership of Anglican Archbishop Desmond Tutu, Chair of South Africa's Truth and Reconciliation Commission (TRC), and of Guatemalan Catholic Archbishop Juan Gerardi, who formed and oversaw an independent truth commission; it is found in the theological writings of Popes John Paul II and Benedict XVI, of Yale theologian Miroslav Volf, of the Jewish scholar Marc Gopin, of the Muslim scholar Mohammed Abu-Nimer, and several others.[6] But if these figures have succeeded in bringing reconciliation into global policy

---

3. On the liberal peace, see Paris "Peacebuilding and the Limits of Liberal Internationalism"; Richmond, "The Problem of Peace: Understanding the 'Liberal Peace.'"

4. Ash, "True Confessions," 37–38; Bhargava, "Restoring Decency to Barbaric Societies," 60–63; Crocker, "Retribution and Reconciliation," 6; Crocker, "Truth Commissions, Transitional Justice, and Civil Society," 108; Gutmann and Thompson, "Moral Foundations of Truth Commissions," 32–33; Ignatieff, "Articles of Faith," 111–13, 21–22.

5. Greenawalt, "Amnesty's Justice," 199; Gutmann and Thompson, "Moral Foundations of Truth Commissions."

6. Abu-Nimer, *Nonviolence and Peace Building in Islam*; De Gruchy, *Reconciliation*; Gopin, *Between*

discourse, none has developed it into an ethic to be practiced in political orders, an ethic that addresses the moral and policy dilemmas that are involved with peacebuilding. How might such an ethic be conceived?

Reconciliation is a concept of justice: this is the ethic's central claim. It will seem a strange claim to citizens steeped in the modern liberal tradition, for whom justice is a matter of rights, fairness, economic equality, and punishment rightly meted out. It is indeed the Bible that grounds the claim. The case for it begins with the linguistic observation that in both the Hebrew of the Old Testament and the Greek of the New Testament, the terms that are translated into the English word *justice* also frequently translate into the English word *righteousness* (*sedeq* and *mishpat* in Hebrew and the family of words beginning with *dik-* in Greek). This righteousness is comprehensive, involving right relationship between all the members of a community, as prescribed by God's covenant, in their political, social, economic, legal, familial, cultic, and professional affairs.[7]

Reconciliation itself appears fifteen times in the New Testament (rendered as *katallage* and *katallosso*), though hardly at all in the Old Testament, and means either the process of restoration of right relationship or the condition of right relationship that results from this restoration.[8] If right relationship, or comprehensive righteousness, is the biblical meaning of justice, then it follows that reconciliation can equally connote the restoration of justice or a resulting state of justice. It is in this sense that reconciliation is a concept of justice. Second Isaiah speaks of justice in just this way—as a "saving justice" in which God comprehensively restores the people of Israel to righteousness, ultimately through a messianic suffering servant. In his Second Letter to the Corinthians, Paul explicitly connects reconciliation with the Greek word that translates to both righteousness and justice, *dikaiosunê*: "God made him who has no sin to be sin for us, so that in him we might become the [*dikaiosunê*] of God" (5:21, NIV)[9]

The biblical concept of reconciliation not only describes justice but is also a vision of peace, just as the ethic of reconciliation developed here aims to build peace in political orders. Isaiah 32:16–17 (NIV) is only one of many passages in scripture that closely links justice, righteousness, and peace: "Justice [*sedeqah*] will dwell in the desert and righteousness [*mishpat*] live in the fertile field. The fruit of righteousness [*sedeqah*] will be peace [*shalom*], the effect of righteousness [*sedeqah*] will be quietness and confidence forever." *Shalom*, the Hebrew word for peace, in fact means something much like comprehensive righteousness, prescribing a vision for the life of the entire Jewish community that involves health and prosperity, economic and political justice, and honesty and moral integrity in relations between persons.[10] *Eirene*, the New Testament word for peace, is the direct translation of *shalom* into Greek, and connotes similarly "a condition reaching into almost any aspect of human life, communally or individually considered,"

Eden and Armageddon; Torrance, "The Theological Grounds for Advocating Forgiveness and Reconciliation in the Sociopolitical Realm"; Volf, *Exclusion and Embrace*.

7. See Achtemeier, "Righteousness in the OT"; Marshall, *Beyond Retribution*.

8. De Gruchy, *Reconciliation: Restoring Justice*, 46, 51.

9. Scriptural references are taken from the New International Version unless otherwise indicated.

10. Yoder, *Shalom*, 10–23; Zehr, *Changing Lenses*, 130–32.

involving material welfare, justice, and good order.[11] Peace is that aspect of reconciliation which entails a state of right relationship.

That virtue which animates the process of restoring right relationship is mercy. Mercy, here, is biblical mercy, a far wider, far more restorative virtue than mercy in the Enlightenment tradition, which is primarily a release from justly deserved punishment. As Pope John Paul II explained in his second encyclical, *Dives in misericordia*, mercy in the scriptures is "manifested in its true and proper aspect when it restores to value, promotes and draws good fall the forms of evil existing in the world and in man."[12] Such a concept of mercy complements and indeed quite resembles the biblical concept of saving justice. Only thus could Micah 6:8 consistently declare: "He has showed you, O man, what is good. And what does the LORD require of you? To act justly [*mishpat*] and to love mercy [*hesed*] and to walk humbly with your God."[13]

Reconciliation as a concept of justice—and of peace, and of mercy—is manifested not only in the Bible's language but also in its accounts of God's response to evil. It is a response that differs quite distinctly from the intellectual "solutions" to the problem of evil that Enlightenment philosophers proposed. God's response to evil is rather one of action, action that restores the nation of Israel through forgiveness, reinstatement of the rights of the poor, the renewal of creation, and even punishment.[14] In the Jewish scriptures of the Old Testament these actions make up *tikkun olam*, the repair of the universe through which God renews his covenant. The Gospels later identify Jesus as the one who fulfills Isaiah's prophecy of the suffering servant who "leads justice to victory."[15] This justice of victory, which, here again, involves forgiveness, a judgment upon evil, hope for the poor, and the renewal of creation, climaxes in his death on the cross and his resurrection.

The meaning of this death and resurrection—the atonement—theologians have interpreted in quite different ways over the course of church history. For early church fathers, most vividly perhaps St. Irenaeus and St. Athanasius, Christ's death and resurrection were both a victory in a battle with sin, evil, and death as well as a restoration of humanity and creation—a "recapitulation," as Irenaeus put it. Far less supportive of a ethic of reconciliation is an interpretation that St. Anselm adumbrated in the Middle Ages but that reached its climax in some strands of the Protestant Reformation, one holding that Christ paid to God the penalty that humanity deserves for its sin and in so doing procured a not-guilty verdict for humanity and appeased the wrath of God the Father, but did not at the same time restore persons, relationships, and creation.[16] Far more

11. Mauser, *The Gospel of Peace*, 33.

12. Pope John Paul II, *Dives in Misericordia*, encyclical, November 30, 1980, §6.

13. The Jewish Study Bible translates *hesed* here as goodness rather than mercy. Other translations of the Bible, like the NIV, which I use here, render it as "mercy."

14. See Levenson, *Creation and the Persistence of Evil*; Neiman, *Evil in Modern Thought*.

15. Matt 12:20. See also Wright, *Evil and the Justice of God*, 64. Jesus' restorative mission is also revealed in the words with which he inaugurates his ministry in the Gospel of Luke: "The Spirit of the Lord is on me, because he has anointed me to preach good news to the poor. He has sent me to proclaim freedom for the prisoners and recovery of sight for the blind, to release the oppressed, to proclaim the year of the Lord's favor" (4:18). Here, he quotes from Isaiah 61:1–2; see also Isaiah 58:6.

16. See Schmiechen, *Saving Power*, 37–45.

hopeful for an ethic of reconciliation was the revival in the twentieth century of thinking much along the lines of the early church's victory interpretation but with an additional stress upon the implications of Christ's death and resurrection for the restoration of the social and political realm. Unsurprisingly, much of this revival came in response to war and carnage on a level unseen for centuries. It can be discerned in the writings of nineteenth-century Protestants like Albrecht Ritschl and twentieth-century Protestants like P. T. Forsyth, Karl Barth, Dietrich Bonhoeffer, Jan Milic Lochman, and Miroslav Volf, who have argued that Christ's justification begets the transformation and reconciliation of political orders.[17] Among popes, it can be seen in the arguments for forgiveness, apology, and mercy in politics proposed by Pope Benedict XV, who commended forgiveness to European states at the end of World War 1, by Pope John Paul II, who advocated forgiveness and reconciliation in the political realm in the closing sections of *Dives in misericordia* and subsequent addresses for the World Day of Peace, and more recently by Pope Benedict XVI. Catholic theologian Gustavo Gutiérrez has made the case that salvation involves the transformation of unjust social structures and the liberation of the poor from their confinement.[18] Protestant theologian Jürgen Moltmann has developed a theology holding that on the cross, Jesus acted in solidarity with the poor, the tortured, the murdered, and the marginalized, but also with perpetrators.[19] This thinking resonates strongly with the restorative justice movement, one that first arose in juvenile criminal law in the West, was been championed by the Mennonite tradition but also endorsed by the U.S. Catholic bishops, and was famously applied to national political orders by Archbishop Tutu in his leadership of South Africa's Truth and Reconciliation Commission. From all of these sources and strands, the building blocks of a biblically based ethic of reconciliation have emerged.

Importantly for building a consensus around principles of reconciliation in a context like Iraq, many of these same building blocks can be found in Islam, As they appear in Islamic scriptures and tradition, Arabic words for justice, reconciliation, peace, and mercy are far closer to Jewish and Christian understandings than to those of the Enlightenment. With some interpretive effort, the Qur'an's words for justice, *'adl* and *qist*, can be understood to mean comprehensive right relationship. The Arabic *sulh* means settlement of differences through a restoration of relationship, while *musalaha* translates directly to reconciliation and carries a connotation of comprehensiveness. Further, *salaam*, the Arabic word for peace, refers to a general state of harmony, not just a cessation of hostility, much like the Jewish *shalom*. Likewise, the words for mercy, *rahma, rahim,* and *rahamin,* connote a broadly construed compassion, a general will to restore.[20] Whereas the Qur'an contains no notion of divine atonement—it does not teach that humanity collectively fell through Adam's sin in the Garden of Eden, nor that Jesus is the Son of God who saves humanity from this plight—it does portray God as restoring relationship with sinful humans through

---

17. De Gruchy, *Reconciliation: Restoring Justice,* 44–76.

18. See, among his many other writings, Gutiérrez, *Theology of Liberation,* trans. Inda and Eagleson.

19. See Gutiérrez, *Theology of Liberation*; and Moltmann, *The Crucified God.*

20. Abu-Nimer, *Nonviolence and Peace Building,* 60; Khadduri, *The Islamic Conception of Justice,* 3–12; LaHurd, "'So That the Sinner Will Repent'," 28; Omar, "Between Compassion and Justice," 9.

their repentance and his forgiveness.[21] At least some portions of Islamic criminal law arguably contain a notion of restorative justice.[22] Most powerfully, traditional Arab Muslim rituals of *sulh* and *musalaha*, employed to restore relationships within villages and communities in the wake of serious crimes, entail richer notions of restoration than virtually any comparable communal rituals that I have found in the Christian or Jewish traditions.[23] My claim is not that Islamic notions of justice, peace, mercy, and reconciliation are univocal with Christian conceptions, but rather that meaningful dialogue and achievement of consensus around the principles of reconciliation that I set forth here can occur both in Muslim contexts and in contexts where Muslims and Christians mingle.

If reconciliation as a conception of justice is rooted in ancient theological texts, what form might it take in modern politics? Modern political orders, at least ones characterized by human rights, democracy, and limited constitutional government, will promote less than the whole range of relationships involved in *sedeq* and *shalom*—they attend primarily to these relationships embodied in public law. (Human rights, for instance, are a legal guarantee but also a complex form of relationship among persons, involving specific claims and duties among citizens and between citizens and states.) But if political reconciliation promotes less than *sedeq* and *shalom*, it involves much more than the mere restoration of rights and institutions. It also involves a wide range of measures aimed at healing the wide range of wounds that political injustices inflict.

Just what are these wounds? The definition of political injustice arises from contemporary transitions themselves: political injustices are violations of the human rights and the laws of war that are spelled out in international conventions. But if these norms define political injustices, they do not describe the multiform and textured ways in which they wound their victims. There are at least six:

1. *The violation of the victim's basic human rights.* This first form of woundedness indeed resembles the very definition of a political injustice. But since the legal guarantee of a person's human rights is a key aspect of what he or she is entitled to vis-a-vis the community of citizens in the state, this violation is one of the forms of woundedness that arises from a political injustice.

2. *The many forms of harm to the victim's person.* Among these are death, the death of loved ones, permanent bodily injury, grief humiliation, trauma, the loss of wealth and livelihood, the defilement of one's race, ethnicity, religion, nationality or gender, sexual violation, and many other harms.

3. *Victims' ignorance of the source and circumstances* of the political injustices that harmed them.

4. *The failure of community members to acknowledge victims' suffering*, either through ignorance or indifference.

---

21. Sachedina, *The Islamic Roots of Democratic Pluralism*, 106.

22. Ammar, "Restorative Justice in Islam."

23. Abu-Nimer, *Nonviolence and Peace Building*, 102–8; Irani and Funk, "Rituals of Reconciliation: Arab-Islamic Perspectives."

5. *The "standing victory" of the perpetrator's political injustice.* It is not only harms to the victim's person that political injustices leave behind, but also an unchallenged, undefeated message of disregard for the victim's dignity—a message that consumes an additional harm to the victim and to the shared values of the community.

6. *The wounded soul of the perpetrator.* Deep in several religious and philosophical traditions is the idea that evil injures the soul of the perpetrator. Often, this injury will redound in severe psychological damage.

Because these six forms of wounds are inflicted directly by political injustices, they may be called "primary wounds." But they also result in "secondary wounds"—acts of further injustice and withdrawals of assent from new regimes that arise from the emotions of fear, hatred, resentment, and revenge that emanate from memories of the original injustices themselves. As the experiences of countries like Bosnia, Ireland, and Rwanda attest, these secondary wounds further stunt the project of building just and stable political orders—sometimes for generations.

Correspondingly, an ethic of political reconciliation aspires to heal the range of primary and secondary wounds that political injustices inflict. Reflecting the sense in which the religious traditions view reconciliation as action every bit as much as they view it as principle, it is through practices that the ethic is realized: indeed, it is through six multiple and interdependent practices that the ethic is realized—building institutions for social justice, acknowledgment, reparations, punishment, apology, and forgiveness—each of which manifests reconciliation's core logic of restoration of right relationship and heals a distinct dimension of woundedness.[24] Inasmuch as they heal primary wounds, these practices effect what can be called "primary restorations." These restorations, though, can then effect "secondary restorations": certain forms of "social capital," including an increase in popular trust in the political order, democratic participation, and identification with the nation. It is important to remember that in the political realm, as the experience of the past generation has shown, these restorative practices will always be achieved only in part, always hampered by power and unresolved differences over the meaning of justice, and limited by their sheer size and complexity. But as the past generation has also shown, the practices are not merely the brainchild of theorists. Each of the six that I describe below has in fact taken place in numerous settings over the past generation, however messily, and might now contribute to the building of peace in Iraq. It is just this predicament that calls for an ethic, one that would be irrelevant if the practices never occurred and that would be unnecessary if they occurred without difficulty.

Reconciliation in Iraq

Is not all talk of reconciliation in Iraq naive and utopian, especially a concept of reconciliation whose endpoint is *shalom* or *salaam*? Admittedly, it is rather a Hobbesian peace that U.S. policymakers have overridingly prioritized in recent years—an end to levels of political violence that they neither anticipated nor planned for when they first

---

24. On the importance of practices ethics, see MacIntyre, *After Virtue*, 187.

went to war and a securing of a degree of order that will allow them to begin to withdraw U.S, troops. Yet, is it not also true that the very sources of violence are just the sort that reconciliation addresses?

A 2003 *New York Times* story tells of a Shiite Iraqi, Sadri Adab Diwa, whose younger sister, Hamaa, was abducted and killed by Saddam Hussein's regime in 1980 for giving a Qur'an to a classmate. "If I catch Saddam," Diwan promised, "I won't kill him. That won't be enough. I'll suck his blood. And if he escapes, I'll follow him to the ends of the earth."[25] Such pursuits of revenge on the part of Shiites as well as Kurds, both of whom were subordinated by Sunnis since the beginning of the Ba'athist regime and brutally suppressed by Saddam, have been common since Saddam's fall and have redoubled with subsequent stacks and killings. Sunnis have responded in kind. After the February 2006 destruction of the Shiite Golden Mosque of Samarra and the wave of retaliation that it sparked, observers began to speak of a full-fledged civil war. It is a conflict between partisans with religious, national, and other identities driven by communal loyalties, fear of the other's domination, and the emotions of revenge and hatred that memories of past injustices have generated—royalties, fears, and emotions whose moderation and assuagement are indispensable to any achievement of stability in Iraq.[26]

Far from being confined to academics and church leaders, reconciliation has indeed risen to become arguably the most frequent and most salient principle to which policy-makers—U.S. and European but also Iraqi—make reference in their proposals for Iraq. The *Iraq Study Group Report* of November 2006, a landmark set of recommendations by a bipartisan commission appointed by the U.S. government, mentions reconciliation sixty-three times and devotes a major section to it. The term has shown up frequently in the benchmarks that Congress has set for U.S. policy and that the U.S., government has set for the Iraqis, and has been proffered vigorously in the speeches of former secretary of state Condoleeza Rice, U.S. ambassador Zalmay Khalilzad and his successor, Ryan Crocker, and other voices in the U.S. government like Congressman Chris Smith. Former UN secretary general Kofi Annan, Special Envoy Lakhdar Brahimi, and heads of state like Tony Blair and Sylvio Berlusconi have also urged it. Iraqis themselves have taken up the concept as well. Not least is Prime Minister Nouri Al-Maliki, who, in June 2006, unveiled a twenty-eight-point comprehensive plan for reconciliation, one said to be inspired by South Africa's Truth and Reconciliation Commission, that received wide support from several parties in the Iraqi government as well as Turkey.[27] Conferences of Iraqi civil society, including religious leaders, have advocated reconciliation, too.[28]

25. Sachs, "Iraqis Seek Justice, or Vengeance, for Victims of the Killing Fields."

26. On religion and nationalism in Iraq, see Cole, "The Rise of Religious and Ethnic Mass Politics in Iraq."

27. Al-Maliki, "Iraq PM Unveils National Reconciliation Plan." News reports differ about exactly how many points the reconciliation plan contains. On the South Africa influence, see Hasni, "Iraq Reconciliation Plan Inspired by South Africa."

28. In October 2006, 50 *ulema* (religious scholars) from both the Sunni and Shiite communities convened under the auspices of the fifty-seven-state Organization of the Islamic Conference to develop and use the Makkah Document, a call for reconciliation and an end to violence among Muslims that elicited the approval and endorsement of Prime Minister Maliki and top religious leaders Ali Al-Sistani and Moqtada Sadr. Then, in December 2006, a "National Reconciliation Conference" brought together

None of these initiatives, nor reconciliation's establishment in political discourse, means that reconciliation has been successful or even effectual. At the present writing, U.S. policymakers and other analysis widely believe that violence in Iraq has waned and that prospects for settlement have improved, but also that stability is unlikely without reconciliation.[29] When they speak of reconciliation, what political officials both inside and outside of Iraq mean is usually some combination of the following: a greater incorporation of Sunnis into the constitution and the national government; a reversal of the de-Baathification policies through which the Bush administration widely purged the Iraqi government of Ba'athist party members shortly after the end of the formal war in 2003; a sharing of oil revenue among Sunnis, Shiites, and Kurds; provincial elections to boost local autonomy; a wider amnesty for both members of Saddam's security forces and more recent insurgents; a pension plan for former officials; and great autonomy for Kurds.[30] Recently, U.S. political and military officials have come to place the adverb "political" before reconciliation, perhaps to distinguish their approach from a more ambitious and realistic one involving religion, civil society, and hearts and minds.

But is "political reconciliation" enough to bring peace and stability to Iraq and allow the United States to pull its troops out—America's central foreign policy goal? Can the goals of political reconciliation themselves be achieved apart from a broader array of measures conducted by a broader array of actors with a broader array of goals, including a significant transformation of the memories, emotions, and desire for revenge that brought about the current violence in the first place? The top negotiator of the 1993 Oslo Accords between Israel and Palestine, Dennis Ross, made much the same point in a speech six years later when he attributed the subsequent breakdown of the settlement to its failure to take hold in the attitudes of the population. The same insight also lies behind the truth commissions that over thirty countries have undertaken in the wake of dictatorship and civil war in the past generation. The argument is one of simple realism: an Iraq that the United States can plausibly exit requires stable institutions, which in turn require legitimacy in the eyes of the population, which turn requires dealing with the wounds that give rise to the desire to withhold such legitimacy and to take up arms.

Providing the moral framework for the job that is required is an ethic of reconciliation grounded in biblical and Qur'anic conceptions of justice, mercy, and peace and enacted through a set of six practices that transform the wounds of injustice. The first practice,

---

major Iraqi government and religious leaders, including Prime Minister Maliki, to attempt to settle differences. In October 2007, the United States Institute of Peace, in partnership with the U.S. military, the State Department, and the United States Agency for International Development, convened in Baghdad a reconciliation conference of thirty-one tribal sheikhs from Mahmoudiya. On the latter, see United States Institute of Peace, "USIP-Facilitated Iraq Reconciliation Agreement a Key Breakthrough for Stability Effort in South Baghdad's 'Triangle of Death.'"

29. U.S. Deputy Secretary of State John D. Negroponte said in December 2007 that "the security surge had delivered significant results. . . . Now progress on political reconciliation, including key national legislation as well as economic advances, is needed to consolidate the gains. If progress is not made on these fronts we risk falling back toward the more violent habits of the past." Quoted in Graff and Ibrahim, "U.S. Seeks Political Gains; Sunnis End Boycott."

30. The most thorough description of an official political approach to reconciliation that I have found is that of the Iraq Study Group, *Iraq Study Group Report: The Way Forward—A New Approach.* See pp. 64–70 in particular.

building socially just institutions, is the one that corresponds most current U.S. policy in Iraq and with the ideals of global institutions: the liberal peace. It includes the rule of law based on a constitution that promotes democracy and human rights and a commitment to economic growth and a just distribution of goods. The wounds that it heals are the lack of recognition of the rights and dignity of the person that existed under the regime of Saddam. Today, basic human rights are guaranteed in law but not in practice. It is to secure these goals that U.S. forces ought to remain in Iraq.

But far more is required. Acknowledgement is the practice of conferring recognition upon the suffering of victims of human rights violations. It seems to overcome the community's ignorance of this suffering and sometimes even the victim's own ignorance of the circumstances in which the violations took place. Accounts of transitional justice from around the world show that victims are often willing to forego revenge and give their assent to a new political regime—a "secondary restoration"—once they have received recognition for their suffering. Discovering and exposing the injustices of the past creates legitimacy for the regime of the future.

In recent transitions away from war and dictatorship, states have practiced acknowledgment through a novel form of institution: the truth commission, an official body charged with investigating and producing a public record of past injustices. Truth commissions practice acknowledgment best when the recognition they confer is most personal, occurring through public hearings or other opportunities for witnessed testimony. Respected voices in the international community have indeed put forth proposals for an Iraqi truth commission.[31] At present, Iraq is not stable enough to conduct a national truth commission. But global practice has shown that acknowledgment can also be practiced effectively—and all the more personally—through community-level forums, which are now thinkable in many Iraqi cities and villages.[32] A remarkable survey of Iraqis conducted by the International Center for Transitional Justice and the Human Rights Center of the University of California, Berkeley, shows broad popular support for truth-seeking processes, especially local forums and ones conducted by nongovernmental organizations. "That the Iraqi people need to learn from the lessons of the past to be able to create the future—not merely that we remember the past," is a typical sentiment voiced by a Sunni man from Baghdad.[33] Acknowledgment might also take place through documentation centers, the unearthing of mass graves, museums, and memorials, for which the same report shows strong support and which leaders like the prominent Iraqi exile Kanan Makiya have vigorously promoted.[34]

The logic behind the third practice, reparations, is much like the argument for acknowledgment: it is a form of recognition that the state or even the perpetrator himself

31. See, e.g., Bassiouni, *Iraq Post-Conflict Justice.*

32. By the end of 2007, the death rate in Iraq had fallen to one-fifth of what it was a year earlier and ethno-sectarian violence was mostly limited to areas west of Baghdad and Rusala. See U.S. Department of Defense, *Measuring Stability and Security in Iraq*, 18.

33. International Center for Transitional Justice and Human Rights Center, University of California, Berkeley, *Iraqi Voices*, 38; also see 37–40.

34. International Center for Transitional Justice and Human Rights Center, University of California, Berkeley, *Iraqi Voices*, 40; Worth, "The Struggle for Iraq."

confers on victims. The difference is that reparations are material, taking the form of money, mental and health services, access to education and employment, and the like. The wound that they address is in part lack of recognition for the victim but also the victim's material loss—economic, physical, and psychological. Understood, no amount of reparations could reverse the loss of a loved one or a permanent injury. But often, reparations can both compensate in part for the material dimension of the loss and symbolically communicate recognition to the victim. Like acknowledgment, reparations might help to reduce victims' resentment and elicit their assent for the new regime.

Among respondents to *Iraqi Voices*, support was widespread for material and symbolic compensation.[35] Former deputy secretary of state Stuart E. Eizenstat has proposed that a compensation fund, overseen by both Iraqi and international representatives, be established for victims of torture, assassination, or other human rights abuses. European foundations for victims of Nazi injustices can serve as a model. Eizenstat also proposes a property commission to resolve the claims—often complex and conflicting—of the tens of thousands of Iraqis who were displaced from their homes under Saddam's rule.[36]

The fourth practice, punishment, might at first seem like a strange one in an ethic of reconciliation. In settings of transitional justice all over the world, reconciliation is pitted against punishment, restorative justice against retributive justice, and forgiveness against imprisonment and accountability. Punishment, though, need not be at odds with reconciliation—but only if it is justified differently than through the logics of retributivism and consequentialism between which Western arguments about criminal justice have oscillated for the last couple of centuries. It is rather what theologian Christopher B. Marshall calls "restorative punishment," grounded in biblical texts, that can contribute to reconciliation.[37] Addressing the wounds of the "standing victory" of the human rights violator's message of injustices and the disorder in the soul of the wrongdoer himself, restorative punishment seeks to repair persons, relationships, and political orders in the wake of massive political injustices.

Restorative justice may involve long-term imprisonment for the top masterminds of human rights violations and jail for politically motivated acts of murder, rape, torture, and assault. In Iraq, this means Saddam's top leaders and those who have committed terrorist acts since his fall. Lower-level perpetrators might receive amnesty, but amnesty that is conditional on participation in public forums like truth commissions and other public rituals that perform other dimensions of the repair of wounds. Even those who have committed the most serious crimes might face such a public forum in addition to trials and imprisonment. It is hard to imagine a less restorative form of punishment than the public hanging of Saddam Hussein, which inflamed tensions between Sunnis and Shiites not only in Iraq, but through the Arab world.[38] Restorative punishment also implies a version

---

35. International Center for Transitional Justice and Human Rights Center, University of California, Berkeley, *Iraqi Voices*, 40.

36. Eizenstat, "Reconciliation, Not Just Reconstruction."

37. Marshall, *Beyond Retribution*, 97–144.

38. For an excellent analysis of the justice in Saddam's trial and execution, see Carlson, "Discerning Justice in the Trial and Execution of Saddam Hussein."

of vetting that involves far more careful scrutiny of past complicity with Saddam's crimes than the Bush administration's sweeping de-Ba'athification.

The fifth practice, apology, and especially the sixth practice, forgiveness, are the most distinctly theological of the six—and the rarest in global politics today. Through a public apology, an individual perpetrator or head of state or other leader can nullify his or his group's ongoing commitment to its injustices, delegitimize the political injustice of the previous regime or faction in war, and contribute to the legitimacy of a new regime. Apologies by former Ba'athist leaders, or by today's heads of Sunni and Shiite armies and factions for their members' acts of terrorism, might go a long way toward defusing tensions. Through its own apology for the abuses perpetrated by its armed forces, especially those at Abu Ghraib prison, the United States might also gain legitimacy for the remainder of its stabilizing operation and contribute noticeably to reconciliation in Iraq.

Forgiveness complements apology. In Christianity, forgiveness is an imitation and participation in God's own redemptive act on the cross. Theologians are divided over whether victims ought to initiate it or perform it in response to a prior apology. In Islam, God forgives the repentant sinner and commands the victim to forgive a wrongdoer who apologizes, as the Qur'an stresses over and over. When practiced toward political injustices, forgiveness might strengthen the agency of victims, defeat the wrongdoer's message of injustice by condemning and then overcoming it, defuse cycles of revenge, and greatly facilitate the building of a new political order. In the context of transitional justice, forgiveness has occurred more commonly in the context of truth commissions or other forums where the acknowledgment of victims' suffering and the apology of perpetrators has first occurred. *Iraqi Voices* shows significant support for forgiveness among ordinary Iraqis, though far less when it is seen as an amnesty that would replace the punishment of top perpetrators. Indeed, it need not be. If punishment is justified restoratively, then forgiveness can supplement it as a common restorative practice.

Again, the six practices all manifest the restorative logic of an ethic of political reconciliation. As such, each of them manifests mercy understood as a broad will to restore, peace as a broad state of right relationships, and the justice of reconciliation, a justice that restores right relationships in a political order. In Iraq, this ethic implies a far wider set of activities than what policymakers now mean by political reconciliation, but these activities may well be vital to the success of political reconciliation.

Reconciliation and Realism

But the skeptic may persist: does not such an ambitious vision strain an already burdened U.S. military mission? Reconciliation's success, in fact, depends on these activities being conducted by a far wider array of actors than the U.S. military. The U.S. armed forces themselves have recognized this conclusion insofar as they have sought to construct "Provincial Reconstruction Teams," "Concerned Local Citizens Programs," and bottom-up reconciliation programs that coordinate U.S. efforts with those of local Iraqi citizens.[39] What is needed, though, and what the United States would do well to

39. U.S. Department of Defense, *Measuring Stability and Security in Iraq.*

recognize, is a much broader incorporation of both international institutions and civil society actors in reconstruction and reconciliation efforts. "Reconciliation must be an Iraqi process, led by Iraqis. But to give the political process the greatest possible chance at success, the United States must remain actively involved in shoring up the security situation," concludes analyst James Phillips.[40]

The UN and the legitimacy that it confers can bolster the work of a truth commission or a reparation board. The International Criminal Court would provide a far better mode for trying and punishing top Iraqi war criminals than Iraqi national courts, helping to alleviate the divisive perception of victor's justice. NGOs, especially ones that focus on transitional justice, could provide both expertise and objectivity. Religious leaders are an assert that has been overlooked, especially by a still-secularized U.S. foreign policy establishment. Prestigious voices in a religious society like Iraq, they are potential carriers and promoters of a faith-based ethic of reconciliation. The Iraqi Study Group—hardly outside the policy mainstream—drew just this conclusion in its report.[41] Religious leaders have already gathered in a handful of major conferences designed to bring together divided factions. Dramatic here is the work of Anglican Canon Andrew White, who created an Iraqi Interreligious Initiative that brings together high-level Shiite and Sunni leaders as well as representatives of minority groups, including Iraqi Christians.[42] The support of a united front of religious leaders for the practices of reconciliation that I have outlined could crucially enable their occurrence and their success.

To envision such an array of actors conducting the portfolio of practices that make up an ethic of reconciliation is not to invoke easy optimism but to offer an approach that can improve the prospects of a most difficult operation. Not an alternative to U.S. military efforts, this approach is rather a broader framework for peacebuilding that includes these efforts but situates them in partnership with other players and stratagems. Broadest of all, it is an alternative conception of justice, one whose roots lie in the texts of the Abrahamic religious traditions. But it is a conception with concrete operational implications, ones that might well contribute to stability in Iraq and the opportunity for American troops to exit Iraq having achieved success.

40. Phillips, "Proposed Timetables for U.S. Withdrawal Would Sabotage Reconciliation in Iraq."

41. Iraq Study Group, *Iraq Study Group Report*, 68.

42. On the other gatherings, see note 8. On the work of Canon White, see McFarlane, "The Iraqi 'Nation'"; and Foundation for Relief and Reconciliation in the Middle East, "Peace Progress in Cairo."

"A Theology of Peace in the Context of the Gulf War"

GEORGE WEIGEL[1]

Needed: A Theology of Peace

THE KEY WORD . . . is, of course, "theological." Alienation from the American experiment shaped the *politics* of the religious Left during the war, as I argued above. But the root problem of the churches' engagement with the public moral argument that preceded U.S. military action in the Gulf, and that all bedeviled some church leaders' discussion of the future of Christian-Islamic relationships (particularly in the context of the politics of the Middle East), should not be located at the level of historical or political analysis, but in terms of doctrine. Mainline/oldline Protestantism and a considerable part of the Catholic leadership, having abandoned Christian Realism of the sort taught by Reinhold Niebuhr, Paul Ramsey, and John Courtney Murray, have substituted in its place psychologized and quasi-utopian understandings of international public life, which suggest the possibility of a world without conflict. What has been lost in this doctrinal shuffle is the classic Christian tradition's understanding of "peace" as *tranquillitas ordinis*: rightly ordered and dynamic political community, in and among nations, in which legal and political institutions provide effective means for resolving the inevitable conflicts that will define public life under the End Time.

While certain minority currents in the long, complex history of Christian social thought have argued for the possibility of man's building the promised Kingdom of peace and righteousness here on earth, mainstream Christian tradition, even in its more optimistic reading of human possibilities (as in the Thomistic, Anabaptist, and Wesleyan traditions), has been resolutely anti-utopian, which is to say, Augustinian. The collapse of this Augustinian realism about human propensities for evil, cruelty, and injustice is one root of liberal Protestantism's and radical Catholicism's extreme skepticism about the just war tradition, whose origins are, of course, to be found in Augustine himself. And to jettison the just war tradition is to jettison the worldly concept of peace that, as has been argued so frequently in this essay, is embedded in it. But peace, according to Christian self-understandings, must still be pursued: which means, to come

---

1. "Theology of Peace" is excerpted from chapter 2 in Johnson and Weigel, eds., *Just War and the Gulf War*.

full circle, substituting for various utopianisms the peace of *tranquillitas ordinis*, the worldly peace of politics and law.

Biblical Peace and World Peace

The path to a reformed American Christian address to the problems of war and peace in the post-Cold War world will run through a far more sophisticated theology of peace than is presently informing Christian activism on these issues. Such a theology would have several defining characteristics.

It would understand the biblical peace of *shalom*—the peace of the Kingdom of God established in its fullness, the peace in which swords are beaten into plowshares, the lions rest with the lambs, and the nations stream to the mountaintop of the Lord (Isaiah 2:2–4)—as an eschatological horizon toward which humanity is called, and against which the brokenness of the present world can be measured.

But it would also understand that the peace of *shalom* in its fullness is a matter of God's work, not man's, and it would thus eschew utopian notions of the mundane achievement of the peace of *shalom* through human agency—especially human political agency. *Shalom*-as-eschatological-horizon is thus an essential complement to the quotidian task of building the peace of *tranquillitas ordinis*—the peace of dynamic and rightly ordered political community, within and among nations—in this world, this side of the coming of the Kingdom. *Shalom* reminds us of the limits of the political, and thus clarifies just what is possible—and thus obligatory—for political life. A reformed theology of peace within which *shalom* and *tranquillitas ordinis* stand in creative tension would reposition the just war tradition precisely as a moral calculus oriented toward the pursuit of peace with freedom, order, security, and justice. It would take as one of its primary tasks the development of the concept of statecraft implied by the just war tradition, and in doing so it would help establish, in the wider public debate over war and peace, that there is no escape from the rigors of moral reasoning on facing questions of America's role in world affairs. It would link concepts of national interest to concepts of national purpose and national responsibility. And thus it would challenge both Wilsonian moralism and those forms of realpolitik which seem to suggest that a sufficiently tough-minded construal of "the national interest" absolves one from further reflection on the "ought" questions in the foreign policy debate.

Reclaiming an Understanding of Justice

A reformed theology of peace would resist the temptation—still widespread in religious circles influenced by the theologies of liberation—to pose the achievement of "justice" as the absolute precondition to peace. The reformed theology of peace envisioned here would have a far more subtle and complex understanding of the relationship between these two moral ends of politics. It would reclaim the triadic conception of justice—as commutative, distributive, and legal—that once characterized Christian thought on these matters. And it would develop the notion that legal justice—questions of the constitutional and legal right-ordering of societies and policies—is fundamental to the pursuit of peace as *tranquillitas ordinis*.

A reformed theology of peace would thus reflect far more seriously on the experience of the Revolution of 1989 in Central and Eastern Europe—a revolution built primarily on demands for the protection of basic human rights and on demands for democratic governance, as the preconditions to the pursuit of more equitable economic arrangements. It would also understand that in a world in which there will always be conflicts over what is "just" in given situations, a key moral issue for those concerned about the pursuit of peace is the availability of nonviolent legal and political instruments for adjudicating those conflicting claims without mass violence.

The Lay Vocation in the World

A reformed theology of peace would also challenge the clericalism that was one of the notable characteristics of the churches' address to the Gulf crisis. It would understand that holy orders, however construed in the various Christian ecclesial communities, confer no special charism of worldly wisdom. It would take far more seriously the teaching of the Second Vatican Council that "on the national and international planes the field of the apostolate is vast; and *it is there that the laity more than others are the channels of Christian wisdom*." In making the Council's teaching real in the life of the ecumenical Church, religious leaders, theologians, and Christian political theorists would engage a far wider array of fellow-Christian interlocutors in government, the military, and the relevant academic and policy disciplines than was the case with both the National Council of Churches and the United States Catholic Conference during the Gulf crisis. At the practical level, this will inevitably involve a reform of the bureaucratic processes by which denominations and ecumenical agencies gather information, form judgments, and make public statements on matters of war and peace.

A reformed theology of peace would take up another, and related, ecclesiological issue, namely, the appropriate roles of the Church in public moral argument about war and peace. The National Council of Churches' approach—reams of (usually tendentious and often partisan) policy analysis and prescription, preceded by a modicum of biblical/theological language—is clearly inadequate, and indeed ecclesiologically misconceived. The National Conference of Catholic Bishops made a serious effort in November 1990 to shape the public moral argument over the Gulf crisis according to the canons of the just war tradition, but Archbishop Roach's subsequent testimony before the Senate Foreign Relations Committee fell back into the familiar pattern, in which lengthy historical and policy analysis obscures and in some respects marginalizes the moral arguments being made.

The right "mix" of moral-framework setting and illustrative policy application is not easy to define in the abstract. But surely further conversation and debate on the balance here is in order. The churches are not perceived, by the wider political community (or indeed by many of their congregants), as wise moral counsellors or, as the Catholic bishops like to put it, as "pastors and teachers." They are perceived, and not without reason, as political, and indeed partisan, actors. The formal leadership of the churches has to face this fact, and it has to engage a serious debate about the ways in which religious leaders (and others, particularly the laity) embody the "public Church" in the public arena. The alternative to that conversation is a "public Church" that, in many respects, continues to drive itself to the margins of the debate, all the while consoling itself with the notion that it is being prophetic.

Neither Victims Nor Executioners

Finally, a reformed theology of peace would insist that there is no escape from moral responsibility when the nation is faced with a challenge and a threat like that posed by Saddam Hussein's invasion and occupation of Kuwait. Those who, in the name of the peace of order in international public life, urged a proportionate and discriminate use of armed force against Saddam Hussein took on a moral responsibility for their actions—which included, inescapably, the killing of innocents. But it should also be understood that those who rejected the use of military force were not absolved from moral responsibility for what would have followed had their counsel been taken, which would have included the killing of innocents, and in large numbers. The gruesome stories of what was going on in Kuwait while we were "giving sanctions a chance" should have made that clear, and beyond reasonable argument.

Amid all the talk of a "new world order," it is well to remember Albert Camus's challenge to men of conscience in the immediate aftermath of the Second World War: the task, Camus wrote, was to create an international order in which decent men might be "neither victims nor executioners." That remains a noble goal. It is not a goal that embodies the fullness of "peace" in Christian theology. But it is fully congruent with classic Christian understandings of peace as *tranquillitas ordinis*. It is a goal America's religious institutions might well take as their own.

"A Clash of Rival Apostasies? The Religious Problem and the Clash of Civilizations at 25"

Robert Joustra[1]

WHAT THE FRENCH CALL *la revanche de Dieu* is now so firmly established in the canon of international relations and the politics of the day-to-day that it can be somewhat taken for granted. Religion is back, not as "epiphenomenal," not as a catalyst for other, more real, underlying material concerns, but as a motivator and meaning maker itself. But, as the word "revenge" implies, this is not a universally celebrated reversal. If the social science has settled that religion is back, that it matters, that it is a power in its own right, it is anything but decided upon *how* it matters, whether this is *good* or *bad*, and—indeed—whether, as Talal Assad's disciples like Saba Mahmood and Elizabeth Shakman Hurd argue,[2] we know what it is we are talking about when we say "religion" anyway. On the twenty-fifth anniversary of Samuel P. Huntington's much debated thesis on the "clash of civilizations" in *Foreign Affairs* in 1993, which this issue of *The Christian Scholars Review* considers ("celebrates" might be a bit strong), I therefore revisit how Huntington himself proposed for us to think about religion and global politics. Several things stand out, in this analysis. First, Huntington did not think of religion merely as one of a perhaps-forgotten list of causal factors in international relations. Religion was not, for Huntington, like other sorts of factors that could be simply recalled, catalogued, and fit into existing paradigms of politics. In fact, I argue in this article that religion was not a simple causal factor at all; it was *constitutive* of international order. That is, to *miss* religion, as those like Daniel Philpott say we have done (only perhaps to find it again),[3] is not simply to be out a set of important variables; it is to have the wrong formulas. This is because religion is a defining, constitutive category of political communities, a fundamental marker that sets out the terms and conditions upon which we even engage in politics. To even define, for example, the *religious* and the secular, and how these relate to political legitimacy, is a religious but

1. This article appeared originally in *Christian Scholar's Review* 48, no. 3 (1965).

2. See Mahmood, *Religious Difference in a Secular Age*, and Shakman Hurd, *Beyond Religious Freedom*.

3. Philpott, "Has the Study of Global Politics Found Religion?" 183–202.

also *political* statement.[4] Thus, Huntington says that religion, culture, and language are the fundamental material out of which world civilizations arise. Civilizations do not produce religion, language, and culture; rather, *out of* religion, language, and culture civilizations arise. Says Huntington, quoting Christopher Dawson, "the great religions are the foundations on which the great civilizations rest."[5]

This, I argue, is an important recovery of a tradition of Christian social thought on the nature of the religious, one which Huntington rightly finds in historians like Dawson, but I think can most effectively be drawn out through an engagement with Abraham Kuyper (1873–1920). Kuyper shows both how original and important this "religious" insight of Huntington's is, but he will also showcase a second, critical problem with Huntington's thesis: the problem of political pluralism. To say, as Huntington does, that civilizations are founded in religion, culture, and language creates a special problem for plural societies, or indeed for plural religions (as is often pointed out about "political Islam"). If, indeed, the integrity and vitality of a civilization depends on being deeply in touch with its religious, cultural, and linguistic roots, as Huntington does, the subsequent conclusion that the real problem with societies like America is multiculturalism (that is, a loss of such cohesion and vitality), which he also does, is not hard to reach. And so, we come to the heart of the one of the enduring criticisms of Huntington's proposal, not a kind of fussing around with how he draws civilizational boundaries, or what coheres "Africa" and so on, but a *fundamental* problem from which can spring a hive of nationalism, racism, xenophobia, and more: the problem of pluralism in civilizations defined by common religion, language, and culture. This is a challenge for which Huntington's proposal is less well equipped, but again in dialogue with Kuyper and the English School, I propose a way to salvage his core insight into the religious foundation of civilizations, while attaching to it a more pluralist politics, an attachment which may remedy both Huntington's sometimes slippery nationalism, and his occasionally rough generalizations of inter/intra-civilizational diversity. These, I think, are key insights which update Huntington's arguments in such a way as to offer, especially the Christian thinker, a helpful way to navigate the politics of the global resurgence of religion.

Many, many problems have been made of Huntington's clash thesis. Musharraf purportedly blamed the world's attention on Christian-Muslim rivalry on him. Recalled by Jeffrey Goldberg, "Well, you know this is all Sam Huntington's fault. Before this book, no one ever talked about Islam and Christianity in competition. So, it really goes back to Samuel Huntington!"[6] Though a bit overstated, Musharraf's criticisms echo a large swath of academic literature on Huntington's clash thesis, especially the way he deals with religion, and most especially the way he talks about Islam. This clash thesis, between Huntington's pessimistic perspective on Islam and his somewhat rosier perspective on the

---

4. For a longer argument, see Joustra, *The Religious Problem with Religious Freedom*.

5. Huntington, *The Clash of Civilizations*, 47. For an outstanding resource for Christopher Dawson on his historiography and philosophy of history. I recommend *Dynamics in World History*. I have designed and taught an introduction world history (to 1914) around Dawson's historiography (also C. T. McIntire) for several years.

6. "Religion, Culture, and International Conflict after September 11: A Conversation with Samuel P. Huntington." Available online at: http://www.jamesbowman.net/articleDetail.asp?pubID=1209.

Christian West, became so influential, hardly a person could take a podium, presidents included, without needing to repudiate it on some level. Jeffrey Haynes boils it down to this: there is a "synergy between Christianity and liberal democracy, key foundations of a normatively desirable global order built on individualistic, liberal values." Huntington contrasts this with what he calls Radical Islam (including Islamism, Islamic extremism, Islamic fundamentalism) which he called a fundamentally political movement aimed at anti-democratic religious and cultural changes to global order.[7] Huntington was hardly alone in this argument, and indeed the events of 9/11 fed into his thesis that a militant, fundamentalist Islamism sought systemic transformation of the international system with violent resistance to the West (especially America). The problems with this, however, were many. First, it is one thing to argue that political Islam and Christianity may diverge in their approaches to liberal democracy, but quite another to say that therefore Islam was poised, en masse, to violently challenge or overthrow liberal democracy. Second, it is also unhelpful to the point of a critical error to conflate Islam and political Islam, and the diversity within Islamism and political Islam itself.[8] The atrocities with which the world has become only too familiar in the past several decades on the behest of radical Islamist groups are perpetrated by terrorist organizations which should not be conflated with Islamic party politics in Malaysia, or the crown in Morocco, or Muslim-democrats in Tunisia. Third, logically following from this recognition of deep diversity in the world of political Islam, we might expect rather than finding Islam's "bloody borders" with other civilizations, that, in fact, bloody politics are often *intra-civilizational*, that is in spaces like Yemen, Syria, Iraq, and so on. The worst offenders and the worst atrocities of Islamist violence are often against other Muslims, fundamentally challenging Huntington's prediction that "fault line" conflicts between civilizations would be the major challenges of the future. It is rather fault-line conflicts *within* civilizations that seem to have produced the worst violence. Civil war, not state-state war, is the general rule in the twenty-first century.

All of this amounts to just a little throat clearing even to talk about Huntington's thesis. These are not insignificant problems for either the explanatory or predictive power of religion in his clash thesis, and the complaint that Huntington's thesis has contributed to the outsized perception of the radical Islamist threat to the West, versus the more real, urgent threat it poses to Islamic peoples and regimes, has some truth to it. Tragic as the events of New York, Paris, London, Marseilles, and the list goes on, are, they are exceptions and not the rule of the day-to-day tragedies in places like Lahore, Aceh, Mosul, Sana'a, and so on. The people who suffer the worst under the threat of radical Islamism are often other Muslims.

Huntington, in other words, has an Islam problem, and his civilization thesis has some "fault lines" of its own regarding the coherence of its political and cultural units. But does this mean his representation of religion itself is wrong, or that talking about civilizations as rooted in religious, cultural, and linguistic categories is therefore

---

7. Haynes, *Religion, Politics and International Relations*, 99.

8. See a very fine recent book from Hamid, *Islamic Exceptionalism: How the Struggle Over Islam Is Reshaping the World* for some helpful distinctions here.

incoherent or untenable? I do not think it does. In fact, I find the model itself for thinking about global politics an especially helpful one for thinking through the power of
religion in international relations, not merely as a causal factor (one of many) but as a
constitutive factor (fundamental to its structure and order). Here it is worth considering Huntington's approach in his own words.

Samuel P. Huntington was a student of the great historians, philosophers of history,
and even Christian thinkers on the nature of and meaning of this contested word "civilization." He marked out several broad distinctions that are worth recalling.

First, he said, a distinction exists between civilization "in the singular and civilization in the plural."[9] The idea of civilization, although dating as far back as the Greek
polis or Qin dynasty in China, was a French term which was meant to demarcate a border
with "barbarism." Civilization meant culture, it meant order, society, law, skilled trades,
economics, so on. In other words, there were common ordering principles which set it
apart from different ordering principles (other civilizations in the plural, the concern of
Huntington) or no ordering principles (anarchy).

Second, Huntington referred to civilizations as a "cultural entity," and both "refer
to the overall way of life of a people, and a civilization is a culture writ large."[10] This
includes things like norms, values, institutions, ways of thinking. Quoting Braudel,
Wallerstein, Dawson, Durkheim, Maus, Spengler, and more, Huntington calls up to our
attention something *like* what Charles Taylor will come to call a "social imaginary." By
social imaginary Taylor means more than just a theory or intellectual framework, he
means the whole way human beings imagine themselves, and the practices that sustain
and provide meaning to that imagination.[11] This is not unique to the modern age, although Taylor says there is something special and unique about the *modern* social imaginary.[12] Writes Taylor, "humans operated with a social imaginary well before they ever got
into the business of theorizing about themselves."[13] I call this a friendly amendment to
Huntington's list of sources on defining civilization, because I believe it gets at the more
fundamental character of what Huntington calls "culture." Indeed, he writes that of the
objective elements which define civilizations, "the most important usually is religion."[14]
To a very large degree, writes Huntington the historian, "major civilizations in human
history have been closely identified with the world's great religions." Ethnicity, language,
customs, all of these are important reinforcing factors for the work of civilization, *but*
religion, he argues, is by far the most important, often capable of overcoming barriers in
language, race, custom, and so on. This is because religion is fundamental to the kind of
world and life view that Taylor calls a "social imaginary"; it arranges the very cognitive
furniture we sit and debate upon, it is there before we even begin to theorize about it,
and it has powerful, society-shaping, world-changing assumptions built into our politics.

9. Huntington, *The Clash of Civilizations and the Remaking of World Order*, 40.

10. Huntington, *The Clash of Civilizations and the Remaking of World Order*, 41.

11. Taylor, *A Secular Age*, 156.

12. A conversation for another day, but for which I recommend Joustra and Wilkinson, *How to
Survive the Apocalypse: Zombies, Cylons, Faith, and Politics at the End of the World*.

13. Taylor, *Modern Social Imaginaries*, 26.

14. Huntington, *The Clash of Civilizations*, 42.

Inter-civilizational dialogue is difficult, if not sometimes impossible, for this very reason, as Alasdair MacIntyre argues in the legacy of his own important book, *Whose Justice? Which Rationality?*, because the very context and content of what is considered rational is sometimes not shared. This is why he argued, along with what Huntington, that "mythology, in its original sense, is at the heart of things."[15]

Third, civilizations are comprehensive; that is, its many parts cannot be understood apart from or with reference to its broader civilization. Civilization is the "broadest level of identification with which [one] strongly identifies." They are the "biggest 'we' within which we feel culturally at home as distinguished from the other 'thems' out there."[16] A question for Huntington, to which we will attend shortly, is whether such large groupings might not be of states, but rather of *people* across states: do rural, conservative Catholics in Quebec have more "civilizational" affinity to Catholics in Nigeria, or with their urban, secular Quebecois neighbors 100 miles away in Montreal, with whom they share things like political citizenship? Is it possible, for example, that the pluralism of modern nation-states has reached such a crescendo that Castell's vision of a "network society" now functions to cohere a minority "civilization" of secular-elites with more affinity between Paris, Tokyo, Dubai, and Sao Paolo, than between the residents of villages and towns just a few miles outside their metropolitan boundary? Given the results of the American election in 2017, it is more than a merely academic question whether significantly different social imaginaries (mythologies in the "original sense") may now persist in previously presumed homogenous outposts of a civilization.

Fourth, Huntington says that while civilizations are mortal they are also very long lived. This is because civilizations are not simply empires or states; they are a whole way of understanding the world, a way of life, and it takes a truly significant challenge to change or conquer that. And these changes do not usually "end" a civilization, eradicate a whole way of life overnight, but rather shift understandings and practices slowly over decades or centuries. This predicts the complaint of conservative Christians (and many non-Christians) who might argue that calling the United States, or Canada (and so on) *Christian* states is wrong, since these are in effect secular, or if they are Christian in any way they are a kind of adaptation of Christian ideals, or even what Scott Thomas calls an "apostasy of Christendom." But we do not need to agree on what *true* Christian politics are to agree largely that many of the ideals, values, and principles of Western society come by way of the Christian tradition, and that indeed we in the West live among the political legacy of that great religion. The moral and social architecture of western Christianity may be rejected, in disrepair, and so on, but it cannot be erased overnight, any more than children can "disown" their parents; even their categories of opposition are defined against their lineage.

Fifth, since civilizations are not merely cultural or political entities, they are not usually coterminous with one state or empire. A civilization, says Huntington, "may thus contain one or many political units."[17] It is here that I often wonder if Huntington

15. MacIntyre, *After Virtue*, 216.

16. Huntington, *The Clash of Civilizations*, 43.

17. Huntington, *The Clash of Civilizations*, 44.

would have been clearer if had chosen a slightly different term than "civilization." The much beloved British term "commonwealth" has an old, even Augustinian history, which does some of the heavy lifting for us conceptually that Huntington must lay out more laboriously. A commonwealth is, by definition, not only one political unit, and it is usually bound together by common culture, understandings, and—to offer the Augustinian point—*loves*. The historical example of the Byzantine Commonwealth, a favorite phrase of noted historian Dimitri Obolensky, serves us well.[18] Here we could talk about a "core state," as Huntington does, but one at the center of a commonwealth of nations, some of whom resent, challenge, and even periodically attack the Byzantine state. And yet they share this common Orthodox civilization, not always peaceably, not always coherently, but there are some *basic loves*, and therefore some common moral and political concepts, to which these plural sometimes enemy societies are pointed. That, I think, gets at what Huntington means when he talks about civilizations as many political units, and this may go some of the distance to recovering from sharp criticism his "Islamic civilization." The fight to define, redefine, and defend what is meant by a civilization, over against others within it, can be just as bloody, if not bloodier than, that same fight outside. None of this means Islamic societies cannot practice democracy, or capitalism, or liberal human rights and so on, it just means that if they do so it will tend to be for *Islamic* rather than Christian-secular rationale.

Finally, Huntington lays out his own reading of civilizations in the world today, which is probably the easiest in retrospect to criticize. I will hold my criticisms of his system of nine Civilizations because I first want to correct more fundamentally how he operationalizes religion. To this point in his argument, Huntington might be considered a student of many of his widely cited historians and historiographers, men like Christopher Dawson or Arnold Toynbee. But when it comes time to talk about what he means by religion and how he categorizes them, we end up with a rather flat perspective. He writes that "a universal religion is only slightly more likely to emerge than a universal language," and that while we have seen an "intensification of religious consciousness" this has mainly "reinforced the differences among religions."[19] His data on world religions is a capture of religious adherents showing progression in world population adhering to major religious traditions, including Western Christian, Eastern Christian, Muslim, Hindu, Buddhist, Chinese folk, Tribal, Atheist, and Nonreligious. But where did the world-historical, civilization-shaping, imagination-transforming, society-making power of religion go? Why did it suddenly get transferred into the banal categories of secular twentieth-century social science to be robbed of all its creative, civilization-making energies? If, indeed, by "religion" we come to mean something like an ordering of our loves, a basic cognitive and social orientation that makes sense of the world, a mythology (in its original sense), then these categories do not begin to touch, with the kind of sophistication that, say, *A Secular Age* does, *civilizational imaginaries*. In other words, just when we were on the cusp of a kind of architectonic critique, which would endeavour to understand systems, institutions, and societies by their affective, worshipping orientations, we quit the field for a

18. Obelensky, *The Byzantine Commonwealth: Eastern Europe, 500–1453*.

19. Huntington *The Clash of Civilizations*, 64.

mundane restatement of what secular social science categorizes as "religion." What about what Bob Goudzwaard would call the presumptive religion of the modern age, "capitalism and progress" or what Christian Smith calls "therapeutic moral Deism?" These, arguably, are as *religiously* defining of the so-called Christian West as historic Christianity is. And could not the same argument be made for Dubai, or Qatar, whose banks and legislatures are very busy accommodating capitalist logic out from under Islamic laws on finance? Could the bankers of Qatar, though Muslims, have more *religious affinity* with the Christian hedge fund managers of Wall Street than the Wahabis down the road in Riyadh? These are provoking questions, but they are meant, in a way, to push Huntington on his own logic. The problem for Huntington, I propose, is not that he is too radical in his talk about religion shaping global politics. It is that he is *not radical enough.*

And, partly for failing to extend this radicalism, Huntington also gets caught in a nationalist trap; by aligning single-coherent states within single-coherent civilizations, the problem of plural politics is immediately magnified since "multiculturalism carries an inherent danger."[20] As Huntington puts it, "multiculturalism at home threatens the United States and the West" just as "universalism abroad threatens the West and the World. Both deny the uniqueness of Western culture."[21] If Western society is a Christian society, or Indian society is a Hindu society, or Russian society is an Orthodox society, then we must be busy both excavating, recovering, and then applying those foundational religious principles. Some in India, Russia, and indeed Western societies, have been very busy doing just that, and the results have been populist nationalism which are very far from the kind of plural politics that most would wish for. In fact, by humbly offering a corrective to Huntington on an otherwise brilliant application of religion as a constitutive rather than simply causal factor, I believe the problem of pluralism itself can be resolved in a less troubling fashion. To do that, I enlist the pastor turned politician, and great theorist of political pluralism, Abraham Kuyper, and key voices from the tradition in which I think Kuyper can be reasonably situated: Christian Realism and the Early English School.[22]

Abraham Kuyper and the English School's Radical Religion and Political Pluralism

If there is one figure to whom we can retreat for a needed religious radicalism *and* political pluralism, it is surely the tireless man of religion and politics, Abraham Kuyper. Kuyper's own forays into foreign policy, as I have written at greater length elsewhere, were a nearly comedic routine of failures,[23] but he also contributed, in my opinion, at least two fundamental insights that augment and reorient Huntington's operationalization of religion in foreign affairs, and might creatively adapt his "civilizational" paradigm for present-day

20. Chaplin and Joustra, eds., *God and Global Order*, 10.

21. Huntington, *The Clash of Civilizations*, 318.

22. Or perhaps "Augustinian Realism," a term that also fits well for Dawson, Butterfield, and Kuyper. Also see Joustra, "Post-Secular Prophets."

23. Joustra, "Abraham Kuyper among the Nations."

politics.[24] These are his emphases on the inescapably *religious nature* of nations and how best to consider the problem of pluralism in international law.

At least one common denominator between Kuyper, Butterfield, Dawson, and others that Huntington appreciatively cites, is the work of Augustine. Here we can see a common presumption that the national character of a people is fundamentally derivative of their religion, what they worship, and the truer the form of that worship, the more coherent and resilient their national life. Religion, for both Kuyper and Huntington, is not a by-product of a national life, but it is rather the wellspring from which national life emerges. To even *do* foreign policy is first, then, to ask the question: what is it my neighbor loves? And how have they arranged their social and national life around the objects of their worship? This is not a purely cognitive or philosophical task of investigating histories, policies, and religious texts. It is a more *anthropological* task than that, for the *organic* nature of nations must be observed, and maybe lived, not simply intellectual dissected. True worship springs up, observed in practice, not merely preached from pulpits or delivered in national assemblies.

Like Huntington, Dawson, Kuyper, and Butterfield would have been skeptical of any national project that can be held together by purely secular ideals. Kuyper could, and did, come to terms with Islamic nations, as he did in his journeys around the Mediterranean,[25] but he would find the denial of religious character of *any kind* baffling and incoherent for a nation. It is, he might wonder, strange that nations should work so diligently to occlude the common objects of their love and worship, and dangerously shallow that religious protagonists should be discouraged from articulating their own rationale for those loves. Indeed, nothing could more assure the installation of some new authoritarian politics than to occlude debate upon its most fundamental questions about who we are, what we love, how that matters—or—to the point of pluralism, *why* we believe these things. The important point of the Kuyperian tradition of *principled pluralism* is nations or states are necessarily engaged in robust religious-political debates about what kinds of principles or loves to hold in common, while keeping open by pluralist necessity that we may *disagree* on *why* we love them commonly. To collapse any state's or even civilization's identity with one purely religious identity is to expose it to not only the worst of radical nationalism, but also anti-pluralism. This was a powerful lesson Kuyper, in his last days, took from the experience of the Great War: that baptizing any nation's foreign policy with the will of the Lord was a sure recipe for disaster. Certainly, we may say historiographically, "God uses peoples in history," as he used Rome or Babylon, or Assyria. As Kuyper wrote in *Pro Rege*:

> Therefore, when we consider Christ's kingship in its relation to the state, we must look not only to Christ's power over sovereigns and statesmen as individuals, nor only to the spirit that he causes to arise in the law, nor only to the

24. For a popular summary of this argument, see Joustra, "Globalization and the Kingdom of God," which itself is covered in more detail in Joustra, "Abraham Kuyper among the Nations." Thanks to both *Politics & Religion* and the *Public Justice Review* for allowing parts of these arguments to be reproduced here.

25. A translation of Kuyper's journeys "Around the Old-World Sea" is currently underway into English. A popular eight-part documentary series, with George Harinck, has, however, already been aired in both Dutch and English. See also Kuyper, *On Islam*.

conflicts that he raises in the nations' hearts through the political system, nor only to the influence he exercises through the colonial possessions of Christian powers and through the awakening of that international orientation. Rather, over and on top of all these things we must consider also the relationships in which the states are placed with respect to each other, and the historical outcome to which the relationships between these states, great and small, will lead. It is from Above that bonds are woven between these states. It is these bonds, which are woven, then untied, and finally rewoven into a new configuration, that produce what we call the history of the nations.[26]

But to say that a nation's identity is divinely ordained as coterminous with Christ's Kingship itself is to risk the kind of egoistic, Christian imperialism that unseats the *sovereignty of God* and exchanges it for the idol of the nation. Kuyper concludes the thought:

> His [Christ's] kingdom is not of this world. What he is now realizing is and remains the kingdom of heaven, but the history of the kingdoms of the world must be placed in the service of the coming of that kingdom, and it is our King himself who brings this about. His church is in the world, and not cut off from it. The destiny and future of his church would depend on a power foreign to him, if it were indeed the earth's kings that determined the course of history in the life of the world.[27]

Kuyper saw firsthand the clash of idolatries in the Great War, and we would do well to remember that despite his enduring passion for Calvinistic Christianity as a sure foundation for national life, the simplistic identification of one nation's life with the will of God was a great and terrible evil from which the world did not soon recover.

International law, for Kuyper, was about recognizing the constraints under which power, even great global power, operates. The laws among nations, then, may be thought of as a kind of *functional stewardship* of deeper norms, most significantly the norms of Christ and his Kingdom. Kuyper wrote in *Pro Rege*:

> It may seem like everything in history is worked by human beings alone, but in reality the entire theatre of the world is God's majestic workplace, and the rulers, counselors, and commanders who accomplish those changes are no more than instruments in his hand.[28]

This, of course, is where broadly secular theory would demur from Kuyper's political theology. For law to be law, to be not only binding but also morally coherent, Kuyper believed it must be rooted in the Christian Gospel. Can, for example, laws be made and maintained between Hindu and Muslim countries, Christian and Buddhist nations? Kuyper might have been skeptical. What for him, at the close of the Great War, was the cataclysm of *European* Christianity did not shake his confidence in the need for the Gospel as the cornerstone of political life. If anything, it retrenched his conviction that the laws among nations had broken down precisely *because* of the egoistic imperialism which had so blasphemously gripped the people of once-Christian Europe. The Europeans had prostrated

---

26. Kuyper, *Pro Rege: Living under Christ's Kingship: Volume 3*, 336.
27. Kuyper, *Pro Rege: Living under Christ's Kingship: Volume 3*, 342.
28. Kuyper, *Pro Rege: Living under Christ's Kingship: Volume 3*, 334.

themselves before idols, and the consequences of that idolatry were made manifest in the breakdown of international law and the cataclysm of war.

Kuyper then, like Dawson and Butterfield, would unswervingly confess the need to root international law in *Christian* principles and confessions, *but* in the here and now he may well have time, patience, and even some fascination with other-religious traditions articulating their own, indigenous rationales for those same principles. I think that for Kuyper there could be no *other* way of imagining international law in a plural world: for while Christians may well strive for all nations to know the Gospel, as one of those "necessary adjustments to reality" the Christian *foreign policy maker* must know that it is both impractical and naïve to wait for the new heavens and the new earth to make policy and partnership with non-Christian neighbors and nations. And, further, because of Dawson and Kuyper's strong emphasis on religion as the ground motive and life force of a civilization, I believe the work of international law, particularly in a post-secular world order, becomes as much *inter-religious dialogue* as it does politics. There is, in that sense, no set of laws between plural nations that is purely secular. All laws, per Kuyper's thought, have their root in religion. The key, then, is finding what *common* cause we may among rival root systems, while never excusing ourselves from confessing that the Calvinistic-root system is the surest and the best.[29]

One can imagine, then, a kind of Augustinian correction from the English School to Huntington's model, that narrower groupings of political communities might have more "commonwealth" affinities (read: more specific loves) which unite them, and broader civilizational groupings would have much narrower, or thinner affinities (perhaps like the Universal Declaration of Human Rights). It is about a hierarchy of loves, not all of which can be reasonably shared, but *some* of which might be, and might provide the basis for things like international law and global order. This also creates a kind of space for the sort of intra-civilization diversity I imply above, where belonging to a larger "we" does not preclude real diversity and debate *within*, some of which can and will get bloody as groups fight to define and redefine the concepts and practices of their politics and culture.

Conclusion: A Clash of Rival Apostasies?

So how would this English School intervention on the religious character of nations and the interreligious nature of international law adjust Huntington's civilizational paradigm? At least two such adjustments seem, to me, to be critical from putting Huntington in dialogue with Kuyper.

First, we must accept Huntington's more radical definition of the religious, as he covers it himself in the opening pages of *The Clash of Civilization*, as the ground from which world civilizations emerge, as a *constitutive* rather than only *causal* factor global affairs. This means that operationalizing religion to construct discrete civilizations is no simple task. Human societies and nations, like human hearts, do not have perfectly ordered

---

29. This would be a "Kuyperian" argument not foremost for utility (that is, Christianity is a kind of socio-economic catalyst), but rather primarily because it is true and that in exercising obedience to truth and the norms latent in creation, social and political benefit may follow.

interior lives, where it is simple to show in practice that what we love is exactly and in what order we say we do. If the human heart, as John Calvin would be quick to remind us, is an idol factory then international society is an idol industrial complex.

And yet, to say that Russia has an "Orthodox" imprint on its social and political imagination is also not entirely unhelpful. It is not complete, there is quite a lot of social, historical, and theological plurality that have packaged under that one rather generic label, but as a kind of approach we could do worse than to pay attention to the Orthodox religion as constitutive of the moral and social architecture of the Russian state and its sense of self. But to offer Russia the exclusive identity of Orthodox politics seems, to me, to play rather generously into the hand of the nationalist and populist sentiments of Vladimir Putin's *Russkiy Mir* and his irredentist arguments for "repossessing" Orthodox religious and cultural peoples back into their "natural" civilization. Putin even used the liberal international doctrine of the Responsibility to Protect for his annexation of Crimea from Ukraine. Could it be that Huntington's unreconstructed civilizational approach dangerously undermines religious and political minorities within a "civilization's sphere" of influence? No matter what our affinity for Huntington's thesis, we should never say that one state or even group of states has only "one" social and political heritage, if we mean to safeguard the nature of pluralist democracies. It can be expedient, useful, even insightful to study certain political-theological trajectories (as in Orthodox ones) when doing foreign policy (say in Eastern Europe), but to allow those categories to exhaust those societies puts their minorities in a very dangerous place, and enables a kind of nationalist politics that, at least the convicted Christian, should find very troubling.

What we might find, instead, is that there are majority and minority reports on careful study of political-theological traditions, some of which fade, some of which resurge, and so on. Societies are not one thing, and if we conflate latent worldviews, culture, and *religion* with the most fashionable or powerful ideologies of the day in a state, we will have missed much history, and be robbed of explaining why and how those societies change (or might change).

Operationalizing religion in this way may also shift categories of what counts as a civilization, as I suggested earlier in the essay. Could it be that modern, technocratic capitalism is as *religious* a mythology as Hinduism? Bob Goudzwaard certainly thinks so.[30] James Skillen thinks so too, arguing that:

> what Huntington missed in his analysis . . . is that driving motives of earlier state-to-state warfare and ideological crusades were not nonreligious and unrelated to the clash of civilizations. It is just that nineteenth and twentieth century warfare among states in the grip of competing nationalism, socialisms, communism, and liberalism represented clashes within Western civilizations, *clashes that were as deeply religious as anything we are witnessing today.*[31]

And if this is the case then might not a "world civilization" (so religiously defined) be cropping up from under our noses defined, for one of the first times, not along historic

30. Goudzwaard, *Capitalism and Progress.*

31. Emphasis added. Skillen, *With or Against the World,* 16. See also Koyzis, "Westernization or Clash of Civilizations?"

geographical boundaries, but along highly networked, high financed, highly travelled urban corridors? This is also Scott Thomas' argument, that:

> There *is* a clash of civilizations, but it is not between Islam and the West. The real clash is between what Alasdair MacIntyre calls tradition-based modes of rationality and visions of the common good and those modes and visions based on the Enlightenment project. If so, then the real clash is between, on the one hand, orthodox Islam and Christianity, and, on the other, all modern forms of fundamentalism, whether they are faith based or secularist. . . . The clash of civilizations is really a sibling rivalry since the apostate West and radical global Islamism spring from a similar source of apostasy: post-Enlightenment modernity.[32]

Less sensationally, perhaps, we could talk, as Jonathan Fox does, of the increasing (and increasingly violent) "Secular-Religious Competition" in global affairs.[33] What we would be left with, then, is an even stronger case for so-called civilizational diversity *within* contemporary states, *within* Huntington's blocks of civilizations as he described them. The problem of cohesion is real, as Huntington himself rightly intuited, but the answer lies probably not in a false and troubling coercive claim to religious, linguistic, and cultural homogeneity within states, but rather in a clearer, bolder, and—yes—even more plural religious expression about the *principles* or *loves* around which these states revolve.

Second, as I have already implied above, we must make some adjustments for pluralism both in the form of "inter-civilizational" dialogue abroad and freedom of religion or belief as fundamental to the character of just societies at home. This makes religion more, not less, important in global and domestic affairs, putting it at the forefront of efforts not only to build consensus around issues of significant global concern[34] but also to provide the heavy moral vocabulary[35] around which common action, if not common conviction, can take place. And this is exactly what we would expect to need and find if religion was a constitutive rather than merely causal factor in international relations. That insight remains, in my opinion, one of the most fundamental approaches that Huntington offers. We would not want to adopt his categories wholesale, and we might want to quibble (more than a little) with his uneasy demarcations of states and civilizations with one whole political-theological tradition, but amended and nuanced, his core insight into the challenges that face twenty-first-century politics, and the categories and vocabularies we will use to face them, are as helpful today as they were when he first put pen to paper in 1993.

---

32. Thomas, "The Clash of Rival Apostasies amidst the Global Resurgence of Religion" 202–3.

33. Fox, *Political Secularism, Religion, and the State.*

34. See in a special issue, Barbato and Joustra, eds., "Popes on the Rise: The Modern Papacy in World Affairs."

35. Philpott, *Just and Unjust Peace.*

3–12

"Blessed are the Peacemakers"

Marc LiVecche[1]

THE BIBLICAL CONCEPT OF peace is hardly touched when defined simply as the absence of external conflict or war, or the simple presence of inner tranquility. The operative word in Hebrew is *shalom,* which traces its roots to several Semitic languages. At its core, *shalom* designates a state of wholeness, harmony, and completeness—it points to the way things *ought* to be.

The prophets used *shalom* to convey the blessings for God's people associated with the coming of the Messiah. Grounded in the presence of justice and order, conditions required for human flourishing, biblical peace is comprehensive welfare extending in every direction. Following the prophets, Thomas Aquinas understood that peace cannot be present where there is no justice (Isa 5:9). Peace, then, is not a virtue, per se; it is the fruit of virtue (Isa 48:18).

The Septuagint—the Greek translation of the Bible—renders *shalom* as *eirene.* One Dominical mandate for Christ followers, therefore, is to be irenic—to be aimed at peace. Christians are called to be peacemakers.

This does not always mean what we think it means. Consider the pacifist preference for the red-letter bits of scripture including, above all else, the Sermon on the Mount (Matt 5). Many pacifists will agree that of all the Beatitudes of Jesus, the call to be peacemakers has a unique muscularity. Whereas the others point to an attitude to be cultivated, the call to be peacemakers demands a particularly concrete action. The Christian realist can agree with this. But that is where agreement ends.

The Christian understanding of peace has largely withered. Overly spiritualized, peace too often is predominately identified as an inner feeling of serenity and, externally, of conflict avoidance—or, at least, of that kind of conflict that requires confrontation, coercion, or force. The muscularity of the injunction *to be* a peacemaker has atrophied. Rendered maudlin, peacemaking is sanitized of anything deemed morally uncomfortable, including the necessity of the peacemaker to stand in judgment.

This is a far cry from the Sermon on the Mount. Peacemakers, remember, look a lot like God. "Blessed are the peacemakers," Jesus proclaims, "for they will be called sons

---

1. This article appeared in *Providence Magazine* on March 28, 2018 at https://providencemag.com/2018/03/blessed-peacemakers-sermon-mount-just-war/.

of God." Presented as a cumulative character description, the constituent elements of the Beatitudes—the poor in spirit, the meek, those who mourn, those who hunger and thirst for righteous, the merciful, the pure in heart, and the peacemakers—roll together, each gathering one into the others, until they form a comprehensive aggregate able to be recognized as "a son of God." This is really saying something.

In Semitic thought, "sonship" is used figuratively to signify the idea that a person shares the qualities—the nature—of the fatherly figure specified. So, when exploring what it means to be a peacemaker, the first question to ask is what kind of peacemaker is God? Doing so reveals that, at the very least, peacemakers are those willing to confront hard issues with integrity in order to end hostilities and to allow the conditions required to bring the contending adversaries back together.

As God's career in this regard makes plain, the establishment of right relationships between fallen people—and between fallen people and their God—is never easy. The biblical scholar Frederick Dale Bruner alerts us to the nature of peacemaking:

> Struggle, confrontation, and partisan engagement . . . we bring peace today when we enlist people in warfare against evil struggles. . . . The circle of right relations that is peace will often, in a crooked world, be relations that pass through struggle and confrontation.

Similarly, Reinhold Niebuhr, writing just after the horrors of WWII, chided those Christians who had shrunk from the hard duty—the struggle and confrontation—of opposing Nazi and Japanese tyranny with military force. The peace of God, he insisted, must never be equated with the peace of detachment. In this, at least, Niebuhr was following in the line of Augustine, who understood war to be sometimes tragically necessary for the recovery and continued maintenance of a peace durable enough to hold firm against the conditions of the world. It pays to remember, as Jean Elshtain often asserted, that Augustine was talking about the peace of the *Pax Romana*. This compelled or ordered peace was, however, unjust in the full light of eschatological *shalom*, nevertheless very real and very significant. More than any competitor then on the market, the Roman *pax* was capable of keeping neighbor from eating neighbor, and of preserving the interconnected web of culture, civilization, art, and tradition that, by Augustine's day, was well in jeopardy. The approximate good of ordered peace is most often better than unadulterated anarchy.

Much better still is Augustine's notion of *tranquilitas ordinis*—the tranquility, or peace, of order. Such peace is not externally compelled but rather internally prompted by love of God and neighbor. This peace, Augustine writes in *The City of God*, is born of a commitment that "one will be at peace, as far as lies in him, with all men." The basis of this commitment is "the observance of two rules: first, do no harm to anyone, and, secondly, to help everyone whenever possible." This will not result, Elshtain cautioned, in "the perfect peace promised to believers in the Kingdom of God, the one in which the lion lies down with the lamb." Against this vain hope Elshtain frequently reminded us that "on this earth, if the lion lies down with the lamb, the lamb must be replaced frequently."

Nevertheless, Elshtain saw this pursuit of a *tranquilitas ordinis* running in a bright line from Augustine to the US Constitution and beyond. The establishment of measures to ensure security and public safety promoted "domestic tranquility" as central to what the new order being created after the American Revolution was all about. Peace was to be the product of order and justice, without which no other political goods could long perdure. What political goods did she have in mind? As she noted in *Just War Against Terror,* simply the quotidian ones:

> Mothers and fathers raising their children; men and women going to work; citizens of a great city making their way on streets and subways; ordinary people flying to California to visit their grandchildren or to transact business with colleagues—all of these actions are simple but profound gods made possible by civic peace. They include the faithful attending their churches, synagogues, and mosques without fear, and citizens—men and women, young and old, black, brown, and white—lining up to vote on Election Day.

In such a vision, the Beatitudes and founding principles enter the same conceptual orbit. The term "blessing" in Christ's sermon requires some excavating. In the Vulgate, the Latin term for "blessed" can be translated "happiness." But this does not point to a subjective feeling, but rather an objective fact. Just so, the Founder's declaration that all people are endowed by our Creator with the right to the "pursuit of happiness" points to something similar. The Founders aren't pledging their lives and sacred honor to the right of Americans to enjoy a gassy kind of happiness that can be attained in this, that, or any old way. "Happiness" has a peripatetic connotation—it points to the enjoyment of those conditions that allow human beings—made in the image of God—to enjoy eudaimonia; that is, to flourish. Eudaimonia requires a specific eco-system built for both body and soul. So, Jesus and Jefferson want us to be happy, but both are pointing to an objective reality, not merely a subjective feeling. Wonderful is the life or occasion in which both the objective and subjective align. But, as an earlier Beatitude assures us, even those who mourn can be happy.

Glossing on what can be gleaned from the Beatitudes, there are obvious attitudinal characteristics of the peacemaker that can be drawn from Augustine. Looking at his letter to Boniface, the military commander of the Roman army in North Africa, we see Augustine cautioning the commander to "cherish the spirit of the peacemaker." Augustine exhorts him to recognize that it is necessity, and not one's own will, which prompts the conscientious warrior to "slay the enemy" who fights against him. Force is always only the form love takes against sufficiently grave evil when in the last resort nothing else will protect the innocent, restore justice, and bring about the conditions for peace. The old Chestertonian nugget obtains: "The true soldier fights not because he hates what is in front of him, but because he loves what is behind him."

Moreover, the peacemaker, when compelled to fight, doesn't do so in the negation of peace, but rather with the end of peace foremost in mind as the chiefly desired object. While fighting with the aim of peace promotes awareness that there are certain ways of fighting that better allow for the possibility of presently warring peoples to come together in concord at the cessation of belligerence, it does not negate the belligerence. Responsible sovereigns—the authority over whom there is no one greater charged with the care of the political community—might sometimes determine that nothing else will retribute evil, take back what has wrongly been taken, or protect the innocent. Nor does it mean that belligerence won't be terribly violent.

Gen. Douglas MacArthur understood this. When he announced his retirement in 1951 to a Joint Session of Congress, he declared that he considered himself simply "an old soldier who has tried to do his duty as God gave him the light to see that duty." That duty, he understood, was "to destroy" in order "to build up." Nowhere was such a sense of duty more on display than in the Pacific. The war with the Japanese was a bloodletting best characterized by its staggering brutality. After Pearl Harbor, Bataan, Guadalcanal, Iwo Jima, Okinawa, Hiroshima, and Nagasaki, the peace that now exists between America and Japan is almost miraculous.

MacArthur had no doubt of the task that followed the Japanese surrender. He knew that despite the government finally agreeing to stand down, there was no guarantee that the proud soldiers, sailors, airmen, and civilians of Japan would not match their pride with defiance and insurgency. Surrender, the cessation of open conflict, did not yet mean peace. But MacArthur understood that the Allied treatment of Emperor Hirohito, the divine authority for the Japanese, would have a tremendous influence on the prospects of real peace and reconciliation. He warned against the impulse of some among the Allies who wanted to prosecute the emperor for war crimes. MacArthur won out. He left Hirohito in his imperial position—if with only a modicum more than symbolic power—and utilized the emperor to ensure continuity of control and authority over the Japanese people, both military and civilian. MacArthur's demonstration of respect for core Japanese values and his understanding of the benefits of forgiveness and appropriate absolution allowed the once-warring nations to move on—and to face the new communist threats arrayed against their mutual interests.

This is the same MacArthur who always argued for a strong US military, a robust forward presence, a credible nuclear arsenal, and the martial resolve to convince adversaries of our willingness to fight to protect our interests. This is what peacemaking looks like. Warfighting can be a divine vocation.

Of course, just as the peacemaker is not to avoid the obligation to use force when the obligation confronts him, neither is he to eagerly employ it. Christians are not to use the inevitability of tension within the world as an excuse to seek, encourage, or unnecessarily stoke conflict. When either non-violence or violence will properly retribute a gross injustice, vindicate victims, or protect the innocent, the Christian will choose non-violence. Nor will a peacemaker ever inaugurate new violence. But it remains that there is often no choice to be made between violence or non-violence. Sometimes our enemies have already made violence a fact, and nothing but fighting will stop them. Paul's injunction, "In so far as it depends on you, be at peace with all men," is a commitment to force as last resort. We are to do whatever we legitimately can to make peace with our enemies, including praying that God would bless them and work in their conscience to stand down. More than this, we are to take those early and positive steps to do good in the world, alleviating, where we are able, cause for animosity. Nevertheless, there are, indeed, no sure ways to soften hard hearts, and the practice of peace has restrictions.

Peace at the price of truth is not asked for. The Christian, because he is a Christian, cannot do such things. "As far as it depends on you" is not just a goad toward peace, but also a limit: you, given who you are, redeemed by Christ and created to carry the image of God, are called to preserve peace. But you, given who you are, have no call—nor right—to trump the veto of those who refuse to reciprocate your peaceful endeavors. Our enemies have a vote whether peace will prevail.

For Augustine, the impossibility of peace was a tragedy. He lamented: "A just war is justified only by the injustice of an aggressor, and that injustice ought to be a source of grief to any good man, because it is a human injustice." Given the heavy nature of this task, the demeanor of the Christian soldier was paramount; Augustine insisted that "no one is fit for inflicting this punishment except the man who, by the greatness of his love, has overcome that hatred wherewith those are wont to be inflamed who wish only to avenge themselves."

For Aquinas, standing in the Augustinian stream, the goal of conflict was clear. "[B]e peaceful, therefore, in warring," he said, "so that you may vanquish those whom you war against and bring them into the prosperity of peace."

And then let us be happy together.

3–13

"A Robust Nuclear Deterrent: A Force for Peace and Justice"

REBECCAH L. HEINRICHS[1]

OVER THE PAST SEVERAL decades, the number of Christian churches that support the goal of global denuclearization and oppose U.S. nuclear policies has grown considerably. The World Council of Churches, which includes more than 300 evangelical and Protestant churches, has urged global disarmament, although the member churches have varying positions on what that means practically. The more theologically liberal churches like the Methodists and Episcopalians oppose the very possession of nuclear weapons, even for deterrence purposes. It is more common for Christian churches concerned about nuclear weapons to hold positions similar to that of the Roman Catholic Church, which opposes the use of nuclear weapons, urges eventual global disarmament, but allows for nuclear weapons to exist for the purpose of deterrence based on the "balance" model of strategic stability. Pope Francis, however, has made denuclearization one of his personal top priorities. Archbishop Benedito Auza, the Holy See's Ambassador to the UN, recently explained, "Today there is no more argument, not even the argument of deterrence used during the Cold War, that could 'minimally morally justify' the possession of nuclear weapons. The 'peace of a sort' that is supposed to justify nuclear deterrence is specious and illusory."[2]

To the contrary, to support moving toward a small arsenal of nuclear weapons is to necessarily embrace the immoral and highly unstable policy of Minimum Deterrence and its corollary policy of Mutually Assured Destruction. Not only is the United States morally justified to possess nuclear weapons and to credibly threaten their employment, it would be *immoral* and inimical to the principles of Christian just war theory for the U.S. government to adopt the disarmament agenda.

First, it is important to keep in mind the explicit purpose of government as instituted by God. The Scriptures show that God's purpose for government is to commend what is good and punish what is evil. In other words, it is to seek justice and, thereby,

---

1. Rebeccah Heinrichs, "A Robust Nuclear Deterrent: A Force for Peace & Justice" first appeared in *Providence Magazine*, August 15, 2016.

2. Dias, "Pope Francis's Latest Mission: Stopping Nuclear Weapons."

protect the innocent. God has given government the prerogative to use lethal force in its path of obedience.[3] Christian just war theory remains the guide for how Christians have traditionally thought about how and when the government can wield the sword in the way God intended. Just war theory allows for the use of force as long as it meets the criteria for justly entering into war (*jus ad bellum*) and the criteria for justly waging the war (*jus in bello*).

Antinuclear Christians often argue that the employment of nuclear weapons necessarily violates at least two principles that disqualify the just use of nuclear weapons— discrimination and proportionality. The use of force must discriminate combatants from noncombatants and, furthermore, take into consideration what is being destroyed for the sake of what is being protected.[4] However, it is possible, and in fact necessary, to uphold those principles and maintain a preeminent nuclear force. Unfortunately—and dangerously—ideological opposition to nuclear weapons often precludes a reasoned discussion on the matter.

Minimum Deterrence Based on Ideological Opposition to Nukes Rather than Desire To Protect Innocent

The antinuclear agenda is based on the premise that nuclear weapons are inherently evil, that their use is never ethically justified, and that their very existence is dangerous; therefore, antinuclear idealists argue that lowering the number of nuclear weapons worldwide, regardless of where they are located, is a noble objective and increases the prospects for peace.

But nuclear weapons possess no moral agency. The regime leaders in possession or in pursuit of them do. The purpose of U.S. nuclear weapons is, and ought to remain, to deter catastrophic war and preserve relative peace and stability. Ultimately, they are to protect innocents. Nuclear weapons have served as the bedrock of U.S. deterrence since the nuclear attacks that brought WWII to a close. There are now nine countries in possession of nuclear weapons.[5] And missiles, the delivery systems for mass casualty warheads, continue to rapidly increase in quantity and sophistication. In contemplating the best policy for U.S. nuclear deterrence and the appropriate force structure, the stakes have never been higher. Rather than beginning with the assumption that nuclear weapons are evil—regardless of the kind or consideration of the nature of the regime that possess them—one should begin with asking the question: how can the United States government, in fulfilling its highest responsibility as instituted by God, most effectively protect innocents from the threat of the most catastrophic kinds of war?

Instead of asking this most basic question, antinuclear idealists jump right to denuclearization, and therefore advocate for what is called a Minimum Deterrence policy. This policy is based on the belief that the United States ought to move towards zero

3. See, for example, 1 Pet 2:14 and Rom 13:1–7.

4. Payne and Coleman, "Christian Nuclear Pacifism and Just War Theory: Are They Compatible?"

5. There are also at least forty-four nuclear capable states, which are listed in Annex 2 of the misguided, and fully ratified, Comprehensive Nuclear-Test-Ban Treaty.

nuclear weapons and can right now safely cut current deterrent capabilities to significantly lower numbers, perhaps even as low as 100 nuclear warheads. In 2009 President Barrack Obama, while admitting that a world without nuclear weapons would not happen in his lifetime, stated his intention to lead the initiative to move the world toward zero nuclear weapons. Part of his agenda would entail cutting the U.S. force, which he successfully went on to do when he secured the New START Treaty with the Russian Federation. According to the Obama Administration,[6] the treaty stipulates that the United States and Russia will cap their accountable deployed strategic nuclear warheads at 1,550 and deployed delivery vehicles at 700, a 74 percent reduction in the allowed limits of the 1991 START Treaty and a 30 percent reduction in the allowed number of real deployed strategic warheads under the 2002 Strategic Offensive Reductions Treaty (the Moscow Treaty).[7] Only months after the treaty went into effect, and without so much as offering up a single study that might support the assumptions, the President flippantly remarked that the U.S. has "more nuclear weapons than we need,"[8] signaling that he intended another round of cuts in the near future.

But, with the resurgence of an expansionist Russia, the President's diplomatic team, however sympathetic to the antinuclear idealists, concluded it could not continue cutting U.S. deterrent capabilities without taking on unacceptable levels of risk. To put a finer point on this, the reality of the threat and the behavior of other regime leaders forced the Obama Administration to halt its efforts to further implement a Minimum Deterrence policy. This abrupt change in policy lays bare one of the fundamental flaws of the Minimum Deterrence policy they advocate.

Antinuclear idealists claim that simply lowering the number of nuclear weapons increases security and, critically, that other countries will be persuaded to devalue nuclear weapons if the United States does. In fact, as the United States has gone to lower numbers of nuclear weapons, has self-imposed testing limitations, and placed a unilateral prohibition on developing new nuclear capabilities, nuclear proliferation has exploded across the globe. More countries have determined that possessing nuclear weapons serves their own national security needs. One has only to look to North Korea, China, and Iran for evidence. But since many proponents of Minimum Deterrence dismiss the possibility of a nuclear war with Russia,[9] it is particularly useful to look more closely at Russia's recent nuclear-related activities.

Russia has moved nuclear weapons to the center of its military strategy. While the United States continues to punt on overdue nuclear modernization efforts, the Russians are in the middle of an ongoing and massive modernization campaign. Moreover, the Russians do not place limits on their own capabilities. For example, while the United

6. There are loopholes in the treaty, that make some of the Obama administration's assessments of the treaty's limits unrealistic. For more on this, please see Payne and Scheber, "The Threat of New START."

7. Baker and Heinrichs, "Deterrence and Nuclear Targeting in the 21st Century."

8. Remarks by President Barrack Obama at Hankuk University, Seoul, Republic of Korea, March 26, 2012.

9. For one such example of the tendency of antinuclear idealists dismissing the plausibility of conflict with Russia, please see the Global Zero U.S. Nuclear Policy Commission Report, "Modernizing the U.S. Nuclear Strategy, Posture, and Force Structure," May 2012.

States does not place multiple independently targetable reentry vehicles (MIRVs) on its Intercontinental Ballistic Missiles (ICBMs) because they fear they would be provocative, Russians aggressively utilizes them.

What is perhaps most concerning is that the Russians have changed their nuclear doctrine in recent years. In Congressional testimony, while serving as the Vice Chairman of the Joint Chiefs of Staff, Admiral Winnefeld, explained that Russian military doctrine supports the employment of nuclear weapons in order to *de-escalate* a non-nuclear conflict. As the admiral explained, NATO can overwhelm Russia in conventional weaponry, but nuclear weapons have a psychological effect in addition to a technical one, and this can change calculations. NATO's understandably strong aversion to even threaten the employment of nuclear weapons gives Russia leverage. Russia has no qualms about exploiting the especially acute fear of nuclear conflict held by Western countries to further its national objectives. Should Russia employ a nuclear weapon, most likely a low-yield battlefield nuclear weapon,[10] against a NATO country with the intent to de-escalate what Russia claims is aggression, that NATO country would no doubt invoke Article V of the NATO Treaty, and the United States with its allies would be required to respond. It doesn't take much of an imagination to see how Russia's miscalculation could lead to a nuclear exchange that may, horrifically, escalate from there.

It is clear that nuclear weapons will continue to influence global affairs as long as national leaders desire to shape events to meet their own perceived interests. Thus, the United States must continuously invest the intellectual capital to determine how best to deter and defend against nuclear conflict.

The great paradox of deterring mass casualty warfare including nuclear conflict is that it requires the United States to make unmistakably clear that it is willing to employ nuclear weapons to preserve the lives of its citizens and those of its allies. As such, it makes no sense for a state to possess nuclear weapons that it claims it will never employ. Conversely, it makes no sense for the United States to threaten retaliation with nuclear weapons when the kind of force it possesses is such that in reality it would never employ it. Enemies of the United States should be made to conclude that aggressing on the United States or its primary interests could actually invite a U.S. nuclear response, and any perceived gains are not worth the cost. But, in order for an enemy to make this calculation, the U.S. nuclear threat must be credible.

Minimum Deterrence and Mad at the Heart of Antinuclear Agenda

The case for a credible and therefore effective U.S. nuclear deterrent is where we find the strong moral case for building and maintaining a robust, flexible, and resilient nuclear force. As previously stated, Christian antinuclear idealists, adopting the arguments of the secular pacifists, wrongly assume that nuclear war necessarily means the indiscriminate targeting of thousands of civilians. This is simply false.

10. For more on the plausibility of Russian employment of tactical nuclear weapons, please see Dr. Matthew Kroenig, testimony before the Senate Armed Services Committee, February 25, 2015 and Heinrichs, "NATO's Nuclear Nightmare Over Ukraine."

One of the reasons many Christian antinuclear idealists continue to wrongly believe that the existence of nuclear weapons necessarily means the nuclear targeting of civilians is because this was once a common way secular strategists discussed deterrence. For example, during the early 1960s, Jerome Wiesner, science adviser to President John F. Kennedy and President Lyndon B. Johnson, testified before Congress that the U.S. could establish deterrence based on a threat to destroy six of the ten largest Soviet cities. This kind of deterrence policy, relying on what is called in nuclear parlance "countervalue targeting," only requires a small arsenal of nuclear weapons because cities are large targets and easy to hit with only a few warheads and delivery systems. It is the only deterrence policy that requires a small number of nuclear weapons.

But, under no circumstances should the United States target civilian populations. Targeting civilians violates the fundamental principles that define the character of the United States of America and fails to meet the just war criteria *jus in bello*. Moreover, even from the perspective of cold realism, claiming to target civilian populations and maintaining a force structure designed to do this would likely not serve American interests, for some enemy leaders do not value the lives of their civilian populations the way that the United States does. In fact, it is reasonable to assert that American policymakers value the lives of enemy countries' civilians more than their dictators do.

But antinuclear idealists, in seeking a Minimum Deterrence policy, advocate moving towards a small force, for placing restrictions on the kinds of nuclear weapons the United States can build and deploy, prohibit testing, and oppose nuclear modernization. This inflexible, and less accurate, limited force cannot optimally hold the spectrum of enemy military and regime facilities at risk, nor can it guarantee minimal collateral damage. Indeed, according to Dr. Keith Payne, "Strategic systems of the 1960s and 1970s tended to combine relatively high yields and low accuracy that reduced the prospects for discriminate nuclear employment."[11] Continued improvement since the 70s has increased the accuracy of the delivery systems and decreased the yield of the warhead. Continued modernization with the freedom to test and develop new capabilities will improve the ability of the United States to make them more controllable, more accurate, and able to minimize collateral damage. A Minimum Deterrence policy cannot minimize collateral damage, and is best suited for a countervalue targeting strategy.

Minimum Deterrence fails to meet the criteria for just war theory on another front. It requires the U.S. government to leave American cities vulnerable to nuclear attack. During the Cold War, this doctrine, Mutually Assured Destruction (MAD), held that the Soviet Union and the United States would be deterred from launching a nuclear weapon out of fear of retaliation. If either country built defenses to protect their population, those antinuclear idealists argued that the other country would be provoked to build up its offensive arsenal, thereby precipitating an unstable environment and arms race.

By the 1980s the United States had shifted to a counterforce targeting policy, meaning it would no longer target civilian populations and would instead target military assets, including nuclear forces. This could only remain true as long as the U.S. nuclear force remained large enough and diverse enough to hold the enemies' military assets

---

11. Payne and Coleman, "Christian Nuclear Pacifism and Just War Theory: Are They Compatible?"

at risk. But even after this shift to a counterforce targeting policy, nuclear deterrence policy had not yet totally moved away from the doctrine of MAD. U.S. officials made clear in public statements that American cities would intentionally remain undefended from missile attack. This kept in place the imaginary, mechanistic "strategic balance" or "balance of terror." Illustrating this principle, Secretary of State Henry Kissinger, arguing in favor of the 1972 Anti-Ballistic Missile (ABM) Treaty, which codified that neither the U.S. nor the Soviet Union would build effective missile defenses, noted that it gives missiles "a free ride" to their intended targets.[12]

A Nuclear Posture Consistent with and Required by Just War Doctrine

The United States should finally and fully adopt a strategic posture that provides optimal protection of the American people, beginning with the goal of deterring war and maintaining peace. It should reject the immoral balance of terror policies proffered by the secular antinuclear idealists and adopted by many Christian churches. The George W. Bush Administration rightly moved further away from this anti-just war, balance-of-terror formulation when he withdrew the United States from the ABM Treaty in 2002 in the wake the September 11th attacks. President Bush then set out to adapt the U.S. strategic posture to take advantage of the full spectrum of available weapons, including non-nuclear offensive weapons, nuclear weapons with a variety of delivery systems and a spectrum of nuclear yields, and purely defensive weapons with the ability to intercept missiles of all ranges in all phases of flight to provide the strongest possible defense of the American people should deterrence fail.

Since then, the United States has developed and deployed a layered ballistic missile defense system comprised of sensors and missile interceptor systems based on land and at sea. Still, U.S. policy unofficially endorses a missile defense policy that seeks to only defend against the "limited" threats posed by rogue states like North Korea and Iran, and intentionally leaves U.S. cities and bases vulnerable to Russian and Chinese missile attack, out of a misguided belief that to fully defend against Russian and Chinese attack might provoke those countries to build up their offensive systems. First, this is still the immoral policy of MAD. Moreover, as discussed, Russia is moving forward with a massive nuclear modernization effort, regardless of U.S. missile defense systems, and as almost daily press reports show, Russia continues threatening the U.S. and our allies without provocation.

And, while the United States takes great care in not defending against Russian missiles, Russia has been modernizing its missile defense system to defend against a potential attack from the United States. In a January 15, 2014 letter to then Chairman of the Armed Services Committee, Howard "Buck" McKeon, and the Chairman of the Joint Chiefs of Staff, General Martin Dempsey, said that "Russia's objective with its ballistic missile defense (BMD) capabilities is to ensure defense of critical political and military targets in the Moscow area from a ballistic missile attack, either by the United States or any other nation with nuclear or conventional ballistic or cruise missile capabilities."

12. Please see Dr. Keith Payne, "U.S. Strategic Arms Control Objections," Testimony before the U.S. Senate Foreign Relations Committee, May 5, 1999.

And, in a document provided to Congress, Under Secretary Frank Kendall III warned that China is "developing and testing several new classes and variants of offensive missiles, forming additional missile units, upgrading older missile systems, and developing methods to counter ballistic missile defenses." Mr. Kendall also described China's development and successful testing of anti-satellite capabilities and said "PLA [People's Liberation Army] writings emphasize the necessity of 'destroying, damaging, and interfering with the enemy's reconnaissance and communications satellites,' suggesting that such systems, as well as navigation and early warning satellites, could be among the targets of attacks designed to 'blind and deafen the enemy.'"

A moral and truly effective strategic posture must include a robust missile defense system that provides the best defense of innocent Americans as technically possible. Such a missile defense system would complement U.S. offensive weapons.

The U.S. strategic posture must also include a nuclear policy that is in keeping with the character of the United States, which is also consistent with just war theory. Therefore, there should be a counterforce targeting strategy, intentionally seeking to minimize collateral damage. As previously discussed, counterforce requires that the United States have the ability to hold at risk what the enemy values. These specific targets will vary with each enemy state, but in general, they are the facilities and objects that maintain the regimes and their means of holding power and oppression. They will certainly include the deeply buried and hardened military facilities in Russia, North Korea, Iran, and China, for example.

The U.S. nuclear deterrent force must have the ability to hold at risk all of current enemies and potential enemies' crucial facilities and arsenals central to their regimes and military, taking into account the possibility of enemy alliances as well. It must also have the ability to adapt to the changing global landscape. It should never constrain future American Presidents' options by limiting the system based on today's global threat environment or the hopes of a less complex and more peaceful future global environment. History and human nature instruct us that we should, in fact, expect and prepare for the opposite. Therefore, the United States should not move to levels below the limits codified in the New START Treaty. Moreover, the United States should fully modernize the aging nuclear force, including all three legs of the nuclear triad (bombers, ICBMs, and submarines), and reserve the right to develop new nuclear weapons if the threats require it. It should also refuse to ratify the Comprehensive Nuclear-Test Ban Treaty, which would preclude the United States from resuming explosive nuclear testing. In order to maintain a credible and reliable force, leaders at the U.S. national labs may one day advise testing once again.

In closing, nuclear weapons are the backbone of the U.S. strategic posture, even if they are only one component. As instructed by the latest Nuclear Posture Review Report, nuclear weapons should be complemented by a mix of conventional weapons and missile defense systems.[13] But the United States must first firmly reject the arguments

13. Some antinuclear idealists argue that a conventional strike weapon can technically do what a nuclear weapon can do and, therefore, can substitute nuclear weapons. This is false for several reasons. First, nuclear weapons have a psychological component to them that gives them a different quality even apart from technical capability. Second, nuclear assurance, that is, the promise to retaliate on

of antinuclear idealists, including those who wrongly do so in the name of just war theory. Christian teaching requires the U.S. government to exact justice and to protect the innocent, and it can best do this with a credible nuclear posture. A credible nuclear posture requires that it is compatible with Christian ethics, and therefore cannot target an enemy state's civilians, nor can it intentionally leave American citizens exposed to nuclear attack. Therefore, Christian churches and U.S. defense planners have no choice but to reject the policies of Mutually Assured Destruction and Minimum Deterrence, and to embrace a strategic posture that includes a robust missile defense system and an adaptable, resilient, and robust nuclear deterrent.

---

behalf of an ally under the nuclear umbrella, must take into consideration what is necessary to assure allies. Allies have expressed that only a nuclear response would satisfy the necessary conditions for assurance. Last, in order to penetrate the most hardened targets, nuclear weapons are still technically required. Or, as Greg Weaver, the deputy director for plans and policy for U.S. Strategic Command stated at a February symposium in 2012, "You can't replace nuclear weapons today with conventional capability. . . . They don't have the same effects on targets, but as a result they don't have the same effects on people's decision calculus."

3–14

"The Responsibility of Nations: A Moral Case for Coercive Justice"

Jean Bethke Elshtain[1]

DEBATES ABOUT INTERNATIONAL JUSTICE typically range over the well traversed terrain of distribution and redistribution. From Dame Barbara Ward's *Rich Nations, Poor Nations* published in the early 1960s, to calls during the Jubilee year of 2000 for forgiveness of the Third World debt, justice has been conceived of in economic terms, in terms of righting the balance between the world's wealthy and impoverished.

I am not going to revisit this question, in part because I believe a more exigent matter lies today before the international community: namely, the need to bring about the political stability—the minimal civic peace—requisite to attain and secure fundamental human goods, including a measure of distributive justice. Absent political stability, every attempt to prop up impoverished countries must fail; justice demands accountability and there is no political accountability where there is no structure of power and laws. Without such a structure, the likelihood of what we now routinely call "humanitarian catastrophes" is magnified many-fold.

Emblematic of the ills attendant upon political instability is the disaster of so-called failed states, in which human beings are prey to the ruthless and the irresponsible. Although the raison d'être of states ought to be maintaining stability and civic peace, many become disturbers of that peace, even agents of injustice. What follows is an argument for meeting one essential precondition of international justice: securing political stability, if necessary by the use of outside force. Such efforts are today often understood in terms of international peacekeeping and "humanitarian intervention." We would be better off, I think, if we understood these efforts in terms drawn from the Christian tradition of thinking about when and where coercive armed intervention is justified in order to protect innocent victims of political instability.

One thing is clear: in recent years, stopping brutality and arbitrary violence—including the growth of terrorism and what Michael Ignatieff has dubbed "apocalyptic nihilism"—has become both a strategic necessity and a moral requirement of the highest priority. In

---

1. This article originally appeared in *Daedalus* 132, no. 1 *On International Justice* (2003).

too many nations—one thinks of Rwanda and Bosnia—political chaos, often instigated by ruthless ideologues or feckless profiteers, has claimed thousands of lives.[2]

Without political stability, justice is an empty ideal. In Ignatieff's words, "freedom becomes an issue only after order has been established." My argument for using outside force, if necessary, to protect innocent victims is complex, and not without complications. And what I am calling for is bound to be controversial—namely, the use of force as a remedy under a justice claim based on equal regard for inviolable human dignity. As a claim applying to all peoples without distinction, this principle is by no means universally affirmed.

But I believe that a principle of equal regard, based on the right to make a claim for armed intervention rather than simply for humanitarian assistance, establishes a framework for the achievement of a decent, stable international order as the necessary prelude to both freedom and distributive justice. And I also believe that there are times when a principle of equal regard will override the reluctance to take up arms. The upshot is a presumptive case in favor of the use of armed force by a powerful state or alliance of states that has the means to intervene, interdict, and punish on behalf of those under assault.

If you are a political theorist, as I am, your starting point is almost invariably the ancient Greeks and, more particularly, the life of the citizen in the Athenian polis. But what happens when you explore the contrast between the rules that applied to citizens within the polis to the justice norms and practices that governed their dealings with foreigners? As it turns out, justice lies at the heart of the matter. Athenians, like most other Greeks, made a sharp distinction between internal and external affairs: justice obtained among citizens within the polis, while force governed relations with others. Accordingly, what would be counted a wrong against a citizen was not necessarily so counted if another polis, or a foreigner, was the victim of it. Perhaps the most shocking example of how this distinction was applied in practice is the so-called Melian dialogue, familiar to readers of Thucydides' *The Peloponnesian War*. After the hapless citizens of the island of Melos refused to give up their seven-hundred-year-old tradition of civic liberty, the Athenian generals proclaimed that the strong do what they will and the weak suffer what they must; the Athenians attacked the island, slew its men, and sold its women and children into slavery.[3] To be sure, among the ancient Greeks diplomacy and arbitration might be called upon to mediate the rule of force in relations with external others. But acts of generosity toward the foreigner were an exception, and in general the Greeks maintained a sharp presumptive divide between justice as an internal norm, and force as an external rule.

2. It should be obvious from my description that the instability to which I refer is not the disturbance to civic peace attendant upon social and political contestation. In such cases, including those involving widespread civil disobedience, a structure of laws and accountability is in place—and it is precisely this structure that becomes a target for protesters to the extent that they believe the law encodes specific injustices. I am referring to law-less situations of cruelty, arbitrariness, violence, and caprice—and these abound at present.

3. Thucydides, it must be noted, did not present the Melian dialogue as a depiction of exemplary behavior on the part of the Athenian generals; indeed, it presaged disaster for Athens. Oddly enough, however, contemporary realists often identify this extreme instance of the use of force as a case in point for their perspective.

From its inception, Christian doctrine embodied a dramatic challenge to this Greek approach to justice. Christianity put pressure on the notion that good or ill treatment should depend on tribal or political affiliations; hospitality was supposed to be extended to all without exception. The Christian parable of the Good Samaritan illustrates this claim: if a Samaritan, with whom the Jews of Jesus' day had no neighborly contact, could treat a beaten and robbed Jew with tenderness and mercy, was it not possible for a Samaritan to be good and for the normative presumptions to be reversed? Hospitality—caritas—became a duty for all Christians, whether the one to whom aid was proffered or from whom it was received was a family or tribal member, or a stranger.

Where moral obligation is concerned, the Christian teaching is in many ways counterintuitive. It is, after all, not surprising that we feel foremost obligated to family and friends; second, to members of our own culture, clan, or society—with foreigners and strangers coming in a distant third. An injustice meted out against one of our own pains us more keenly than an injustice perpetrated against those far removed from us by language, custom, and belief—and separated from us by borders and geographic distance. Even by St. Augustine's account in *The City of God,*

> The diversity of languages separates man from man. For if two men meet and are forced by some compelling reason not to pass on but to stay in company, then if neither knows the other's language, it is easier for dumb animals, even of different kinds, to associate together than these men, although both are human beings. For when men cannot communicate their thoughts to each other, simply because of difference of language, all similarity of their common human nature is of no avail to unite them in fellowship. So true is this that a man would be more cheerful with his dog for company than with a foreigner.

Mutual unintelligibility to the contrary notwithstanding, Christian theology endorses equal consideration for all human beings, whatever the lamentable shortcomings of Christian practice over the centuries.

Of course, the ancient Greek distinction between justice and force never disappeared. It made a powerful comeback in the writings of Machiavelli and other so-called civic republicans, and was reencoded by the Peace of Augsburg (1555) and the Treaty of Westphalia (1648). With Westphalia, the norm of justice pertaining to members of a particular territorial entity received official sanction in its recognizably modern form, marking the beginning of the international state system. The presumption of state sovereignty held that the state alone was the arbiter of what counted as justice, law, freedom, and everything else within its bounded territory. Efforts at softening sovereign autonomy (associated with Hugo Grotius and the notion of international law) were observed most often when adherence to international norms and state self-interest could be reconciled, and were only partially successful.

Meanwhile, Christian universalism remained alive not only in theological and moral arguments now advanced within a divided Christendom, but also in several traditions of theologically grounded political practice. Where the matter of international justice is concerned, the most important of these is the justified, or "just," war tradition.

Many will find this claim surprising. How can a method of assessing whether a resort to war is justified bear directly on contemporary debates about international justice? The argument, simply put, is this: the just war tradition is not just about war. It is a theory of comparative justice applied to considerations of war and intervention. Indeed, in my view, the post-World War II universalization of human rights has deepened and enhanced the importance and reach of the just war perspective.

But in order to understand what the notion of justice with universal applicability precisely means within the just war tradition, a précis of the basics of just war doctrine is required.

From the perspective of the just war tradition, no unbridgeable conceptual or political divide exists between domestic and international politics. Most thinkers within the just war tradition assume that while it would be utopian to suppose that relations between states could ever be governed by the kind of care apposite in our dealings with family, friends, and fellow citizens, it does not follow that an unbridled war of each against all may legitimately commence as soon as one crosses the borders of one's country. Just war thinking is perhaps best known today for some of its concrete injunctions. For example: a war must be openly and legally pursued; a war must be a response to a specific instance of unjust aggression or to the certain threat of such aggression; a war may be triggered by an obligation to protect the innocent (noncombatants)—rather than simply the members of one's polity—from certain harm; a war should be a last resort. These are the so-called *ad bellum* criteria. Just war theorists also insist that means must be proportionate to ends (the rule of proportionality) and that a war be waged in such a way as to distinguish combatants from noncombatants (the principle of discrimination), the most important *in bello* criterion.

Note that one cause that justifies a forceful response, if other criteria such as last resort are also met, is sparing the innocent from certain harm. A response to a direct attack is similarly exigent. Acts of aggression, whether against one's own people or against those who cannot defend themselves, are stipulated as cases of injustice that warrant the use of force. This does not mean one must respond with force, but rather that a justice claim has been triggered and a resort to force is justifiable, without being automatic. Herein lies the rub, the point at which just war and international justice as equal regard make contact. Because the origins of just war thinking lie in Christian theology, the view that human beings are equal in the eyes of God underscores what is at stake when persons are unjustly assaulted—namely, that human beings *qua* human beings deserve equal moral regard. Equal regard means that one possesses an inalienable dignity that cannot be revoked arbitrarily by governments or other political bodies or actors. It follows that the spectacle of people being harried, deported, slaughtered, tortured, or starved en masse constitutes a *prima facie* justice claim. Depending on the circumstances on the ground, as well as on the relative scales of power, an equal regard claim may trigger a movement toward armed intervention on behalf of the hounded, tortured, murdered, and aggrieved.

If such a claim is warranted, some might cavil, ought not an international institution respond? Perhaps. But all too often UN "peacekeepers" are obliged by their rules of engagement (rules of "disengagement" would be more like it) to stand by as people are being slaughtered.

International bodies have tended to avoid using coercive force in order to protect innocent victims of political chaos. As a result, in many cases it will be other political institutions that must respond to the grievances and horrors at hand, provided they can do so in a manner that avoids—to the extent that this is humanly possible—either deepening the injustice at hand or creating new instances of injustice, doubly difficult to sort out.

Let's tackle the first difficulty—what it means to make a claim under the equal regard norm—before turning to the second vexation, namely, who can be called upon to use coercive force on behalf of justice.

Defining and defending international justice as the equal right to have force deployed on one's behalf means that an aggrieved group is obliged to make the case that it is a just cause of substantial gravity.

Genocide is the most obvious case in point. But there are others, including many man-made disasters that are now the occasion for "humanitarian intervention"—a devastating famine, for example. As Amartya Sen has demonstrated, famine on a catastrophic scale is most often the conjunction of natural factors (many years of drought, for example) and starvation maneuvered by cruel political actors to further their own ends.

In such circumstances, it makes far more sense to speak of intervention in a just cause—and to call it justified war—than to obfuscate with the term "humanitarian relief": if attack helicopters, armored personnel carriers, automatic weapons, and the like are involved, it is a war of one sort or another. If famine is the *casus belli*, one interdicts and punishes those responsible for preventing food from reaching starving people.[4] Calling such a situation "humanitarian intervention" only clouds the issue. The real problem is a political one, and coercive force remains an extension of politics by other means.

Let's unpack further an equal regard claim to the deployment of armed force on behalf of a victim of systematic injustice. One implication of this claim is that a third party may be justified in intervening with force in order to defend those unable to defend themselves, to fight those who are engaged in unjust acts of harming, and to punish those who have committed unjust harm. On these grounds, a war would be justified in order to halt the kind of unlimited violence exemplified by Osama bin Laden's fatwa calling on all Muslims everywhere to kill all Americans wherever they may be found. Force that observes limits is frequently called upon to fight force without limits.

At the same time, it is important to note what the equal regard argument does not mean. It does not mean that any one nation or group of nations can or should respond to every violation of the innocent, including genocide, that most horrific of all violations. The just war tradition incorporates a cautionary note: Be as certain as you can, before you intervene in a just cause, that you have a reasonable chance of success. Don't barge in and make a bad situation worse.

---

4. I would not use U.S. military personnel to respond to authentic natural disasters, like flood relief. International humanitarian relief agencies, including non-military U.S. personnel and NGOs, should be deployed in such instances. In light of the current war on terror, deploying our military to respond to the aftermath of hurricanes and the like will stretch us too thin. Humanitarian relief and coercive force must be kept distinct, in part to limit coercive force rather than bury it under the humanitarian rubric.

A prudential warning that intervention in a just cause might exacerbate the harm, that this intervention will itself constitute unjustifiable injustice—such as massive damage to the civilian population of a country or group being harmed by another country or group—must be addressed within the equal regard/just war framework.[5] In such sad situations, those called upon to intervene are obliged to affirm the equal regard norm even as they spell out explicitly how and why they are unable or unwilling to undertake the risks of intervention with force. The reasons for standing down must themselves be grounded in the equal regard norm—for example, in the high probability that more innocents would die as a result of armed intervention on their behalf than would likely suffer if such intervention is not mounted. This approach is better by far than the strategies of evasion and denial applied during the 1994 slaughter of Rwandan Tutsis by Rwandan Hutus. Exculpatory strategies at the time included claims that the full extent of the slaughter was unknown. Or that, as bad as the slaughter was, it wasn't as bad as other cases of genocide, so action that might put American (or other) soldiers in harm's way wasn't warranted. In this and other well-known cases, one is confronted frequently with the spectacle of officials who speak boldly about universal human rights, only to revert to a narrow doctrine of national self-interest in order to evade the implications of embracing these rights.

The safe havens for beleaguered Bosnian Muslims established under a UN umbrella during the Bosnian war were another tragic case of evasion and ineptitude. Bosnian Muslims flowed into these "safe havens" and were there shot to pieces as UN peacekeepers, impotent understanding rules of engagement, stood by. The United States, fearing unfavorable domestic political reaction, temporized, making promise after promise it never kept. As Samantha Power writes, "First, they [administration officials] wanted to avoid engagement in conflicts that posed little threat to American interests, narrowly defined. And second, they hoped to contain the political costs and avoid the moral stigma associated with allowing genocide." Because the Americans had turned the issue into one of *international peacekeeping* rather than *just war-making*, ethnic cleansing proceeded apace and its results were ratified with the Dayton Accords.

Suppose one state does intervene on behalf of a victimized state or people: does this in and of itself mean that the principle of equal regard is being honored in full? Not necessarily.

Take, for example, U.S. intervention in Kosovo under the rubric of NATO authority. The rules of NATO engagement in Kosovo exemplify the failure to abide by the central norm of the just war tradition that maintains that it is better to risk the lives of one's own combatants than those of enemy noncombatants. With its determination to keep American combatants out of harm's way—to enjoy a zero-casualty war for our soldiers—the Clinton administration embraced a principle I call *combatant immunity*, not only for our own combatants but also indirectly for Serbian soldiers. No attempt was made to interdict the Serbian forces on the ground, even as Kosovar civilian casualties escalated with NATO bombing. In a hard-hitting piece on "War and Sacrifice in Kosovo," Paul W.

---

5. Here precision-guided weaponry has rolled back many arguments that modern war and the just war tradition are by definition incompatible. This is surely true of a total war absent restraint. It is not true of a limited war fought, with restraint, in order to punish egregious aggression, to interdict terrible violence, and to prevent further harm.

Kahn scored the administration's violation of the equal regard norm. His comments are worth quoting at some length:

> If the decision to intervene is morally compelling, it cannot be conditioned on political considerations *that assume an asymmetrical valuing of human life*. [The emphasis is mine.] This contradiction will be felt more and more as we move into an era that is simultaneously characterized by a global legal and moral order, on the one hand, and the continuing presence of nation-states, on the other. What are the conditions under which states will be willing to commit their forces to advance international standards, when their own interests are not threatened? Riskless warfare by the state in pursuit of global values may be a perfect expression of this structural contradiction within which we find ourselves. In part, then, our uneasiness about a policy of riskless intervention in Kosovo arises out of an incompatibility between the morality of the ends, which are universal, and the morality of the means, which seem to privilege a particular community. There was talk during the campaign of a crude moral-military calculus in which the life of one NATO combatant was thought to be equivalent to the lives of 20,000 Kosovars. Such talk meant that those who supported the intervention could not know the depth of our commitment to overcoming humanitarian disasters. Is it conditioned upon the absence of risk to our own troops? If so, are such interventions merely moral disasters—like that in Somalia—waiting to happen? If the Serbs had discovered a way to inflict real costs, would there have been an abandonment of the Kosovars?

The doctrine of "humanitarian intervention" not only builds in no barriers to the kind of crude calculus Kahn condemns, but also tacitly encourages a situation of unequal regard, by making the case for relief in terms of international victimization. The more powerful are moved by a sense of pity, at best empathy—not by a sense of obligation to achieve justice for those we perceive as equals. The humanitarian relief model in such circumstances is somewhat analogous to the bureaucratic welfare model of a needy client dependent upon the largesse of a powerful and remote provider. This creates a bizarre situation—one we witnessed frequently in the 1990s—of American soldiers, the best equipped and trained in the world, deployed as high-tech social workers.

By contrast, the equal regard doctrine as an elementary requirement of international justice sets up a *citizenship model*. We respond to attacks against persons who cannot defend themselves because they, like us, are human beings, hence equal in regard to us, and because they, like us, are members of nations, states, or would-be states whose primary obligation is to protect the lives of those citizens who inhabit their polities. Thus, all states or would-be states have a stake in building an international civic culture that averts horrors such as those of Rwanda and Kosovo.

When such horrors arise, we should send in soldiers to protect the innocent, unless grave and compelling reasons preclude it. These soldiers should fight under rules of engagement that abide by just war norms, most importantly noncombatant immunity. If we cannot intervene, other means must be resorted to immediately. People should not be slaughtered because powerful nations are dithering, hoping the whole thing will soon be over, and using domestic political considerations as a trump card in refusing to do the right thing.

In her essay "Genocide and America," Samantha Power writes that:

> People victimized by genocide or abandoned by the international community
> do not make good neighbors, as their thirst for vengeance, their irredentism,
> and their acceptance of violence as a means of generating change can turn them
> into future threats. In Bosnia, where the United States and Europe maintained
> an arms embargo against the Muslims, extremist Islamic fighters and pros-
> elytizers eventually turned up to offer support. Some secular Muslim citizens
> became radicalized by the partnership, and the failed state of Bosnia became a
> haven for Islamic terrorists shunned elsewhere in the world. It appears that one
> of the organizations that infiltrated Bosnia and used it as a training base was
> Osama bin Laden's al-Qaeda.

I have long argued in my own work that moral imperatives are not so many nice-
sounding nostrums that we can simply ignore in favor of hardheaded national interest.
Ethical considerations must be a constitutive feature of American foreign policy; it is in
our long-term national interest to foster and sustain an international society of equal
regard. An equal regard standard is central to a well-functioning international system
composed of decent, if not perfect, states that may or may not be democratic, although
constitutional regimes remain the ideal.

And it is not only the United States that should be bound by such moral imperatives.
Many states are capable of responding to regional catastrophes, even if that means sending
their soldiers into a neighboring country. When a minority population within a country
is being destroyed, or threatened with destruction, neighboring countries are obligated
to take action under the equal regard rule. When, say, the unarmed missionaries of a
particular religion are being executed systematically by a state, neighboring countries are
also accountable and, if they have the means, should exert pressure to stop the slaughter.
Faithfulness to the alliance of equal regard with universal human rights means obligations
are not limited to one's own nationals, or tribe, or co-religionists. In this latter instance, it
is not incumbent upon the neighboring country to make the case, but rather to respond,
once the case has been made, with whatever means are at its disposal.

Finally, who is the "we" that can be called upon to protect the innocent from harm, the
"we" to whom a country without the means to intervene must make its case? The United
Nations cannot be ignored, of course, but nor has it proved effective in this regard. Once
a measure of order is restored, UN peacekeepers may indeed be the best body to enforce
a fragile peace, at least in some situations. But the United Nations habitually temporizes,
sends radically mixed signals, and takes so long to gear itself up and put peacekeepers on
the ground that its unreliability in this regard needn't be argued at length. All one needs to
do is look at its reluctance to enforce its own resolutions for inspections in Iraq.

Presently, the likeliest "we," with both the means to enforce international justice
as an equal regard norm and a strong motive to do so, is the United States. The United
States is capable of projecting its power as no other state can. And the United States is
itself premised on a set of universal propositions concerning human dignity and equality. There is no conflict in principle between our national identity and universal claims
and commitments.

The conflict lies elsewhere—between what we affirm and aspire to, what we can effectively do, and what we can responsibly do. Here fundamental human moral intuitions will inevitably come into play. I described these as a powerfully felt human urgency to protect, to care for, and to seek justice on behalf of those nearest and dearest to us.

If the case can be made—and it isn't just an exculpatory strategy to avoid acting under the equal regard principle—that those nearest and dearest will be directly imperiled if one acts, the obligation to act under equal regard may be affirmed even as exigent prudential reasons for why one cannot act in this case are proffered. One arrives at a position of moral regret because a legitimate claim cannot be honored. A reasonable and justifiable departure from the equal regard norm, e.g., a claim that substantial harm will come to one's fellow citizens if one acts—not as a remote possibility but as a nigh-certain probability—does not apply to the anticipated harm to military men and women attendant upon any commitment to coercive force: it is their job to go into harm's way. It is also their honor to fight as just warriors rather than as wanton murderers, like those unleashed by the Athenians at Melos.

It is extraordinarily difficult to articulate a strong universal justice claim and to assign a particular state and its people a disproportionate burden to enforce that claim. But international justice as coercive force on behalf of equal regard does precisely this. At this critical juncture in human history, the United States is a polity that acknowledges universal premises and is sufficiently powerful to act, or to put pressure on others to act, when and where no other state can.

If the United States were to act justly, in short, the brutal Melian maxim would be mercifully reversed: The strong do what they must, in order that the weak not suffer what they too often will.

"Against the New Utopianism"

Jean Bethke Elshtain[1]

The New Utopianism: What's the Problem?

PROPHETS OF THE NEW utopianism take strong exception to the arguments of those they call "the new internationalists," a stance they associate with such thinkers as Michael Ignatieff, Anne-Marie Slaughter, and Jean Bethke Elshtain. Many of these rejoinders are rather angry, as if "the new internationalists" stand in the way of a real possibility to create a new international order in which sovereignty is side-lined, international law triumphs, and nations no longer know war. These are ancient dreams restated in contemporary terms.

Years ago now I raised critical questions about the concept of peace as an "earthly" concept. Well before "Jerusalem the Golden" of Christian yearnings, the dream of an eternal city of peace and joy where there is neither crying nor fighting, the ancient Greeks had represented peace, Eirene, as a female deity of a decidedly subordinate nature, by contrast to Ares, a male god of great power. Whereas Eirene was attendant upon the great gods, Ares dominated, unsurprisingly considering the founding myth that the gods themselves had come to power only after fighting a brutal war against the Titans. For the Greeks, war was a natural state and the basis of society. Manly valor was shown by the spirit with which men pursued honor and fame. The epics of war, of tragedy and triumph, were constructed in and through figurations that have lost none of their power to evoke and provoke the centrality of war-making with its glories, necessities, and often terrible triumphs. Heraclitus deemed war the "father of all things," arguing that it is alone through strife as a natural law of being that anything is brought into being. Those dominated by self-interest, those who refuse to fight, become slaves. Not a philosophy for the squeamish. The valiant—they shall prevail.

The Romans represented peace as a rather vague goddess. The *Pax Romana* tapped notions at once legalistic and teleological—agreements or pacts not to fight together—with images of *tranquilitas, securitas,* repose. In constructing an altar to pax, the Romans feminised the representation as a *Terra Mater* surrounded by fruit, children, sheep, and oxen. Similarly, in ancient Hebrew thought, peace (shalom) is not only the

1. This article originally appeared in *Studies in Christian Ethics* 20, no. 1 (2007).

absence of war but also a state of well-being; a combination of material and spiritual conditions frequently following a war; a sphere of security that requires assured dominion in order to come into view, to manifest itself. The point is that all antique peoples shared a dream of a world without war and the picture of such a world drew—at least part of the time—upon mythologies of a lost golden age of fructifying harmony or full transparency in which none was an enemy to any other, nor, for that matter, even a nuisance. A world without borders, boundaries, strangers, estrangements. In this world one law prevails and the entire world comes under it.

The dream of Elysium was bolstered and reconstructed when Christianity emerged. The Christian gospel proclaims peace as the highest good. Peace is a blessing not reducible to the terms of any earthly order (including, or most especially, the *Pax Romana*); nor is peace a sentimental dream of an era of perfect justice on this earth. Peace is represented as the fruition available to all through the redemptive promise of the Christian savior—the City of God. But earthly "peace" is bound to be an imperfect approximation of this ideal. In other words, Augustinian Christianity distinguished between peace as a transcendent concept and whatever peace might be achieved on this earth—in the immanent realm. The two could never be conflated although the one—the transcendent—surely inspires the other—the immanent.

The Christian New Jerusalem was balm for the weary but a vexation for the impatient determined to bring peace to earth, the sooner the better. Sixteenth- and seventeenth-century Utopians gave vent to the latter urge as social urgency. Not all Utopians are, or were, alike, of course, but all are concerned with contrasting the disorder they find with the more perfect order they seek. To tag a text or political program "utopian," then, is to do more than label in a neutral manner; rather, the term implies an evaluation and a critical one at that. It suggests that the paradisiacal elements of ancient dreams of peace, shalom, or the New Jerusalem, are featured as part of a program for earthly realisation.

Elsewhere I have called this sort of peace "an ontologically suspicious" concept. It never appears without its violent doppelganger, war, lurking in the shadows: the one requires the other. Peace is healing order; war is destructive discordance—the antinomies may be proliferated almost endlessly. There is an impatience with the realistically achievable possibilities of imperfect human beings and the political configurations they create.[2] Much of this impatience historically has yielded horrific terror—one thinks of Marxism with its eschatological "moment," an insistence that once the pure classless society is achieved states themselves will disappear and all will be as one. I will not go into detail on this—or other destructive visions of peace (perhaps, better said, visions that led to destruction once attempts were made to implement them)—here. Instead I want to speak of a possible new international order that contrasts quite strongly with the new utopianism or, as one has called it, modest utopianism with its neo-Kantian proclamations.

Let's join the issue as it manifests itself in contemporary argument. Kant is either foregrounded explicitly or lurking in the backdrop for many of the "old internationalists" that I tag the "new Utopians" in present dialogue. Kant, you may recall, celebrates

---

2. There have been and are feminist variations on these views of peace. For a discussion, see my *Women and War*.

republican commonwealths. A constitution is Law in its grandest teleological sense and the true sovereign of the state. Law alone produces a situation in which the rights of individuals are defended and harmony between a Constitution and the Principles of Right pertains. Whatever the given Constitution, the citizens must obey: this is an absolute, formal principle. Should a revolution bring a new supreme law into being, citizens are again enjoined to obey so long as Law takes the form of universalisable principles. Obedient but free subjects: that is the story.

The title of his great essay on "Perpetual Peace" signifies Kant's metaphysical ambitions. Peace that is not perpetual is a mere truce. A genuine peace must nullify *all* existing causes of war. Kant writes: "No treaty of peace that tacitly reserves issues for a future war shall be valid."[3] Peace derives from republican civil constitutions; its origins, like those of bourgeois *Privatrecht*, are pure—the concept of right. A league of purely constituted republics will end war forever. Kant's grand design is laced through and through with a grand teleology, willed by Nature, a somewhat capricious "She" who has nevertheless offered up all the necessary preconditions, even using war to gain the absolute of perpetual peace.

"Peace," Kant continues, is the end of all hostilities so that even to modify it by "perpetual" smacks of pleonasm, or superfluous use, more than necessary.[4] I should add here that many who evoke Kant avoid or ignore his metaphysical and ontological arguments, as if they could sever the plan for perpetual peace from what, for Kant, was the necessary foundation for such. By definition, peace is perpetual. Kant also attacks "Jesuistical casuistry," a reference to the just war tradition that offers an account of comparative, not absolute, justice of the sort Kant seeks in the form of "perpetual peace."[5] Kant's articles of perpetual peace require that all codes of conduct must go to the purity of the will or motive. The Law must penetrate to the level of intentionality lest a "doctrine of prudence" triumph, which amounts to a "denial that morality exists at all." Kant criticises all treaties of peace that end particular wars but do not end the state of war—again, diminishing such cessation of hostilities achieved through the usual political means.[6] Moreover, all dealings between states must be submitted to full transparency; nothing can be held in reserve; no card can be played close to the chest; and no secret diplomacy, for nomolatry detests secrecy.[7]

It is unsurprising, perhaps, that should a statesman be in doubt about the right thing to do, he is to turn to moral philosophers who form a separate objective class that is, by definition, incapable of forming cliques so it "cannot be suspected of being the formulator of propaganda."[8]

This is good for a laugh, of course, to anyone who has spent decades in the academy, for we all know that philosophers form cliques more or less routinely. In contemporary

---

3. Kant, *Perpetual Peace and Other Essays on Politics, History and Morals*, 107.
4. Kant, *Perpetual Peace and Other Essays on Politics, History and Morals*, 107.
5. Kant, *Perpetual Peace and Other Essays on Politics, History and Morals*, 109.
6. Kant, *Perpetual Peace and Other Essays on Politics, History and Morals*, 116–17.
7. Kant, *Perpetual Peace and Other Essays on Politics, History and Morals*, 139.
8. Kant, *Perpetual Peace and Other Essays on Politics, History and Morals*, 125–26.

neo-Kantian versions of peace, international law and its tribunals play something of the part Kant assigned to moral philosophers—they are allegedly above the fray; no one would suspect them of being self-interested; they are incapable of forming cliques, and so on. There can be no conflict, he argues, between a theoretical and an applied doctrine of right. If this be not true, then morality is just prudence and this is no morality at all. We see quite clearly the anti-political thrust of Kantianism, its inability to abide conflict between two goods, let's say, or greater or lesser evils.

Neo-Kantianism, of whatever stripe, is rather a far cry from arguments some of us have mounted that aspires to a world of "minimally decent states" and a commitment to the principle of "equal moral regard" for human beings. This "equal moral regard" sounds rather Kantian, to be sure, but it is not an absolute principle in practice—it is an aspiration. One appreciates the tragedy that on this earth even good and decent principles cannot be wholly realised. Surprisingly, even this rather more modest call for minimally decent states—and the assumption that such states will in one way or another likely be democratic—is taxed with a disguised form of moral imperialism, with ethnocentrism, and the encouragement of the use of force. I suspect this has happened because "the new internationalists," myself included, point out that American constitutional principles constitute universal claims, not particular ones, and that these universal claims, e.g., "all persons are created equal," really means all persons. As everyone knows, much of the domestic history of American political life involves contestation to achieve in practice the universalism embedded in the American experiment in principle.

Further, I and others argue that there is no way around American power. The question is whether, on balance, it is used for good or ill. For the new Utopians, American power is often the problem and in the wilder forms of European anti-Americanism, America functions as the repository of all that is disgusting, crass, wicked, manipulative, etc., in the world. The mere existence of American power somehow stifles and strangles the rest of the world—on and on in this vein. For example, Anthony Burke claims that the new internationalism traffics in "fear-soaked rhetoric," and labels the war against Saddam's republic of fear an "unimaginable break" with international norms; Abu Ghraib is construed as the norm rather than an aberration (which makes criminal prosecution of the perpetrators rather inexplicable—if indeed their disgusting display was the norm we would give them medals, not indict them); the idea of state sovereignty is blasted as "violent and exclusivist . . . lingering like a latent illness in the very depths of modern cosmopolitanism."[9] The metaphor of disease is fascinating here. But who are the physicians to heal the international order? For Kant they are the moral philosophers. For Burke and so many others, it is a fantasy United Nations—quite unlike the one we actually have—and international law, universally accepted and endorsed and enforced—although their arguments are often rather thin concerning how just these laws are to be enforced and by whom. Given that the United Nations today is composed of delegates who lopsidedly represent undemocratic and corrupt regimes, this strikes me as a not terribly helpful argument. Moreover, why should an International Court

9. Burke, "Against the New Internationalism," 76, 86, 88, 74. For feminist internationalists, one repetitive theme is that the state is somehow "male" and therein lies the problem or the etiology of the disease of sovereignty.

of Justice dominated by Europeans be any more "universal" than claims launched by a democratic state premised on universal propositions? In sum, the Kantian vision relies on a dualistic contrast between "perpetual peace" and "perpetual war" that is a chimera. The new Utopians ignore or downplay moral and political ambiguity and nuance, the smudginess of real human lives and history.

Those of us who believe the universe is not "heal-able" (if there is such a word) are often taxed with being imperialists if we express the hope that American power can help to stabilise and provide order in international affairs and, at the same time, defeatists precisely because we—or at least I—share St Augustine's conviction that on this earth it will remain impossible to perfectly reconcile human wills. Pace the critics, this is not a counsel of defeatism at all; rather, it represents hope by contrast to optimism. Hope that the world can be made less brutal and less unjust, and this means more respect for human rights and more democratic forms insofar as democracy involves respect for persons *qua* persons. Saying this does not dictate any particular form of government save that no one is born to be a slave, to be tormented, or to be slaughtered because of who he or she is—whether American or Israeli or Palestinian, whether Jew or Christian or Muslim, whether male or female. The new neo-Kantian universalism—or new utopianism—is a mixture of untethered idealism, hoping for the triumph of good will and a world in which international bodies supplant states, international law supersedes multiple civic laws, and there is at some point a definitive abandonment of the use of force in international affairs.

For us "new internationalists"—if we accept the designation and I am not wild about it—we have a real challenge to our position not so much from the new Utopians—I believe their arguments can be rather readily answered—but from serious classical realists who set the bar lower, insisting that the best we can do is to forestall the worst and not hope for some good. There is great wisdom in this posture—forestalling the worst is no small achievement—but, contrary to some interpreters of Augustine, I believe there is also warrant for a measure of hopefulness within his arguments concerning political life and order.

A Summary of "the New Internationalism"

I obviously cannot speak on behalf of all those thinkers now lumped together as "the new"—and troubling, to their critics—"internationalism." But I want to provide a quick summary of my thinking here in order to pave the way for what St. Augustine brings to this inquiry. I find myself rather pained that some critics believe I have abandoned Augustine for a triumphant liberal internationalism when, for my part, Augustinianism forms the set of background assumptions for my entire argument.

In a nutshell, I have argued in several papers that we require a new standard of international justice (based on very old beliefs). Embodied in this justice is a claim to the use of coercive force deployed on one's behalf if one is the victim of systematic, egregious, and continuing violence. The political questions—not philosophic propositions or legalistic ones, for that matter—are central here. Absent political stability, every attempt to prop up impoverished regimes must fail. This, indeed, has been the story in sub-Saharan Africa where corrupt one-party dictatorships have become the norm. Foreign aid to such bodies is eaten up by corruption. Justice demands accountability and there is no accountability where there is no structure of power and laws. Instead one sees disasters like Darfur where human beings are prey to the ruthless, the inflamed, and the irresponsible.

Absent such a structure, culminating in some form of political sovereignty—another name for "responsibility" of collective bodies in the world as we know it—the likelihood of what we now routinely call "humanitarian catastrophes" is magnified many-fold. A paradigm example of the ills attendant upon political instability absent a central, legitimate locus of power and authority is the disaster of so-called "failed states." It is, of course, the case that states themselves, whose very reason to exist is to maintain stability and a measure of internal civic peace, may become disturbers of the peace. But because sovereignty is the way we "name" responsibility, such states can and should be held to account. We still don't do a very good job of doing that but it is one that seems a reasonable aspiration.

I have drawn the just or justified war tradition into a discussion of international justice, demonstrating the ways in which the just war tradition embeds a theory of comparative justice applied not only to war and intervention but to politics more generally. Further, the just war tradition helps to secure a *citizenship model* by contrast to the model of dominator/victim that underlies the humanitarian intervention model, the latter being one that invites a kind of welfare program by contrast to the possible use of force as one way to strengthen or to secure a polity within which accountable officials are responsible for securing civic order and minimal decency.

The victimiser/victim model or modality too often incorporates a form of patronising pity rather than recognition of those in trouble as citizens who, by definition, have the right to expect a minimally decent state. Perhaps one might call this "putting politics first"—something, oddly, that is infrequent in so many discussions mounted by the new Utopians whose faith tends to be placed in a fantasy United Nations (as I have called it) and a neo-Kantian international law. If one believes with the political theorist Hannah Arendt, in a number of her major works, that it is impossible to be something as vague as a "citizen of the world" in anything like the robust way one can be a citizen of a particular state, then you will more likely be drawn to the political, citizenship model.

Just war thinking, of course, is best known as a cluster of concrete injunctions: what it is permissible to do; what it is not permissible to do, where the resort to, and the use of, force is concerned. For example, a war must be openly and legally pursued; a war must be a response to a specific instance of unjust aggression or the certain threat of such aggression; a war may be triggered by an obligation to protect the innocent (non-combatants), including those who are not members of one's polity, from certain harm; a war should be the last resort: these are the so-called *ad bellum* criteria. As a set of strictures about war fighting, just war insists that means must be proportionate to ends—the rule of proportionality—and that a war be waged in such a way as to do one's best to distinguish combatants from non-combatants—the principle of discrimination: these are the *in bello* criteria.

Just war and international justice as equal regard make contact precisely because the origins of just war thinking lie in Christian theology, a view of human beings as equal in the eyes of God. This underscores what is at stake when persons are unjustly assaulted, namely, that human beings *qua* human beings deserve equal moral regard. Equal moral regard means one possesses an inalienable dignity that is not given by governments and must not be revoked arbitrarily by governments. It follows that the spectacle of people being harried, slaughtered, or starved en masse constitutes a *prima facie* justice claim. Depending on the circumstances on the ground as well as the relative scales of power—who can bring force effectively to bear—an equal regard claim may trigger armed intervention on behalf of the hounded, murdered, and aggrieved. For there are times when the claims of justice may override the reluctance to take up arms. An implication of this claim is that a third party may be justified in intervening with force in order to defend those unable to defend themselves, to fight those who are engaged in unjust acts of harming, and to punish those who have engaged in systematic unjust harm in order to diminish their capacity to continue on a path of systematic and egregious violence.

The equal regard argument does not mean that any one nation or group of nations can or should respond to every instance of violation of the innocent, including the most horrific of all violations—genocide or ethnic cleansing. It is important to note that the just war tradition incorporates a cautionary note. Be as certain as you can, before you intervene in a just cause, that you have a reasonable chance of success. Don't barge in and make a bad situation worse. Considerations such as these take us to the heart of the *in bello* rules, those restraints on the means deployed even in a just cause. The damage should not be greater than the offenses one aims to halt—in full recognition that even this cannot be an absolute requirement as no one ever knows for certain what the use of force may invite "down the line." This approach, I insist, is better than the strategies of evasion and denial visible but one example—in the Western reaction to the 1994 slaughter by Rwandan Hutus of Rwandan Tutsis; indeed, in President Clinton's administration word went down that the term "genocide" should never be used by administration spokespersons to characterise what was happening in Rwanda as that term might incite the American people to want to "do something"—even though genocide was an accurate designation of what was happening.

This must suffice as a truncated version of my international justice and equal regard argument. Now it is time to turn to St Augustine.

What Does Augustine Bring to This Discussion?

As one who believes that St Augustine can be brought to bear profitably on nearly every discussion, it comes as no surprise that he should appear here. Although he is not a natural law thinker in the classic sense, Augustine nonetheless believes that there is a naturalist morality written on the hearts of God's sentient creatures. By nature, no man has dominion over any other.[10] Moreover, we are not by nature evil. Evil entered the world through an act of free will and is the burden all successive generations bear and one to

---

10. For a full discussion of this point see my *Augustine and the Limits of Politics*.

which they add their own deposit of sin. Neither are we political by nature, although we are indeed social creatures. The call of nature may move us into fellowship with one another. But nature's reign is not sufficient unto itself. Human projects must be enacted, and they will be driven either by *caritas* or *cupiditas* or some admixture of the two. So there is a *human* nature. We cannot be or become just anything we want to be. Our natures do not dictate any particular way of life if one's reference point is a type of political regime. But Augustine's approach does underscore the naturalness of certain social arrangements, most especially the family. Our dependencies and interdependencies—all flow from our natures. But we either act in obedience to God or we disobey.

Of particular interest to political theology is Augustine's thinking on issues of war and peace. He holds that an imperfect but nonetheless real earthly peace lies within the realm of the possible. At the same time, peace can never be endorsed uncritically. For Augustine offers a withering critique of the injustices that traffic under the name of peace. And justice is what is at stake in any discussion of war and peace—a justice that repairs our fragile bonds of sociality and seeks to mend bonds that have already been broken or frayed by violent acts. In a fallen world, filled with imperfect human beings, we cannot achieve anything remotely approaching perfection in earthly dominion, or religious life, or anything else. At the same time, we all bear responsibility to and for one another to serve and to love our neighbors. One implication for reflecting on Augustine's theology as it applies to "international relations" lies in the fact that if our neighbor is being slaughtered and continuingly crushed by the heavy hand of an intolerable oppression, the just use of force and the vocation of soldiering rise to the fore as options to which we may be urged, perhaps even commanded, by a God of justice.

What is forbidden to the individual—use of lawless violence against another—is sanctioned for the social body in the form of the rule-governed use of force in and through the offices of statespersons and soldiers. In this way, justice is driven by charity and this, in turn, means one must determine the circumstances under which justice may demand penalising those guilty of massive and egregious injustices. For Augustine, one can never get away from original sin but that does not preclude seeking right order—justice—between peoples and between peoples and God. The force brought to bear as an instrument of justice cannot be uncontrolled violence. It is not private violence. It is the use of force at the behest of right authority.

In the interest of summing things up following this much-too-brief discussion, let me just indicate that an Augustinian approach both enables the use of force in the name of justice and simultaneously limits it. Perfecting our natures is beyond our reach. So is "perpetual peace." In the realm of force, a drive to achieve perfect justice, to create a world of neo-Kantian republics, may also erode limits to the justifiable use of force; limits, therefore, to what we are permitted to do even in the name of justice. This Augustinian wisdom exerts—or should—a chastening influence on even the most hopeful ideals lifted up by human beings. I suspect that I have myself, from time to time, been rather too exuberant about the prospects for democracy—by which I mean basic rights-respecting regimes, the most fundamental right being the right to life itself implied by innate human dignity. I have, in other words, associated myself with a tradition in American political thought resoundingly articulated by so many of our twentieth- and now, twenty-first-century presidents: Franklin Delano Roosevelt, Harry Truman, Dwight D. Eisenhower (though rather less so), John F. Kennedy, Ronald Reagan, William Clinton (in an uneven way), and the second George Bush. It has been a bi-partisan commitment for decades—until the very recent past when the "left" and many American liberals, quite astonishingly, have abandoned universal aspirations for human decency and justice. Just recently a leading Democratic Senator called for a return to "fortress America," classic isolationism. It is either that or the new utopianism that emanates from the left nowadays in America—developments that would stun the Democratic Presidents in my list above. In Great Britain, the so-called "Euston Manifesto" provides a stirring restatement of the values at stake in the war against radical extremist Islamism and why the abandonment of a robust stance in opposition to this totalitarian mind-set should [not] be endorsed.

Naming aspirations for decent democracies is a good and understandable thing. At the same time, one must be continually aware of the barriers to the completion of such acts. The aspiration must be strong enough, and the moral imprimatur robust enough, to require us to take up our responsibilities for action. At the same time, the chastening recognition of human imperfection, finitude, and sinfulness should create barriers to utopianisms of any kind. Thus I have determined to speak primarily of "minimally decent states" rather than democracy as such in the future and, continually, to spell out what sort of democracy I have in my sights as the regime or regimes most compatible with human dignity. This suggests an argument that must await another day.

Select Bibliography

Abu-Nimer, Mohammed. *Nonviolence and Peace Building in Islam*. Gainesville, FL: University Press of Florida, 2003.

Achtemeier, Elizabeth. "Righteousness in the OT." In *The Interpreter's Dictionary of the Bible*, vol. 4, edited by G. A. Buttrick, 80–85. Nashville: Abingdon, 1962.

Ammar, Nawl H. "Restorative Justice in Islam: Theory and Practice." In *The Spiritual Roots of Restorative Justice*, edited by Michael L. Hadley, 169–73. Albany, NY: State University of New York Press, 2001.

Amstutz, Mark. "The Bush Doctrine: A Niebuhrian Assessment." *The Review of Faith & International Affairs* 5, no. 4 (2007) 25–33. https://www.tandfonline.com/doi/abs/10.1080/15570274.2007.9523308.

Arendt, Hannah, and Margaret Canovan (introduction). *The Human Condition*, 2nd ed. Chicago: The University of Chicago Press, 1998.

Arnall, Elliss Gibbs. *The Shore Dimly Seen*. Philadelphia: Lippincott, 1946.

Ash, Timothy Garton. "True Confessions." *New York Review of Books* 44 (1997) 37–38.

Augustine of Hippo. *Augustine: Political Writings*. Translated and edited by E. L. Fortin and D. Kries. Indianapolis: Hackett, 1994.

Axelrod, Robert. "The Emergence of Cooperation among Egoists." *American Political Science Review* 75 (1981) 306–18.

Baer, H. David. *Recovering Christian Realism: Just War Theory as a Political Ethic*. Lanham, MD: Lexington, 2015.

Baldwin, David. "The Concept of Security." *Review of International Studies* 24, no. 1 (1997) 5–26.

———. "Security Studies and the End of the Cold War." *World Politics* 48, no. 1 (1995) 117–41.

Barbato, Mariano. *Pilgrimage, Politics, and International Relations*. London: Palgrave, 2013.

Barbato, Mariano, and Robert Joustra. "Popes on the Rise: The Modern Papacy in World Affairs." *The Review of Faith and International Affairs* 15, no. 4 (2017) 1–5.

Barber, Benjamin. *Jihad vs. McWorld: Terrorism's Challenge to Democracy*. New York: Ballantine, 1996.

Bassiouni, M. Cherig. *Iraq Post-Conflict Justice: A Proposed Comprehensive Plan*. Chicago: DePaul University International Human Rights Law Institute, 2004.

Bennett, John C. "Process Theology, Christian Realism, and Liberation Theology." Unpublished paper, The Center for Process Studies, Claremont School of Theology, CA, October 3, 1982.

Berlin, Isaiah. "Two Concepts of Liberty." In *Four Essays on Liberty*, 166–217. New York: Oxford University Press, 1970.

Betts, Richard. "The Delusion of Impartial Intervention." *Foreign Affairs* 73, no. 6 (1994) 2–33.

Bhargava, Rajeev. "Restoring Decency to Barbaric Societies." In *Truth v. Justice: The Morality of Truth Commissions*, edited by Robert Rotberg and Dennis Thompson, 45–67. Princeton: Princeton University Press, 2000.

Biggar, Nigel. *In Defence of War*. Oxford: Oxford University Press, 2013.

Blocq, Daniel. "The Fog of UN Peacekeeping: Ethical Issues Regarding the Use of Force to Protect Civilians in UN Operations." *Journal of Military Ethics* 5, no. 3 (2006) 201–13.

Bonhoeffer, Dietrich. "After Ten Years." In *Letters and Papers from Prison*, enlarged ed., edited by Eberhard Bethge, 16–17. New York: Macmillan, 1971.

Boniface, Pascal. "Reflections on America as a World Power." *Journal of Palestinian Studies* 29, no. 3 (2000) 5–15.

Boyle, Joseph. "Traditional Just War Theory and Humanitarian Theory." In *Humanitarian Intervention*, edited by Terry Nardin and Melissa S. Williams, 31–57. New York: New York University Press, 2006.

Bundy, McGeorge. "Foreign Policy: From Innocence to Engagement." In *Paths of American Thought*, edited by Arthur M. Schlesinger, Jr. and Morton White, 293–308. Boston: Houghton Mifflin, 1961.

Burke, Anthony. "Against the New Internationalism." *Ethics and International Affairs* 19, no. 2 (2005) 73–89.

Butterfield, Herbert. *Christianity, Diplomacy and War*. Nashville: Abingdon-Cokesbury, 1953.

———. *International Conflict in the Twentieth Century: A Christian View*. London: Routledge and Kegan Paul, 1960.

Buzan, Barry, Ole Wæver, and Jaap de Wilde. *Security: A New Framework for Analysis*. Boulder, CO: Lynne Rienner, 1998.

Calvin, John. *Institutes of the Christian Religion*. In *A Compendium of the Institutes of the Christian Religion*, edited by H. T. Kerr, Jr. Philadelphia: Westminster, 1939.

Caporaso, James. "International Relations Theory and Multilateralism: The Search for Foundations." *International Organization* 46, no. 3 (1992) 599–632.

Carlson, John D. "Discerning Justice in the Trial and Execution of Saddam Hussein." In *Enemy Combatants, Terrorism, and Armed Conflict Law: A Guide to the Issues*, edited by David K. Linnan, 37–326. Westport, CT: Praeger Security International, 2008.

———. "What Is Christian about Christian Realism? Reinhold Niebuhr and the Ethics of War." *Religion and the Realist Tradition: From Political Theology to International Relations Theory and Back*, edited by Jodok Troy, 37–61. London: Routledge, 2014.

Carlson, John D., and Jonathon H. Ebel, eds. *From Jeremiad to Jihad: Religion, Violence, and America*. Berkeley: University of California Press, 2012.

Carr, E. H. *The Twenty Years Crisis, 1919–1939*. London: Macmillan, 1940.

Cavanaugh, William T. *Migrations of the Holy: God, State, and the Political Meaning of the Church*. Grand Rapids: Eerdmans, 2011.

———. *The Myth of Religious Violence: Secular Ideology and the Roots of Modern Conflict*. Oxford: Oxford University Press, 2009.

Cha, Victor. "Globalization and the Study of International Security." *Journal of Peace Research* 37, no. 3 (2000) 391–403.

Charles, J. Daryl. "The Ethics of Humanitarian Intervention." In *God and Global Order: The Power of Religion in American Foreign Policy*, edited by Jonathon Chaplin and Robert Joustra, 145–69. Waco, TX: Baylor University Press, 2010.

———. "Toward Restoring a Good Marriage: Reflections on the Contemporary Divorce of Love and Justice and Its Cultural Implications." *Journal of Church & State* 55, no. 2 (2013) 367–83.

Christopher, Paul. *The Ethics of War and Peace*. Upper Saddle River, NJ: Prentice Hall, 1991.

Coates, Anthony J. "Is the Independent Application of *Jus in Bello* the Way to Limit War?" In *Just and Unjust Warriors: The Moral and Legal Status of Soldiers*, edited by David Rodin and Henry Shue, 176–92. Oxford: Oxford University Press, 2008.

Cole, Darrell. "War and Intention." *Journal of Military Ethics* 10, vol. 3 (2011) 174–91.

Cole, Juan R. I. "The Rise of Religious and Ethnic Mass Politics in Iraq." In *Religion and Nationalism in Iraq*, edited by David Little and Donald Swearer, 43–62. Cambridge, MA: Harvard University Press, 2006.

Cooper, Robert. *The Postmodern State and the New World Order*. London: The Foreign Policy Centre/Demos, 2000.

Corey, David, and J. Daryl Charles. *The Just War Tradition: An Introduction*. Wilmington, DE: ISI Books, 2012.

Croatto, J. *Exodus: A Hermeneutics of Freedom*. Translated by Salvator Attanasio. Maryknoll, NY: Orbis, 1981.

Crocker, David A. "Truth Commissions, Transitional Justice, and Civil Society." In *Truth v. Justice: The Morality of Truth Commissions*, edited by Robert Rotberg and Dennis Thompson, 3–21. Princeton, NJ: Princeton University Press, 2000.

Dawson, Christopher. *Beyond Politics*. London: Sheed and Ward, 1939.

De Gruchy, John W. *Reconciliation: Restoring Justice*. Minneapolis: Fortress, 2003.

De Pury, Roland. *Journal from My Cell*. Translated to English. London: Latimer house, 1948.

De Vitoria, Francisco. "On the American Indians." In *Vitoria: Political Writings*, edited by Anthony Pagden and Jeremy Lawrance, 231–92. Cambridge: Cambridge University Press, 1992.

Diamond, Larry. "Is the Third Wave of Democratization Over? An Empirical Assessment." *Kellogg Institute for International Studies Working Paper Series*, no. 236 (March 1997) 2–43.

Dodd, C. H. *The Parables of the Kingdom*. London: Nisbet, 1935.

Dooyeweerd, Herman. *Critique of Theoretical Thought*. Philadelphia: Presbyterian and Reformed Publishing Co., 1955.

———. *Roots of Western Culture: Pagan, Secular, and Christian Options*. Translated by John Kraay and edited by Mark Vander Vennen and Bernard Zylstra. Toronto: Wedge Publishing Foundation, 1979.

Dorrien, Gary. "Communitarianism, Christian Realism, and the Crisis of Progressive Christianity." *Cross Currents* 47.3 (1997) 364–78.

Doyle, Michael. *Ways of War and Peace*. New York: Norton, 1997.

Edwards, Michael. *NGO Rights and Responsibilities: A New Deal for Global Governance*. London: The Foreign Policy Centre/NCVO, 2000.

Elshtain, Jean Bethke. *Augustine and the Limits of Politics*. Notre Dame, IN: University of Notre Dame Press, 1995.

———. "Ethics beyond War's End." In *Ending Wars Well*, edited by Eric Patterson, 123–44. New Haven, CT: Yale University Press, 2012.

———. "Just War and the Ethics of Responsibility." In *Ethics Beyond War's End*, edited by Eric Patterson, 123–44. Washington, DC: Georgetown University Press, 2012.

———. *Just War Against Terror*. New York: Basic, 2002.

———, ed. *Just War Theory: Readings in Social and Political Theory*. New York: New York University Press, 1992.

———. "Where Is the Legacy of Tillich and Niebuhr." In *Just War Against Terror*, 99–111. New York: Basic, 2003.

———. *Women and War*. New York: Basic, 1987.

Elshtain, Jean Bethke, Michael Walzer, George Weigel, et al. *But Was It Just: Reflections on the Morality of the Persian Gulf War*. New York: Doubleday, 1992.

Epp, Roger. "The 'Augustinian Moment' in International Politics: Niebuhr, Wight and the Reclaiming of a Tradition." International Politics Research Paper Number 10, Department of Politics, University College of Wales, Aberystwyth, 1991.

Flescher, Andrew. "Love and Justice in Reinhold Niebuhr's Prophetic Christian Realism and Emmanuel Levinas's Ethics of Responsibility: Treading between Pacifism and Just-War Theory." *Journal of Religion* 80.1 (2000) 61–82.

Fox, Jonathan. *Political Secularism, Religion, and the State: A Time Series Analysis of Worldwide Data*. Cambridge: Cambridge University Press, 2015.

Frank, Andre. *Crisis: In the World Economy*. London: Heinemann, 1980.

Friedman, Thomas. *The Lexus and the Olive Tree: Understanding Globalization*. New York: Farrar, Straus and Giroux, 1999.

Fukuyama, Francis. *The End of History and the Last Man*. New York: Free, 1992.

Garrard, L. A. *Duty and the Will of God*. Oxford: Blackwell, 1938.

Geren, Paul. *Burma Diary*. New York: Harper and Row, 1943.

Glieck, Peter. "Water and Conflict: Fresh Water Resources and International Security." *International Security* 18, no. 1 (1993) 79–112.

Godwin, William. *Enquiry Concerning Political Justice and Its Influence on Morals and Happiness*. London: G. G. J. and J. Robinson, 1793.

Gopin, Marc. *Between Eden and Armageddon: The Future of World Religions, Violence, and Peacemaking*. Oxford: Oxford University Press, 2000.

Gordon, Evelyn. "The Pitfalls of Multilateralism." *The Jerusalem Post*, October 26, 2004.

Gore, Charles. *The Philosophy of the Good Life*. London: Dent, 1935.

Goudzwaard, Bob. *Capitalism and Progress: A Diagnosis of Western Society*. Toronto: Wedge Publishing Foundation, 1979.

Grotius, Hugo. *The Rights of War and Peace*. Edited by Richard Tuck. Indianapolis: Liberty Fund, 2005.

Gutiérrez, Gustavo. "The Hope of Liberation." *Mission Trends No. 3: Third World Theologies*, edited by Gerald H. Anderson and Thomas F. Stransky, 64–69. New York: Paulist, 1976.

———. *Liberation and Change*. Atlanta: John Knox, 1977.

———. "Notes for a Theology of Liberation." *Theological Studies* 31 (1970) 249–50.

———. *A Theology of Liberation: History, Politics and Salvation*. Translated and edited by Sister Caridad Inda and John Eagleson. Maryknoll, NY: Orbis, 1973.

Gutmann, Amy, and Dennis Thompson. "The Moral Foundations of Truth Commissions." In *Truth v. Justice: The Morality of Truth Commissions*, edited by Robert Rotberg and Dennis Thompson, 22–44. Princeton, NJ: Princeton University Press, 2000.

Halperin, Morton. *Limited War in the Nuclear Age*. Cambridge, MA: Center of International Affairs, Harvard University, 1962.

Hamid, Shadi. *Islamic Exceptionalism: How the Struggle Over Islam Is Reshaping the World.* New York: St Martin's Griffin, 2016.

Hardin, Russell. *Collective Action.* Baltimore: Johns Hopkins University Press, 1982.

Hauerwas, Stanley, and Michael Broadway. *Wilderness Wanderings: Probing Twentieth Century Theology and Philosophy.* Boulder, CO: Westview, 1997.

Haynes, Jeffrey. *Religion, Politics and International Relations.* London: Routledge, 2011.

Held, David. *Global Transformations.* Cambridge: Polity, 1999.

Hinze, Christine Firer. "The Bonds of Freedom: Feminist Theology and Christian Realism (Book Review)." *Journal of Religion* 84.1 (2004) 116–17. doi:10.1086/382308.

Hobbes, Thomas. *Leviathan.* Translated and edited by Christopher Brooks. Penguin Classics, 2017.

Hooft, Visser. "The Christian in World Affairs." *The Student World* 2 (1948) 109–25.

Hughes, Emmet J. *The Church and Liberal Society.* Princeton, NJ: Princeton University Press, 1944.

Huntington, Samuel P. *The Clash of Civilizations and the Remaking of World Order.* San Francisco: Simon & Schuster, 1993.

———. *The Third Wave: Democratization in the Late Twentieth Century.* Norman, OK: University of Oklahoma Press, 1991.

Hurd, Elizabeth Shakman. *Beyond Religious Freedom: The New Global Politics of Religious Freedom.* Princeton, NJ: Princeton University Press, 2015.

Ignatieff, Michael. "Articles of Faith." *Index on Censorship* 25, no. 5 (1996) 110–22.

———. "State Failure and Nation-Building." In *Humanitarian Intervention: Ethical, Legal, and Political Dilemmas*, edited by J.L. Hozgrefe and Robert O. Keohane, 299–321. Cambridge: Cambridge University Press, 2003.

International Center for Transitional Justice and Human Rights Center, University of California, Berkeley. *Iraqi Voices: Attitudes Toward Transitional Justice and Social Reconstruction*, Occasional Paper. New York: International Center for Transitional Justice, May 2004.

Irani, George E., and Nathan C. Funk. "Rituals of Reconciliation: Arab-Islamic Perspectives." *Arab Studies Quarterly* 20, no. 4 (1998) 53–73.

Iraq Study Group. *Iraq Study Group Report: The Way Forward—A New Approach.* New York: Vintage, 2006.

Jervis, Robert. "Understanding the Bush Doctrine." *Political Science Quarterly* 118, no. 3 (2003) 365–88.

———. "Why the Bush Doctrine Cannot Be Sustained." *Political Science Quarterly* 120, no. 3 (2005) 351–77.

Johnson, James Turner. "Humanitarian Intervention, Christian Ethical Reasoning, and the Just War Idea." In *Sovereignty at the Crossroads? Morality and International Politics in the Post-Cold War Era*, edited by Luis E. Lugo, 127–43. Lanham, MD: Rowman & Littlefield, 1996.

———. "Just War, as It Was, and Is." *First Things*, February 2005, 14–24.

———. "Moral Responsibility after Conflict." In *Ethics Beyond War's End*, edited by Eric Patterson, 17–34. Washington, DC: Georgetown University Press, 2012.

Johnson, James Turner, and Eric Patterson, eds. *Ashgate Research Companion on Military Ethics.* Edited by James Turner Johnson and Eric Patterson. London: Ashgate, 2015.

Johnson, James Turner, and George Weigel. *Just War and the Gulf War.* Washington, DC: Ethics and Public Policy Center Press, 1991.

Joustra, Robert. "Abraham Kuyper among the Nations." *Politics & Religion* (September 2017) 146–68.

———. "Globalization and the Kingdom of God: A Christian Perspective on International Relations." *Public Justice Review* 5 (2017). https://www.cpjustice.org/public/public_justice_review/article/56.

———. "Post-Secular Prophets: Abraham Kuyper, Herbert Butterfield, and the Early English School." In *The Routledge Handbook of Postsecularity*, edited by Justin Beaumont, 190–200. London: Routledge, 2019.

———. "Public Justice after the Resurrection." *Public Justice Review* 8, no. 2 (2018). https://cpjustice.org/uploads/Joustra_FINAL.pdf.

———. *The Religious Problem with Religious Freedom: Why Foreign Policy Needs Political Theology.* London: Routledge, 2017.

Joustra, Robert J., and Alissa Wilkinson. *How to Survive the Apocalypse: Zombies, Cylons, Faith, and Politics at the End of the World.* Grand Rapids: Eerdmans, 2015.

Kant, Immanuel. *Perpetual Peace and Other Essays on Politics, History and Morals.* Translated by Ted Humphrey. New York: Hackett, 1983.

Khadduri, Majid. *The Islamic Conception of Justice.* Baltimore: Johns Hopkins University Press, 1984.

Klugman, Jeni. *Social and Economic Policies to Prevent Complex Humanitarian Emergencies: Lessons from Experience.* New York: United Nations University World Institute for Development of Economics Research, 1999.

Knock, Thomas. *To End All Wars: Woodrow Wilson and the Quest for a New International Order.* Princeton: Princeton University Press, 1995.

Koyzis, David T. "Westernization or Clash of Civilizations?" *Comment Magazine* (September 2004). https://www.cardus.ca/comment/article/westernization-or-clash-of-civilizations/.

Krause, Keith, and Michael Williams. "Broadening the Agenda of Security Studies." *Mershon International Studies Review* 40, no. 2 (1996) 229–54.

Krieger, Evgeny. *From Moscow to the Prussia Frontier.* London: Hutchinson, 1945.

Kuiper, D. Th. "Historical and Sociological Development of ARP and CDA." In *Christian Political Options*, 10–32. The Hague: AR-Partijstichting, 1979.

———. *De Voorman: Een Sociaal-Wetenshappelijke Studie over Ideologie, Konflict an Kerngroepvorming binnen de Gereformeerde Wereld in Nederland tussen 1820 en 1930.* Kampen: Kok, 1972.

Kuyper, Abraham. *Calvinism: Six Stone Lectures.* Grand Rapids: Eerdmans, 1931.

———. *Lectures on Calvinism.* Grand Rapids: Eerdmans, 1943.

———. *Pro Rege: Living under Christ's Kingship: Volume 3.* Translated by Albert Gootjes and edited by John Kok and Nelson D. Kloosterman. Bellingham, WA: Lexham, 2017.

LaHurd, Carol Schersten. "'So That the Sinner Will Repent': Forgiveness in Islam and Christianity." *Dialog* 35, no. 4 (1996) 287–92.

Levenson, Jon D. *Creation and the Persistence of Evil.* Princeton, NJ: Princeton University Press, 1988.

Lewis, C. S. "The Conditions for a Just War." In *God in the Dock: Essays on Theology and Ethics*, edited by Walter Hooper, 325–27. Grand Rapids: Eerdmans, 1970.

———. "Why I Am Not a Pacifist." In *The Weight of Glory and Other Essays*, edited by Walter Hooper, 64–90. New York: HarperCollins, 2001.

Locke, John. *Two Treatises of Government.* London: Awnsham, Churchill, 1689.

Lovin, Robin. "The Limits of Freedom and the Possibilities of Politics: A Christian Realist Account of Political Responsibility." *The Journal of Religion* 73, no. 4 (1999) 559–72.

Lukács, Georg. *History and Class Consciousness: Studies in Marxist Dialectics*. Cambridge: MIT Press, 1971.

Luther, Martin. *Secular Authority: To What Extent It Should Be Obeyed*. In *Works of Martin Luther*. Translated by C. M. Jacobs. Philadelphia: Muhlenberg, 1930.

Machiavelli, Niccolo. *The Prince*. 2nd ed. Translated by Harvey C. Mansfield. Chicago: University of Chicago Press, 1998.

MacIntyre, Alasdair. *After Virtue: A Study in Moral Theory*. South Bend, IN: University of Notre Dame Press, 2007.

Mackinder, H. J. *Democratic Ideals and Reality*. London: Pelican, 1944.

Mahmood, Saba. *Religious Difference in a Secular Age: A Minority Report*. Princeton, NJ: Princeton University Press, 2015.

Major, C. J., H. D. A. Manson, T. W. Wright. *The Mission and Message of Jesus*. New York: Dutton, 1946.

Marshall, Christopher D. *Beyond Retribution: A New Testament Vision for Justice, Crime and Punishment*. Grand Rapids: Eerdmans, 2001.

Martin, Lisa. "Interests, Power, and Multilateralism." *International Organization* 46, no. 4 (1992) 765–92.

Mauser, Ulrich. *The Gospel of Peace: A Scriptural Message for Today's World*. Louisville, KY: Westminster John Knox, 1992.

Mazzini, Giuseppe. *The Duties of Man*. New York: Funk & Wagnalls, 1844.

McCann, Dennis P. *Christian Realism and Liberation Theology: Practical Theologies in Creative Conflict*. Maryknoll, NY: Orbis, 1981.

McGiffert, A. C. *Protestant Thought before Kant*. New York: Scribner's, 1911.

Mearsheimer, John J. *The Tragedy of Great Power Politics*, Updated ed. New York: Norton, 2014.

Míguez-Bonino, José. *Christians and Marxists*. London: Hodder and Stoughton, 1976.

Moltmann, Jürgen. *The Crucified God: The Cross of Christ as the Foundation and Criticism of Christian Theology*. Minneapolis: Fortress, 1993.

Montefiore, C. G. *Rabbinic Literature and Gospel Teachings*. New York: Macmillan, 1930.

Murray, John Courtney. *We Hold These Truths: Catholic Reflections on the American Proposition*. New York: Sheed and Sheed, 1968.

Nardin, Terry. "The Moral Basis of Humanitarian Intervention." *Ethics & International Affairs* 16, no. 1 (2002) 57–58.

Neiman, Susan. *Evil in Modern Thought: An Alternative History of Philosophy*. Princeton, NJ: Princeton University Press, 2002.

Newman, J. H. "Waiting for Christ." In *Parochial and Plain Sermons*, vol. 6, 234–54. London: Riving Tons, 1875.

Niebuhr, Reinhold. "Augustine's Political Realism." In *Christian Realism and Political Problems*, 119–46. New York: Scribner's Sons, 1953.

———. "The Blindness of Liberalism." *Radical Religion* 1 (1936) 4–5.

———. *The Children of Light and the Children of Darkness: A Vindication of Democracy and A Critique of Its Traditional Defense*. New York: Scribner's, 1960.

———. *Christianity and Power Politics*. New York: Scribner's, 1940.

———. *Discerning the Signs of the Times*. London: SCM, 1946.

———. *An Interpretation of Christian Ethics*. Cleveland, OH: Meridian, 1956.

————. *The Irony of American History.* New York: Scribner's Sons, 1952.

————. *The Nature and Destiny of Man.* 2 vols. London: Nisbet, 1941–43.

————. "Repeal the Neutrality Act!" In *Love and Justice: Selections from the Shorter Writings of Reinhold Niebuhr,* edited by D. B. Robertson, 177–78. Philadelphia: Westminster, 1957.

————. *The Structure of Nations and Empires.* New York: Scribner's Sons, 1959.

————. "Why the Christian Church Is Not Pacifist." In *The Essential Reinhold Niebuhr: Selected Essays and Addresses,* 102–20. New Haven, CT: Yale University Press, 1986.

Obelensky, Dimitri. *The Byzantine Commonwealth: Eastern Europe, 500–1453.* New York: Praeger, 1971.

Omar, A. Rashied. "Between Compassion and Justice: Locating an Islamic Definition of Peace." *Peace Colloquy* 7 (2005) 9–10.

Paris, Roland. "Human Security: Paradigm Shift or Hot Air?" *International Security* 6, no. 2 (2001) 87–102.

————. "Peacebuilding and the Limits of Liberal Internationalism." *International Security* 22, no. 2 (1997) 54–89.

Patterson, Eric. *Ending Wars Well: Just War Theory in Post-Conflict.* New Haven, CT: Yale University Press, 2012.

Patterson, Eric, ed. *Christianity and Power Politics Today: Christian Realism and Contemporary Political Dilemmas.* New York: Palgrave-Macmillan, 2008.

————. *The Christian Realists: Reassessing the Contribution of Niebuhr and His Contemporaries.* Lanham, MD: University Press of America, 2004.

————. "The Enduring Value of Christian Realism." *Philosophia Reformata* 80, no. 1 (2015) 27–39.

————. "Rewinding Rwanda: What If? (A Counterfactual Approach)." *Journal of Political Science* 33 (2005) 123–42.

Patterson, Eric, and Kendra Puryear. "Outlaws and Barbarians: The Bush Administration's Revolution in Sovereignty." *Journal of Diplomacy and International Affairs* 7, no. 1 (2006) 199–211.

Pavlischek, Keith. "Proportionality in Warfare." *The New Atlantis,* Spring 2010, 21–34. https://www.thenewatlantis.com/publications/proportionality-in-warfare.

————. "Reinhold Niebuhr, Christian Realism, and Just War Theory: A Critique." In *Christianity and Power Politics Today,* edited by Eric Patterson, 53–71. New York: Palgrave-Macmillan, 2008.

Payne, Keith B., and Jill E. Coleman. "Christian Nuclear Pacifism and Just War Theory: Are They Compatible?" *Comparative Strategy* 7, no. 1 (1988) 75–89.

Payne, Keith B., and Tom Scheber. "The Threat of New START." *National Review Online,* November 15, 2010. https://www.nationalreview.com/2010/11/threat-new-start-keith-b-payne-tom-scheber/.

Phillips, James. "Proposed Timetables for U.S. Withdrawal Would Sabotage Reconciliation in Iraq." *Heritage Foundation* WebMemo #1632, September 31, 2007. https://www.heritage.org/middle-east/report/proposed-timetables-us-withdrawal-would-sabotagereconciliation-iraq.

Philpott, Daniel. "Has the Study of Global Politics Found Religion?" *Annual Review of Political Science* 12 (2009) 183–202.

————. *Just and Unjust Peace.* Oxford: Oxford University Press, 2015.

Podhoretz, Norman. "In Praise of the Bush Doctrine." *Commentary*, September 2002. https://www.commentary.org/articles/norman-podhoretz/in-praise-of-the-bush-doctrine/.

Polinder, Simon, and Govert Bujis. *Christian Faith, Philosophy, and International Relations: The Lamb and the Wolf*. Amsterdam: Brill, 2019.

Pope John Paul II. *Dives in Misericordia*, encyclical, November 30, 1980.

Radhakrishnan, S. *The Hindu View of Life*. London: Allen and Unwin, 1931.

Ramsey, Paul. *Basic Christian Ethics*. New York: Scribner's Sons, 1950.

———. *The Just War: Force and Political Responsibility*. New York: Rowman & Littlefield, 1968.

———. "Love and Law." In *Reinhold Niebuhr: His Religious, Social and Political Thought*, edited by Charles W. Kegley, 143–188. Reprint, Eugene, OR: Wipf & Stock, 2009.

———. *War and the Christian Conscience: How Shall Modern War Be Conducted Justly?* Durham, NC: Duke University Press, 1961.

Rasmussen, Larry. *Reinhold Niebuhr: Theologian of Public Life*. London: Collins, 1989.

Reichberg, Gregory M., Henrik Syse, and Endre Begby, eds. *The Ethics of War: Classic and Contemporary Readings*. Malden: Blackwell, 2006.

The Republic of Plato. 3rd ed. Translated by Allan Bloom with introduction by Adam Kirsch. New York: Basic, 2016.

Rice, Daniel F. *Reinhold Niebuhr, and John Dewey: An American Odyssey*. Albany, NY: State University of New York, 1993.

Richmond, Oliver P. "The Problem of Peace: Understanding the 'Liberal Peace.'" *Conflict, Security & Development* 6, no. 3 (2006) 291–314.

Ruggie, John. "Multilateralism: The Anatomy of an Institution." *International Organization* 46, no. 3 (1992) 561–98.

Sachedina, Abdulaziz Abdulhussein. *The Islamic Roots of Democratic Pluralism*. New York: Oxford University Press, 2001.

Sachs, Susan. "Iraqis Seek Justice, or Vengeance, for Victims of the Killing Fields." *The New York Times*, November 4, 2003.

Schmiechen, Peter. *Saving Power: Theories of Atonement and Forms of the Church*. Grand Rapids: Eerdmans, 2005.

Schelling, T. C. "Nuclear Strategy in Europe." *World Politics* 14, no. 3 (1962) 421–32. https://www.jstor.org/stable/2009360/.

Scott-Craig, T., and K. Scott-Craig. *Christian Attitudes to War and Peace*. New York: Scribner's Sons, 1938.

Seybolt, Taylor B. "The Myth of Neutrality." *Peace Review* 8 (1996) 521–27.

Singer, Peter. *The President of Good & Evil: The Ethics of George W. Bush*. New York: Dutton, 2004.

Skillen, James W. *With or Against the World: America's Role among the Nations*. Lanham, MD: Rowman & Littlefield, 2005.

Smith, Adam. *Wealth of Nations*. London: W. Strahan and T. Cadell, 1776.

Sowell, Thomas. *A Conflict of Visions: Ideological Origins of Political Struggles*. New York: Basic, 2002.

Spring, Baker, and Rebeccah Heinrichs. "Deterrence and Nuclear Targeting in the 21st Century." *Heritage Foundation*, November 30, 2012. https://www.heritage.org/arms-control/report/deterrence-and-nuclear-targeting-the-21st-century.

Stein, Walter, ed. *Nuclear Weapons and Christian Conscience*. London: Merlin, 1961.

Strand, Daniel. "We Have an Expectation Problem in Afghanistan." *Providence Magazine*, December 13, 2019. https://providencemag.com/2019/12/expectation-problem-afghan istan/.

Taylor, Charles. *Modern Social Imaginaries*. Durham, NC: Duke University Press, 2003.

———. *A Secular Age*. Cambridge: Harvard Belknap, 2007.

Taylor, Michael. *The Possibility of Cooperation*. Cambridge: Cambridge University Press, 1987.

Tesón, Fernando R. "The Liberal Case for Humanitarian Intervention." In *Humanitarian Intervention: Ethical, Legal, and Political Dilemmas*, edited by J. L. Holzgrefe and Robert O. Keohane, 93–129. Cambridge: Cambridge University Press, 2003.

Thomas, Scott. "Response: Reading Religion Rightly—'The Clash of Rival Apostasies' amidst the Global Resurgence of Religion." In *God and Global Order*, edited by Jonathon Chaplin and Robert Joustra, 187–204. Waco, TX: Baylor University Press, 2010.

Thompson, Kenneth. "Moral Reasoning in American Thought in War and Peace." *The Review of Politics* 39 (1977) 386–99.

———. "The Nuclear Dilemma—A Discussion." *Christianity and Crisis*, November 27, 1961, 203.

———. "The Political Philosophy of Reinhold Niebuhr." In *Reinhold Niebuhr: His Religious, Social and Political Thought*, edited by Charles W. Kegley, 223–52. Eugene, OR: Wipf & Stock Publishers, 2009.

Thucydides, and P. J. Rhodes. *The Peloponnesian War*. Edited by Martin Hammond. Oxford: Oxford University Press, 2009.

Tolstoy, Leo. *On Life, and Essays on Religion*. Translated by Aylmer Maude. Oxford: Oxford University Press, 1950.

Torrance, Alan. "The Theological Grounds for Advocating Forgiveness and Reconciliation in the Sociopolitical Realm." In *Politics of Past Evil: The: Religion, Reconciliation, and the Dilemmas of Transitional Justice*, edited by Daniel Philpott, 45–86. Notre Dame, IN: University of Notre Dame Press, 2006.

U.S. Department of Defense. *Measuring Stability and Security in Iraq: Report to Congress in accordance with the Department of Defense Appropriations Act 2007*. Washington, DC, 2007.

Van Prinsterer, Groen. *Unbelief and Revolution*. Marlton, NJ: Lexham, 2018.

Volf, Miroslav. *Exclusion and Embrace: A Theological Exploration of Identity, Otherness, and Reconciliation*. Nashville: Abingdon, 1996.

Waltz, Kenneth. *Man, the State, and War: A Theoretical Analysis*. New York: Columbia University Press, 2001.

Waltzer, Michael. *Just and Unjust Wars: A Moral Argument with Historical Illustrations*. 4th ed. New York: Basic, 2006.

———. "The Politics of Rescue." In *Arguing about War*, 67–81. New Haven, CT: Yale University Press, 2004.

Watson, Adam. "Toleration in Religion and Politics." In *Herbert Butterfield: The Ethics of History and Politics*, 71–86. Washington, DC: University Press of America, 1979.

Weber, Theodore. "Vengeance Denied, Politics Affirmed: Applying the Criterion of Just Intention." *Societas Ethica Jahresbericht* (2000) 170–76.

Weigel, George. "Theology of Peace." In *Just War and the Gulf War*, edited by James Turner Johnson and George Weigel, 85–90. Washington, DC: Ethics and Public Policy Center Press, 1991.

Weiss, Thomas G. "Principles, Politics, and Humanitarian Action." *Ethics & International Affairs* 13 (1999) 1–21.

Werpehowski, William, and Stephen D. Crocco, eds. *The Essential Paul Ramsey: A Collection.* New Haven, CT: Yale University Press, 1994.

Wight, Martin. "The Church, Russia, and the West." *The Ecumenical Review* 1.1 (1948) 25–45.

Wolterstorff, Nicholas. *Justice in Love.* Grand Rapids: Eerdmans, 2011.

———. *"Reason within the Bounds of Religion.* Grand Rapids: Eerdmans, 1976.

———. *Until Justice and Peace Embrace.* Grand Rapids: Eerdmans, 1983.

Wright, N.T. *Evil and the Justice of God.* Downers Grove, IL: InterVarsity, 2006.

Yoder, Perry. *Shalom: The Bible's Word for Salvation, Justice, and Peace.* Newton, KA: Faith and Life, 1987.

Zehr, Howard. *Changing Lenses.* Scottdale, PA: Herald, 1990.

Zelikow, Philip. "The Transformation of National Security: Five Redefinitions." *The National Interest* 71 (2003) 17–28.